Relational Formations of Race

Relational Formations
of Race

THEORY, METHOD, AND PRACTICE

Edited by Natalia Molina,
Daniel Martinez HoSang,
and Ramón A. Gutiérrez

UNIVERSITY OF CALIFORNIA PRESS

University of California Press, one of the most distinguished university presses in the United States, enriches lives around the world by advancing scholarship in the humanities, social sciences, and natural sciences. Its activities are supported by the UC Press Foundation and by philanthropic contributions from individuals and institutions. For more information, visit www.ucpress.edu.

University of California Press
Oakland, California

Library of Congress Cataloging-in-Publication Data

Names: Molina, Natalia, editor. | HoSang, Daniel, editor. | Gutiérrez, Ramón A., 1951– editor.
Title: Relational formations of race : theory, method, and practice / edited by Natalia Molina, Daniel Martinez HoSang, and Ramón A. Gutiérrez.
Description: Oakland, California : University of California Press, [2019] Includes bibliographical references and index. | Description based on print version record and CIP data provided by publisher; resource not viewed.
Identifiers: LCCN 2018040746 (print) | LCCN 2018051806 (ebook) | ISBN 9780520971301 (ebook and ePDF) | ISBN 9780520299665 (cloth : alk. paper) | ISBN 9780520299672 (pbk : alk. paper)
Subjects: LCSH: Race relations. | Immigrants—United States—Social conditions.
Classification: LCC HT1521 (ebook) | LCC HT1521 .R455 2019 (print) | DDC 305.8—dc23
LC record available at https://lccn.loc.gov/2018040746

Manufactured in the United States of America

26 25 24 23 22 21 20 19
10 9 8 7 6 5 4 3 2 1

CONTENTS

ILLUSTRATIONS

ACKNOWLEDGMENTS

Barbara Tomlinson and George Lipsitz remind us that the "structures of professional validation and reward" in academic research often "promote desires to be the one to have the first word or the last word" on a particular subject or discourse. This fixation on innovation and authority, however, ignores the role of "the middle word" or "building on what came before and setting the stage for what will follow."* We understand this volume, *Relational Formations of Race,* and all the collaborative work that brought it to fruition, to be the kind of "middle word" counseled by Tomlinson and Lipsitz. As we describe in the introduction, the race concept itself has been relational from the moment it entered the political vocabulary of modernity; the drive to sort, rank, and compare is constitutive of colonialism and white supremacy itself. And the efforts to resist and transform these ways of knowing and being have also always been relational, witnessed in the practices and analyses of groups struggling for their liberation to find others whose freedom is linked to theirs. Following Lipsitz and Tomlinson, we hope this volume serves as a kind of accompaniment to this deep and wide-ranging body of knowledge and collective action.

Our editor at the University of California Press, Niels Hooper, originated the idea for this volume. As the editor of the press's American Crossroads series, Niels has a keen understanding of the relational dimensions of much of the work in contemporary ethnic and American studies, and of the contribution that a volume organized around such themes could make. Thank you, Niels.

* Barbara Tomlinson and George Lipsitz, "American Studies as Accompaniment," *American Quarterly* 65, no. 1 (2013): 22.

The initial discussions with Niels led us to organize a conference, "Studying Race Relationally," hosted by the University of Chicago in May 2016, that laid the groundwork for this volume. The dynamic conversations and enthusiastic response from presenters, respondents, and the audience sharpened our vision. We thank all the presenters who helped shape the discussions found in this volume: Eric Avila, Michael Dawson, Laura E. Enriquez, Roderick Ferguson, Claire Jean Kim, Julie Lee Merseth, Michael Rodríguez-Muñiz, Catherine Ramírez, Antonio T. Tiongson Jr., Laurie Green, and Jeffrey T. Yamashita. The conference was generously supported by Chicago University's Center for the Study of Race, Politics and Culture (CSRPC), Franke Institute for the Humanities, and History Department. We also thank colleagues at the University of Chicago, including Marco Garrido, Larissa Brewer-García, and Edgar García. And thanks to Richard Jean So for providing thoughtful commentary at the conference, as well as to the CSRPC staff for their support in hosting the event.

The volume received generous institutional support from Yale University and the University of Oregon, as well as an Academic Senate Research Grant from the University of California, San Diego.

We are especially grateful to four readers—Evelyn Hu-DeHart and the three who remained anonymous—who reviewed the initial manuscript for UC Press. Their in-depth knowledge of the field yielded insightful questions that pushed us to make the volume stronger.

Students in Daniel Martinez HoSang's Yale graduate seminar, "Studying Race Relationally" (Timothy Byram, Ambre Dromgoole, Alex Ikeuchi, Isadora Milanez, Héctor Peralta, Daniella Posy, Robbie Short, Alex Williams, and Alex Zhang) worked with an early version of the manuscript and related essays and shared their perceptive readings, questions, and suggestions. The introduction in particular benefited from their careful engagement. Jason Oliver Chang of the University of Connecticut also presented his generative work at the seminar, helping us think the role of state formation and transnational migration within a relational framework.

We are also indebted to our graduate student researchers, Alina Méndez, Ever Osorio Ruiz, Annie Titus, and Héctor Peralta, for their research, editing, and production acumen. Harold Colson, librarian extraordinaire at the University of California, San Diego, helped track down rare photos and documents, as well as many sources related to the nascent and quickly growing field of relational studies of race.

Isabella Furth is both an editor and interlocutor. We thank her for her editorial sharpness and probing questions.

Along with Niels Hooper, we would like to thank the extraordinarily resourceful and helpful staff at University of California Press. Editorial assistant Bradley Depew deserves special mention for his good counsel and for helping us decipher and navigate the ins and outs of the publishing world, from copyright permissions to pixel counts.

We would also like to give a special acknowledgment to George L. and George S. (Lipsitz and Sánchez, respectively). Their scholarship and mentorship have been invaluable to us and to many of the contributors to this volume. Along with Kelly Lytle Hernández, they took time out of their busy schedules to sit down and answer questions about the foundations of studying race relationally and about new directions for inquiry. That conversation, which yielded the roundtable discussion published in the first chapter of this volume, was a touchstone for our work. We are grateful for their *accompaniment*—intellectual, personal, and professional—which has made this book possible.

Finally, as coeditors, we appreciate the cooperation, trust, and generosity that have sustained our collaboration. These are the qualities and commitments of academic life at its best, and they are what have allowed us to contribute a "middle word" to this collective project.

Introduction

TOWARD A RELATIONAL CONSCIOUSNESS OF RACE

Daniel Martinez HoSang and Natalia Molina

In April 1963, Dr. Martin Luther King Jr. composed his celebrated "Letter from Birmingham Jail," a retort to a group of Alabama clergyman who had publicly denounced the nonviolent civil disobedience that Dr. King had helped bring to the city. These clergy, Dr. King explained, had dismissed the civil rights protests as the work of "outsiders coming in," an unwarranted intrusion into local affairs. Dr. King rejected the premise of this charge and the firm boundaries on social and political worlds that it inscribed. It was, he countered, the "inter-related structure of reality" that compelled him to leave his home in Atlanta to join the demonstrations in Birmingham. "Whatever affects one directly, affects all indirectly."[1] Four years later, Dr. King would expand the geographic reach of this "inescapable network of mutuality," condemning the U.S. war in Vietnam and linking the fate of the civil rights movement in the United States to the freedom and self-determination of the Vietnamese people (see figure 0.1). Particularized struggles against domination and exploitation—from the cotton fields of the Mississippi Delta to the coal mines of Appalachia to the hollowed-out villages of Southeast Asia—could not be understood in isolation. They necessitated instead "allegiances and loyalties which are broader and deeper than nationalism."[2]

Dr. King's understanding of the "interrelatedness of all communities and states" frames the political and intellectual bearing of this volume. Scholarship across the humanities and social sciences now commonly conceptualizes race as a social construction shaped in specific historical, social, and political contexts. The dominant paradigm of this work examines the experiences, struggles, and characteristics of subordinated groups (e.g., African Americans, Native Americans, Latino/as, and Asian Americans) and their standing within white supremacist and colonial structures of power.

FIGURE 0.1. Dr. Martin Luther King Jr. marches arm in arm with *(from left)* Dr. Benjamin Spock, Wallace Black Elk, and Monsignor Rice, at the Spring Mobilization to End the War in Vietnam, New York City, April 15, 1967. The march took place a few days after Dr. King's "Beyond Vietnam" speech, in which he laid out the connection between the struggle for self-determination for all peoples, the fight for civil rights, and the war's toll on America's poor.

Groups are studied primarily in relationship to whiteness and through a white/nonwhite binary. By contrast, the essays brought together in *Relational Formations of Race* consider the racialization and formation of subordinated groups in relation to one another. These studies conceptualize racialization as a dynamic and interactive process; group-based racial constructions are formed in relation not only to whiteness but also to other devalued and marginalized groups. By studying race relationally, and through a shared field of meaning and power, scholars can make visible the connections among such subordinated groups and the logic that underpins the forms of inclusion and dispossession they face.

For example, Chinese immigrant communities on the West Coast in the late nineteenth century shared some distinct characteristics of class organization, diasporic identifications, and language, family, and gender formation. But from the moment they arrived in the United States in significant numbers, they entered a field of racialization that was shaped by many different social forces: abolitionist politics and worldviews; the consolidation of white political identity in relation to both capital and nonwhite labor; the changing relationship of Mexico and its economy to the United States; the military conquest of Native lands and the assertion of Native sovereignties; and imperial expansion across the Pacific, including in the Philippines, Hawai'i, and Alaska. Thus, to understand how Chinese migrants became "excludable" subjects ineligible for citizenship, one must also attend to the formation of other racialized groups.

The collection of scholarship brought together in this volume helps to define, map, and formulate a set of theoretical and methodological touchstones for the relational study of race. The volume builds on a growing body of work—generated from American studies, ethnic studies, history, sociology, cultural studies, and literary studies—that emphasizes the relational dimensions of race making in the United States. The Further Reading section at the end of this volume captures a measure of this growing scholarship.

Following Dr. King, scholars employ a relational understanding of race to trace the "inter-related structure of reality" in ways that exceed prevailing theoretical and disciplinary boundaries. The modes of exploitation, control, and hierarchy developed in the last five hundred years could not have been secured through a single or unitary regime of racialization. For example, the logics undergirding Black racialization (the "one drop" rule) and Native racialization ("blood quantum") in the United States are in one sense antithetical. But as Patrick Wolfe and Kimberley TallBear have demonstrated, the conjoined imperatives of labor exploitation and territorial expansion make these modes not only fully compatible but also mutually dependent. While the legacies of eighteenth- and nineteenth-century racial science and contemporary practices of enumeration condition us to think of racial categories as discrete, independent, and bounded, a relational approach reveals them to be coproduced and coconstitutive, and always dependent on constructions of gender, sexuality, labor, and citizenship.[3] Colonialism and white supremacy have always been relational projects. They rely on logics of sorting, ranking, and comparison that produce and naturalize categories of racial difference necessary for the legitimation of slavery, settler colonialism, and imperial expansion.

As several of the essays make clear, this work has a long history, both in terms of scholarly analysis and political practice; relational frameworks themselves are not new. A relational framework lies at the heart of a long history of women of color scholarship and political practice centered on relational understandings of race, featured most notably in collections such as *This Bridge Called My Back,* first published in 1981, as well as Vicki Ruiz and Ellen Carol DuBois's *Unequal Sisters* anthologies, first published in 1990. Other works from that period anticipate many of the themes of this volume, works such as Jack Forbes's *Africans and Native Americans: The Language of Race and the Evolution of Red-Black Peoples* (1993); Tomás Almaguer's *Racial Fault Lines: The Historical Origins of White Supremacy in California* (1994); and Evelyn Hu-DeHart's investigations into the racialization of Asians in Mexico and Latin America. More recently, there have been edited volumes by Roderick Ferguson and Grace Hong and by Alyosha Goldstein,[4] the journal *Kalfou: A Journal of Comparative and Relational Ethnic Studies,* and a growing body of critical scholarship associated with the critical ethnic studies formation. Relational frameworks are also an important component of the broadly transnational and diasporic turn within U.S. ethnic studies and American studies, as well as Indigenous studies ascendant in the last twenty years.

We can trace commitments to a relational study of race, as a political practice, within an expansive tradition of Black internationalist and anti-imperialist politics. Richard Wright's book *The Color Curtain,* reporting on the conference of representatives of Asian and African nations gathered in Bandung, Indonesia, in 1955, offered an early articulation of Third World solidarities within a relational framework, a connection explored in more detail in Roderick Ferguson's essay in this volume. And more than a half century before that, the Black press generated incisive critiques of U.S. imperialism through a logic of relationality. Consider this excerpt from an 1899 editorial in the *Coffeyville (Kansas) American* newspaper, which opposes the U.S. occupation of the Philippines and understands imperial expansion in relation to racialized violence against Black, Chinese, and Native people:

> The matter of the treatment of these people who belong to the dark-skinned races is a matter which concerns us. The conduct of men in the future can only be determined by observing their conduct in the past. Experience and not promises weighs more potently in these matters, and the treatment which the Indians, the Chinese, and the Negroes have received at the hands of white Americans speaks in no uncertain tone—it would be deplorable to have inhabitants of the Philippine Islands treated as the Indians have been treated or the people of Cuba or Puerto Rico ruled as the Negroes of the South have been ruled. . . . This kind of civilization has very little to commend it and it is doubtful whether it ought to be extended to our newly-acquired territory. It is the plain duty of this government to remedy our own scandalous abuses rather than to extend the system under which they have arisen to other people.[5]

The commitment to understand and relate the specificities of racialized experiences to other modes of racial domination expressed so powerfully here animates a growing body of contemporary scholarship within critical ethnic studies and American studies. As we detail in this introduction, *Relational Formations of Race* makes three critical interventions in this developing body of work. First, it advances theoretical work on race and racialization, and the insights produced when racial formation is examined within a relational framework. Second, the essays draw on and help develop a shared methodological framework for the relational study of race across multiple disciplines. Third, the volume stakes out the political and ethical commitments emphasized in relational studies of race, and the important oppositional and liberatory commitments they bear.

THEORIZING RACE RELATIONALLY

In 1899, W. E. B. Du Bois published his classic work *The Philadelphia Negro: A Social Study,* deploying a theoretical framework that would become ubiquitous to a tradition of "community studies" within sociology, anthropology, political science, history, and ethnic studies. Du Bois surveyed a sample of the city's Black residents to understand patterns of housing, education, family life, work, health, and political participation in the context of systematic white discrimination and exclusion. By collecting, aggregating, and analyzing this data, Du Bois made visible the particular experiences, traits, and characteristics that made Philadelphia's Black community distinct from the city's white majority, or what he described as "the real conditions of this group of human beings."[6]

Thousands of invaluable studies have followed in this tradition, documenting the particular experiences, practices, insights, and worldviews of racialized groups in diverse locations: in the segregated neighborhoods of Detroit and Cleveland; the barrios of Chicago and New York; within World War II internment camps and nineteenth-century Chinatowns; and in Native American boarding schools and reservations. And while Du Bois himself would go on to produce a wide-ranging body of scholarship and analysis that was often international and relational in its orientation, the dominant research and teaching paradigms continue to be organized around the model of examining racialized groups in isolation and in relation to whiteness. The approach stems in part from the ways that fields of ethnic studies developed from the distinct social movements each group waged in the 1960s in order to bring greater recognition to their particular and distinctive experiences and histories. Thus, many introductory and survey courses on race are organized around discrete group-based rubrics, introducing the experiences of Asian Americans in one week and those of African Americans in another. Thematic courses in many disciplines follow similar conventions, explicating the literary archives of Mexican American writers in one seminar and those of Native American authors in another. These race-based "subfields" (e.g., "Asian American sociology" or "Latino/a history") have played a central role in pluralizing many disciplines in the last forty years.

Even in the interdisciplinary field of ethnic studies, this framework predominates. While ethnic studies scholars have traced the relationships between dominant systems of power, such as slavery, colonialism, imperialism, and genocide, group-based experiences are typically examined within distinct units or courses. Thus, in studying a topic like "the peopling of the Americas," the material might cover colonialism and genocide (Native Americans); slavery and abolition (African Americans); and immigration and restriction (Asian Americans and Latinos). Such approaches allow students to understand social relations and their histories not only from the "bottom up" but also from the perspective of different groups.

The specialized forms of knowledge, practice, and analysis undergirding this scholarship are invaluable; they have admitted and made legible a broad range of histories, experiences, and struggles long excluded from mainstream academic discourse and public knowledge. At the same time, these paradigms can reproduce a theoretical understanding of race in which racialized groups are conceptualized as discrete and atomized entities that possess internally determined essences and characteristics. Researchers may thus preconstitute a particular group (e.g., "Asian Americans") as their object of inquiry, conceptualizing race as a "thing" or a property. This framework, described by social theorists in other contexts as rooted in a "substantialist" perspective, presumes that racialized groups are intrinsic entities that bear singular, unitary, and distinctive attributes.[7]

As the scholars in this volume demonstrate, racialized meanings, identities, and characteristics are always constituted through relationships and are always dependent on a shared field of social meaning; they are never produced in isolation. Race is not legible or significant outside a relational context. From this perspective, race does not define the characteristics of a person; instead, it is better understood as the space and connections between people that structure and regulate their association. To inhabit, claim, or be ascribed a particular racialized identity or grouping is to be located in an assemblage of historical and contemporary relationships. For example, sociologist Michael Rodríguez-Muñiz has elsewhere argued that the "focus on individual groups encourages a conception of ethnoracial politics populated by isolated and autonomous constituencies—as if racial projects, such as the Black Lives Matter movement and Latino civil rights advocacy, arise in an ethnoracial and political vacuum."[8] By contrast, he explains herein, a relational approach "does not presume the existence of independent, already formed groups" but "holds that ethnoracial boundaries, identities, and political affiliations do not precede, but rather are the *effects* of these relations."

This relational understanding of race draws heavily from Michael Omi and Howard Winant's theory of racial formation, which conceptualizes the production of racial meaning and identity as "always and necessarily a social and historical process."[9] Omi and Winant foreground the role of particular "racial projects" within both micro and macro settings that become generative of racial meaning and power. Racial projects, they explain, "connect what race *means* in a particular discursive practice and the ways in which both social structures and everyday experiences are racially *organized,* based upon that meaning."[10] From this perspective, race can never be isolated from the contextual processes and relationships that shape its meaning. Racialization describes the formation and reformation of these relationships, legible through a range of cultural categories including sexuality, bloodlines, propriety, innocence, fitness, violence, citizenship, savagery, morality, and freedom.[11]

An understanding of racial formation as constituted through different racial projects is fundamental to understanding race as a relational concept. When distinct racial projects are analyzed within the same field of meaning and power, new insights are revealed about the nature of those projects and the broader field of racial formation in which they take shape. As Tiya Miles explains in her essay in this volume, "Uncle Tom Was an Indian: Tracing the Red in Black Slavery," "if we look at African American history and Native American history side by side rather than in isolation, we will see the edges where those histories meet and begin to comprehend a fuller and more fascinating picture. At the intersections of Black and Native experiences, we gain greater understanding of the histories of both groups."

George Lipsitz similarly argues in the roundtable discussion (chapter 1) with George Sánchez and Kelly Lytle Hernández that examining the relationships and articulations between and among subordinated groups requires scholars "to break with this notion of a one-at-a-time relationship with white-ness for each aggrieved group." For Lipsitz, relational frameworks can disrupt "an uninterrogated privileging of whiteness" that typically asks, "How does each group deal with the white center?" rather than exploring the ways that "polylateral relations among aggrieved communities of color" develop and cohere.

As Natalia Molina demonstrates in her essay, a relational framework of analysis is not necessarily the same as a comparative one. A comparative treat-ment of race typically compares and contrasts the characteristics and experi-ences of different racialized groups, often treating their boundaries as stable and produced independently. For example, comparative models have sought to chart the similarities and differences in the patterns of racial hierarchy and formation between different nations, or to chart such similarities and differ-ences between minoritized groups in the United States.[12] An important tradition of scholarship has relied on this comparative framework, including transnational studies by George Fredrickson, Anthony Marx, and Howard Winant.[13] But by taking inventory of the particular attributes or experiences of a group or across differing contexts, such frameworks can reify the assump-tion that racialized groups are operating in autonomous and distinct social, political, and cultural spheres and within isolated, self-contained worlds. Relational frameworks, by contrast, often incorporate but go beyond the logic of comparison to examine the intersections and the mutually constitutive forces between/among what is compared. To study race relation-ally is to acknowledge the limits of examining racialized groups in isolation. As sociologist Matthew Desmond contends, "Locality must be ancillary to relationality."[14]

A relational treatment of race thus conceptualizes racial formation as a mutually constitutive process; racial meanings, boundaries, and hierarchies are coproduced through dynamic processes that change across time and place. Thus, popular discourses on race that appear on the surface to be autonomous and self-generating are in fact legible only through a relational understanding of race. The political scientist Claire Jean Kim has noted that even when scholars attend to the differential trajectories of racialized groups, they can nonetheless "impute mutual autonomy to respective racialization processes that are in fact mutually constitutive." Thus, Kim explains, the "respective racialization trajectories" of different "groups are profoundly interrelated."[15]

In this volume, Perla Guerrero extends this argument by examining the racialization of Vietnamese refugees in Arkansas since the 1970s, charting how American nationalism and militarism, discourses of Christian benevolence, and the long-standing dynamics of Black/white racialization produce particular representations and understandings of Vietnamese refugees. Guerrero argues that this process "explain[s] the elasticity of racialization, as a single group can be defined in shifting and competing ways." Similarly, political scientist Julie Lee Merseth explores the racialization of Arab and Muslim Americans since September 11, 2001, a process that was made legible through their relational positioning in the field of U.S. racial and ethnic politics. The essays by Guerrero, Merseth, Ferguson, and others also reveal the transnational and global underpinnings of the relational study of race.

METHODOLOGY

In academic discourse, the researcher's authority is often established by satisfying or demonstrating mastery or expertise in a particular field. Such conventions of expertise and authority are important to the collective process of building academic fields and shared knowledge, establishing research norms, and generating a shared language to advance collective projects of learning and research. But they can also limit the kinds of questions that can be posed when our objects of study and research questions do not obey the boundaries of our areas of expertise. Scholars employing relational frameworks of race often forgo a claim to expertise to develop a methodology guided by inquiry, rather than expertise, in pursuing research questions that take them beyond their credentialed areas of expertise.

Such new orientations take time. This methodology inherently requires scholars to push beyond their areas of expertise, acknowledging that one can make important contributions to particular research areas without demonstrating mastery of them. George Sánchez observes in the roundtable discussion in this volume that such work "means you have to really enmesh yourself into historiographies, into literatures, traditions that you may not have been trained in. And for many of us, that's a real limitation. It doesn't mean that we shouldn't do it; it just means that to be serious about it is going to take some time." As sociologist Laura Enriquez notes in her essay, "Border-Hopping Mexicans, Law-Abiding Asians, and Racialized Illegality," research questions drive these shifts. Enriquez explains that she found her way to the relational study of race because of the questions I was asking about the role of race in the lives of undocumented immigrants. Most of the literature on undocumented youth focuses on Latinas/os and the structural limitations created by their immigration status; few discuss how intersecting social locations, like race, differentiate experiences of illegality. To fill this gap, I sought to assess how race emerges to structure and differentiate the experiences of Latina/o and API undocumented students. I found that a relational framework was a productive tool for imagining the dynamic and multifaceted production of racialized illegality.

Relational studies of race are thus not limited to studying the interactions of stigmatized groups with one another. Relational frameworks can provide purchase and insight even when different groups are not in frequent or direct contact. These groups share social fields and participate in and react to mutual social processes and practices even as they might inhabit distinct positions within shared structures. As Molina puts it,

> We need to ask who else is (or was) present in or near the communities we study—and what difference these groups' presence made (or makes). This is no less than what Chicana/o historians have been asking those who study the mainstream to do for decades. Just as the prevailing version of U.S. history was incomplete without an examination of the influence of racialized groups, the study of any single racialized group calls for an understanding of the impact of the experiences of other similarly situated groups.

As Lisa Lowe demonstrates in *The Intimacies of Four Continents,* the structure of the historical archive itself often makes such work challenging by masking the relational interdependencies and connections of different groups and places, requiring scholars to read against such absences. Lowe explains,

> The organization of the archives discourages links between settler colonialism in North America and the West Indies and the African slave trade; or attention to the conjunction of the abolition of slavery and the importing of Chinese and South Asian indentured labor; or a correlation of the East Indies and China trades and the rise of bourgeois Europe.

Lowe finds that "in order to nuance these connections and interdependencies, one must read across the separate repositories organized by office, task, and function, and by period and area, precisely implicating one set of preoccupations in and with another."[16]

Many of the essays in this volume take up this imperative, pushing back against the inherent logic of categorization and typology that organizes the archive to reveal such dependencies. For example, Alyosha Goldstein's essay, "Entangled Dispossessions: Race and Colonialism in the Historical Present," considers how African Americans and Native Americans experienced land dispossession and its redress under the Claims Resolution Act of 2010. As Goldstein explains, "The scope and logic of juridical settlement strive to make illegible the interconnections of the colonial taking of Native peoples' lands, the genocide and displacement of Native peoples, the abduction and enslavement of African peoples, and the constitutive force of differential racialization and anti-Blackness as primary social, economic, and political conditions of the United States." Thus, he contends, "studying racial formation as material practices of relational racialization rather than as distinct taxonomies provides a way of confronting how white supremacy in the United States continues to sustain colonial possession and the social exploitation and disposability of racially devalued people as mutually constitutive today."

By making these kinds of relational connections, scholars can also comprehend the ways power operates within a much wider framework. For example, in her contribution, "Indians and Negroes in Spite of Themselves: Puerto Rican Students at the Carlisle Indian Industrial School," Catherine Ramírez reconceptualizes the construct of assimilation within a relational framework. Ramírez's background and expertise lie primarily in Latino/a and Latin American studies. But to understand the complexity and nuance of the lives of Puerto Rican students sent to a boarding school for Native students famously organized around the promise to "Kill the Indian, Save the Man," Ramírez draws on analytics in Indigenous studies and history. She explains,

> If we approach assimilation as a relational process, one organized around ranking, entering, and being situated in a regime of difference, then we see that assimilation is often one and the same as subordination, marginalization, or even, paradoxically, exclusion (differential inclusion, in other words). By studying the experiences of African Americans, Native Americans, and Puerto Ricans at Carlisle and Hampton in relation to one another, I seek to offer a glimpse of assimilation's prehistory and show that assimilation is more than the process whereby the boundary between mainstream and margin blurs or disappears; it is also the process whereby that boundary is, paradoxically, reinforced.

These insights and observations also apply to the use of relational frameworks in the classroom, as they push instructors to engage material that might be beyond their recognized areas of authority. To make use of a relational framework in this way subverts the notion that instructors are always the masters of the subjects they teach, modeling instead an ethic of shared inquiry rooted in the social production of knowledge. For example, to engage students in the work of Jeffrey Yamashita's chapter, "Becoming 'Hawaiian': A Relational Racialization of Japanese American Soldiers from Hawai'i during World War II in the U.S. South," requires instructors to enter into dialogue with a diverse array of historical concepts and theoretical constructs, including the complicated histories of European and Asian settler colonialism in Hawai'i, U.S. regimes of militarism in the nineteenth and twentieth centuries, and the institutionalization of Jim Crow in the U.S. South in the mid-twentieth century. But the payoff is rich, as students gain new insights about the interdependence of U.S. imperialism abroad and the hardening of racial hierarchies at home.

Another important methodological concern advanced in this volume is the imperative to recognize the distinctiveness and at times singularity of particular racial formations within a relational framework, rather than attempting only to identify commonalities of experience or position. Andrea Smith has argued elsewhere, for example, that white supremacy is structured through discrete pillars of domination rooted in the logics of genocide and land acquisition, labor exploitation and slavery, and war.[17] Here, racial difference is constituted through these distinctive yet mutually imbricated modes of domination. To study race relationally requires one to be attentive to such variance. But even as groups are differently positioned with regard to the logics of slavery, genocide, or war, a relational framework can help illuminate these distinctions and the shared logic that undergirds different modes of racialization.

For example, Steven Salaita's essay, "How Palestine Became Important to American Indian Studies," reveals the generative inquiries made possible when Native studies scholars bring their political and intellectual frameworks to bear on the issue of Palestine. Salaita observes that these possibilities are "tremendously rich and accommodate complicated sites of material politics (by which I mean economic systems, activist communities, electoral processes, educational paradigms, and modes of resistance). Accessing those sites enables us to aspire to relationships that go beyond theoretical innovation by concomitantly emphasizing the practices and possibilities of decolonization."

Yet Salaita also cautions against simplistic analogies or comparisons to Native experiences, which can erase the specificity of Indigenous struggles in the United States, particularly when they are invoked to legitimize the subordination of another group. Thus, contributors across the volume outline the ways that relational frameworks must always be grounded in the unevenness of differential racial formations, attentive to what Cherrié Moraga has described as "the danger . . . in failing to acknowledge the specificity of the oppression."[18]

A final methodological emphasis concerns the ways that the relational study of race must remain attentive to the distinctive labor of gender and sexuality through intersectional readings of racial formations. Following the work of Kimberlé Crenshaw, scholars using such frameworks understand all racialized groupings as marked by internal distinction and hierarchy related to gender and sexuality, which are coconstitutive of racial meaning and power.[19] As Ferguson notes in his essay herein, such relational frameworks have long been at the center of women of color politics and practice. In their volume *Strange Affinities: The Gender and Racial Politics of Comparative Racialization*, Ferguson and coeditor Grace Hong explain that women of color feminism and queer of color critique "reveal the ways in which racialized communities are not homogenous but instead have always policed and preserved the difference between those who are able to conform to categories of normativity, respectability, and value, and those who are forcibly excluded from such categories."[20]

REENVISIONING POLITICS AND SOLIDARITY THROUGH RELATIONAL FRAMEWORKS OF RACE

A final emphasis of many of the essays in this volume concerns the new political and ethical insights revealed through the relational study of race. If racism, colonialism, and white supremacy are understood as relational in their logic and operations, effective antiracisms must also operate from a relational premise. Relationality here works through an understanding of both similarity and difference. Audre Lorde explains that "unity does not mean unanimity—Black people are not some standardly digestible quantity. In order to work together we do not have to become a mix of indistinguishable particles resembling a vat of homogenized chocolate milk. Unity implies the coming together of elements which are, to begin with, varied and diverse in their particular natures." Relational antiracisms are most generative when they are rooted in the difficult labor of what Lorde describes as the "unromantic and tedious work necessary to forge meaningful coalitions . . . recognizing which coalitions are possible and which coalitions are not."[21]

With Lorde, previous work has demonstrated the challenges, insights, and dynamics of this work at a variety of theoretical and historical sites. For example, geographer and ethnic studies scholar Laura Pulido has examined key groups in the Third World left movement in Los Angeles representing African Americans, Chicana/os, and Asians, including the Black Panther Party, the Center for Autonomous Social Action, and East Wind, beginning in the 1960s. Her interviews reveal the ways participants in one movement learn from participants in other movements. Relationality can thus operate at a more intimate scale and can serve as a resource when engaging in larger social and political acts.

In his essay, "The Relational Revolutions of Antiracist Formations," Ferguson discusses both the Third World politics that arose from postcolonial nations in the 1950s and 1960s as well as the long history of writing and analysis by women of color, and how these relational frameworks bear important oppositional and liberatory commitments. Ferguson argues that a genealogy "for a relational understanding of race came out of the great social movements of anticolonialism and antiracism in the twentieth century." In the "histories and literatures of national liberation and women of color feminist formations," Ferguson finds "models for antiracist relational analyses and politics, models that were not comparing discrete cultural groups but the implementation and effects of racial processes on various communities within the Global North and the Global South." Ferguson sees a "shift toward relations and connectivity" driven by these formations that "represents one of the great epistemic shifts in the politics and study of race."

Vijay Prashad's 2001 monograph, *Everybody Was Kung Fu Fighting: Afro-Asian Connections and the Myth of Cultural Purity,* similarly foregrounds the ways in which anticolonial struggles led by African and Asian diasporic communities have always been intertwined and mutually constituted. These cultural and political traditions have never been discrete, thus requiring scholars to trace out these relationships and interconnections rather than presuming the existence of fixed primordial histories. Prashad analyzes the realm of cultural production, including the heterogeneous roots of reggae music in Jamaica, as one important mode through which these intertwined histories and contexts are made visible. Other scholars, including Gabriel Solis, Sohail Daulatzai, Loren Kajikawa, and Gaye Theresa Johnson, have similarly demonstrated the role of music as a particular site of relational antiracist consciousness and solidarity.[22] Theater studies scholars such as Diana Paulin have tracked similar connections in relation to Black drama and fiction.[23]

The volume contributes to a growing body of scholarly work and political activism that traces the connections between and among differentiated processes of colonization and racialization. Such work, for example, puts insights from analyses of settler colonialism in dialogue with interrogations of transnational migration in both the Atlantic and Pacific worlds. It also considers the connections between the assertions of immigrant rights and claims for justice in the United States and conceptualizations of Black subordination and freedom.

These connections must be made with care and attention to historical and political difference if they are to produce new political imaginaries. For example, Tiffany Willoughby-Herard critiques the limitations and closures produced by facile and shallow comparisons between slavery and the contemporary struggle for immigrant rights. A rich and sophisticated tradition of Black-led freedom struggles and abolitionist thought all too often becomes flattened though such comparisons by unwittingly trading in "that old canard of modernity that Black political consciousness . . . is too outmoded for contemporary politics." Willoughby-Herard envisions a relational politics in which "we can articulate our serious concern for the plight of undocumented workers, deported students, people who can secure citizenship only by serving in American military misadventures, the millions residing in immigrant detention centers, and immigrant laborers—*and* witness and name the violent murder and criminalization of Black people in every arena of social experience through the enduring nature of slavery, lynching, convict lease conditions, and the sexual violence that links them."

Implicit in the analysis of Ferguson, Willoughby-Herard, and other contributors to the volume is a commitment to move within and across differing political traditions, histories, and frames of analysis. M. Jaqui Alexander has described this process in regard to the formation of women of color politics as the need to become "fluent in each another's histories . . . to unlearn an impulse that allows mythologies about each other to replace knowing about one another . . . [and] to cultivate a way of knowing in which we direct our social, cultural, psychic, and spiritually marked attention on each other." She sets this ambition plainly: "We cannot afford to cease yearning for each other's company."[24]

Situating one's experiences and struggles in this way yields new relations of solidarity and horizons of justice by showing how racial discourses and projects inform one another, and by denaturalizing and exposing the logics of violence and dispossession that undergird diverse forms of racial subordination. We don't live isolated lives; these relationships and articulations already exist. As Lorde explains, "Our struggles are particular, but we are not alone." Racism is always already relational. The question is whether our scholarship and politics attend to this relationality—in all its challenges and complexity—and take seriously the ways it operates in our world.

ORGANIZATION OF THE VOLUME

The volume is divided into four parts. The first, "Theorizing Race Relationally," considers a set of theories and methods used to study race relationally, as well as the new analytic insights produced through these frameworks. The second part, "Relational Research as Political Practice," uses a relational framework to make broader interventions into the critical study of race and distinct fields within ethnic studies, foregrounding the distinct political insights and analyses that can be produced through this work. The third part, "Historical Frameworks," examines relational formations of race across time, foregrounding the ways that particular historical forces and events contest and transform racial meanings, identities, and power through relational frameworks. The essays in this part disrupt more familiar histories of discrete racialized groups by examining the coproductive character of racial formation. The essays in the final part, "Relational Frameworks in Contemporary Policy," are rooted in social scientific traditions and conventions that examine relational race in contemporary settings. The essays also demonstrate the ways that a relational framework can be brought to bear on different qualitative methodologies within the social sciences, including content analysis, interviews, and studies of racial group formation.

NOTES

1. Martin Luther King Jr., "Letter from Birmingham Jail," in *Why We Can't Wait* (New York: Signet, 1963), 65.
2. Martin Luther King Jr., "Beyond Vietnam: A Time to Break Silence," April 4, 1967, Riverside Church, New York City, archived at the Martin Luther King, Jr. Research and Education Institute, Stanford University, https://kinginstitute.stanford.edu/king-papers/documents/beyond-vietnam.
3. Patrick Wolfe, "Settler Colonialism and the Elimination of the Native," *Journal of Genocide Research* 8, no. 4 (2006); Kim TallBear, *Native American DNA:*

Tribal Belonging and the False Promise of Genetic Science (Minneapolis: University of Minnesota Press, 2013).

4. Alyosha Goldstein, ed., *Formations of United States Colonialism* (Durham, NC: Duke University Press, 2014); Grace Kyungwon Hong and Roderick A. Ferguson, eds., *Strange Affinities: The Gender and Sexual Politics of Comparative Racialization* (Durham, NC: Duke University Press, 2011).

5. *Coffeyville American,* February 11, 1899, in *The Black Press Views American Imperialism (1898–1900),* edited by George P. Marks (New York: Arno Press), 114.

6. Du Bois, *The Philadelphia Negro* (1899; repr., New York: Schocken Books, 1967), 5.

7. Matthew Desmond, "Relational Ethnography," *Theoretical Sociology* 43 (2014): 550–51.

8. Michael Rodríguez-Muñiz, "Racial Arithmetic: Ethnoracial Politics in a Relational Key" (paper presented at the "Studying Race Relationally" conference, University of Chicago, May 13, 2016).

9. Michael Omi and Howard Winant, *Racial Formation in the United States: From the 1960s to the 1980s* (New York: Routledge, 1986).

10. Michael Omi and Howard Winant, *Racial Formation in the United States: From the 1960s to the 1990s,* 2nd ed. (New York: Routledge, 1994), 56.

11. Roderick Ferguson, "Race," in *Keywords for American Cultural Studies,* ed. Bruce Blodgett and Glen Hendler (New York: New York University Press, 2007), 191–95.

12. Hong and Ferguson, introduction to *Strange Affinities,* 9. See also Antonio Tiongson Jr., "Afro-Asian Inquiry and the Problematics of Comparative Critique," *Critical Ethnic Studies* 1, no. 2 (2015).

13. Anthony Marx, *Making Race and Nation: A Comparison of the United States, South Africa, and Brazil* (Cambridge: Cambridge University Press, 1997); Howard Winant, *The World Is a Ghetto: Race and Democracy since World War II* (New York: Basic Books, 2001); George M. Fredrickson, *The Comparative Imagination: On the History of Racism, Nationalism, and Social Movements* (Berkeley: University of California Press, 2000).

14. Desmond, "Relational Ethnography," 559.

15. Claire Jean Kim, "The Racial Triangulation of Asian Americans," *Politics & Society* 27, no. 1 (1999): 106.

16. Lisa Lowe, *The Intimacies of Four Continents* (Durham, NC: Duke University Press, 2015), 5.

17. Andrea Smith, "Indigeneity, Settler Colonialism, White Supremacy," in *Racial Formation in the 21st Century,* ed. Daniel Martinez HoSang, Oneka LaBennett, and Laura Pulido (Berkeley: University of California Press, 2012), 66–90.

18. Cherríe Moraga and Gloria Anzaldúa, "Introduction, 1981," in *This Bridge Called My Back: Writings by Radical Women of Color,* 4th ed., ed. Cherríe Moraga and Gloria Anzaldúa (Albany: State University of New York Press, 2015), 24.

19. Kimberlé Crenshaw, "Mapping the Margins: Intersectionality, Identity Politics, and Violence against Women of Color," *Stanford Law Review* 43, no. 6 (1991).

20. Hong and Ferguson, introduction to *Strange Affinities*, 2.

21. Audre Lorde, "Learning from the 60's," in *Sister Outsider: Essays & Speeches by Audre Lorde* (Berkeley, CA: Crossing Press, 2007), 134–44.

22. Sohail Daulatzai, *Black Star, Crescent Moon: The Muslim International and Black Freedom beyond America* (Minneapolis: University of Minnesota Press, 2012); Loren Kajikawa, "The Sound of Struggle: Black Revolutionary Nationalism and Asian American Jazz," in *Jazz/Not Jazz: The Music and Its Boundaries,* ed. David A. Ake, Daniel Goldmark, and Charles H. Garrett (Berkeley: University of California Press, 2012), 190–216; Gabriel Solis, "The Black Pacific: Music and Racialization in Papua New Guinea and Australia," *Critical Sociology* 41, no. 2 (2015); Tamara Roberts, *Resounding Afro Asia: Interracial Music and the Politics of Collaboration* (Oxford: Oxford University Press, 2016).

23. Diana Rebekkah Paulin, *Imperfect Unions: Staging Miscegenation in U.S. Drama and Fiction* (Minneapolis: University of Minnesota Press, 2012).

24. M. Jacqui Alexander, *Pedagogies of Crossing: Meditations on Feminism, Sexual Politics, Memory, and the Sacred* (Durham, NC: Duke University Press, 2006), 269.

PART ONE

Theorizing Race Relationally

The chapters in this section explore the theories and methods that undergird the relational study of race, as well as the new analytical insights produced through these frameworks. In the "Race as a Relational Theory" roundtable discussion, George Lipsitz, George Sánchez, and Kelly Lytle Hernández reflect on the personal and professional experiences that led them to study race relationally. Their dialogue sheds light on how such work often requires scholars to go beyond their immediate area of expertise organized around the histories, cultures, and politics of specific racialized groups. To study race relationally is to place one's work in a dialogue with events, people, and literature that may not immediately seem to resonate with or influence the conventional frameworks of one's scholarship. In doing so, scholars often need to cede the conceit that they can entirely master a broad range of new literature, archives, or other primary sources. Instead, scholars must ask new questions about their object of study in order to acknowledge the limitations of their scholarly training, field, methods, and sources.

Along with shedding light on how studying race relationally works as theory and method, Lipsitz, Sánchez, and Lytle Hernández highlight how studying race relationally can help us know and better address social justice issues in collaboration with the communities we serve. As Lytle Hernández says, "[I saw] that to unravel anti-Blackness, I was going to have to take on what was happening with the undocumented folks, and antibrownness, and also think through indigeneity. It is [a sense of] solidarity but is also an understanding that it's not just relationships. It's that your freedom is my freedom. Your struggle is my struggle. Your sacrifice is my sacrifice."

Some of us in this volume have come to a relational approach to race by necessity. We may have not started out thinking of the need to study race relationally, but the complexities of our subjects, respondents, or other actors in our narratives all called for a more complex lens than one that tackled one racialized group at a time. This is the subject explored by Natalia Molina in her essay, "Examining Chicana/o History through a Relational Lens." Molina argues that we should examine Chicana/os in relation to other racialized groups in order to develop a fuller understanding of how racial categories form and operate. The chapter highlights different models of relational work by examining key works in Chicana/o history that have also employed a relational methodology. In addition, the chapter demonstrates how we can use organizing principles other than race to find links between racialized groups. By revisiting key events in Chicana/o history and examining them through a relational lens, Molina demonstrates the new insights we gain when we interrogate how groups are racialized in relation to one another. She argues for the necessity of pulling back the lens and adopting a relational approach even when examining the experiences of a single racialized group, because "the very framework that comprises our understanding of race is necessarily and inseparably drawn from the experiences of racialized groups vis-à-vis other racialized groups." Chicano/a historians have long argued that histories of the mainstream are incomplete if they do not consider the influence of racialized groups; similarly, she says, "the study of any single racialized group calls for an understanding of the impact of the experiences of other similarly situated groups."

In his essay, "Entangled Dispossessions: Race and Colonialism in the Historical Present," Alyosha Goldstein illuminates how studying race relationally can serve as the glue that connects seemingly disparate histories/moments in time. Goldstein's essay examines the historical entanglements of U.S. colonialism, racial capitalism, and the economies of expendability as they extend into the present. The primary focus of the chapter is the Claims Resolution Act (CRA) of 2010, legislation that brought together and financed a series of milestone U.S. civil rights and Native American class-action lawsuit settlements. The chapter considers how and why the CRA brings into proximity discrepant yet connected histories of dispossession and racism and attempts to situate them within an overarching teleology of progress in the face of economic volatility and social instability. The analysis reveals the significance of the differential devaluation of racialized groups and the dynamics of settler colonialism for understanding the relationship between anti-Black racism and the dispossession of Indigenous peoples.

Studying race relationally allows us to see how systems of power, such as settler colonialism and white supremacy, operate in interlocking ways. Goldstein turns to legal cases to examine how ethical and juridical reconciliation shed light on—as well as attempt to erase and contain—a history of racist discriminatory laws. It is only by examining African Americans and Native Americans in relation to one another that we can see the interconnections among their histories of dispossession, colonization, enslavement, and differential racialization, and how these histories continue to shape the present, even as the logic of juridical settlement strives to obscure such connections. This work is vital. As Goldstein reminds us, "Studying racial formation as material practices of relational racialization rather than as distinct taxonomies provides a way of confronting how white supremacy in the United States continues to sustain colonial possession and the social exploitation and disposability of racially devalued people as mutually constitutive today."

ONE

Race as a Relational Theory

A ROUNDTABLE DISCUSSION

George Lipsitz, George J. Sánchez, and
Kelly Lytle Hernández, with Daniel Martinez HoSang
and Natalia Molina

This roundtable features three scholars who have produced some of the most groundbreaking and generative work on the relational study of race: George Lipsitz, George Sánchez, and Kelly Lytle Hernández. Recorded at the University of Southern California in December 2016,[1] their wide-ranging discussion addresses the particular role of Los Angeles and California in relational studies of race; the challenges of teaching and research using a relational framework; and the importance of such frameworks beyond the academy.

George Sánchez, author of the award-winning *Becoming Mexican American* (Oxford University Press, 1993), has spent more than two decades chronicling the complex multiracial relationships in the Boyle Heights neighborhood of Los Angeles through an array of research, teaching, and public impact projects, including collaborations with several local museums and history projects.

George Lipsitz has authored dozens of articles and books that incorporate a relational framework, including many works that address the particular role of music, the arts, and other forms of cultural production in this process. He is also the editor of *Kalfou: A Journal of Comparative and Relational Ethnic Studies,* one of the first scholarly journals to explicitly foreground a relational framework.

Kelly Lytle Hernández is the author of the celebrated *Migra! A History of the U.S. Border Patrol* (University of California Press, 2010) and *City of Inmates: Conquest, Rebellion, and the Rise of Human Caging, 1771–1965* (University of North Carolina Press, 2017). Both works exemplify the most far-reaching and sophisticated insights that can be produced through relational studies of race.

DANIEL MARTINEZ HOSANG AND NATALIA MOLINA: *Can you describe for us how your teaching and research came to address and incorporate relational frameworks of race?*

GEORGE LIPSITZ: I don't think there are many people who set out to say, "I am going to do a comparative and relational ethnic studies project." I think they found it in the complexity of the world. And I think that had two ramifications. One, it meant that they had to break with this notion of a one-at-a-time relationship with whiteness for each aggrieved group. We didn't know until we were doing the comparative and relational work that there was an uninterrogated privileging of whiteness that had been there—the issue was [always] "How does each group deal with the white center?" not "How are polylateral relations among aggrieved communities of color formulated?"

There is this line in a Chester Himes article in the *Crisis*.[2] He was writing about the Zoot Suit Riots and the Japanese internment. And he basically said, "I came to Los Angeles, and it hurt me worse than Cleveland. And it hurt me racially worse than any place I have seen. But until I saw the Zoot Suiters getting attacked, I secretly thought it was something wrong with us. When I saw what they were doing to the Japanese, saw what they were doing to the Mexicans, I realized it was them, not us. And rather than apologizing or explaining ourselves, we had to basically see that there is a system at work there." Himes reiterated this line of thought in his 1945 novel *If He Hollers Let Him Go,* where he describes "little Riki Oyana" singing "God Bless America" and being hauled off to the internment center at the Santa Anita racetrack the next day.[3] I think most of the work that will come to the fore of the studies we talk about comes from the ways in which race becomes transposed into mass incarceration, environmental racism, descriptions of nonnormative sexual and gender behavior, and low-wage labor. None of these issues can be solved one group at a time. So part of the difficulty of [most] racial studies is that you take the tort model of law and say, "There but for race, people would have been OK." But we know that race is intersectional. It's the life of the party; it never goes anywhere alone. Because race has to do with differential citizenship, lesser citizenship, premature death, disproportionate exposure to violence, it makes you look at more than one group. But I also think it's important for us not to privilege one way of looking at things and say we always want things to be comparative and relational. There is a time to [look at things] together; there is a time to [look at them] apart. There are things that are enabled by looking comparatively and relationally, and there are things that are inhibited by it.

GEORGE SÁNCHEZ: I didn't enter looking for relational approaches, but I was drawn there by the consistency of what I kept finding. And so my first book, *Becoming Mexican American,* though now people look at it and they think, "Oh, relational this, relational that." I didn't see that at all. To me, [getting to the idea of the relational] was a learning process of having been trained in an older ethnic studies model and attempting to stay focused on the subject at hand and constantly being pushed. But also realizing that while on the one hand [relationality] did happen everywhere, on the other hand, it manifested itself in certain places in certain kinds of ways. So that was, for me, an eye-opening thing. And then I wanted to systematically go back and think about how we write this different kind of history. What are the various ways one can approach that?

For me, the other big revelation came from the 1992 LA riots. Experiencing that in Los Angeles, experiencing it at the end of publishing my first book, meant that I had to deal with a real-time historical event that I kept seeing as completely multiracial. And seeing where whiteness fits into all this. It was easy to point to [Police Chief] Darryl Gates . . . and [Mayor] Tom Bradley [in terms of speaking to the Black-white dynamics]. But I like microstories, so I turned to those on the ground. Their own individual stories said volumes about where they fit into different kinds of racial orders. You know, at those moments, you don't simply sort of raise your hand and offer a history lesson. You actually have to deal with what it means to be in the moment.[4]

I was taken aback by how much everyone wanted to reframe the LA riots as a two-dimensional thing. Whether you were framing it from the perspective of Koreans or from the perspective of African American young men or from [the perspective of] law and order. It was almost impossible for people to frame it in its full complexity: to me that was very instructive. This is not an easy task. It's one of the most difficult tasks, and we haven't mastered the way in which we have to understand it. And literally this was something happening right before our eyes. And so I never bemoaned the fact that there are a lot of different models at work in ethnic studies, because this complex relational analysis seemed really difficult to do when you are actually trying to interpret something that's happening right in front of you in real time.

For me, teaching is maybe the easiest way to try to understand something, because you are trying to process things at a whole bunch of different levels. So you are trying to put stories together at similar times.

To teach the history of Los Angeles is, for me, to teach a history that is constantly unknowing itself. You have to constantly push out. Why are you using that framework? Doesn't that framework come from somewhere else? Isn't that something that you don't know? How do you deal with what Patty Limerick would call the "legacy of conquest"? If you understand Indigenous stuff, how do you put African American history into that? So it's a constant kind of trying to get students to feel that they don't know what is familiar.

LIPSITZ: Part of what's interesting about Sánchez as a scholar is that he carried Los Angeles with him to Harvard [as an undergraduate], and to [graduate school at] Stanford. And you can see it in *Becoming Mexican American.* There is this place where he talks about the Asian dentists in the East Side [of Los Angeles] because they couldn't practice on the West Side. And so Asians became important in the Chicano community as professionals because white racism kept them out of the West Side. The Repertorio Musical Mexicana record store [he wrote about] was of interest because it was a business that was an ethnic-specific site, but it resonates with the ways in which Black culture, especially Black pop, became a point of entry into America for Mexican immigrants in a way that white Anglo society for the most part didn't.[5] And the issues of the internment—which is always considered a footnote on the East Coast—have a different meaning here. And it's a powerful meaning, not just because of what happened to Japanese Americans but because it maintains [the age-old] trick: "We won't let you assimilate, and now we'll lock you up because you are unassimilable." And so there is something about the state's relationship to racism that becomes evident from that. And then the additional thing that Sánchez did is this amazing discussion of northern Mexico and U.S. capital's penetration into it. There is already baseball instead of bull fighting and beer instead of tequila and Protestant churches all over the place.[6] So Sánchez didn't [start with an assumption about] a blank slate of coming to America and becoming Americans. The ethnic studies that was taught at the institutions where he was, was [like] Mary Antin's *The Promised Land:*[7] "I was nobody; I lived in the dark ages. And now that I am an American, here is my American story." [Sánchez] didn't do that. I think part of it is because you walk around Los Angeles and it's not the Lower East Side Jewish, Polish, Irish, Italian kind of immigration thing. You are forced to see the whole thing differently.

SÁNCHEZ: I think the specific things that I brought were a kind of immersion in a particular racialization of Mexicans in Los Angeles that didn't fit any other patterns that I saw. For me the relationship between

Mexicans and Blacks was a very vibrant, powerful experience. So making sense of the diversity of all that was a fundamental thing for me. I started to see in that experience what was unique about Los Angeles. Part of it was the relationship with Blacks. Part of it was a sense that to my family, Los Angeles did not seem foreign. So discussions like [Oscar] Handlin's about moving to a place and cutting off from [the past] and having to start anew and that sort of stuff—that made no sense to me, being from Los Angeles.[8] My parents felt very comfortable in Los Angeles. It wasn't that it was the same as Mexico, but it was familiar in a very particular way, place names and everything else. So I had to make sense of that very fundamental history—and then I had to ask, How do other groups deal with that? So there were a lot of those kinds of questions coming at me that I knew didn't fit in the paradigms that were being set up on the East Coast.

HOSANG AND MOLINA: *Kelly, can you talk about how your experiences growing up near San Diego shaped the relational focus of your scholarship?*

KELLY LYTLE HERNÁNDEZ: I grew up as a Black girl on the border and part of a very small Black community, where our frame of reference wasn't back East or South. Certainly, there is the weight of the South, but we are always looking toward Mexico. And these are areas of escape, of possibility, of solidarity. That was really what brought me to this way of studying race—our relationships with Mexicans and the way that our possibilities for love and community and survival rested with understanding the Mexican community and the Mexican American community and building with them. That's the history I need to understand: Who are my neighbors? How did they get here? I saw how me and my friends were being policed by drug police in particular, and that gave me a frame of reference for how undocumented folks are being policed on the border, a real critical frame. So that's where *Migra!* came from—from trying to understand what the hell is going on here. What is this process of race that allows the Border Patrol to come on to a bus, pick out everybody who looks Mexican, take them off the bus, and scare them to death, and only half of them come back? I got that as a Black kid. And the other thing I got was, they weren't coming after us. The Border Patrol were the only armed officers who weren't coming after us.

I grew up speaking quite a bit of Spanish. My parents simply said, "You are going to learn. We live near the border. You are going to learn." And my parents enforced that. So the Spanish language comes from a family that said, "At every opportunity we will send you with our friends to spend the day to speak, to be—to travel back and forth across the border, but you will also learn the academic level of it as well." I have carried that with me. After my undergraduate years, I went to live in South Africa and did a typical teaching-abroad program. And it was in South Africa that I began to think more seriously about indigeneity and about the relationships between Blackness and indigeneity, and I came back to the States wanting to think and do a dissertation on African Americans, Native peoples, and land. But when I was in graduate school, I started looking ahead [and trying to figure out], What can you commit yourself to thinking about for 10 years, 20 years? I knew that it was the passion and the politics that I learned in the undocumented labor camps around Proposition 187 [in 1994] that was going to carry me through the dissertation.[9] And [the other thing that pushed me through was] this question that I always had about the bogeyman or the Border Patrol that defined so many people's lives. The personal experiences [that drove me] were much like George [Sánchez]'s. Simply coming up in a diverse community and thinking about how our neighbors were being impacted in ways that were specific to them but that had carryovers or scripts for ourselves. [I saw] that to unravel anti-Blackness, I was going to have to take on what was happening with the undocumented folks, and antibrownness, and also think through indigeneity. It is [a sense of] solidarity but is also an understanding that it's not just relationships. It's that your freedom is my freedom. Your struggle is my struggle. Your sacrifice is my sacrifice. And that, I think, came to me growing up in this small Black community on the border. And a family that was really rooted in the Black radical tradition of internationalism. I really owe them so much.

LIPSITZ: I do think for a lot of people, Black internationalism is an important part of this. So often the Black radical tradition is misconstrued as being a desire for a temporal homeland along the [lines of Marcus] Garvey, but it was really a form of world-transcending citizenship. This is an ingredient that's important to a lot of the people doing this work.[10] The whole tradition of Dr. W. E. B. Du Bois's "common cause of the darker races" held the belief that the U.S. global empire was a consequence of slavery and segregation and that anticolonialism was important to Black freedom. When I was in high school in Paterson, New Jersey, the stores around the high school would get Black newspapers like the *Baltimore Afro-American* and the *Pittsburgh Courier*—and this is a tradition that goes back to the 1930s that considered [Indian prime minister Jawaharlal] Nehru a part of the Black community. The Indian National Congress was a part of Blackness in a way that made no phenotypical or bloodline sense, but it was a family of resemblance that was clearly there. And as Robin [Kelley] and Betsy Esch wrote, the tremendous prestige of the Chinese revolution in Black communities, the Panthers' interest in China and North Korea, was an important part of everyday life in those circumstances.[11] In [pianist] Horace Tapscott's discussion of this collective that he had in South Los Angeles, he says newspapers from all over the world just showed up. Immigrants and exiles came through the door. By contrast there have been tremendous institutional philanthropic subsidies since then for separate groups for encouraging Black capitalism, for encouraging a Mexican American center, but not a Third World Studies center. It almost makes us forget how interconnected these things were. But I do think that for everybody, even when Blacks don't appear, Blackness becomes an important epistemological tradition for people to draw on. So what comes with great difficulty in our scholarly categories flows inexorably in the life of aggrieved communities.

SÁNCHEZ: I am interested in the nature of each of these relationships [as I work on] my next book, on [the LA neighborhood of] Boyle Heights, [which is] particularly focused on the Black-Mexican relationship with Boyle Heights. I am interested in the intergenerational learning. [One of the subjects of the story is] a Mexican Filipina woman named Paula Crisostomo, whose mother turns out to have been active with Black women in public housing battles in the 1950s, which I had never heard about. So I explore that issue of Black women and Mexican women fighting together [for public housing] in Ramona Gardens in order to understand what its possible impact was on Paula, who later became so active in the 1968 walkouts led by Mexican American students. [The walkouts] are something that is often interpreted as very nationalist with no relation to the Black movement; but those relations are obvious to me. How do you trace these stories across time? What are the different ways people learn from different communities? Again, there's not one story. For me it's very important to get at the multiple ways that communities affect each other. Sometimes the relational works across eras. We have just begun to explore the multiple ways that this kind of interrelationship can occur. To me it's really important to explore all sorts of different ways in which this comparative and relational work can actually happen over time. We don't know enough. There's all these side stories that people have uncovered that have to be explored. What does it mean to have your parents' history affect you? It's a very basic but critical question that we haven't done enough work on. For migrants, that's important. For people that are international migrants, what does it mean to have something that your parents did in another country affect the way that you approach a certain problem in this country? We are the front end of that exploration.

LYTLE HERNÁNDEZ: It pushes us to think more expansively about where knowledge is produced. Diversifying the academy is very important as a place where we produce knowledge. But we must also acknowledge the many ways in which worker struggles, communities, organizations, youth are asking new questions that can produce new knowledge. So I am curious to move into the conversation about the work we have all been doing that is beyond the academy; in my experience, it's been working outside the academy that has been the most transformative for how I think and the questions that I pose, and methodologically how I do my work.

LIPSITZ: Walter Rodney said that scholars who think along with social movements have more urgency in the questions that they ask and answer. They also have their antenna out to things that have not yet been codified and not yet been written into the dominant archives and institutions. [I'm thinking of] Dr. W. E. B. Du Bois, Ida B. Wells, and Oliver Cromwell Cox. Working along with social movements exists in a broad range of fields. Ruth Wilson Gilmore can't deal with Black incarceration separate from Latino incarceration. Diane Fujino wants to write a biography of Asian American activists, and she winds up writing about Richard Aoki and Yuri Kochiyama, who are in the Black movement. It's a connection to activism that does this. Paula Ioanide's book *The Emotional Politics of Racism: How Feelings Trump Facts in an Era of Color Blindness,* which is an exemplary kind of understanding of the comparative and relational dimensions of these things, came out of her work dealing with issues of police brutality and incarceration. She writes about the Abner Louima beating and the ordinance in Escondido, California, meant to keep immigrants out, and she sees these things as related because in activism [those connections] come to the fore.[12] The archive becomes broader because you are not stuck with just the records, which are structured in dominance, but you have new archives that are opened up from that kind of connection. A different series of questions come to the fore. I also think that part of what social history opens up is the possibility to think that the details of everyday life have meaning, that they are representative of a broader social frame. It lets you recognize things as significant even when they don't have institutional power. When you are representing a complex social world, it's harder to think that one change—changing the people in power, passing one law—is going to make things better. And yet in liberal scholarship this is constantly the thing. Kimberlé Crenshaw says we are trained to think these problems are like cracking open an egg. You hit it once and it opens up. But for us it's more like peeling an onion. And for a scholar, that's a better disposition to have than trying to find the one primordial cause and cure. Look at the complex social world and see the layers and interconnections. Don't have a metaphor of root and branch, but think rhizomatically about things going back and forth across different territories. I think that the work that we like has a fidelity to the complexity of the evidence, and it refuses some of these simpler explanations. We can criticize the groups we are writing about because we are not political operatives. We are not cheerleaders. We have a broader commitment to a morally just world and to represent the lives of the people that we are dealing with. And that is what Barbara Tomlinson and I call accompaniment.[13]

SÁNCHEZ: A lot of my thoughts on this come principally from working with students. My entry into this is not by exiting the academy but by embedding myself in it as a community that is particularly focused on the people who are the first in their families here or [who] present something that is really different in terms of the struggles they are encountering. I have had a lot of interaction with students from Central America, particularly Guatemala. But [the window of understanding is in] learning the history of Guatemala and learning the history of coming from genocide and asking the question, what impact does that have generationally? It's understanding families where genocide has been rooted into the very fabric of what they know of their past. And the students who I am dealing with—some of their relatives were killed because they were guerrillas. Some of their relatives were part of the military. And it's the same family. So it's the embeddedness in a society in which genocide has affected everything that I am interested in long term. And I think what has drawn me to other places in the world— South Africa is one of those places—is to understand the reverberations of those societies across national frameworks and the very deep meaning that history has had inside of families and therefore inside of communities. It then allows you to go back in time and see other situations and get at the meaning of an event when that event is over, or when that event is not over but its time frame is passed on to questions of memory and understanding and what you need to forget and what you need to remember. And all those issues that keep coming up in people's own lives.

LYTLE HERNÁNDEZ: I really want to respond to two of the things you lifted up right now. The first is the ways in which immigration historians historically have grappled with African American history and with Blackness, which have been very problematic and troubling. What was so revelatory and liberatory about first reading *Becoming Mexican American* was that it was the first immigration history I had read that didn't use the story of immigrants as a bat against African Americans. It wasn't the instructive story about what the Black community is doing wrong to not incorporate into America, and that was because of your attention to race and racialization in particular. So I was very thankful to read your book at that moment in time. For me so much of U.S. immigration history hasn't done that—it is about immigrants, but it's also about Blackness and trying to explain away ongoing Black subjugation. Your book offers another way of looking at that. The second thing I want to speak to is the question of genocide. I too have been thinking a lot about genocide in recent years. I have been thinking about settler colonialism and, as Audra Simpson and Andrea Smith say, what it means for all of us. What does it mean to build systems, to build institutions, to build schools and hospitals in a site formed and framed for the elimination of the Native? What kind of possibilities does that create for any of us and all of us? This is not to flatten out the particularities of settler colonialism for Native peoples—we have to keep that in the front of our minds—but to think through seriously what that means for peoples of African descent in particular who were brought here as labor. I think Los Angeles is really important to this because African Americans have not always been needed as labor. So I think that we are really on the cutting edge of what happens to Black folks in the space of elimination when they are not needed for labor. We were needed during that short moment during World War II. But before that moment and after it, Blacks have not been core to the labor force here. And I think what you see happening on the streets in Los Angeles today has a lot to do with that story of genocide and the possibilities that were created through Native elimination.

LIPSITZ: We are not simply adding on information about neglected groups to what's already known and fleshing out the picture. What we actually are exposing is the parochialism of the academy, of its curriculum, of its epistemology, its archives, its ontologies. If you neglect Indigenous dispossession, you will never get to the full answer. The very fact that the issue is there compels you to do a more serious kind of work that actually exposes the narrowness of the archive. Look at the roster of history departments. Look at the parts of the world that are studied most. Ten percent of the world has 90 percent of the historians studying it. And what that means is that genocide is always the Holocaust and never Indigenous dispossession, never Guatemala, never Cambodia. And whether it's exactly genocide or not isn't the issue. The issue is that we have a very impoverished notion of how racialized violence works. It goes back to that great observation by Aimé Césaire.[14] He says, essentially, that Europe was surprised by Hitler, but Burma was not surprised. Martinique was not surprised. Senegal was not surprised. There is a way in which we are trying to ask and answer better questions by taking the long way around, and the presence of previously unrepresented groups puts pressure on the curriculum so that these kinds of conversations can go on. And it's not that George or Kelly knew in advance [that the key would be] Indigenous dispossession or Guatemalan or Cambodian history, but a dialogue with Audra Simpson, a discussion with a student who comes into your class, forces you to be a different kind of historian. Not out of sympathy to those folks but to realize your own limitations of what you have been taught. So in some ways comparative and relational ethnic studies is actually the quality control arm of scholarship. It's the way to deal with the insufferable class, linguistic, and national narrowness that is inscribed in the curriculum and repeated over and over again and will always stand at the center of the disciplines even though it's actually produced very few credible explanations of racial subordination. When you desegregate the faculty and the students, that opening up isn't automatic. You can learn anything from anybody—intelligence and nonintelligence are equal-opportunity employers. But [opening up the faculty and students] opens up the possibility for different kinds of work being done. Anybody could have disassembled the universal category "woman" by looking at the way women of color have to do housework for white women. But it was Evelyn Nakano Glenn who did it. Anybody could have shown how rights for Black men are not rights for Black women, but it was Kimberlé Crenshaw who did.[15] And there was a time when Glenn and Crenshaw wouldn't have been in these institutions. So the fact that you make that possible—and of course I am not making a one-to-one relationship between somebody's embodied identity and their scholarship—but I am saying that scholarship is innately cosmopolitan. It needs to draw from the broadest possible pool of interlocutors. The truth is that the academy itself is criminally complicit in the social relations it sometimes pretends to critique because of its narrow race, class, linguistic, and identity base.

SÁNCHEZ: [Relational studies of race] are actually pushing at the boundaries that have been presented and saying, "Wait a second. This doesn't make much sense." I think that's what people in this work do when they do it well. They are rooted from wherever they came from and that always shapes them. But at the same time they are pushing, saying, "This category or this boundary doesn't make sense, and I am going to push beyond it. I am going to try to ask more fundamental questions that let me get beyond that." When people start doing [that], then we really have new knowledge. So you have got to give people experiences that allow them to push at those boundaries. You have got to give inquisitive people the opportunities that allow them to ask those additional questions. And if we keep simply sending them through certain categories, and all you get is this box, then that's not going to happen.

LIPSITZ: [Nurturing and promoting that kind of scholarship] requires a counterculture within the academy. The credentialing system requires that in order to be admitted to graduate school, in order to get degrees and be published, you have to win the approval of the people who dominated the previous paradigms. [There is] something innately conservative and backward looking about that. We don't want to foolishly throw out knowledge from the past. We want to respect all knowledge, but those forms will reproduce themselves if there isn't a conscious effort to disrupt them and to create different kinds of curricula, different kinds of pedagogy, different understandings of what an archive is, and uncomfortable conversations that go across disciplinary boundaries.

HOSANG AND MOLINA: *What do you see as the main limitations or challenges of relational scholarship on race?*

SÁNCHEZ: Most of us don't have Lipsitz's encyclopedic knowledge across all different sorts of groups. I certainly don't have it. What does that mean when we want to do some serious comparison? It means you have to really enmesh yourself into historiographies, into literatures, traditions that you may not have been trained in. And for many of us, that's a real limitation. It doesn't mean that we shouldn't do it; it just means that to be serious about it is going to take some time. And we live in an academy that doesn't give us the time. [Becoming tenured] gave me the opportunity to take my time, to get trained in certain areas, whether it's Jewish American history or Japanese American history, and to produce serious scholarship that can have an impact in those fields. But there is a limitation to that. There is a limitation in terms of time, effort, and all the other ways that we get pulled around. But for me that's what brings me joy—being able to enmesh myself and engage with scholars in that field in a serious way. At the beginning of this process I felt like there wasn't enough out there doing the kind of relational work in the way I wanted to do it. And therefore I wanted to explore methodologically what it means to do relational work. I learned from a lot of my students—letting folks explore different ways of understanding relations. So for me it's also about allowing for different methodologies to be employed and celebrating those differences. You see this new generation of folks who are doing this in wonderfully rich ways and having conversations that I think are relatively new. We are at the beginning of that process to really understand the richness of doing history in this way. It is not easy, but if you think it's important and you're willing to slog through a lot of stuff, it can have some real impact.

LYTLE HERNÁNDEZ: Let me tell you a story about my new book, *City of Inmates*. It looks at Los Angeles to explore the rise of mass incarceration and its impact on a variety of communities—how criminalization and incarceration became so big in the late twentieth century through this incredible foundation that was built in the nineteenth century, of Native elimination, immigration control, and police brutality, anti-Black police brutality in particular. I spent about seven or eight years deep in the archives researching this book. The Los Angeles Police Department and the sheriff's department had all thrown away all their records, so I had to go and find all these different records. I went to Mexico City, Washington, DC, through the American South, reading slave censuses and lots of different records. And when I was done reading all those records and I found these stories that I thought had been hidden away, I started putting the pieces together and [realized] this new field of study, this new field of scholarship, settler colonialism, helps me to understand all this. I thought I had really hit something [new], that we have understood mass incarceration primarily through the plantation-to-prison story line and that we need to also look at it through settler colonialism. And I wrote up this book and I came out of the archive and I talked to community activists: Pete White in Los Angeles at Community Action Network, Kim McGill at the Youth Justice Coalition, and many others. And they said, "Kelly, we have been talking about extermination and genocide for years." And I thought, "Oh my

God." The methodology I have been using, going solo deep into the archive, wasn't right. It wasn't right at all. [It goes to show that] it is fundamental to follow this long method of developing relationships not just within the academy but also outside it, with the people who have been fighting and grappling and opposing these structures. So I think methodologically the lesson I learned through *City of Inmates* is that in some ways the rush that had kept me very insular in writing the book and the urgency I felt about the story of elimination and extermination would have been greatly enhanced by improved conversations beyond the academy. So this relational race lens that we are talking about today is something that's very much happening on the streets and in the community.

And what I have learned most of all from these organizers is that we have got a twenty-four-year plan. We have got until 2040, when the demographics of this country will have changed dramatically. The white majority is going to be eclipsed. The U.S. empire is most likely going to be eclipsed, and we have got to dig in for a very, very long battle and prepare ourselves for the turning point. For me, that was revelatory and liberatory because a lot of the work that we are doing right now feels like we are constantly battling and fighting and maybe even losing. But the point is to protect ourselves, to love one another, and prepare ourselves and our students for 2040. And the relational race lens is going to be so critical because in 2040, we are going to have to do this together.

SÁNCHEZ: To me that issue also looms large in this work—thinking about 2040 but in a different way. For me, I think white supremacy is going to be fairly constant in the years to come. I worry a lot more about the juxtaposition of all these groups that will emerge as the majority in 2040. When I think about having a twenty-four-year plan, I don't assume that those groups are going to be on the same page—I ask, how do you create that possibility? Because they are not on the same page now. They haven't been on the same page in the past, and in fact 2040 looms large as a time when they may not be on the same page. Different regions and different places. Mexicans will want to say, "Well, hell, we have been fighting here in California for a long time. Now we are the majority and we are going to call the shots." And elsewhere it will be other groups. That to me is a much scarier proposition. So when I think about this issue of 2040, I wonder how we can do our work in such a way that we can expose the fallacy of that kind of competition but also show the possibilities of what it means to know each other's past, know each other's histories in a rich way in order to work together in a different way. It's always been about fighting white supremacy—but it's now [also] about how do we create a different context for the kinds of relationships we want to grow. So when I think about Chicano nationalism, I think about a lot of the rough edges of what may happen as people feel that they are empowered. And empowered not in a good way but in negative ways vis-à-vis other groups that I care deeply about. And that has always been part of the nature of this work for me.

LIPSITZ: The import of the question starts with an academic concern [as to whether] comparative and relational work undermines the possibilities for breadth and depth. So if you have too much breadth, do you sacrifice depth? If you have too much depth, do you miss the opportunities for breadth? And as scholars we are trained, and rightly so, to try to have mastery over evidence and to have complexity in our arguments. But there is a third part of what we do, and that is scholarship as also an act of intervention. Research is a social, discursive act that frames a conversation and invites people to respond. If you are thinking that you want to have the once-and-for-all answer, this is a misunderstanding of what scholarly work is. It's legitimate to say, "How much do you need to know about two societies if you are going to compare them?" But you could never do a comprehensive and encyclopedic comparison. You can't do a comprehensive and encyclopedic understanding of your own society, much less two. What you can create through this work is a dialogic homology where you stick one body of knowledge up against another and you say, "What do we learn from this?" And it's always incomplete, particularly in historical work where you can't make your own database and you can't limit the variables. You are dealing with the complexity of an infinite number of actions, events, and ideas about which you have a terribly slender thread of evidence that you try to make reasoned speculations from. It's always limited. It's always incomplete. But it's valuable because there are patterns, there are clues, there are ways in which the conversation and discussion can get better.

We don't want to challenge the reification of separate racial and ethnics studies with an equal reification and dogmatic attention to comparative and relational work. Everything that enables also inhibits. And in fact sometimes the worst thing you can do is to make comparisons. We have to deal with the illusion of completeness and the irresponsibility that's involved in comparison, but I think these things can be tempered by friendliness, humility, respect, and by scholarship that doesn't say "I am right," but "I am trying to be right," and "I am not providing you the first or last word." Barbara Tomlinson and I have been trying to argue that everything we write is the middle word. You are taking something from somebody and you are passing it on to somebody else. And you are trying to make the conversation better through your particular contribution to it. There is enormous responsibility in doing this kind of work, which as Kelly and George have pointed out, is tremendously difficult because it has historical impact. It's not only a discussion about history; it's a part of history. How people will live, what will happen, in part, depends on what they think has happened, the ways in which they recognize the patterns of the past impeding or promoting change in the present. We are not the final arbiters of that, but we can make provocations that will enable people to see these things in different ways. If my discussion of locking people up doesn't resonate with [community activist] Pete White, who has so much more experience with that than I have, then I really ought to question my view—more so than if it doesn't resonate with James Q. Wilson, who is considered to be the scholarly expert on that subject.[16] You have got to put the stuff out. And if we are wrong, nobody should be happier to hear criticism of us than ourselves because that's how we will make it better. There is no scientific law that hasn't at some point been disproved. There is no historical argument that hasn't been improved on by somebody else. To think that there is a once-and-for-all fix is a mistake. To contribute honorably and honestly to an ongoing conversation and to share the responsibility to broaden it with a lot of people who think but don't have the status in society where they are recognized as thinkers— that is the role we can play.

HOSANG AND MOLINA: *How do relational frameworks of race play out in the public impact of your work?*

LIPSITZ: We write books that become part of a curriculum, that become part of the work that the university does in society. The university is an important institution in society. It helps shape what the teachers teach and what the advertising copywriters write and what the parents tell their children, so there is an important and honorable public role to be played there. It has to do with the writing, the teaching, the criticism, all that. But part of our job [also] ought to be to promote and foreground and publicize the work of our colleagues, the work that might not be recognized as important. And as you get more status in the profession, you can lose touch with this, and you think one more statement from you is the most important thing when the first statement from another generation might be much more valuable. Sánchez is a master at remembering this. But I also think we need to promote venues for distributing the ideas, experiences, and perceptions of people who never set foot in universities unless it's to clean the floors or cook the food. So there is a kind of public work that needs to be done of getting artists and activists to write books and get those books published. To have books of student writing be distributed. To encourage dance troupes and bloggers to invent new polities, new politics, and to create new publics. It's not unrelated to what we do. When the Ferguson uprising took place, part of what happened was that people recognized that Black Twitter was this enormous public sphere that a lot of people didn't know was out there. I saw on Black Twitter, I saw tweets from Ferguson that said, "Nobody who stood with the queer transwomen on West Florissant Avenue can deny that intersectionality matters." [Insersectionality] was an academic concept that was printed in law journals that none of these folks read, but in a moment of danger, in a moment of crisis, it became a tool that crystallized for them the experiences that they had had. At that moment of intersection, nobody controlled that dialogue, but it was an important moment of coming together. This is a society that suffers terribly from a lack of democracy, from what James Baldwin called "the brutal anonymity of American life," where people think they don't count or they think their words don't count, so they just don't say anything. Creating spheres of mutual accountability, responsibility, dialogue, learning, is something we can do, and I think we tremendously undervalue that.

SÁNCHEZ: I want to talk a little about institutions and how important it is to think about the transformation of existing institutions but also the creation of new ones in very traditional ways. For example, I return all the time to Japanese American internment as a learning tool and how much the Japanese American community, through the Japanese American National Museum, through people like [actor and activist] George Takei, through other entities, raise Japanese American internment of the 1940s as the context for current anti-immigrant legislation and detentions as critical not just for Japanese Americans but for [all of us today and] Muslims in particular. That dialogue is so important, because what has been nourished is institutional life in the Japanese American community that has kept the story alive and allowed for people to draw from it in order to make sure that it is not forgotten and [that] those lessons can be learned by new generations. Here is this institution that over generations has said, "We are going to tell this story. We are going to keep this information alive. We are going to do it not for just the Japanese American community but also for this broader notion of American democracy." And these days it's about Muslims. So that to me is a very powerful story about the impact solid institutions with a historical bent can have on other issues over historical time.

One story I love to tell is giving talks at synagogues and giving people the 1939 Federal Housing Administration description of [Boyle Heights], from the time they lived there but that they have never seen. So you have these people who were nostalgic about the community they lived through in Boyle Heights realizing that the federal government had said, "This is hopelessly heterogeneous, and every block is full of subversive racial elements." And here they are at eighty or ninety years old, having to struggle [to understand] the place that had been such an important part of their growing up, maybe a place they left in the 1940s but they don't really know why they left. And they have got to put pieces together late in life that they had been thinking of in very different ways. That's a very powerful experience. The learning keeps taking place at every age. These things are really important to share. Sometimes as historians we have access to materials, we have access to learning tools that have to be put in the hands of people of every generation, from the youngest to the oldest. People have to be able to understand themselves if relational history is to work. People don't know that [things] occurred. Even if they were literally there experiencing it, they don't know why it occurred. They are trying to understand. And so the power of that is at really local levels, wherever it is, is really important. We live at a time when a lot of local histories are getting torn asunder through gentrification, through all kinds of forces that want us to ignore that that history actually ever took place, that consciously are trying to destroy that historical understanding. Therefore, we have got to fight for the public space that says, "No. This community is going to know its history in all its complexity—and is going to make room for people's own memories of that history and actually put it in dialogue with everybody else's understanding of what was happening at this place at a given moment." To me that's a different kind of public impact. It's a public impact that has to occur at every level from national to international to the very, very local—whether through dance or theater or traditional museum space or online or in elementary school classrooms. All those venues are really important, and we have new tools to be able to make use of that.

LIPSITZ: Part of what you have been so successful at, George, is having people see themselves as part of history. I sometimes tell my students,

"You might not be interested in history, but history is interested in you." And there is a way in which reckoning with that is an important part of self-knowledge.

LYTLE HERNÁNDEZ: I often think about teaching as a public act and how important it can be for a lot of my students when they have a Black woman teaching them about Mexican and Mexican American history or Asian American history. Teaching the large general education cluster class on immigration history and talking about Chinese exclusion, and what does it mean for them to learn that history from this woman standing in front of them? Many of them may have walked in the door and dismissed me automatically, but they learn to respect the knowledge that I am bringing to the table through my connections with what they see as intimately theirs. I see it as mine as well. In the beginning they have a usually much more narrow approach to the material. I think that, when we talk about race relationally, it can be very important to talk about the work that we are doing in the library and in the archives and bring it back out to public spaces and articulate it for diverse audiences from our own embodied position. I am always aware of that when I stand up in front of a group—not just what I am putting forth but how I am putting it forward. So I will be very attentive to my cadence, to the particular language that I am using, and the world that I am representing for them as a Black woman standing in front of them. So that's one thing in terms of the public impact of thinking about race relationally. The other one is, I have become very invested in engaging in public inquiry with community members. So acknowledging my own lack of knowledge and working through and developing questions together and conducting research together. There is also something about being willing to expose ourselves as professional scholars to not knowing much and working with diverse communities on the issues and the struggles that we confront together.

LIPSITZ: My friend David Kim teaches religious studies. He starts every seminar going around the room, asking, Who are you associated with and who are you accountable to? And it turns out to be a really interesting question. You get to know a lot about people the way they answer that prompt. If he were here, my answer would be, *this* is who I am associated with. *This* is who I am accountable to. *This* is where I want to be. It's amazing with all the fear and anger at this moment and how hard our work is going to be, it's important to savor how far we have come and who we have come here with. I wouldn't trade it for anything.

NOTES

1. Recorded at the University of Southern California on December 19, 2016. Transcribed by Vicki Parent for Litivate, February 3, 2017.

2. Chester Himes, "Zoot Riots Are Race Riots," *Crisis* 50, no. 7 (July 1943): 200–201.

3. Chester Himes, *If He Hollers Let Him Go* (New York: Thunder's Mouth Press, 2002), 3.

4. Read the insightful dialogue between Sánchez and Lipsitz on this topic, George J. Sánchez, "Reading Reginald Denny: The Politics of Whiteness in the Late Twentieth Century," *American Quarterly* 47, no. 3 (1995): 388–94; George Lipsitz, "The Possessive Investment in Whiteness: Racialized Social Democracy and the 'White' Problem in American Studies," *American Quarterly* 47, no. 3 (1995): 369–78.

5. George J. Sánchez, *Becoming Mexican American: Ethnicity, Culture, and Identity in Chicano Los Angeles, 1900–1945* (New York: Oxford University Press, 1993), 182; see also 141, 261.

6. Sánchez, *Becoming Mexican American,* 23.

7. Antin's autobiography recounted her emigration from Russia to the United States and her experiences of assimilation and Americanization. Mary Antin, *The Promised Land* (Boston: Houghton Mifflin, 1912).

8. Oscar Handlin, *The Uprooted: The Epic Story of the Great Migrations That Made the American People* (Boston: Little, Brown, 1973).

9. Proposition 187 was a 1994 statewide ballot measure in California that sought to bar unauthorized immigrants from a wide range of health, educational, and social services. It was approved by a wide margin of the electorate but later overturned by the courts.

10. In the longer transcript, Lipsitz cited Arlene Dávila, *Barrio Dreams: Puerto Ricans, Latinos, and the Neoliberal City* (Berkeley: University of California Press, 2004); Vivek Bald, *Bengali Harlem and the Lost Histories of South Asian America* (Cambridge, MA: Harvard University Press, 2013); Eric Tang, *Unsettled: Cambodian Refugees in the New York City Hyperghetto* (Philadelphia: Temple University Press, 2015).

11. Robin D. G. Kelley and Betsy Esch, "Black Like Mao: Red China and Black Revolution," *Souls* 1, no. 4 (1999): 6–41.

12. Paula Ioanide, *The Emotional Politics of Racism: How Feelings Trump Facts in an Era of Colorblindness* (Stanford, CA: Stanford University Press, 2015); Diane Carol Fujino, *Heartbeat of Struggle: The Revolutionary Life of Yuri Kochiyama* (Minneapolis: University of Minnesota Press, 2005); Ruth Wilson Gilmore, *Golden Gulag: Prisons, Surplus, Crisis, and Opposition in Globalizing California* (Berkeley: University of California Press, 2007).

13. Barbara Tomlinson and George Lipsitz, "American Studies as Accompaniment," *American Quarterly* 65, no. 1 (2013): 1–30.

14. Aimé Césaire, *Discourse on Colonialism* (New York: Monthly Review Press, 1972), 36.

15. Kimberlé Crenshaw, "Demarginalizing the Intersection of Race and Sex: A Black Feminist Critique of Antidiscrimination Doctrine, Feminist Theory, and Antiracist Politics," *University of Chicago Legal Forum* 1 (1989): 139–67; Kimberlé Crenshaw, "Twenty Years of Critical Race Theory: Looking Backward to Move Forward," *Connecticut Law Review* 43, no. 5 (2010): 1253–352; Evelyn Nakano Glenn, *Issei, Nisei, War Bride: Three Generations of Japanese American Women in Domestic Service* (Philadelphia: Temple University Press, 1986).

16. James Q. Wilson and Joan Petersilla, *Crime and Public Policy,* 2nd ed. (New York: Oxford University Press, 2011).

TWO

Examining Chicana/o History through a Relational Lens

Natalia Molina

I remember in graduate school having a conversation with a fellow Chicano student about how difficult it was to be one of the few Chicana/os in our program.[1] He argued that it was particularly challenging for us because we had grown up in predominantly Mexican, working-class *barrios*. He suggested that we were used to being members of a community where it was not necessary to explain our positions because of shared experiences. It was true that I had grown up in a working-class neighborhood and that it was home to a large Mexican community, but it was also home to Chinese immigrants, Vietnamese refugees, Filipino nationals, and working-class whites. Growing up in such diversity, I was accustomed to finding commonalities with kids from backgrounds different from mine. We shared similar experiences as working-class youth. We got ourselves ready for school in the morning because our parents had already left for work, we rode the city bus together to and from school, and we let ourselves back into our homes in the afternoon because our parents worked late. When we hung out on the corner and the police, who drove by regularly, stopped to ask us questions, we *all* felt ill at ease. Being from a working-class neighborhood produced a kind of solidarity among us that cut across the color line.

But, of course, there were also differences. In school, my white counterparts were more likely to be tracked into programs such as honors classes, band, ROTC, and theater. I, on the other hand, despite completing the prerequisites and maintaining a high GPA, was told explicitly that I could not enroll in Advanced Placement classes. The school took the position that because English was my second language, I would likely have difficulty succeeding in these courses.[2] Together, my experiences in the neighborhood and at school provided some of my first lessons in intersectionality.[3]

It is probably because of these early formative experiences that when it came time to write my dissertation, I chose to look at race relationally. Even after further work on my dissertation resulted in the publication of my first book, I continued my efforts to demonstrate the importance of placing Chicana/o studies in a relational framework. By "relational," I do not mean comparative. A comparative treatment of race compares and contrasts groups, treating them as independent of one another. It can also leave the construction of the categories themselves unexamined, thus, even if unintentionally, reifying them in the process. A relational treatment of race recognizes that race is a mutually constitutive process and thus demonstrates how race is socially constructed, hence fighting essentialist notions of race. Furthermore, it attends to how, when, where, and to what extent groups intersect. It recognizes that there are limits to examining racialized groups in isolation.[4]

In this chapter, I discuss the advantages of a relational perspective and urge others to join me in looking at race relationally. I am certainly not asking scholars to jump ship and abandon Chicana/o history or its counterpart fields (e.g., Asian American history). These fields make an invaluable contribution, first by providing social and cultural histories of groups, and second, by documenting the buildup of structural discrimination, including the development and dissemination of cultural representations of these groups that have simultaneously hidden and facilitated such discrimination. What I am asking is that, using the foundational understanding of race as a social construction, we pull the lens back as we research, write, and teach. We need to ask who else is (or was) present in or near the communities we study—and what difference these groups' presence made (or makes). This is no less than what Chicana/o historians have been asking those who study the mainstream to do for decades. Just as the prevailing version of U.S. history was incomplete without an examination of the influence of racialized groups, the study of any single racialized group calls for an understanding of the impact of the experiences of other similarly situated groups.

In the first part of this chapter, I examine the literature that has made a strong case for centering race in the American West and that has discussed what is at stake in such a project. I then turn to key works that have moved in the direction of a relational understanding of race. In the second part, I provide possible directions and strategies for those who wish to engage in a relational project. I also revisit some well-known cases in Chicana/o history and bring in new primary sources from my research to read these cases through a relational lens in order to show what can be gained from such an approach.

Earlier works in Chicana/o history have made possible the methodological and theoretical move toward a relational study of race. The authors of these earlier studies did history "from the bottom up." They dug through community newspapers (*before* they were digitized!), combed city directories, and compiled census data; they were the first to locate sources in the vast labyrinth of the National Archives. They also provided ways to think about the relationships among race and power, institutionalized racism, segmented labor markets, community formation, segregation in the urban landscape, and civil rights outside a Black-white binary.[5]

Despite these scholarly contributions, Chicana/o history continued to be marginalized. In an effort to gain a wider audience and create a more inclusive dialogue, some historians urged a rethinking of the paradigms and parameters of the field that would provide an overarching rationale for centering race in our historical narratives.[6] For example, in 1992, Antonia Castañeda made an early, but largely unheeded, call for studying race relationally. While more scholarship on women and communities of color had been produced in the 1980s than in previous decades, Castañeda argued that much of it tended to be descriptive, or looked only at people of color vis-à-vis whites, instead of in relationship to and with one another. Consequently, these works generally ended up replacing a Black-white binary with another type of binary.[7] Castañeda asserted that we should center women of color in our studies, not for the sake of inclusion, but because by centering them we would have to acknowledge the presence and importance of issues of power and decolonization. My call for a greater focus on relational notions of race, like Castañeda's, goes beyond arguing for a more inclusive narrative history. I maintain that the very framework that comprises our understanding of race is necessarily and inseparably drawn from the experiences of racialized groups vis-à-vis other racialized groups and thus it is imperative that we pull the lens back even when examining the experiences of one racialized group.

Two books that emerged in the 1990s in Chicana/o history are standouts, both for their relational perspective on race and for their success in going beyond a Black-white paradigm. Neil Foley's *The White Scourge: Mexicans, Blacks, and Poor Whites in Texas Cotton Culture,* a study of race relations in central Texas, examined how Anglos who migrated from the southern United States to central Texas brought with them a racial ideology shaped by Reconstruction discourse meant to preserve whiteness as a bastion of privilege.

These whites' interactions with Mexicans alongside African Americans complicated their prior understandings of race, which had developed within a Black-white paradigm, thus disrupting this binary racial stratification.[8]

Similarly, Tomás Almaguer's *Racial Fault Lines: The Historical Origins of White Supremacy in California,* which focuses on nineteenth-century California and the racialization of Native Americans, Asians, and Mexicans, shows that examining racial groups in a continuum sheds light on how the racial construction of various groups affect one another. Almaguer's study of California empirically grounds Michael Omi and Howard Winant's theory that region and historical period are key in understanding how we come to think of bodies as racialized.[9] Race relations in the nineteenth-century United States were heavily framed by the Black-white paradigm, but the small population of African Americans in California, coupled with the diverse populations of Natives and immigrants, resulted in a racially stratified hierarchy among Mexicans, Asians, Native Americans, and Anglos that defied binary racialization.[10]

My own work is committed to a similar recognition of the importance of the differential racialization of groups, a specific interest in California, and a commitment to moving beyond conceptualizing race as a Black-white binary. I chose to focus on Chicana/os and Mexican immigrants, hoping to contribute to this important literature. I was broadly interested in what went into constructing the category "Mexican" and decided to look at public health practices, institutions, and discourses to demonstrate the structural and cultural ways that public health helped shape what it meant to be "Mexican." I settled on Los Angeles as the place of study because of its large Mexican population. Historically, Los Angeles had once been part of Mexico (El Pueblo de Nuestra Señora la Reina de los Ángeles de Porciúncula) until it was annexed, along with much of northern Mexico, in the aftermath of the Mexican-American War (1846–48). For the next six decades, the Mexican population in the United States declined rapidly. Beginning in the 1910s, Mexicans immigrated to Los Angeles in large numbers, fleeing the Mexican revolution, lured by the many opportunities presented by the growth of large-scale farming, and facilitated by the ease of movement resulting from the completion of railroad networks. By 1930, Los Angeles could claim a Mexican population second in size only to that of Mexico City.[11]

But it was Los Angeles's ethnoracial diversity that ended up having the most impact on my study. Early twentieth-century Los Angeles was a rapidly growing metropolis, fueled by the completion of railway systems, by the frenzy to build its iconic California bungalows for a bourgeoning population, and by the ease of agricultural development achieved by importing water from the Owens Valley. It needed laborers and thus attracted a diversity of groups, such as Japanese farmers, Mexican bricklayers, and midwestern white-collar workers. The result was a segmented labor force. It became clear to me that it would misrepresent the experience of Mexican immigrants if I ignored the diverse racialized communities that composed Los Angeles. Indeed, to be Mexican in Los Angeles meant to be just one part of a multiethnoracial setting that in no small part shaped how people understood the social, cultural, racial, and political meaning of "Mexican" in Los Angeles.

In researching the medical racialization of Mexicans in the nineteenth century, I became convinced that, to understand how the category of "Mexican" was shaped, I needed to look at other racialized groups. Even though mine was a mainly twentieth-century study at the time, I decided to follow the lead of Albert Camarillo's precedent-setting *Chicanos in a Changing Society* to see if the experiences of Mexicans in the nineteenth century shaped their successors' experiences in the twentieth century.[12] Yet, Mexicans were eerily absent in the nineteenth-century science-based historical records, as if, in keeping with the ideologically and biologically influenced Manifest Destiny lore, they all had dutifully died off. The Mexican population that continued to live in the United States after annexation did not seem to come to the attention of scientists and health officials as other groups did.[13] Instead, the city health officer's inaugural report in 1879 revealed that it was Chinese residents, not Mexicans, who were imagined as the greatest threat to the city's well-being.[14] In that first report, Health Officer Dr. Walter Lindley assured his listeners that Los Angeles had "everything that God could give" a city.[15] Among Los Angeles's many virtues, the doctor emphasized "the health giving sun [present] almost every day in the year ... the ocean breeze just properly tempered by hills and orange groves ... pure water pouring down from a mountain stream [and] ... the most equable temperature in the civilized world."[16] In stressing the importance of improving sanitary conditions in Los Angeles, he called for the construction of a municipal sewer system and appealed to the city council to eradicate Chinatown, "that rotten spot [that pollutes] the air we breathe and poisons the water we drink."[17] These comments mark the beginning of what became a long tradition among city health officials of tracing any blemish on the pristine image of Los Angeles—including all forms of disease and any manner of disorder—to the city's marginalized communities, not solely Mexicans.

By the 1910s, with the increase of Mexican immigration, Mexicans increasingly captured the attention of health officials.[18] Mexicans, of course, were by no means solely a new immigrant wave to the area. But in the intervening years between the Mexican-American War and this new wave of immigration from Mexico, other immigrant groups (as seen above) had shaped the racial terrain on which Mexican immigrants would now be understood. They followed in the footsteps of the Chinese, who immigrated in the mid to late nineteenth century, and then the Japanese, who came as laborers after Chinese immigration was severely restricted after the passage of the Chinese Exclusion Act of 1882. Beginning in 1907, the Gentleman's Agreement seriously limited Japanese immigration by allowing only nonlaborers, workers already living in the United States, and their family members to immigrate. Decades before more Mexicans arrived, LA officials had used racial stereotypes and negative representations of Asian groups to guide their decisions regarding the distribution of city resources, including where they built (or failed to build) important infrastructure, like sewer systems, and whom they let live and work in certain areas of the city. In short, now in the early twentieth century, Mexicans became targets of the personal racism once directed at the earlier groups and bore the burden of the structural racism embedded in the city.

Though my first book, *Fit to be Citizens?*, focused primarily on Mexicans, I also examined their connections to the experiences of the city's Asian residents, demonstrating how immigrants were racialized in relation to one another, which often resulted in the institutionalization of a racial hierarchy. How health officials came to view and treat Mexicans was directly tied to these officials' assumptions about and experiences with the city's Asian residents. Indeed, from 1869 to 1920, the city health department used only two racial categories: "Chinese" and "the rest of the population."[19] "Mexican" was a category constructed from what it was not: not white, not Chinese, not Japanese. A relational examination of all three groups clarifies how racialization projects can differ in their intent, application, and impact, depending on the specific group targeted.[20]

METHODS AND MODELS

By now you might be saying to yourself, "That all sounds interesting, but how would I go about thinking about race relationally?"[21] A good way to start is to consider a few basic methodological principles and become acquainted with some model studies. It is important to recall a basic guiding principle for doing research: how you define your research *subject* shapes your research *process and question*. Thus, when it comes to choosing your research subject, I advocate using units of analysis or organizing principles other than solely racial categories. If we choose to question the history of Chicana/os and, for example, their relationship to a specific institution (e.g., the public school system, the Catholic Church, or the police), we are likely to turn to well-known and heavily used sources. This in turn may put us at risk of going down only previously blazed trails.

Scholars of Chicana/o history know the "usual suspects" archives: for example, the Ernesto Galarza Papers at Stanford, the Carey McWilliams Papers at UCLA, the Immigration and Naturalization Service (INS) Records at Laguna Niguel, California, and Washington, DC, and the Mexican Consulate records in Mexico City. There are many very good reasons for using these archives, but doing so primarily because they are repositories of records on Chicana/os can be intellectually limiting. I almost fell victim to this hidden danger when I received a fellowship at the Huntington Library while researching my dissertation topic.

At the Huntington, I was consistently introduced as doing Chicana/o history and thus was repeatedly directed to the John Anson Ford Papers, a collection routinely mined by scholars of Chicana/o history because of Ford's involvement with racialized communities in Los Angeles. It is a rich collection, but it contains relatively little that was relevant to my research *question* (how does public health inform our ideas about race?); instead, there was a great deal of information about my research *subject*. Conversely, when I contacted the Los Angeles Department of Public Health, different staff members forewarned me that the department did not have many materials on Mexicans. Once I started digging into their records, however, I found that they held a lot more of interest than my contacts realized. The staff's lack of awareness reflected the fact that no one before me had used the department records for this purpose. Moreover, while the records did not include as many materials on my research *subject* as some of the well-known archives in Chicana/o history, they did contain a lot on my research *question*.

This example underscores the importance of finding more creative ways to locate new sources and of being tenacious when mining all sources. Particularly for our first major project, most of us tend to locate potentially relevant archives by following leads found in footnotes. If we are exclusively or mainly doing and reading Chicana/o history, we will follow the same leads and keep reproducing the same types of histories. We need to be reading LGBT, Native American, African American, and Asian American histories alongside Chicana/o history. We need to attend conference panels even if— no, *especially* if—we are not in these fields. If race is the only organizing principle we use when answering a research question, we will miss the way other factors may affect the topic we are interested in. If we follow strategies that expand our horizons and take us into new areas, we might find new information about the subject of our studies in unexpected places: African Americans' experiences are described in INS records, and histories of Native Americans in Japanese internment records, to cite just two real examples.[22]

Reconsidering the Unit of Analysis

Another way to approach the question of thinking about race relationally is to consider using an organizing principle other than race. Let's take space as a model and Boyle Heights, an East LA neighborhood, as an example.[23] Boyle Heights is known for having been a very diverse community from the early 1900s through the 1950s, after which it gradually became a neighborhood with a predominantly Mexican population. During the first half of the twentieth century, other areas of Los Angeles deliberately buttressed the walls of segregation around their communities by writing deed restrictions into housing developments and permitting only segregated access to public facilities such as swimming pools. By contrast, at the railway station marking the entrance to their neighborhood, Boyle Heights officials hung a banner that read "Eastside Greeting: We Welcome All."[24]

Historian George Sánchez's treatment of Boyle Heights shows us some of the advantages of a more expansive approach to race. By pulling the lens out and studying this neighborhood, rather than solely Mexicans, he is able to get out a host of their interactions and dynamics with other groups and institutions. Sánchez has long been attracted to this LA community. He examined the area in his multi-prize-winning first book, *Becoming Mexican American* (1993); he served as a consultant for the Japanese American National Museum's exhibition *Boyle Heights: The Power of Place*, mounted in 2002; and he has chosen Boyle Heights as the subject of his forthcoming book.[25] Sánchez is especially interested in how issues of diversity like those evident in Boyle Heights complicate models of Americanization and assimilation. His work also reminds us that even when we focus on the local level, we need to consider the impact of larger structural and institutional factors: in 1939, the Federal Housing Administration officially declared the celebrated diversity of Boyle Heights as "literally honeycombed with diverse and subversive racial elements" which impeded funding to the area and had long-term implications for its development.[26]

A different example of Sánchez's approach to looking at race relationally is evident in a 1994 article on Boyle Heights he coauthored with Sally Deutsch and Gary Okihiro.[27] Here we learn another valuable lesson about how to do relational work—collaborate! In this simultaneously accessible and insightful piece, the three authors, each drawing on her or his distinct area of specialization, worked together to portray this diverse neighborhood without resorting either to a simplistic melting-pot paradigm or to a celebration of bucolic multiculturalism. Instead, in their examination of this community composed of Mexicans, Jews, Japanese, and others, Deutsch, Sánchez, and Okihiro showed how the lived experience of one group dramatically affected the experience of others. Seventeen years after first reading this piece, I am still struck by these scholars' treatment of Japanese internment and its effects on Boyle Heights' residents, Japanese and non-Japanese alike. The local high school lost one-third of its senior class to internment. An English teacher at the school began a round-robin letter-writing campaign to encourage her students to write to their fellow classmates interned in the camps. In another notable case, a Mexican teenager went to live in the camps to demonstrate solidarity with his friends. These stories add a different experience from the prevailing ones of racism directed toward the Japanese in the aftermath of Pearl Harbor. Perhaps the difference here is that these folks lived in the same neighborhood, went to the same schools, shared favorite family food, and could thus form ties more readily in the face of adversity.[28] Examples such as these are startling reminders that internment had profound reverberations beyond the Japanese community. In this sense, a relational study of race provides an impetus for ceasing to consider the experiences of specific groups the provenance of individual area studies, such as Asian American studies, and instead centering them squarely in U.S. history, where they belong.

Being more creative in the way we define our research questions is also likely to make us more open to and interested in potentially valuable new sources. For instance, life histories (e.g., oral histories, autobiographies, memoirs, diaries, and journals) can provide ways to get at intersectionality.[29] Carey McWilliams, noted activist, journalist, and attorney, was well positioned, both in terms of his politics and professions, to do relational work. His life history is a rich example of how an individual's biography can provide a window into relational notions of race. From 1939 to 1942, he served as the director of California's Division of Immigration and Housing, which oversaw the living conditions of migrant laborers. In this capacity, he crisscrossed the state, visiting farms and interviewing workers of many nationalities, including Mexican, Filipino, and Japanese. His criticisms of then governor Earl Warren led Warren to dismiss McWilliams in 1942. Returning to his legal practice, McWilliams worked on some of the most pressing civil rights cases of the time, serving as head of the Sleepy Lagoon Defense Committee (discussed below). Beginning in 1953, he took the helm at the *Nation;* for the next twenty years, he published many dozens of articles and editorials, often on issues of social justice.[30] Moreover, throughout his career, McWilliams wrote monographs centered on various racialized groups: *Prejudice: Japanese-Americans: Symbol of Racial Intolerance* (1944), *Brothers under the Skin* (1944), and *A Mask for Privilege: Anti-Semitism in America* (1948). His book *North from Mexico* (1949) is often credited as the first book-length study of Mexican American history.[31]

In all these writings, McWilliams gave detailed accounts of each group's unique history in the United States and pointed out their shared struggles. But he also had an eye for seeing how the experiences of one group affected others, even when separated by space and time. He argued, for instance, that the "modes of aggression tried against Indians and Blacks easily transferred to the Chinese" and that the immigration policies and restrictions first directed at the Chinese were then directed at "brown" immigrants.[32] McWilliams's works are the first extended U.S. histories to center relational notions of race. Despite these especially fertile conditions, no one has yet used McWilliams to write a substantial study shedding light on relational aspects of race in California during and after World War II, underscoring that there is still much work to do in looking at race relationally and offering almost endless possibilities for interested researchers.

Reconsidering What We Already Know

Of course, when thinking about race relationally, we do not always need to reinvent the wheel or mine new sources. We can take well-known historic moments and look at them in relationship to one another. We can search for areas of overlap, ask what the relationship of one event is to the other(s), and create a sort of timeline "mashup." Consider, for example, two momentous

Mexican Scottsboro boys

Shown above are 10 of the 12 Mexican Sleepy Lagoon boys serving sentences up to life imprisonment. Trade unions and trade union bodies, including the National CIO, say they were victims of racial incitement and discrimination and are working with the Sleepy Lagoon Defense Committee to appeal their convictions. The picture, taken at San Quentin penitentiary where the boys are making excellent records, shows, left to right, standing, Gus Zamora, John Matuz, Angel Padilla, Jack Melendez, Smiles Parra, (front row) Henry Ynostroza, Bobby Telles, Bobby Thompson, Chepe Ruiz and Manuel Reyes. Ruiz and Telles, both 18, are serving life sentences; the others from five years to life. Not shown are Henry Leyvas, 20; Manuel Delgado, 19.

FIGURE 2.1. "Mexican Scottsboro Boys," *Los Angeles Tribune*, December 27, 1943.

events in Chicana/o history: the August 1942 Sleepy Lagoon murder and subsequent events (including the trial and its appeal) and the Zoot Suit Riots, which occurred in June 1943. The first was an altercation that broke out at a party and resulted in the death of a twenty-two-year-old, José Díaz. His body was found in an LA reservoir known as the Sleepy Lagoon. Consequently, police rounded up hundreds of Mexican youth and arrested twenty-two, all of whom were tried for murder (see figure 2.1). Everyone—the media, police, prosecution, and judge—blatantly discriminated against the young Mexican defendants. This racism provoked a backlash that resulted in widespread public support from both inside and outside the Mexican American community. A multiethnic coalition, the Sleepy Lagoon Defense Committee, provided support and raised funds for the defense of the Mexican youth. In the second case, the Zoot Suit Riots, long-standing tensions between Mexican youth known as "zoot suiters" (because of the outfits they wore) and military servicemen erupted into a weeklong race riot in Los

FIGURE 2.2. Alice McGrath with Sleepy Lagoon defendants and defense attorney Ben Margolis, Alice Greenfield McGrath Papers (Collection 1490). UCLA Library Special Collections, Charles E. Young Research Library, University of California, Los Angeles.

Angeles. Mobs of white servicemen descended on East Los Angeles, aiming to attack zoot suiters and strip them of their zoot suits, which the military men viewed as un-American and unpatriotic. While most zoot suiters were Chicano, African American and Filipino zoot suiters also were attacked.

A multiracial coalition of important leaders and supporters of the Chicana/o youth, aware that the racism directed at the defendants did not occur in isolation, strove to bring to the public's attention the systematic discrimination occurring at the time. In their model studies of relational notions of race, historians Luis Alvarez and Scott Kurashige detail such coalitions. They also document the extent to which African American community members saw their fates as linked with those of Chicana/os, pointing to the outpouring of support by African Americans for the Sleepy Lagoon defendants.[33] I also found this was the case in my research into the coverage of the case. One African American newspaper, the *Los Angeles Tribune,* compared the treatment of the boys in the Sleepy Lagoon case to those of nine African American youth falsely accused of rape in Scottsboro, Alabama, in

1931. The paper referred to the Chicana/os as the "Mexican Scottsboro boys."[34] In an opinion piece featured in the *Tribune,* columnist Alyce Keys wrote, "You don't have to be a quiz kid to figure out why these boys were made the victims of such a travesty on *[sic]* American justice. Remember our Scottsboro case. It is the same pattern of fascist racism."[35]

In a timeline of the Sleepy Lagoon affair, Alice McGrath, an activist and executive secretary of the Sleepy Lagoon Defense Committee (see figure 2.2), listed events related to Chicana/os during this period, but also reminded her audience that in April, just a couple of months before these landmark events, Japanese and Japanese Americans were relocated to internment camps.[36] Similarly, McWilliams commented, "It was a foregone conclusion that Mexicans would be substituted as the major scapegoat group once the Japanese were removed."[37] Juxtaposing these events forces us to ask what message was meant to be conveyed by this mass containment, displacement, and racialization of both Mexican and Japanese residents, actions that took place just months apart; doing so reminds us that both groups were depicted as enemies of the state during World War II.

WHAT'S THE PAYOFF?

In this chapter, I have argued that we should examine Chicana/os in relation to other racialized groups in order to develop a fuller understanding of how racial categories are formed and how they operate. Thinking about race relationally will continue to be of importance in the future, not only for trends in the scholarship but also for the world we live in. Indeed, those of us who study history often do so because we want to make change in our present and because this requires that we understand the relationships between racial representations and structural forces, power and inequality, and how these relationships change over time.

NOTES

This chapter was first published in *Pacific Historical Review* 82, no. 4 (2013): 520–41.

1. I use the term *Chicana/o* throughout this chapter to refer broadly to Mexicans and Mexican Americans alike. I use this term because it references the Chicano

movement of the 1960s and 1970s, and the development of the scholarly field of Chicana/o studies that arose out of it.

2. Although English was my second language, the teachers and administrators had no way of knowing this. I had no accent, and given that all my schooling had been in English, I spoke English better than Spanish by the time I reached high school.

3. The following are foundational works that explain the importance of looking at how concepts of race, class, and gender intersect: Kimberlé Crenshaw, "Mapping the Margins: Intersectionality, Identity Politics, and Violence against Women of Color," *Stanford Law Review* 43, no. 6 (1991); Patricia Hill Collins, *Black Feminist Thought: Knowledge, Consciousness, and the Politics of Empowerment* (New York: Routledge, 1991).

4. Michael Omi and Howard Winant, *Racial Formation in the United States: From the 1960s to the 1980s* (New York: Routledge, 1986).

5. Examples of these foundational works include Mark Reisler, *By the Sweat of Their Brow: Mexican Immigrant Labor in the United States, 1900–1940* (Westport, CT: Greenwood Press, 1976); Albert Camarillo, *Chicanos in a Changing Society: From Mexican Pueblos to American Barrios in Santa Barbara and Southern California, 1848–1930* (Cambridge, MA: Harvard University Press, 1979); Richard Griswold del Castillo, *The Los Angeles Barrio, 1850–1890: A Social History* (Berkeley: University of California Press, 1979); Mario T. Garcia, *Desert Immigrants: The Mexicans of El Paso, 1880–1920* (New Haven, CT: Yale University Press, 1981); Ricardo Romo, *History of a Barrio* (Austin: University of Texas Press, 1983); Rodolfo Acuña, *A Community Under Siege: A Chronicle of Chicanos East of the Los Angeles River, 1945–1975* (Los Angeles: Chicano Studies Research Center Publications, University of California, Los Angeles, 1984).

6. To place this shift in historical perspective, see David G. Gutiérrez, "Significant to Whom? Mexican Americans and the History of the American West," *Western Historical Quarterly* 24, no. 4 (1993): 519–39; Vicki L. Ruiz, "Nuestra América: Latino History as United States History," *Journal of American History* 93, no. 3 (2006): 655–72. See also Adrian Burgos et al., "Latino History: An Interchange on Present Realities and Future Prospects," *Journal of American History* 97, no. 2 (2010): 424–63.

7. Antonia Castañeda, "Women of Color and the Rewriting of Western History: The Discourse, Politics, and Decolonization of History," *Pacific Historical Review* 61, no. 4 (1992): 510–11. Some works stand out as heeding this call, including Gloria Anzaldúa, *Borderlands: The New Mestiza/La frontera* (San Francisco: Spinsters/ Aunt Lute, 1987); Sarah Deutsch, *No Separate Refuge: Culture, Class, and Gender on an Anglo-Hispanic Frontier in the American Southwest, 1880–1940* (New York: Oxford University Press, 1987); Deena J. Gonzalez, *Refusing the Favor: The Spanish-Mexican Women of Santa Fe, 1820–1880* (New York: Oxford University Press, 1999); Susan Lee Johnson, *Roaring Camp: The Social World of the California Gold Rush* (New York: W. W. Norton, 2000); Peggy Pascoe, *Relations of Rescue: The Search for Female Moral Authority in the American West, 1874–1939* (New York: Oxford University Press, 1990); Emma Pérez, *The Decolonial Imaginary: Writing Chicanas*

into History (Bloomington: Indiana University Press, 1999); Vicki Ruiz, *Cannery Women, Cannery Lives: Mexican Women, Unionization, and the California Food Processing Industry, 1930–1950* (Albuquerque: University of New Mexico Press, 1987).

8. Neil Foley, *The White Scourge: Mexicans, Blacks, and Poor Whites in Texas Cotton Culture* (Berkeley: University of California Press, 1997).

9. Omi and Winant, *Racial Formation.*

10. Tomás Almaguer, *Racial Fault Lines: The Historical Origins of White Supremacy in California* (Berkeley: University of California Press, 1994). Other key studies of relational notions of race outside of this field include Claire Jean Kim, *Bitter Fruit: The Politics of Black-Korean Conflict in New York City* (New Haven, CT: Yale University Press, 2000); Tiya Miles, *Ties That Bind: The Story of an Afro-Cherokee Family in Slavery and Freedom* (Berkeley: University of California Press, 2005).

11. George J. Sánchez, *Becoming Mexican American: Ethnicity, Culture, and Identity in Chicano Los Angeles, 1900–1945* (New York: Oxford University Press, 1993), 179.

12. Albert Camarillo, *Chicanos in a Changing Society: From Mexican Pueblos to American Barrios in Santa Barbara and Southern California, 1848–1930* (Cambridge, MA: Harvard University Press, 1979).

13. Reginald Horsman, *Race and Manifest Destiny: The Origins of American Racial Anglo-Saxonism* (Cambridge, MA: Harvard University Press, 1981).

14. Lindley was the first head of the city's public health department. He delivered the inaugural *Los Angeles City Annual Health Officer's Report* on November 13, 1879.

15. *Health Officer's Report* (1879), 1.

16. *Health Officer's Report* (1879), 3.

17. *Health Officer's Report* (1879), 3.

18. Unfortunately, the experiences of Mexican youth can also be found in the state of California's sterilization records. Miroslava Chávez-García, *States of Delinquency: Race and Science in the Making of California's Juvenile Justice System* (Berkeley: University of California Press, 2012).

19. After 1920, the city health department expanded its categories to include "Mexican," "Japanese," and "Negro"; the county health department used "White," "Mexican," "Japanese," and "Other" to keep track of the populations under its jurisdiction.

20. In their highly influential study, *Racial Formation in the United States: From the 1960s to the 1980s,* Omi and Winant define racialization as a "sociohistorical process by which racial categories are created, inhabited, transformed, and destroyed" (56). They emphasize the historically specific and socially constructed nature of racial categories by drawing attention to "*projects* in which human bodies and social structures are represented and organized" (55–56; emphasis in the original).

21. On graduate programs with a relational approach, see Ramón Gutiérrez, "Ethnic Studies: Its Evolution in American Colleges and Universities," in *Multiculturalism: A Critical Reader,* ed. David Theo Goldberg (Cambridge, MA: Blackwell, 1994), 155–67.

22. On the crossed paths of Native Americans and interned Japanese, see Allison Varzally, *Making a Non-white America: Californians Coloring outside Ethnic Lines, 1925–1955* (Berkeley: University of California Press, 2008), 129–36. In my research using INS records, I have come across references to how best to racially categorize African Americans for naturalization purposes, to job competition between African Americans and Mexicans, and to lynching. See Record Group 85, Archives I, National Archives, Washington, DC.

23. Another model study is Albert Camarillo, "Black and Brown in Compton: Demographic Change, Suburban Decline, and Intergroup Relations in a South Central Los Angeles Community, 1950–2000," in *Not Just Black and White: Historical and Contemporary Perspectives on Immigration, Race, and Ethnicity in the United States,* ed. Nancy Foner and George M. Fredrickson (New York: Russell Sage Foundation, 2004), 358–75.

24. Japanese American National Museum, "Exhibition Overview," *Boyle Heights: The Power of Place,* accessed November 18, 2011, http://www.janm.org /exhibits/bh/exhibition/exhibition.htm.

25. Sánchez, *Becoming Mexican American;* George J. Sánchez, *Bridging Borders, Remaking Community: Racial Interaction in Boyle Heights, California, in the 20th Century* (University of California Press, forthcoming). The following chapter and article by Sánchez are also about Boyle Heights and will be included in the forthcoming book: George J. Sánchez, "Disposable People, Expendable Neighborhoods," in *A Companion to Los Angeles,* ed. William Francis Deverell and Greg Hise (Chichester, U.K.: Wiley-Blackwell, 2010), 129–46; George Sánchez, "'What's Good for Boyle Heights Is Good for the Jews': Creating Multiracialism on the Eastside during the 1950s," *American Quarterly* 56, no. 3 (2004).

26. Quoted in George Lipsitz, "The Possessive Investment in Whiteness: Racialized Social Democracy and the 'White' Problem in American Studies," *American Quarterly* 47, no. 3 (1995): 373.

27. Sarah Deutsch, George Sánchez, and Gary Y. Okihiro, "Contemporary Peoples/Contested Places," in *The Oxford History of the American West,* ed. Clyde A. Milner II, Carol A. O'Connor, and Martha A. Sandweiss (New York: Oxford University Press, 1994), 639–70.

28. The oral interviews from the Japanese American National Museum's exhibition, *Boyle Heights: Power of Place,* suggest as much about the solidarity in the neighborhood.

29. For an innovative example of how life histories can contribute to relational notions of race, see Gaye Johnson's work using the biographies of two women who fought for similar causes but for whom no evidence exists of a friendship or alliance. Gaye Johnson, "Constellations of Struggle: Luisa Moreno, Charlotta Bass, and the Legacy for Ethnic Studies," *Aztlán: A Journal of Chicano Studies* 33, no. 1 (2008).

30. Carey McWilliams, *The Education of Carey McWilliams* (New York: Simon and Schuster, 1979).

31. Carey McWilliams, *Brothers under the Skin* (Boston: Little, Brown, 1944); Carey McWilliams, *Prejudice: Japanese-Americans: Symbol of Racial Intolerance*

(Boston: Little, Brown, 1944); Carey McWilliams, *A Mask for Privilege: Anti-Semitism in America* (Boston: Little, Brown, 1948); Carey McWilliams, *Factories in the Field: The Story of Migratory Farm Labor in California* (Hamden, CT: Archon Books, 1969); Carey McWilliams, *North from Mexico: The Spanish-Speaking People of the United States,* rev. ed., updated by Matt S. Meier (1949; repr., New York: Praeger, 1990).

32. McWilliams, *Brothers under the Skin,* 90, 96.

33. Luis Alvarez, "From Zoot Suits to Hip Hop: Towards a Relational Chicana/o Studies," *Latino Studies* 5 (2007); Luis Alvarez, *The Power of the Zoot: Youth Culture and Resistance during World War II* (Berkeley: University of California Press, 2008); Scott Kurashige, *The Shifting Grounds of Race: Black and Japanese Americans in the Making of Multiethnic Los Angeles* (Princeton, NJ: Princeton University Press, 2008).

34. "Mexican Scottsboro Boys," *Los Angeles Tribune,* December 27, 1943.

35. "Key Notes," Alyce Keys, *Los Angeles Tribune,* December 6, 1943.

36. Alice Greenfield McGrath, "Sleepy Lagoon Case—Chronology," 1983, Department of Special Collections, University of California, Los Angeles, accessed July 29, 2011, http://www.library.edu/special/scweb.

37. McWilliams, *North from Mexico,* 206; cited in Kurashige, *Shifting Grounds of Race,* 150.

THREE

Entangled Dispossessions

RACE AND COLONIALISM IN THE HISTORICAL PRESENT

Alyosha Goldstein

In what is now the United States, differential racialization and colonialism have been mutually constitutive in ways that, while changing over time, continue to substantially shape the present. Despite the American exceptionalist premise that inexorable progress makes racism and colonialism history, the devaluation and expropriation of peoples racialized as not white remains deeply entangled with the contemporary dynamics of property and poverty. My focus in this chapter is both on the ongoing relations of racial and colonial dispossession and on the governmental and juridical efforts to convey the appearance of their historical resolution.

This chapter uses the Claims Resolution Act (CRA) of 2010 as a lens through which to examine how jurisprudence as an institutional practice that strives to govern and discipline the past, and monetary compensation as an ostensible means of closure, are relevant for understanding colonialism and racialization today. The CRA funded a series of historic U.S. civil rights and Native American class-action lawsuit settlements. Included in this legislation were *Cobell v. Salazar* and *In re Black Farmers Discrimination Litigation* (also known as *Pigford II* because of its connection to the *Pigford v. Glickman* settlement of 1999). In *Cobell,* the Interior and Treasury Departments were sued for mismanaging American Indian trust accounts, which had been created by the General Allotment Act of 1887, and its final settlement awarded plaintiffs $3.4 billion. *Pigford II* was a suit against the U.S. Department of Agriculture for discriminating in its loan programs against Black farmers and was the single largest civil rights settlement in U.S. history. The chapter's first section explains the specific history of racialization, property, and continental conquest at stake in the CRA's class-action suits, and it analyzes the legislative debates over the CRA, in which policy makers' concerns over the financial crisis of 2008 articulate with the extended historical circumstances addressed in the legal cases themselves. The chapter's second and third sections dwell, respectively, on the *Cobell* and *Pigford II* settlements. The conclusion considers further how the act frames and fore- closes racialized dispossession and settler colonialism and, moreover, what escapes the conciliatory imperative of liberal jurisprudence.

OVERCOMING THE PRESENT

In the broadest sense, *modern colonialism* refers to the techniques and insti- tutions that maintain foreign control over a people and territory, depriving those subjugated of autonomy and self-governance, and justifying this impo- sition in terms of the religious, moral, cultural, or racial superiority of the foreign power. As a particular iteration of this larger formation, settler colo- nialism is especially significant in the United States, where settlers have sought to eliminate and replace Indigenous peoples by force and assimilation rather than extracting resources and revenue on behalf of a distant colonial metropole.[1] Settler colonialism in the United States is a perpetually incom- plete project. It is a logic of possession and inevitability predicated on the disavowal of its own violent displacements and denial of their ongoing con- testation. Such collisions and confrontations have not diminished; they con- tinue unabated in the colonial present.

Slavery and colonialism—property claims to both persons and land— remained explicitly and inextricably entwined from the early national period until the end of the Civil War. The territorial provisions of the *Dred Scott v. Sanford* decision reveal, for example, how slavery's economic logic of property and value has been indispensable to U.S. colonial expansion.[2] Foundational for the United States, the racial terms of property, possession, and belonging are evident as well in the mid-nineteenth-century seizure of northern Mexico, the Chinese Exclusion Act of 1882, and the history of U.S. immigration policy. As Cheryl Harris argues, "The origins of whiteness as property lie in the parallel systems of domination of Black and Native American peoples out of which were created racially contingent forms of property and property rights."[3] Understanding the historical constitution of private property, resource extraction, and speculative investment in and through colonialism and slavery (as well as what Saidiya Hartman describes as the "indebted ser- vitude" of African American peonage and sharecropping that formed slavery's afterlife[4]) is crucial for addressing the present-day displacement of risk, accountability, and culpability from the wealthy to everyone else. This displacement ensures that the cost of economic crisis and collapse is paid for by poor and working-class people, and it has served as yet another mechanism for the accelerated privatization and concentration of wealth.[5] The CRA provides an especially evocative lens through which to address how current juridical, political, and economic projects acknowledge these historically fraught social relations while aiming, simultaneously, to disavow and foreclose their enduring salience.

The role of law in the inscription and mediation of social norms is accentuated by the efforts of neoliberal policy making to reduce the state to a mechanism for administering coercion (such as policing, punishment, and military operations) and enforcing contracts. In this context, the normative adjudication of conflict and the legal grounding of civil society take on a reinvigorated significance as the state is further devolved and dispersed. Even as calls to deregulate markets and to eliminate social and environmental protections increasingly circumscribe the rule of law, jurisprudence assumes a greater burden as the supposedly neutral and dispassionate arbiter of right.[6] Describing how the law functions "as an archive or mode of record keeping," Chandan Reddy argues that "historical and social differences (of gender, race, and sexuality, among others) are subjugated by the law as a precondition for their entrance into the national record, and forced to preserve the liberal narrative of universality on which the legal sphere bases its notion of justice and on which the nation is said to be founded."[7] Law serves as an archive for this chapter not because of the justice it claims to confer, but rather because it stages and registers political and social antagonisms—antagonisms that are in excess of its regimes of precedent and judgment. Against the limits of legal argument, this chapter examines how the CRA highlights various histories of colonial and racialized dispossession in the United States, but it does so— amid an ongoing moment of economic volatility and social instability—only to situate these histories within an overarching teleology of national progress and improvement.

Taking place in the wake of the midterm elections of 2010, congressional deliberation on the CRA clearly registered both the insecurities of the economic crisis and the recent Republican electoral victories. The legislation's Democratic supporters framed their arguments in terms of debt and the moral imperatives of fiscal responsibility. Representative Sheila Jackson Lee (D-TX) asserted that "America is a place of equality. . . . [L]egitimate issues addressing native lands have now been resolved. This is not a handout. This legislation is paid for."[8] According to Representative Ed Perlmutter (D-CO), "America needs to pay its debts and not allow this kind of discrimination to go forward. . . . This country pays its bills."[9] Nick Rahall (D-WV) likewise declared, "I am proud to say that we have been able to resolve these long-standing litigation matters without adding to the Federal deficit."[10] Reiterating the racially inflected and paternalistic language of "handouts" and "responsibility," Democrats emphasized the correlation between legitimacy and solvency as a national imperative.

But, chiding the Democrats sponsoring the bill, Representative Doc Hastings (R-WA) claimed that "the message from the voters in November's election was unmistakable: It's very clear the American people do care about Congress acting in a transparent, open, and fiscally responsible manner." He contended, "At a time of record deficit spending and record Federal debt, it is the duty of Congress to ask questions to ensure that these settlements are in the best interest of the taxpayers."[11] Not surprisingly, neither the taxpayer nor the interest Hastings invokes coincides with the CRA's Native American or African American claimants. Representative Steve King (R-IA) dismissively characterized the *Pigford II* settlement in particular as "modern-day reparations" and, along with Representative Michele Bachmann (R-MN), argued that its claims process was rife with fraud. King bemoaned "spending money that we don't have for causes that don't have the support of the American people." Suggesting that 75 to 90 percent of the Pigford applicants were fraudulent, he declared, "We can't be paying modern-day slavery reparations thinking we compensate what took place in the past. We have the future to worry about."[12] Regrettable as aspects of this past may have been, according to King, racial opportunists now threatened the vitality of the United States by making duplicitous claims that neither served nor had the endorsement of the "American people." Representative Virginia Foxx (R-NC) stated, "The growing deficits under the Democrats' leadership will ultimately lead to a lower standard of living and less opportunity for future generations of Americans. As spending by the Federal Government grows to unsustainable levels, the U.S. will sacrifice its sovereignty by becoming dependent on debt borrowed from foreign countries."[13]

Here, in the aftermath of the 2008 crisis, moral deficit, economic debt, and historical injustice combine to threaten the semblance of national integrity and sovereign authority. During the signing ceremony, President Barack Obama declared that the legislation was not "simply a matter of making amends. It's about reaffirming our values on which this nation was founded—principles of fairness and equality and opportunity. It's about helping families who suffered through no fault of their own get back on their feet. It's about restoring a sense of trust between the American people and the government that plays such an important role in their lives."[14] Representative James Clyburn (D-SC) likewise affirmed that with the CRA "we removed this stain on our country's history. What happened to our nation's African American farmers and Native Americans was wrong, and we have made it right."[15] Congressional debate and presidential decree were symptomatic in this instance of current anxieties not only over insolvency but also over the incapacities of the U.S. nation-state and the persistent failures of the settler colonial project.

At the very moment when the neoliberal fantasy of market-based salvation defaults and the Keynesian model of regulatory remediation appears equally untenable, the foundational violence, territorial seizure, and social obliteration on which settler colonial expansion has been based once again potentially comes into view, in the form of new appeals to "restoring a sense of trust" with Native peoples and African American farmers. That the federal government in fact has specific and legally mandated terms of trusteeship based on treaty agreements with Native American nations that it has regularly disregarded remains unacknowledged in this more intangible appeal to the virtues of restoring trust. During an era of mass eviction and foreclosure, when the national fiction of upward mobility and greater wealth across the generations appears ever more scandalously unattainable for most everyone, the dispossession of Indigenous peoples takes on new significance because their ostensible assimilation and disappearance have been the very conditions on which national progress has been predicated.

EXTINGUISHING FUTURE CLAIMS

In 1996, Elouise Cobell and four other named plaintiffs filed a class-action lawsuit against the federal government on behalf of individual Indian owners of trust lands, lands that were a result of the General Allotment Act of 1887, also known as the Dawes Severalty Act. Following two decades of escalating military and extralegal violence toward Indigenous peoples in North America, the Dawes Act sought to replace the elimination of Natives physically with their assimilation juridically and economically.[16] From the perspective of many non-Indian reformers who considered themselves advocates for Native Americans, allotment amounted to a bulwark against genocide, ensuring Indigenous survival through assimilation to liberal personhood and property norms.[17] At the time, despite its own military campaigns, the federal government decried settler brutality and lawlessness. Commissioner of Indian Affairs Ezra A. Hayt, for instance, contended that the government was "impotent to protect the Indians on their reservation, especially when held in common, from the encroachments of its own people."[18] Legislation such as the Major Crimes Act of 1885, which diminished tribal jurisdiction over non-Indian perpetrators, and Public Law 280 in 1953, which mandated the transfer of federal law enforcement jurisdiction over designated tribes in six states to state governments, ensured that settler violence would continue with impunity.[19]

Yet allotment allowed the federal government to sell off Indian lands that were ostensibly "surplus" to the parcels allocated to Indian individuals in fee simple title, and it precipitated widespread loss of land among Indigenous peoples through tax foreclosure and fraud once the land was divided and privatized. Moreover, Joanne Barker argues that the Bureau of Indian Affairs' "regulations of competency and land title by blood marks the constitutive role of race in Native dispossession." Barker points out that allotment generated census rolls supplied a "federal record of tribal members' blood and lineality," which were then used as the administrative basis for "the institutionalization of the identification of tribal members by blood as a not-so-subtle proxy for race."[20] As David Chang puts it, allotment "reinforced a tendency in the United States to think that it is race, rather than political difference, that defines Indian people and Indian nations."[21] Focusing on the assimilation of individual Indians, allotment further dismantled sovereign nation-to-nation relations—already underway with the unilateral legislation in 1871 that ended U.S. treaty making with tribes—and aimed to transform the "vanishing Indian" into a racial minority. The Dawes Act also stipulated that the United States would operate as the trustee for individual Indians' lands and natural resources and for the monetary assets generated by leases to those lands and resources, as private industry extracted oil, coal, and timber, and held grazing rights. Those assets and lands—of which about eleven million acres remain individually owned—are managed by the Secretary of the Interior and, through the Individual Indian Money (IIM) Trust Fund, by the Treasury Department.

The *Cobell* suit charged the U.S. government with gross neglect of its fiduciary obligations since 1887. Tried repeatedly from 1996 until 2009 in the

U.S. District Court of the District of Columbia, *Cobell* entailed more than thirty-six hundred filings, eighty published opinions, and eleven appellate decisions.[22] It is among the largest such suits ever filed against the federal government. Indeed, the government's mismanagement has been so egregious that the Department of the Interior (DOI) has testified that—in dereliction of its specific statutory mandate and obligation—it cannot render an accurate accounting of the money currently held in the IIM trust. This remarkable failure to account for the money it collected and disbursed was reaffirmed throughout the duration of the suit and in several congressional hearings. For instance, when asked in 2002 about the DOI's capacity to provide an account of the IIM trust funds, Tom Slonaker, then the DOI's special trustee for American Indians, replied that the agency "simply can't produce a full accounting ... a complete and full accounting which the Trustee is obligated to provide to the beneficiaries."[23] Since the creation of the trusts, the Interior Department has been notorious for leasing Indian lands below market rates and for flagrant mismanagement of funds collected and disbursed. A report by the Joint Commission to Investigate Indian Affairs in 1915 described the "great wealth in the form of Indian funds" derived from lands held in trust as "an inducement to fraud, corruption, and institutional incompetence almost beyond the possibility of comprehension."[24] And a study by the American Indian Policy Review Commission in 1977 declared, "Measured by international standards, the leases negotiated on behalf of Indians are among the poorest agreements ever made."[25] Even at the outset of the *Cobell* suit, an operative distinction between the management of the accounts and the administration of the leases shielded the Interior Department from investigation into its long-standing collusion with private industry's exploitation of Indian resources. Focused exclusively on the IIM trust accounts themselves, the terms of the suit entirely exempted the Bureau of Indian Affairs (BIA) leasing practices.

When brought to court, *Cobell* demanded two measures. First, it sought a full accounting of the money owed to about five hundred thousand Indian beneficiaries on whom the United States imposed the IIM trust accounts. Second, it called for a substantial reform of the Interior Department's administration of the Indian trust funds. The settlement ignored both these demands and instead substituted a monetary award to the class-action plaintiffs.[26] The plaintiffs' initial estimate of $137.2 billion in unpaid trust funds from 1887 to 2000 was calculated by cross-referencing the historical records of the oil, gas, coal, and other companies that leased from the BIA and adding the accrual of interest.[27] Rejecting the plaintiff's estimate and supporting the Interior Department's contention that an actual historical accounting was too costly, the final settlement in 2009 was for a vastly reduced total of $3.4 billion, based instead on statistical sampling.[28] Kimberly Craven argued that in this sense an underlying problem with the settlement was the way in which it expanded the class of plaintiffs: "If in the leasing of your land, it was damaged from overgrazing, minerals extracted without your permission, timber cut without payment, soil poisoned from agricultural chemicals or any other reason, you will be paid $500, plus a formula amount, to extinguish these potential claims."[29] And by accepting the settlement payout, plaintiffs relinquished any further recourse against the government for mismanagement. *Cobell* did not intend to extinguish these potential claims when it was first filed, but this was a result of the final settlement.

On November 24, 2012, the *Cobell* settlement appeal period expired, and—the Supreme Court having dismissed the appeals petitions submitted for its consideration—two days later President Obama announced "the final approval of the Cobell settlement agreement, clearing the way for reconciliation between the trust beneficiaries and the federal government."[30] Not only did the settlement claim to resolve more than a century of theft and negligence without providing an accounting and without changing the administrative and juridical conditions that led to the situation, but it also used a considerably reduced payment ($3.4 billion rather than $137.2 billion) to preempt further claims by Indians whose land was mismanaged by the Interior and Treasury Departments.

In effect, the *Cobell* settlement's terms sustained and intensified the individuation and privatization of property that drove the Dawes Act in 1887, which parceled and allotted collective tribal land and thus broke up tribal nations, compelled assimilation, and opened Indian lands to non-Indian purchase and settlement. And the settlement ultimately relieved the United States of any obligation to provide an official record of the funds that it expropriated, or misappropriated, for its own unaccounted uses. It did not hold the government responsible for payment based on such an accurate accounting. It absolved the federal government of its violations of the terms of its fiduciary obligations.

Although a portion of the settlement money is allocated toward the purchase of fractionated interests in allotments (the increasing subdivision of ownership of allotted land created as title is passed on to multiple heirs over generations) and transfers these purchases to tribal governments, it works to shift the burden of proof and accounting from the federal government and its agencies to individual Indian claimants. In doing so, it intensifies the calculations of individuation—and hence diminishes tribal claims—rather than pluralizing sovereign authority. In the wake of the final *Cobell* settlement, arguments that focus on the comparative disadvantage of Native Americans' seeking mortgages because of the liminal status of reservations substitute for more far-reaching claims to tribal sovereignty and U.S. culpability.[31] In other words, any reckoning with the political specificity of tribal sovereignty and the persistence of U.S. treaty obligations is avoided, and that history is instead recast in terms of the illegibility of Indian reservations to real estate and commercial banking—an illegibility that erroneously names tribal sovereignty as the source of poverty and as the obstacle to capital and credit.

ECONOMIES OF RACIAL ATTRITION

If reconciliation in the *Cobell* settlement seems to have been purchased by removing the historical evidence of theft and by abrogating future claims, then the terms of juridical closure and compensation in the case of *Pigford II* remain problematic as well. The president of the Black Farmers and Agriculturists Association, Gary Grant, was among those present at the CRA presidential signing ceremony on December 8, 2010. Decidedly less sanguine than others commenting on the event, Grant observed, "Seemingly forgotten in the process are those Black farmers who are in the Administrative Process or have outstanding court claims, like my parents, not to mention those who filed Civil Rights claims during the 'Bush years' who are now threatened with loss of their claims because of the Statutes of Limitations being used against them since the Bush Administration did pretty much as the Reagan Administration by stripping the office of Civil Rights and not following up on filed claims."[32] He noted that the settlement, as with so many of the federal government's previous Department of Agriculture (USDA) discrimination inquiries, instituted no penalties for the agency or its representatives who were directly culpable for the racist practices identified in the suit. Furthermore, of the African American farmers who will be compensated through the *Pigford* and *Pigford II* settlements, many will pay the money toward costs related to their previous bankruptcy. The settlement also did not resolve the consequences of their past debts, nor did it provide substantially for future possibilities to resume farming. What the settlement affirmed—through a standardized and finite distribution of payments—was the progressive realization of justice presumably immanent to law, specifically that federally institutionalized racial inequality was now past, finished, and resolved.

As U.S. District Court Judge Paul L. Friedman observed in his opinion for the original consent decree for *Pigford I,* which was filed in April 1999, the USDA was created on May 15, 1862, "as Congress was debating the issue of providing land for freed former slaves."[33] And through the signing of the CRA, what Friedman regarded as "a fair resolution of the claims brought in this case and a good first step towards assuring that the kind of discrimination that has been visited on African American farmers since Reconstruction will not continue into the next century" had acquired the full force of historical conclusion.[34] In his formal statement on the CRA, Secretary of Agriculture Tom Vilsack remarked that the legislation would "finally allow USDA to turn the page on past discrimination against black farmers. . . . The process has been long and often difficult, but we can't wait any longer to close this sad chapter in USDA's history."[35] That the legislation would "finally allow" Vilsack and the USDA to "close this sad chapter" implies, of course, a peculiar inversion: here, the USDA—rather than the African American farmers who initiated the lawsuit—was "waiting for justice" and hoping for some juridical end to its long-standing and institutionalized practices of racial discrimination.

Despite the failures of the Freedmen's Bureau and the Southern Homestead Act of 1866 to redistribute property to emancipated African Americans, and despite concerted white hostility and violence, 20 percent of Black farmers managed to purchase at least some arable land by 1880. (By comparison, 60 percent of all Southern white farmers owned their land at this time, which on average was valued at twice as much as their Black counterparts'.)[36] That the formerly enslaved were not the principal beneficiaries of such transfer of "public land" should not minimize the fact that all land ownership by non-Indigenous peoples operated in tandem with settler colonial expansion. Nevertheless, by 1910 African Americans held title to about sixteen million acres of farmland, and by 1920, there were 925,000 Black-owned farms in the United States. During the economic crisis of the 1930s, the USDA created new loan programs that directly contributed to diminishing the hard-won gains of African Americans since Emancipation. And by 1997, the year the first *Pigford* class-action lawsuit was filed, Black farmers owned and operated only 18,451 farms. Even though all small-scale farming declined significantly over the course of the twentieth century, largely because of the industrialization and corporatization of agribusiness, there was considerable disparity between the loss of 98 percent for Black farmers as compared to 66 percent for whites.[37]

New Deal legislation—including the Agricultural Adjustment Act of 1933, the Soil Conservation and Domestic Allotment Act of 1936, and the Bankhead-Jones Farm Tenant Act of 1937—established the USDA's role as the "lender of last resort" and created local county committees to administer loans to select qualifying farmers. The county committees had considerable influence on agricultural development and individual farm capacity. The committees made supervised long-term loans to farmers who were unable to find other financing, and they set limits for the maximum acreage on which farmers could raise their crops. In the South, until as late as the mid-1960s, these committees comprised only white farmers who used their fiscal and planning authority to systematically dispossess and eliminate Black farmers in the South. Loans were especially crucial during the 1930s and after World War II, because of the increasing costs of new agricultural technologies—which were required for modernized production but also had the effect of decreasing farm labor—and because of the increasing competition from corporate agribusiness. Historically, both public and private lenders have cast small farmers, as a group, as uncreditworthy.[38] The Farmers' Home Administration Act of 1946 (which is the source of the USDA's current loan programs) and the Consolidated Farmers' Home Administration Act of 1961 (which sought to address the increasing need for credit as a result of agricultural mechanization) continued to expand and refine the USDA's function as a fiscal safety net, but once again they largely bypassed farmers of color.[39]

Mounting pressure from the civil rights movement compelled a certain degree of institutional adjustment and more public standards of accountability, yet at the USDA, these changes manifested themselves for the most part in a bureaucratic compulsion to conduct repeated evaluations and intermittent official investigations. In the wake of the Civil Rights Act of 1964, the U.S. Commission on Civil Rights initiated an inquiry into the discriminatory practices at the USDA. The commission's report in 1965 found that despite the agency's significant contributions to "raising the economic, educational, and social levels of thousands of farm and rural families," African American farmers were "a glaring exception to this picture of progress."[40] The commission also reported that USDA assistance to Black farmers was "consistently different from that furnished to whites." In 1982 the U.S. Commission on Civil Rights published the results of another inquiry into the USDA, which concluded that since the report in 1965, the agency had—apart from establishing a division for reviewing civil rights violations—made little or no progress in eliminating discriminatory actions against African American farmers.[41] The following year the Reagan administration's response was simply to close the USDA's Office of Civil Rights Enforcement and Adjudication.

In 1997, African American farmers brought two class-action suits contending that the USDA's local county committees, to which they had applied for farm loans and assistance, had denied or postponed their applications on the basis of race from 1983 to 1997 and, further, that the USDA had then failed to investigate their allegations of racial discrimination. These farmers filed complaints stating that they were facing foreclosure and bankruptcy because the USDA denied them timely loans and debt restructuring—a charge that a USDA-commissioned study in 1994 supported. Other findings from this study showed that the largest USDA loans went to corporations (65 percent) and white farmers (25 percent); loans to Black farmers averaged 25 percent less than those given to whites; and 97 percent of disaster payments went to white farmers, while less than 1 percent went to African Americans.[42] The study reported that reasons for discrepancies in treatment between Black and white farmers could not be easily determined due to "gross deficiencies" in USDA data collection, which omitted applicant and demographic information necessary for comparison.[43]

In April 1999, the U.S. District Court for the District of Columbia approved a settlement agreement and consent decree (a judicial decree expressing a voluntary agreement between parties to a suit in return for the withdrawal of a criminal charge) in *Pigford v. Glickman*. The deadline for submitting a claim as a class member was September 2000, but as of November 2010, only 69 percent of eligible class members had final adjudications approved. Many voiced concern about the structure of the settlement agreement, the large number of applicants who filed late, and reported insufficient representation by class counsel. A provision in the farm bill of 2008 permitted any late-filing *Pigford* claimant who had not yet obtained a determination on their claim's merits to petition for such a determination in federal court. A maximum of $100 million was also made available for payment of the original *Pigford* claims. The multiple late-filed claims were then consolidated into a single case, *In re Black Farmers Discrimination Litigation* (commonly referred to as *Pigford II*), which was settled in February 2010 for $1.25 billion. But because only $100 million was made available in the farm bill of 2008, the *Pigford II* settlement was contingent on congressional approval of the additional $1.15 billion in funding. After a series of failed attempts to appropriate funds for the settlement agreement, the CRA provided the full appropriation in 2010.

The framework of "discrimination" that structures *Pigford II* operates through what Lawrie Balfour describes as "a political language of formal equality, which is premised on the erasure of the past." Drawing on the work of W. E. B. Du Bois, Balfour argues that, unlike "discrimination" and the discourse of formal equality, "a language of reparations"—as a language that affirms and refigures the past as a vehicle for social change—"might . . . enable a more democratic refiguration of political time."[44] An exclusive focus on "discrimination" deflects attention from the historical racial formation of capitalism itself, from the ways that race and its depredations are capitalism's constitutive features. *Pigford II* expanded the opportunity for Black farmers to be included in the plaintiff class, but it was, in the final instance, at once belated and premature—both too late to counter the wrongs already done and too early to have yet devised a means to challenge the ongoing dispossession of Black farmers by global agribusiness and financial crisis. The average size of farm operations in the United States grew substantially from the 1920s to the 1970s, as mechanization and capital-intensive agriculture dramatically reduced the number of farms and farmers. During the farm crisis of the 1980s, dependent on credit and severely indebted, small farmers faced massive foreclosures, while large-scale corporate agricultural production exponentially expanded.[45] A focus on discrimination ultimately justifies and reaffirms the underlying system because it makes racism external to capitalism's formation and its functioning, and in this instance, that focus also exempts from consideration the historical inequities of the (global) political economy of agriculture. Congressional efforts to cut funding for the Supplemental Nutrition Assistance Program (food stamps) from the 2013 farm bill is likewise symptomatic of this dichotomization of federal subsidy for corporate agribusiness and agricultural policy addressed to social inequality.[46]

The notion of discrimination that is central to both of the *Pigford* class-action suits works as a corollary to liberal conceptions of diversity and inclusion. In her study of the institutional discourses of diversity, Sara Ahmed makes several incisive points that are directly relevant for understanding both the forms of closure that the CRA performs and the liberal ambivalence that accompanies contemporary calls for settling claims of racial injustice. Ahmed argues that the performative tolerance and social repair institutionally enacted by championing diversity and inclusion recenter whiteness, "whether as the subject of injury who must be protected or as the subject whose generosity is 'behind' our arrival [as people of color]. To show our gratitude, we must put racism behind us."[47] The very admission of guilt broadcast by the settlement of the class-action lawsuits served to recuperate prevailing norms that disavow racism as constitutive and systemic. As Ahmed points out, "Guilt can be a way of performing rather than undoing whiteness. Guilt certainly works as a 'block' to hearing the claims of others as it 'returns' to the white self."[48] Indeed, the very mention of racism or whiteness is taken as evidence of the "stubbornness, paranoia, or even melancholia" of those who are not white, "as if we," writes Ahmed, "are holding onto something (whiteness) that our arrival shows has already gone . . . as a sign of [our] ingratitude, of failing to be grateful for the hospitality we have received by virtue of our arrival."[49] The CRA settlements do not change the underlying conditions or the institutional practices that prompted the lawsuits; instead, the settlements ostensibly serve as evidence of progress and intend to solicit gratitude for unexpectedly fulfilling a compensatory promise of justice.

UNRECONCILED TO REPARATION

The resolution proposed by the CRA is similar in purpose to influential models of ethical and juridical reconciliation, even as it also evokes more mundane forms of reconciliation found in financial accounting. Legal theorist Brenna Bhandar argues, "The much vaunted social and political objective of reconciliation, prevalent in colonial settler societies which attempt to grapple with the injustices that accrued during the course of violent settlement, demands a settled, unified notion of what transpired, which in turn compresses history into a seamless, progressive narrative of nation formation."[50] Acknowledgment and accommodation in this context serve as a means to justify and to invigorate colonial sovereignty. In jurisprudence and legislation, as Bhandar argues, "the injustices of the colonial past and its history of racist discriminatory laws" are acknowledged "only in order to close off and contain this past. The past is remembered only so that it may be forgotten in the push towards maintaining the foundation of the existing economic and social order."[51] The CRA presumes this aspiration to inclusion, and it aims to reaffirm the impartial value of prevailing social and economic norms.[52]

When Representative Steve King denounced the *Pigford II* decision as "modern-day reparations," he did so by claiming that "you cannot fix something that happened a century and a half ago. You can't go back and put the blood back in people's veins when they've paid in blood to put an end to slavery. And you can't hold the generations, six and seven generations hence, responsible for the sins of the great great great great great great grandfathers."[53] Whose blood King refers to here is perhaps deliberately ambiguous, but one connotation is that white people died to end slavery and thus have already paid their debt. As the corollary to such a perspective, Saidiya Hartman argues, "The very bestowal of freedom established the indebtedness of the freed through a calculus of blame and responsibility that mandated that the formerly enslaved repay both this investment of faith and prove their worthiness."[54] Despite arrangements made to fund the CRA from duties collected under the terms of the Continued Dumping and Subsidy Offset Act, King objected to spending money that was "unbudgeted, unauthorized, unacceptable—and not just 41 cents out of every dollar borrowed, a lot of it from the Chinese and the Saudis—but all of this money, all of this unbudgeted funding is a hundred percent borrowed money."[55] One irony here is that although King blatantly misrepresented the specific terms of the lawsuit, his efforts to broadly denigrate and delegitimize the settlement by conflating it with what he believed to be the absurdity of "modern-day reparations" for slavery nevertheless gestured toward the possibilities of such far-reaching demands.

Reparations are quite distinct from settlement and reconciliation. Robert Westley suggests that the movement for slavery reparations potentially conveys the "difference between the past as bygone and the past as prologue"; in other words, the difference between the past as something for which people today bear no responsibility or lived relation, and the past as the living conditions of future possibility.[56] Against the ongoing "devaluation of people of African descent," Westley contends that compensation "entails not mere abolition but a fundamental social revaluation of objects of commerce as subjects, a social transformation in which those same subjects are viewed as persons entitled to restitution and recognition of human rights and, not least of all, an appreciation of the exploitative dimension of slavery across time."[57] Redress in this sense demands a fundamental undoing of present-day racial economies of attrition and colonial dispossession rather than simply making amends and offering recompense aimed at securing business as usual. The relational coconstitution of racial and colonial dispossession thus continues to exceed historical reconciliation and conclusion.

The CRA draws attention to the manifest inequities experienced by Native peoples and African Americans in what is now the United States. Yet, ultimately, its terms of resolution weigh against reckoning with the entangled dispossession and fraught historical relations through which colonization and differential racialization continue to shape the present. The scope and logic of juridical settlement strive to make illegible the interconnections of the colonial taking of Native peoples' lands, the genocide and displacement of Native peoples, the abduction and enslavement of African peoples, and the constitutive force of differential racialization and anti-Blackness as primary social, economic, and political conditions of the United States. Studying racial formation as material practices of relational racialization rather than as distinct taxonomies provides a way of confronting how white supremacy in the United States continues to sustain colonial possession and the social exploitation and disposability of racially devalued people as mutually constitutive today.

NOTES

This chapter was first published as "Finance and Foreclosure in the Colonial Present," *Radical History Review* 118 (Winter 2014): 42–63.

1. Patrick Wolfe, "Settler Colonialism and the Elimination of the Native," *Journal of Genocide Research* 8, no. 4 (2006); Audra Simpson, "Settlement's Secret," *Cultural Anthropology* 26, no. 2 (2011): 205–17; Robert Nichols, "Indigeneity and the Settler Contract Today," *Philosophy and Social Criticism* 39, no. 2 (2013): 165–86.

2. Don E. Fehrenbacher, *The Dred Scott Case: Its Significance in American Law and Politics* (New York: Oxford University Press, 1978), 152–208.

3. Cheryl Harris, "Whiteness as Property," *Harvard Law Review* 106, no. 8 (1993): 1714. See also Jenny Reardon and Kim TallBear, "'Your DNA Is *Our* History': Genomics, Anthropology, and the Construction of Whiteness as Property," *Current Anthropology* 53, supplement 5 (2012): S233–45.

4. Saidiya V. Hartman, *Scenes of Subjection: Terror, Slavery, and Self-Making in Nineteenth-Century America* (New York: Oxford University Press, 1997), 125–63.

5. Financial Crisis Inquiry Commission, *The Financial Crisis Inquiry Report: Final Report of the National Commission on the Causes of the Financial and Economic Crisis in the United States* (New York: Public Affairs, 2011), 400–403.

6. Chandan Reddy, *Freedom with Violence: Race, Sexuality, and the US State* (Durham, NC: Duke University Press, 2011), 50.

7. Reddy, *Freedom with Violence,* 165.

8. *Congressional Record,* November 30, 2010, H7656.

9. *Congressional Record,* November 30, 2010, H7654, H7657.

10. *Congressional Record,* November 30, 2010, H7686.

11. *Congressional Record,* November 30, 2010, H7686.

12. *Congressional Record,* December 1, 2010, H7845, H7850. King's allegations were inspired by Andrew Breitbart and have been reiterated in Sharon LaFraniere, "U.S. Opens Spigot after Farmers Claim Discrimination," *New York Times,* April 25, 2013.

13. *Congressional Record,* November 30, 2010, H7656.

14. "Obama Signs the Claims Resolution Act of 2010," speech transcript, Washington, DC, December 8, 2010, http://projects.washingtonpost.com/obama-speeches/speech/521/.

15. As quoted in Ashley Southall, "Black Farmers Settlement Approved," *The Caucus* (blog), *New York Times,* November 30, 2010, http://thecaucus.blogs.nytimes.com/2010/11/30/black-farmers-settlement-approved/.

16. Patrick Wolfe, "Against the Intentional Fallacy: Logocentrism and Continuity in the Rhetoric of Indian Dispossession," *American Indian Culture and Research Journal* 36, no. 1 (2012): 1–46.

17. Wilcomb E. Washburn, *The Assault on Indian Tribalism: The General Allotment Law (Dawes Act) of 1887* (Philadelphia: J. B. Lippincott, 1975); Leonard A. Carlson, *Indians, Bureaucrats, and Land: The Dawes Act and the Decline of Indian Farming* (Westport, CT: Greenwood Press, 1981); Jessica A. Shoemaker, "Like Snow in the Spring Time: Allotment, Fractionation, and the Indian Land Tenure Problem," *Wisconsin Law Review* 4 (2003): 729–88; Kristin T. Ruppel, *Unearthing Indian Land: Living with the Legacies of Allotment* (Tucson: University of Arizona Press, 2008); C. Joseph Genetin-Pilawa, *Crooked Paths to Allotment: The Fight over Federal Indian Policy after the Civil War* (Chapel Hill: University of North Carolina Press, 2012).

18. As quoted in Washburn, *Assault on Indian Tribalism,* 7.

19. See, for instance, Julie Evans, "Where Lawlessness Is Law: The Settler-Colonial Frontier as a Legal Space of Violence," *Australian Feminist Law Journal* 30 (June 2009): 3–22; Kimberly Robertson, "Righting the Historical Record: Violence against Native Women and the South Dakota Coalition against Domestic Violence and Sexual Assault," *Wicazo Sa Review* 27, no. 2 (2012): 21–47.

20. Joanne Barker, *Native Acts: Law, Recognition, and Cultural Authenticity* (Durham, NC: Duke University Press, 2011), 90.

21. David A. Chang, "Enclosures of Land and Sovereignty: The Allotment of American Indian Lands," *Radical History Review* 109 (Winter 2011): 109.

22. Michelle Tirado, "Obama Signs Cobell Settlement," *American Indian Report,* December 9, 2010, http://www.americanindianreport.com/wordpress/2010/12/obama-signs-cobell-settlement/.

23. U.S. Senate Committee on Indian Affairs, *Individual Indian Money Accounts: Hearing before the Committee on Indian Affairs, United States Senate,*

One Hundred Seventh Congress, 2nd session on the July 2, 2002, Report of the Department of the Interior to the Congress on the Historical Accounting of Individual Indian Money Accounts, July 25, 2002 (Washington, DC: Government Printing Office, 2002), 11.

24. United States Joint Commission to Investigate Indian Affairs, Bureau of Municipal Research, *Business and Accounting Methods, Indian Bureau: Report to the Joint Commission of the Congress of the United States, Sixty-Third Congress, Third Session, to Investigate Indian Affairs, Relative to Business and Accounting Methods Employed in the Administration of the Office of Indian Affairs* (Washington, DC: Government Printing Office, 1915).

25. American Indian Policy Review Commission, *Final Report* (Washington, DC: Government Printing Office, 1977), 339.

26. Interviews by J. Kēhaulani Kauanui, "Episode #6: Is the Cobell Settlement a Scam?," *Indigenous Politics: From Native New England and Beyond,* WESU-FM, September 7, 2010, http://www.indigenouspolitics.com.

27. Lori Townsend, "Cobell Plaintiff Attorney's Make Argument for $137 Billion," *News from Indian Country,* February 10, 2003.

28. John Files, "One Banker's Fight for a Half-Million Indians," *New York Times,* April 20, 2004.

29. Kimberly Craven, "Cobell Lawsuit Not Good for All American Indians," *Billings (MT) Gazette,* July 8, 2010, http://billingsgazette.com/news/opinion /guest/article_5330a9ee-8a2d-11df-93f7-001cc4c03286.html.

30. Rob Capriccioso, "Indians Pull Appeal to Cobell Settlement," *Indian Country Today,* November 8, 2012, http://indiancountrytodaymedianetwork.com /article/indians-pull-appeal-to-cobell-settlement-government-says-payments-by-years-end-144690; "Statement of the President on the Final Approval of the Cobell Settlement," November 26, 2012, http://www.whitehouse.gov/the-press-office /2012/11/26/statement-president-final-approval-cobell-settlement.

31. See, for instance, Elizabeth Laderman and Carolina Reid, "Mortgage Lending on Native American Reservations: Does a Guarantee Matter?," *Journal of Housing Economics* 19, no. 3 (2010): 233–42.

32. As quoted in Earnest McBride, "Black and Indian Farmers Gain from Largest Civil Rights Settlement in History," *Jackson (MS) Advocate,* December 16, 2010.

33. "Civil Actions, Nos. 97–1978, 98–1693 [1999]: Opinion," in *Redress for Historical Injustices in the United States: On Reparations for Slavery, Jim Crow, and Their Legacies,* ed. Michael T. Martin and Marilyn Yaquinto (Durham, NC: Duke University Press, 2007), 666.

34. "Civil Actions [1999]," 667.

35. Tom Vilsack, "Turning the Page on Discrimination at USDA," November 30, 2010, http://blogs.usda.gov/2010/11/30/.

36. Pete Daniel, *The Shadow of Slavery: Peonage in the South, 1901–1969* (Urbana: University of Illinois Press, 1972); Christopher Clark, "The Agrarian Context of American Capitalist Development," in *Capitalism Takes Command: The Social*

Transformation of Nineteenth-Century America, ed. Michael Zakim and Gary J. Kornblith (Chicago: University of Chicago Press, 2012): 13–37.

37. Kristol Bradley Ginapp, "Jim 'USDA' Crow: Symptomatic Discrimination in Agriculture," *Drake Journal of Agricultural Law* 8, no. 2 (2003): 237–49; Pete Daniel, *Dispossession: Discrimination against African American Farmers in the Age of Civil Rights* (Chapel Hill: University of North Carolina Press, 2013).

38. Cassandra Jones Havard, "African-American Farmers and Fair Lending: Racializing Rural Economic Space," *Stanford Law and Policy Review* 12, no. 2 (2001): 333–60.

39. Valerie Grim, "The Politics of Inclusion: Black Farmers and the Quest for Agribusiness Participation, 1945–1990s," *Agricultural History* 69, no. 2 (1995): 257–71; Valerie Grim, "Black Participation in the Farmers Home Administration and Agricultural Stabilization and Conservation Service, 1964–1990," *Agricultural History* 70, no. 2 (1996): 321–36.

40. U.S. Commission on Civil Rights, *Equal Opportunity in Farm Programs: An Appraisal of Services Rendered by Agencies of the United States Department of Agriculture* (Washington, DC: Government Printing Office, 1965), 8.

41. U.S. Commission on Civil Rights, *The Decline of Black Farming in America: A Report* (Washington, DC: U.S. Commission on Civil Rights, 1982).

42. Tadlock Cowan and Jody Feder, *The Pigford Cases: USDA Settlement of Discrimination Suits by Black Farmers* (Washington, DC: Congressional Research Service, March 12, 2013), 3.

43. D.J. Miller & Associates, Inc., *Producer Participation and EEO Complaint Process Study for the Farm Service Agency (FSA) of the U.S. Department of Agriculture,* Contract No. 35–3151–5-00001, March 4, 1996, III-15

44. Lawrie Balfour, *Democracy's Reconstruction: Thinking Politically with W.E.B. Du Bois* (New York: Oxford University Press, 2011), 26, 43.

45. Bill Winders, *The Politics of Food Supply: U.S. Agricultural Policy in the World Economy* (New Haven, CT: Yale University Press, 2009); John J. Green, Eleanor M. Green, and Anna M. Kleiner, "From the Past to the Present: Agricultural Development and Black Farmers in the American South," in *Cultivating Food Justice: Race, Class, and Sustainability,* ed. Alison Hope Alkon and Julian Agyeman (Cambridge, MA: MIT Press, 2011): 47–64.

46. Cole Stangler, "Food Stamps on the Chopping Block," *In These Times,* July 11, 2013, inthesetimes.com/article/15135/congress_prepares_to_slash_food_stamps1/.

47. Sara Ahmed, *On Being Included: Racism and Diversity in Institutional Life* (Durham, NC: Duke University Press, 2012), 168.

48. Ahmed, *On Being Included,* 169.

49. Ahmed, *On Being Included,* 43.

50. Brenna Bhandar, "'Spatialising History' and Opening Time: Resisting the Reproduction of the Proper Subject," in *Law and the Politics of Reconciliation,* ed. Scott Veitch (London: Ashgate, 2007), 94.

51. Bhandar, "'Spatialising History,'" 95, 99.

52. For an extended critique of the liberal politics of inclusion, see also Alyosha Goldstein, *Poverty in Common: The Politics of Community Action during the American Century* (Durham, NC: Duke University Press, 2012).

53. *Congressional Record,* December 1, 2010, H7845–46.

54. Hartman, *Scenes of Subjection,* 131.

55. *Congressional Record,* December 1, 2010, H7845.

56. Robert Westley, "The Accursed Share: Genealogy, Temporality, and the Problem of Value in Black Reparations Discourse," *Representations* 92, no. 1 (2005): 85. See also Robin D. G. Kelley, *Freedom Dreams: The Black Radical Imagination* (Boston: Beacon Press, 2002), 110–34; Adjoa A. Aiyetoro and Adrienne D. Davis, "Historic and Modern Social Movements for Reparations: The National Coalition of Blacks for Reparations in America (N'COBRA) and Its Antecedents," *Texas Wesleyan Law Review* 16, no. 4 (2010): 687–766.

57. Westley, "Accursed Share," 84.

___

PART TWO

Relational Research as Political Practice

The essays in this section use a relational framework to make broader interventions into the critical study of race and into distinct fields within ethnic studies, foregrounding the particular political insights and analyses that can be produced through this work. The essays demonstrate how many social movements and subordinated groups have long advanced a relational understanding of race.

Roderick Ferguson's essay, "The Relational Revolutions of Antiracist Formations," examines the anticolonial and antiracist struggles of the twentieth century after World War II to show how revolutionary nationalist, women of color, and queer of color formations have produced relational articulations of antiracism. A relational understanding of race, Ferguson argues, breaks from pervasively nationalist frameworks, generating "a global rather than simply national awareness of its implications." Ferguson's "genealogical" method for understanding race relationally reaches back to the histories and literatures of national liberation and women of color feminist formations. In these histories, Ferguson finds models for antiracist relational analyses and politics that arose not out of comparisons between specific groups but out of a broader awareness of the "implementation and effects of racial processes on various communities within the Global North and the Global South."

Like Ferguson's essay, Steven Salaita's "How Palestine Became Important to American Indian Studies" brings a transnational optic to the relational study of race. The essay is an exposition of the ways in which discrete movements—in this case those of American Indians and Palestinians—can find shared recognition in each other's causes that can amplify their understanding of their own. Even though Palestinian and Native American histories, geographies, systems of governance, and political realities may appear vastly different, Native

American scholars and activists have increasingly turned to the Palestinian experience to gain insight into their own struggles against settler colonialism. This fundamentally relational approach not only sheds light on "Palestine as a crucial site of global struggle," but also underscores "the importance—indeed, [the] centrality—of American decolonization to that struggle."

Tiya Miles's essay, "Uncle Tom Was an Indian: Tracing the Red in Black Slavery," is similarly rooted in the political imperatives of understanding race as a relational concept. Miles describes the ways conventional historiographies can often obscure the intersections and meeting points of Black and Native histories. "Uncle Tom Was an Indian" explores the interrelationship between the enslavement of African Americans and the enslavement of Native Americans in the United States, as well as the legacy of these histories for individual and group identities. The essay traces these connections by examining the coconstitutive history of Black and Native enslavement, intimacies, and freedom. By examining advertisements seeking the return of enslaved people who had run away and Works Progress Administration interviews with freed people, Miles uncovers common lines of kinship as well as inherent tensions. Exploring the interactions between slavery and Native peoples contributes to a richer picture of the American, Native American, and African American pasts. But, as Miles points out, "[this] richer picture is at the same time more complicated, characterized by contradictions and contestations of the familiar and comfortable."

Finally, Tiffany Willoughby-Herard's chapter, "'The Whatever That Survived': Thinking Racialized Immigration through Blackness and the Afterlife of Slavery," seeks to "foreground immigrant rights advocacy that is multi-issue and that refuses the effacement of Black people."

Drawing on literary scholar Saidiya Hartman's concept of the "after-life of slavery," and sociologist Dale Tomich's concept of "second slavery," the essay demonstrates the centrality of racial chattel slavery to the contemporary struggles for immigration rights, and why such struggles must go beyond the call for citizenship rights and national incorporation. Willoughby-Herard uses Hartman's and Tomich's work to show that the post-Emancipation period has far more in common with the period of racial chattel slavery than many immigrant rights advocates typically acknowledge or recognize. The essay sets out to strengthen "that tendency within the immigration rights movement in the United States that is more keenly aware of its relationship to Black survival and the 'antislavery thought and action' that are its main armature."

FOUR

The Relational Revolutions of Antiracist Formations

Roderick Ferguson

World 3 is a collection of stamps put together by the British art collective the Otolith Group. The book is the companion text to an art exhibit that the collective curated to configure "moments from the grand project of mid-twentieth century Pan Africanism, envisaged as the total liberation of the African continent from Europe's empires."[1] The book of stamps is taken from one central work in the exhibition entitled "Statecraft," and it dramatizes the emergence of former colonies into independence through the stamps that commemorated the former colonies' independence.

World 3 includes a picture of a stamp that the Egyptian government issued to recognize Algerian independence. The stamp depicts the green, white, and red Algerian flag planted in the northwestern part of the map of Africa, where Algeria is located.[2] The map of Africa is colored black. In the book, a quote from Frantz Fanon appears above the stamp. The quote reads,

> Among colonized people there seems to exist a kind of illuminating and sacred communication as a result of which each liberated territory is for a certain time promoted to the rank of "guided territory." The independence of a new territory, the liberation of the new peoples are felt by the other oppressed countries as an invitation, an encouragement, and a promise.[3]

The passage from Fanon and the image express a politics of relationality, one that was definitive of the grand political project of anticolonialism. Aesthetically speaking, the red, white, and green Algerian flag is planted in and a part of the symbolic and political territory of liberation represented by the blackened African continent. The flag juts out from the continent as one route in the cartography of liberation. As such, the stamp suggests that Algeria is in relation with other countries on the continent, relating to them through a desire and a demand for liberation. In the language of this volume, the stamp points to how—as the editors put it in this volume's introduction—"group-based racial constructions are formed in relation not only to whiteness but also to other devalued and marginalized groups."

I begin with the stamp because in many ways it contains the genealogy of this volume's inquiry and directive—to study race relationally. Here, I mean to signal the fact that the genealogy of a relational understanding of race came out of the great social movements of anticolonialism and antiracism in the twentieth century. Indeed, the shift toward relations and connectivity represents one of the great epistemic shifts in the politics and study of race. In this sense, my own method for understanding race relationally is a genealogical one that requires a critical return to the histories and literatures of national liberation and women of color feminist formations, both of which provided models for antiracist relational analyses and politics, models that were not comparing discrete cultural groups but the implementation and effects of racial processes on various communities within the Global North and the Global South. As I hope to show, the move toward relations and connectivity because of these social formations represents one of the great epistemic shifts in the politics and study of race.

POST–WORLD WAR II AND THE RELATIONAL OUTCOMES OF BANDUNG

In many ways, the history of national liberation coheres with Natalia Molina's understanding of what it means to engage and study race: "[The] very framework that comprises our understanding of race is necessarily and inseparably drawn from the experiences of racialized groups vis-à-vis other racialized groups, and thus it is imperative that we pull the lens back even when examining the experiences of one racialized group."[4] As a way of grouping histories of exclusion in the Global South, national liberation and self-determination emerged as "frameworks" for understanding the experiences of groups shaped by processes of colonization and racial subordination. For instance, one of the main seedbeds for the emergence of relational understandings of race can be seen in the Bandung conference of 1955. Writing in 1958 in the Algerian newspaper *El Moujahid,* the periodical that was founded to inform the Front de Libération National (FLN) fighters, Fanon states, "The Bandung pact concretizes this carnal and spiritual union at one and the same time. Bandung is the historic commitment of the oppressed to help one another and to impose a definitive setback upon the forces of exploitation."[5] Emphasizing the principles of association promoted by Bandung, Partha Chatterjea notes that the Bandung conference affirmed the "promotion of world peace, namely, mutual respect of all nations for sovereignty and territorial integrity, non-aggression, non-interference in internal affairs, equality and mutual benefit, and peaceful coexistence."[6] As a relational exercise, the Bandung conference would be a way for "the oppressed" to identify with one another through their various and complex histories of racial suppression and exclusion under European colonialism.

For historian and theorist Robert J. C. Young, the conference would provide the conditions for a political and epistemological shift based on the independence of colonized nations: "The Bandung Conference," he says, "gained its great symbolic power from the fact that it was effectively the first postcolonial international conference held by the newly independent countries of the former colonial world."[7] In terms of race, Chatterjea again argues that the discussions at Bandung promoted an awareness and a critique of the ways that race was used to coordinate colonization in various regions of the world. As he states, "In 1955, at Bandung, no one had any doubt about the principal problem of human rights in the world: it was the continued existence of colonialism and racial discrimination. There was little doubt about the chief instrument by which human rights were to be established. It was the principle of self-determination of peoples and nations."[8] Bandung was thus the moment when race and colonialism would become the principles by which to establish relations among colonized nations.

The post–WWII moment would also see the rise of efforts to take the spirit of Bandung and extend it to the question of the United States' expanding role in the historical drama of empire. For instance, Che Guevara, among others in the Latin American context, would take up this interest in using race and colonialism to establish relationships across Africa, Asia, and the Americas, attempting to join the forces against European colonialism with emergent ones aimed at refusing U.S. imperialism. Also in 1965, one year after Guevara's travels to the Congo, Kwame Nkrumah, in *Neo-colonialism: The Last Stage of Imperialism,* would argue that the United States was "foremost among the colonialists,"[9] thereby helping to further illustrate the historical links between European and U.S. imperialisms and their relationship to the grievous circumstances of peoples in Africa, Asia, and Latin America.

Relatedly, the Vietnam War further exposed the United States' links to European imperialism and helped to promote race as a transnational category linking disparate peoples, histories, and cultures. The drama of colonialism and anticolonialism would, as a result, bring about the internal colonial model within the United States as a way of framing those links. Talking about the model's impact on social movements in this country, Ramón Gutiérrez argues, "Internal colonialism offered minorities an explanation for their territorial concentration, spatial segregation, external administration, the disparity between their legal citizenship and *de facto* second-class standing, their brutalization by the police, and the toxic effects of racism in their lives."[10]

As these events demonstrate, the genealogy for studying race relationally arises out of anticolonial and antiracist struggles of the twentieth century, particularly those of the post–WWII moment. These struggles occasioned an epistemological shift, not simply in terms of laying the foundations for postcolonial theory but also in laying the groundwork for understanding race in relational terms that defied national boundaries. To understand the epistemological significance of this, we need only remember that Gunnar Myrdal's 1944 text, *An American Dilemma*, tried to enshrine the study of race as an inquiry confined to the internal workings of race within national borders. It would take the emergence of anticolonial and antiracist movements with internationalist commitments and analytics to disrupt what had become a kind of sociological and national common sense. Put simply, the relational understanding of race meant fostering a global rather than simply national awareness of its implications.

THE GENDER AND SEXUAL CONTRADICTIONS OF ANTIRACISM AND ANTICOLONIALISM

While anticolonial and antiracist struggles helped to articulate race's relationship to the global, the gendered and sexual contradictions of antiracism and anticolonialism would produce even newer relations for the politics and study of race. With regard to cisgender women and the category of gender in general, nationalist movements against racial and colonial exploitation often became the locations by which women could engage in insurgent struggles. For instance, in the United States, African American women and Latinas were prominent participants and organizers in a variety of organizations, including the Student Nonviolent Coordinating Committee, the Black

Panther Party, the Young Lords, La Raza, and so on. In Africa, Asia, and other parts of the Americas, the universal pledge of anticolonial and nationalist movements became a way of radicalizing cisgender women as well. Consider, for instance, the role that Algerian women played in the FLN's war against French colonialism and recall that scene in *The Battle of Algiers* in which Djamila, the young Algerian woman, has taken off her veil and donned Western clothes and makeup. There is a blockade at Rue de la Lyre. The soldiers capture and detain an Algerian man who is without his documents, but they let Djamila proceed. After all, she's just a Westernized Algerian girl with an innocent cosmetics case; little do they know that Djamila is using the cosmetics case to transport explosives. As Barbara Harlow has argued, the scene is significant as an example of how Algerian women participated in the revolution, stating, "Djamila, like many other Arab women in the country, has assumed a role in her social order, one which not only has brought her out of seclusion and into the streets but has refashioned her physical and cultural appearance."[11]

Observing instances like this in nationalist movements, the Turkish and British feminist Deniz Kandiyoti argued in her classic article "Identity and Its Discontents," "On the one hand, nationalist movements invite women to participate more fully in collective life by interpellating them as 'national' actors: mothers, educators, workers, and even fighters."[12] While nationalist movements provided the conditions for disrupting discourses of gender, they also provide the means for reconsolidating gender as well. As Kandiyoti states, "On the other hand, [nationalist movements] reaffirm the boundaries of culturally acceptable feminine conduct and exert pressure on women to articulate their gender interests within the terms of reference set by nationalist discourse."[13]

Queer subjects also contested how nationalist organizations and movements insisted that sexual politics be articulated within the heteropatriarchal terms of reference set by those organizations and movements. For instance, the Black and Latino/a queer group Third World Gay Revolution argued in their 1970 essay "The Oppressed Shall Not Become the Oppressor," "Sisters and brothers of the Third World, you who call yourselves revolutionaries, have failed to deal with your sexist attitudes. . . . Brothers still fight for the position of man-on-the-top. Sisters quickly fall in line behind-their-men."[14] The group ends the essay by addressing the issue of homophobia among nationalists of color: "By the actions that you have taken against your gay brothers and sisters of the Third World you who throughout your lives have suffered the torments of social oppression and sexual repression, have now placed yourselves in the role of oppressor."[15]

Speaking in 1996 about the role that gender and sexual regulations played in radical Black and Latino organizations in the 1960s, Angela Davis argues,

> We know that J. Edgar Hoover identified the Black Panther Party as the greatest threat to the internal security of the country, and that the FBI orchestrated assaults from one end of the country to the other, in collaboration with local police departments. This has been documented. What has not been taken as seriously are the internal struggles within radical Black and Latino organizations. It was also the inability to address questions of gender and sexuality that also led inevitably to the demise of many organizations.[16]

Davis illustrates in this example that the inattention to gender and sexuality was not a mere oversight in radical politics. It was a structural impediment to a fuller articulation of liberation. Indeed, as she goes on to suggest, the notion of antiracist struggle adopted by those organizations was one that rested on heteropatriarchal assumptions and ideals. Referencing Elaine Brown's 1993 book *A Taste of Power: A Black Woman's Story*, Davis states,

> If you look at Elaine Brown's book, which has been abundantly criticized— for good reasons, in part—she does reveal the extent to which the [Black Panther Party] and many of its fraternal organizations were very much informed by masculinist notions of what it means to engage in struggle. These notions of struggle depend on the subordination of women, both ideologically and in practice.[17]

Another way of stating this is to say that the heteromasculinist notions of political struggle could relate to women (and we might add queers) only as subordinates. In this way, gender and sexuality established the relational limit of Black and Latino radical organizations.

These historical accounts are crucial not simply for noting the instances of homophobia and sexism within antiracist contexts. They are decisive because they demonstrate that heteropatriarchal practices and discourses are not slippages in national liberation but part of its progression. Anticolonial movements in Africa, the Caribbean, Latin America, and North America have all demonstrated historical patterns of gender and sexual regulation. These instances not only say something about the historical occurrences of homophobia and sexism, but also point to a constitutive feature of nationalist formations—that is, their predisposition to regulate the terms and relations of antiracist and anticolonial liberation. Thus, nationalist formations have historically acted not only as the promoters and innovators of race as an analytic and as a politics but also as its regulators. For this reason, race has occupied the epistemological role of "woman" in nationalist discourse. To use Kandiyoti's words, race has been lifted up as both the agent of liberation and as the object of regulation whose whereabouts, associations, and relations must be constantly monitored by nationalist formations in order to determine whether the analytical and political correspondences are appropriate. Put otherwise, the gender and sexual contradictions that have constituted the histories of nationalist formations suggest that those formations have never simply been the fulfillment of antiracism's possibilities but have limited its potential as well.

WOMEN OF COLOR AND POSTCOLONIAL FEMINISMS AND QUEER OF COLOR CRITIQUE

If antiracist and anticolonial nationalisms constrained race as the basis of critical analysis and radical politics, as I have just argued, and thereby disciplined race's relational character and agency, then the 1970s, 1980s, and 1990s saw the emergence of formations that attempted to liberate race's analytical and political associations. Given that under anticolonial and antiracist nationalism race took on the epistemological position of woman—that is, having its movements managed and controlled—only a set of critical formations that could address the gendered and sexualized nature of that category's supervision could facilitate its relationship with other social formations and rubrics. Enter women of color feminism and queer of color critical formations.

In her 1981 preface to *This Bridge Called My Back*, Cherríe Moraga expresses the need for a feminism that can help her make sense of the social contradictions and heterogeneities invoked by a subway ride that takes her "from the white suburbs of Watertown, Massachusetts to Black Roxbury" and a bus ride that she embarks on in her "white flesh to Harvard Square, protected by the gold highlights [her] hair dares to take on, like an insult, in this miserable heat."[18] Moraga transfers to another train and goes "underground" and remembers the story of how an ambiguously gendered friend, Julie, is racially profiled because she is Black. While on the train, Moraga witnesses a white cop throw a "Black kid up against the door, handcuff him, and carry him away." Discussing these scenes, Grace Hong in *The Ruptures of American Capital: Women of Color Feminism and the Culture of Immigrant Labor,* reads the journey as a metaphor for the critical associations that women of color feminism was trying to develop:

> For Moraga, to "transfer and go underground" implies an epistemological shift as well as a spatial one. Traveling from one part of a town to another in that particular moment ... is not simply moving through undifferentiated, abstract space but through variegated heterotopic spaces rife with a proliferation of meanings, histories, and material circumstances.[19]

The epistemological shift in Moraga's ride can also be read as a metaphor for reestablishing race's relational horizon, reestablishing it so that the category might address the links between differently gendered and racialized social and subject formations, symbolized here through a Chicana with light-skin privilege, an ambiguously gendered Black queer woman, and a young Black male whose racialized masculinity is understood as the antithesis of normativity and the necessary target of state surveillance. Women of color feminism thus invested race with a new relational life, allowing it to relate to the gender and sexual heterogeneities and the material urgencies that were shaping life in the 1980s.

That relational momentum brought about by women of color feminism could also be seen, for instance, in the German context as well. As Fatima El-Tayeb details in her book *European Others: Queering Ethnicity in Postnational Europe,* a variety of factors enabled notions of political struggle that ran counter to the ones promoted by heteromasculinist liberation movements. One of those factors was the presence of a "transnational feminist network that brought Audre Lorde to Berlin and created a venue of expression through the fledgling female-owned Orlanda press."[20] Lorde's presence would further inspire Afro-German feminists who were attempting to mobilize around issues of race in the German context. That transnational network of feminists saw itself as part of a global circulation of Black radical politics. In addition there was the activism of a "group of young Afro-German feminists who located women across the country and convinced them to share their often painful stories of growing up black in Germany."[21] That activism would culminate in the 1986 book *Showing Our Colors: Afro-German Women Speak Out.* Describing the anthology, El-Tayeb states, "The anthology connected the nation's history to black life stories covering almost a century, contextualizing experiences that had hitherto been perceived as aberrant and individual, pointing to them as collective traits in the life of a part of the population that up to that point was neither perceived nor had defined itself as a community: black Germans."[22]

As El-Tayeb argues, this feminist emergence laid the ground for the Black movement in Germany, producing a situation in which Afro-German feminism set the relational horizons for Black radicalism in that country: "The focus on a female perspective in *Showing Our Colors* as well as its explicitly feminist context made sure that there, black identity was not presented as male; instead it was women's voices that first articulated experiences that laid the groundwork in constituting a larger sense of community."[23] This original feminist focus would set the Afro-German movement apart from other antiracist movements: "This differentiated black Germans from almost any other ethnic, diasporic, or nationalist movement in which typically women, as well as queers, while taking part in the struggle additionally have to fight for their inclusion in a communal We."[24] This would produce not only a different structural context in which Afro-German women and queers would be at the forefront of defining and leading the Black struggle; it would also produce an ideological context that eschewed heteromasculinist models of struggle. As El-Tayeb writes,

> Rather than presenting a different normative experience, the early Afro-German movement rejected the idea of the normative in general, replacing it with a fractured, dialogic, queer subjectivity, presenting a new whole, the Afro-German community, while allowing its parts to stand next to and sometimes against each other, rather than forcing them into a coherent pattern.[25]

In contrast to other settings, the Afro-German movement was one in which antiracism was understood to emerge out of and to reach for feminist and queer contexts and issues. As such it stands as an example of the relational possibilities promoted by intellectual and political frameworks that begin with gender and sexual heterogeneity.

As the German context indicates, women of color feminism and queer of color critical formations caused a kind of epistemic and political revolution in the relational and associative capacities of the category race. Whether we are talking about nuclear proliferation, prison expansion, rape, the curtailment of sexual freedom, poverty, homelessness, environmental destruction, immigration, disfranchisements along the lines of race, gender, transgender, and sexuality; women of color and queer of color cultural and activist formations produced powerful models for connecting with some of the most urgent issues of our time. Moreover, those intellectual and activist formations have fostered gender and sexuality as not only emblems of identity but as catalysts for making connections where presumably none existed. Through the emergence of these formations, we would witness the expansion of the relational possibilities of race—that is, as it was put into other worlds, into other texts, as it was used to invent new relations. While the stamp of the Algerian flag symbolizes the notion that the politics of race must have its stake in the nation-state form as the deliverer of liberation, women of color and queer of color formations were using race to try to think beyond the state as the site of belonging and emancipation, especially since the state—through its investments in gender and sexual regulations—was demonstrating the repetition rather than the end of the master's day.

In doing so, women of color feminism and queer of color critique struck at the very philosophical heart of what is considered to be the relational and associative character of the modern mind. For instance, in his 1748 text *An Enquiry Concerning Human Understanding*, the British philosopher David Hume argued in his chapter "Of the Association of Ideas," "It is evident that there is a principle of connexion between the different thoughts or ideas of the mind, and that, in their appearance to the memory or imagination, they introduce each other with a certain degree of method and regularity."[26] For Hume, the associations—as principles of connection—are based on "resemblance, contiguity in time or place, and cause or effect."[27]

As historian Emma Rothschild states, Hume was steeped in the eighteenth-century Atlantic world of commerce, information flows, war, and slavery.[28] Implying the commercial and cosmopolitan influence that this setting had on Hume, Rothschild argues, "Hume was thought of in his lifetime, and for much of the nineteenth century, as the first great theorist of long-distance commerce, or of what one of his biographers described, in 1846, as 'the social economy of the globe.'"[29] As Rothschild shows, "the social economy of the globe" in eighteenth-century Britain was denoted by global commerce in goods and in people, and it was an Atlantic world that made its way into the interior. This was the background of Hume's propositions about the principles of connection that constitute the modern mind. Hume's ideas about contiguity in time and space, cause and effect, and resemblance were shaped by the conditions of global commerce, by the fact that the distant, the foreign, and the oblique were constituting the realities of the Atlantic world.

For Hume nonwhite peoples could not hold title to the disposition of the Enlightenment, particularly where rationality, sociality, inquisitiveness, and information were concerned. As he argued in an infamous footnote to his classic essay "Of National Characters," "I am apt to suspect the negroes to be naturally inferior to the whites. There scarcely was a civilized nation of that complexion, nor even any individual eminent in either action or speculation. No ingenious manufactures among them, no arts, no sciences." Rothschild observes that the footnote became a "foundational text of late eighteenth- and nineteenth-century racism." Referencing the eighteenth-century Jamaican poet Francis Williams, Hume would opine further in the footnote, "In JAMAICA indeed, they talk of one negroe as a man of parts and learn- ing; but is likely he is admired for slender accomplishments, like a parrot, who speaks a few words plainly." The footnote indicates that Hume excluded the nonwhite races from the principles of the mind, making racial difference the limit of the mind's capacity to associate and relate.

We can think of the work that women of color feminism has done to cultivate the mind's principles of and capacities for association as a direct alternative to those proposed by theorists such as Hume. In the introduction to *Third World Women and the Politics of Feminism*, Chandra Mohanty situ- ates the connections that were made between various groups of women of color in her definition of "third world women" or "women of color." She writes,

> It is a sociopolitical designation for people of African, Caribbean, Asian, and Latin American descent, and native peoples of the U.S. It also refers to "new immigrants" to the U.S. in the last decade—Arab, Korean, Thai, Laotian, etc. What seems to constitute "women of color" or "third world women" as a viable oppositional alliance is a common context of struggle rather than color or racial identifications.[30]

As Mohanty implies, the terms "women of color" and "third world women" signified an emergent associative mode whose principles of connection were different from those that Hume stipulated. Rather than the principle of con- nection being "resemblance," "contiguity [in time and place]," and "cause or effect"—as they are in Hume's text—for Mohanty the principle of connec- tion is the scene of oppositionality. As the principle of connection, the oppo- sitional scene has an immediately political valence inasmuch as it arises out of conditions such as war, prison expansion, forced sterilization, migration, colonialism, and the social regulations of the welfare state.

In this sense, revolutionary nationalist and women of color feminist formations were attempts to supersede the relational limits of liberal capitalism that were partly set by Hume. Moreover, it was women of color feminist and queer of color formations that sought to transcend not only the relational limits of liberal capitalism but revolutionary nationalism as well. Women of color feminist formations advanced racialized gender and sexuality as technologies of connection and associations, technologies that would set the standard for much of the progressive political and intellectual work in the 1970s and thereafter.

· · ·

The question of relationality exists at the heart of several social formations, from the foundations of modern knowledge, as exhibited in Hume's theory of the associations, to the connections between regimes of regulation and domination, as seen in the histories of race, capital, and colonialism, to the political and analytical possibilities of difference as the emergence of feminist and queer formations attest. How race relates, probably more than any other question, has accounted for the mobility of race as an analytical and political construct. It has also defined the horizon of intellectual and political experimentation. This question is the genealogy of interdisciplinarity from which many of us hail. In the *Intimacies of Four Continents,* Lisa Lowe—for example—defines modern liberalism this way: "the branches of European political philosophy that include the narration of political emancipation through citizenship in the state, the promise of economic freedom in the development of wage labor and exchange markets, and the conferring of civilization to human persons educated in aesthetic and national culture."[31] In all their guises, the genres of antiracist relationality have attempted to alienate these aspects of modern liberalism and in doing so have tried to imagine alternatives to its way of ordering the social world.

NOTES

1. *The Otolith Group: World 3*, edited by Kodwo Eshun, Anjalika Sagar, Martin Clark, and Steinar Sekkingstad. Bergen Kunsthall/Casco—Office for Art, Design, and Theory, 2015, published in conjunction with the exhibition "In the Year of the Quiet Sun," shown at Bergen Kunstall, Bergen, Norway, http://otolithgroup.org /index.php?m=current.

2. An image of the stamp can be found here (accessed August 15, 2018): https://www.hipstamp.com/listing/egypt-566-mnh-flag-y214-3/16411022.

3. Kodwo Eshun, *World 3* (Bergen, Norway: Bergen Kunsthall, 2014), 115.

4. Natalia Molina, "Examining Chicana/o History through a Relational Lens," *Pacific Historical Review* 82, no. 4 (2013): 524.

5. Frantz Fanon, *Toward the African Revolution* (New York: Monthly Review Press, 1967), 146.

6. Partha Chatterjea, "Empire and Nation Revisited: 50 Years after Bandung," *Inter-Asia Cultural Studies* 6, no. 4 (2005): 488.

7. Robert J.C. Young, *Post-colonialism: An Introduction* (Oxford: Blackwell, 1999), 191.

8. Chatterjea, "Empire and Nation Revisited," 488.

9. Kwame Nkrumah, *Neo-colonialism: The Last Stage of Imperialism* (New York: International Publishers, 1984), 239.

10. Ramón Gutiérrez, "Internal Colonialism: An American Theory of Race," *Du Bois Review: Social Science Research on Race* 1, no. 2 (2004): 281–95.

11. Barbara Harlow, introduction to *The Colonial Harem,* by Malek Alloula, trans. Myrna Godzich and Wlad Godzich (Minneapolis: University of Minnesota, 1986), x.

12. Deniz Kandiyoti, "Identity and Its Discourses: Women and the Nation," in *Colonial Discourse and Post-colonial Theory: A Reader,* ed. Patrick Williams and Laura Chrisman (New York: Columbia University Press, 1994), 380.

13. Ibid.

14. Third World Gay Revolution, "TWGR Flier," 1970, accessed April 1, 2016, outhistory.org/exhibits/show/gay-liberation-in-new-york-cit/item/1956.

15. Third World Gay Revolution, "Third World Gay Revolution: The Oppressed Shall Not Become the Oppressor," *Come Out! A Liberation Forum for the Gay Community* 1, no. 5 (1970): 13.

16. Lisa Lowe, "Angela Davis: Reflections on Race, Gender, and Class," in *The Politics of Culture in the Shadow of Capital,* ed. Lisa Lowe and David Lloyd (Durham, NC: Duke University Press, 1997), 305.

17. Ibid., 306.

18. Cherríe Moraga and Gloria Anzaldúa, preface to *This Bridge Called My Back: Writings by Radical Women of Color* (New York: Kitchen Table Press, 1981), xii.

19. Grace Hong, *The Ruptures of American Capital: Women of Color Feminism and the Culture of Immigrant Labor* (Minneapolis: University of Minnesota Press, 2006), xii.

20. Fatima El-Tayeb, *European Others: Queering Ethnicity in Postnational Europe* (Minneapolis: University of Minnesota Press, 2011), 66.

21. Ibid.

22. Ibid.

23. Ibid., 67.

24. Ibid.

25. Ibid., 67.

26. David Hume, *An Enquiry Concerning Human Understanding* (Cambridge: Cambridge University Press, 2007), 19.

27. Ibid., 20.

28. Emma Rothschild, "The Atlantic Worlds of David Hume," in *Soundings in Atlantic History: Latent Structures and Intellectual Currents, 1500–1830*, ed. Bernard Bailyn and Patricia L. Denault (Cambridge: Cambridge University Press, 2009): 405–48.

29. Ibid., 405–6.

30. Chandra Mohanty, "Introduction: Cartographies of Struggle, Third World Women and the Politics of Feminism," in *Third World Women and the Politics of Feminism,* ed. Chandra Mohanty, Ann Russo, and Lourdes Torres (Bloomington: Indiana University Press, 1991), 7.

31. Lisa Lowe, *The Intimacies of Four Continents* (Durham, NC: Duke University Press, 2015), 3–4.

FIVE

How Palestine Became Important to American Indian Studies

Steven Salaita

In the nascent days of the millennium, I was a new doctoral student at the University of Oklahoma, attempting to convince potential dissertation committee members of the utility of my proposed project, a comparison of the discourses of colonization in North America and Palestine. It was a difficult sell. The person who would direct my dissertation, Alan Velie, was easygoing, telling me to work on whatever suited me, but other faculty worried that the idea would be too broad or mechanical. Those concerns would later play a critical role in my attempts to manage the focus of the project. Like nearly all doctoral students, I was deeply anxious about my ability to even compose a dissertation. I knew that I knew too little to know how to adequately respond to skeptical authority figures with much greater knowledge.

Eminent scholar Robert Warrior joined the faculty before my third year. I immediately approached him, though with considerable apprehension, not knowing much about his politics or predilections. He expressed enthusiasm about the idea, explaining to me his history with Edward Said and his experiences living and working in Palestine.[1] It quickly became evident in my conversations with Warrior that his interest in my project amounted to more than a corresponding interest in the Middle East. It was also methodological. Warrior existed, and continues to exist, at an intersection of variegated, intercommunal methodologies, a focus extending from his first book, *Tribal Secrets,* to the magisterial volume *The World of Indigenous North America.* This twenty-year period in American Indian studies saw increased focus on the national traditions of individual tribes but also on expansive practices of transnational communication. As I became immersed in the field, I realized that American Indian studies has performed inter/nationalism since its inception, a necessity given the heterogeneity of Indigenous nations in

America. Descriptions of this transnational focus include "intertribal" and the all but obsolete "pan-Indian," but in recent years inquiry in the field has moved beyond tribalism (in the sense of Darcy McNickle's usage) and assessment of pannational affinities, though those subjects remain important.[2] Recent scholarship has exhibited interest in the histories, politics, and cultures of a wide range of non-American geography. For example, American Indian studies has recently forged institutional connections with Palestine— that is, scholars in the field are now producing systematic analyses of Palestine as a geography of interest (and one that is in some ways crucial) to our understanding of decolonization in North America. How does the presence of Palestine in the field shape and define its limits and possibilities? What are the terms and frameworks for useful comparative scholarship? Are there material politics at stake in comparing America and Palestine? This chapter analyzes those questions.

Before I sort out the comparative bases of Natives and Palestinians, let us take a look at some of the reasons comparison of Natives and Palestinians has increased in recent years. I believe there are three primary factors, each with its own set of contradictions and subtexts.

First, the proliferation of blogs and social media wherein people can argue, inform, share, and theorize, however superficially (or, in some cases, sophisticatedly). These platforms lend themselves to all sorts of comparisons, usually for the sake of rhetorical persuasion. The benefits and detriments of social media to activism and scholarship are wide ranging and much contested, so it is difficult to quantify new media's exact level of influence on the surge of comparison among Natives and Palestinians, but social media platforms document the extent to which the comparison has entered into the consciousness of a certain demographic, that of the intellectual engaged in public discourse around decolonization.

Second, Palestine scholars and activists increasingly use the language of indigeneity and geocultural relationships to describe the political, economic, and legal positions of Palestinians. For instance, in referencing Natives and Palestinians, Sa'ed Adel Atshan speaks of "our shared history as Indigenous peoples who have faced ethnic cleansing by European colonists."[3] The adoption of such language is a rhetorical act meant to situate—rightly, based on considerable evidence—Palestinian dispossession in a specific framework of colonial history rather than as an exceptional set of events brought forth by ahistorical circumstances. The language identifies a perceived sociohistorical familiarity with other dispossessed communities, in this case North American indigenes. The declaration that Palestinians are not merely native or original but *indigenous* to the land colonized by Israel, not a completely new phenomenon but one growing in frequency, alters a number of crucial factors of Palestinian strategies of decolonization, in particular the relationship of human rights organizations with international law, the comparative possibilities in fields such as ethnic and Indigenous studies, and both intellectual and physical deployment of Palestinian nationalism into transnational spaces.

And finally, the most important reason for the proliferation of comparative discourses is the boycott, divestment, and sanctions movement (BDS). Boycott of Israeli institutions or of the state itself has a long, albeit uneven, history in the Arab world. When I discuss BDS, I have in mind a specific call for cultural and academic boycott issued in 2005 by nearly two hundred organizations representing Palestinian civil society.[4] Thus BDS is not a governmental or corporate initiative, but neither is it spontaneous or organic, for it arises from a long history of decolonial advocacy on an international scale. Narrowly, BDS can be identified as an initiative of Palestinian civil society to pressure the Israeli state to comply with international laws against colonialism and military occupation, using nonviolent methods of resistance as opposed to traditional diplomatic and dialogic strategies that have repeatedly failed (peace talks, for example, or multicultural programming). This movement continues to grow. What does BDS have to do with American Indian studies? A great deal, actually. Briefly, many Native scholars and activists have taken up the cause of BDS and in so doing have broadened the conditions of studying the decolonization of America and deepened what it means to undertake the types of intellectual and political activities one might perform in the service of Palestinian liberation.

Other reasons for the increase in comparisons of Natives and Palestinians include the ascension of Palestine as a test case of one's decolonial/leftist/scholarly credibility; the success of the Palestinian national movement in convincing greater numbers of people around the world to support or even identify with its cause (aided by increased Israeli belligerence and its dissemination in alternative media); the growth of Arab American studies, a field to which Palestine is central, in the academic spaces of ethnic studies, where it has encountered American Indian and Indigenous studies; and the increased emphasis in American Indian and Indigenous studies on transnational and comparative methodologies, which has led numerous scholars from the Pacific, North America, and South America to Palestine, both intellectually and physically.

In early 2012, a small delegation of U.S.-based scholars visited Palestine, a visit arranged by the United States Academic and Cultural Boycott of Israel, which campaigns for various BDS initiatives and helps set policy around ethical forms of boycott. In the past few decades, delegations to the West Bank and Gaza have been common, usually undertaken by peace groups or students. (Delegations arranged by Zionist organizations to Israel are likewise common; these delegations usually enjoy better funding and attendance.) The 2012 delegation, conceptualized in part as a fact-finding mission, differed from typical delegations in that it was peopled by prominent scholars with expertise in various areas of race and ethnicity. The point of view of the delegation, then, went beyond gathering information that would justify BDS. It also situated Palestinian dispossession in a framework of worldwide neoliberal practices, rather than merely as a consequence of communal strife or historical misfortune. The group was influenced by analysis of iniquity located primarily within U.S. racial paradigms. As a result, we have available an example of how Palestine can be of interest to American Indian studies, in this case through inter/national analysis performed by multiethnic and interdisciplinary academics.

After returning, one of the delegates, Neferti X. M. Tadiar, observed,

> Palestinian life is . . . not the accomplishment of one aberrant state, inasmuch as the latter is supported by a global economy and geopolitical order, which condemns certain social groups and strata to the status of absolutely redundant, surplus populations—an order of insatiable accumulation and destruction that affects all planetary life. The question of Palestine is thus an urgent question of a just and equitable future that is both specific to this context and to this people, and a general and paradigmatic global concern.[5]

Another delegate, J. Kēhaulani Kauanui, reflects on a critical conversation she had about BDS in Haifa with a group of Palestinian citizens of Israel:

> What emerged from the conversation was that '48 Palestinians are attempting to shift the discourse to the paradigm of settler colonialism emerging from their concern with the general framework of discourse around the Palestinian question. This approach to boycott insists on a reframing to open up connections with all Palestinians. I could relate to this. In my work fighting the US occupation of Hawai'i, I routinely challenge the US government's legal claim to Hawai'i, expose the roots of the US as a settler colonial state, and critically engage the history of US imperialism in Native America and the Pacific Islands, insisting on the recognition of US empire as a form of violent, global domination.[6]

Both Tadiar and Kauanui emphasize Palestine as a global issue. Tadiar in particular contests what might be called the regionalization of the Israel-Palestine conflict—that is, the propensity to view (by design or ignorance) the conflict as limited to the regional circumstances of its creation. Kauanui personalizes Palestine, reflecting on her history as a scholar-activist of Hawaiian liberation to better comprehend Zionism's pervasive colonial history. Both writers make clear the need to approach Palestine as a crucial site of global struggle, in the process inherently acknowledging the importance—indeed, the centrality—of American decolonization to that struggle.

The delegation visited Palestine at a salient historical moment and in turn played a critical role in developing that moment into something consequential and sustainable. It was conceived amid a growing awareness of Palestine as a nexus of inter/national possibility, a place where one can encounter the self-perpetuating incarnations of U.S. history. The professors who traveled from America to Palestine illustrated that scholarship limited to the environs of the campus usually overlooks the worldly knowledge in abundance in places whose subjugation enables the accrual of educational status and wealth—such places where so many work so hard to conceptualize status and wealth as a natural condition.

THE NEW CANAAN

There are conditions in which Native scholars have taken up the issue of Palestine. The possibilities of comparison are tremendously rich and accommodate complicated sites of material politics (by which I mean economic systems, activist communities, electoral processes, educational paradigms, and modes of resistance). Accessing those sites enables us to aspire to relationships that go beyond theoretical innovation by concomitantly emphasizing the practices and possibilities of decolonization. If early settlers conceptualized North America as a New Canaan (in perpetual evidence by the numerous towns across the United States with biblical nomenclature), then the role Israel plays in American imperial practices extends the metaphor by using the immutable legitimacy of its colonial enterprise as further justification for the permanence of a federal United States under whose ultimate jurisdiction Indigenous nations will remain. America thus becomes a New Canaan all over again, invigorated by the emergence of a nation-state atop the original Canaan.

Although North America was settled by various national groups, colonization of the so-called New World has been infused with a particular narrative of salvation, redemption, and destiny. Settlers assumed the role of Joshua crossing the river Jordan into Canaan, where God commanded them to exterminate the Indigenous populations and establish for themselves a beatific nation on a land of milk and honey underused and unappreciated by the natives.[7] The English, Puritans most specifically, were the most avid proponents of this view, but vast geographies of North America were overwhelmed by settlers and missionaries animated by godly purpose. Even in acknowledging the variegated, often conflicting, narratives of New World settlement, multitudinous sources illustrate that from its earliest moments, the United States has been beholden to a Holy Land ethos, articulated in various ways throughout the enterprise of European settlement.[8]

The emergence of Zionism in Europe in the late nineteenth century evoked a dialectic with the project of American settlement that remains today in the close relationship between the United States and Israel, apparent in military aid, security cooperation, and foreign policy. It is, however, in the complex discursive and psychological spaces of ideology that the two states most closely align. The relationship is built through particular articulations of belonging that codify national identity into the mythologies of colonial domination and military conquest. Both Israel and the United States are relentlessly exceptional—and they are exceptional, ironically, only together.

Through identification and assessment of those connections, scholars in American Indian studies have made important advances in modes of analysis that inform my inter/national rubric. For instance, there has been much reflection on the relationship of Zionism with global systems of imperialism, militarization, plutocracy, and the neoliberal economies that undercut Indigenous self-determination in numerous parts of the world. U.S. support for Israel tells us much about the breadth of actors and actions involved in the continued occupation of Native lands in North America. Israel's conduct in the world, beyond its mistreatment of Palestinians, affects the health and economies of Indigenous communities worldwide, Indian country among them. Israel participates in the neoliberal corruption that dispossesses Natives of land and resources. Orly Benjamin's "Roots of the Neoliberal Takeover in Israel" illustrates the origins and consequences of Israel's neoliberalism, which partly explains the state's contribution to repression and genocide of Indigenous peoples in Guatemala and El Salvador in the 1980s. As a variety of scholars and journalists have shown, that contribution included logistical oversight and material support.[9] General Efraín Ríos Montt, architect of Guatemala's 1982–83 genocide, which especially affected Ixil communities in the country's highlands, considered Israel an indispensable ally in the global fight against communism, with which he fancifully associated Guatemala's Native communities.

When we think of Israel's effect on American policy, Indigenous communities rarely figure into the conversation, yet, as with the vast majority of state-sponsored or corporate perfidy, Indigenous communities are the ones who most suffer the immanence of iniquity. Latin America is a noteworthy site of Israeli perfidy, which, in keeping with the practice of neoliberal geopolitics, has disproportionately harmed Natives (along with the poor more broadly). Many reasons exist for this disproportionate harm. In general, plutocratic conduct, as Jodi Byrd, Jasbir Puar, and Scott Morgensen illustrate, exists in contradistinction to the practice of Indigenous self-determination.[10] Plutocracy invariably dispossesses Indigenous peoples and further impoverishes them through resource appropriation, military occupation, environmental destruction, and sponsorship of neocolonial corruption.

Israel's covert activities in Latin America have also directly harmed Indigenous peoples. Those activities occur in the framework of U.S. imperialism, for which Israel often acts as interlocutor. Israel likewise offers its police and military for hire as consultants to both industrial and developing states, in some cases supplying arms or tactical support.[11] Israel's most recent foray into Latin America has involved Mexico, although, as Jimmy Johnson and Linda Quiquivix reveal, "Mexico began receiving Israeli weaponry in 1973 with the sale of five Arava planes from Israel Aerospace Industries. Throughout the 1970s and '80s, infrequent exports continued to the country in the form of small arms, mortars, and electronic fences. Sales escalated in the early 2000s, according to research that we have undertaken."[12] Today, Israel provides Mexico with training and weapons in its counterinsurgency against the (Mayan) Zapatistas in Chiapas. Zapatista leader Rafael Guillén Vicente (a.k.a. Subcomandante Insurgente Marcos) has noted Israel's role as a colonial aggressor across the Atlantic: "Not far from here, in a place called Gaza, in Palestine, in the Middle East, right here next to us, the Israeli government's heavily trained and armed military continues its march of death and destruction."[13]

If Gaza, in Marcos's formulation, is "right next" to Chiapas, then it also abuts significant parts of Central America. Israel's role in the 1982–83 genocide of Mayans in Guatemala was more than peripheral. It supplied arms, many captured from the Palestine Liberation Organization, to the Honduran and Guatemalan governments.[14] In Guatemala it offered counterinsurgency training and military logistics. Rodolfo Lobos Zamora, the chief of staff of the Guatemalan army during the 1980s, proclaimed, "The Israeli soldier is the model for our soldiers."[15] In 1982, Montt, then Guatemala's president, "told ABC News that his success was due to the fact that 'our soldiers were trained by Israelis.'"[16] During Montt's 2013 trial for genocide, of which he was convicted, there came to light further evidence of Israeli involvement, including the Guatemalan army's use of helicopters supplied by Israel in addition to various intelligence channels, whose establishment led to the widespread torture and imprisonment of activists and civilians.[17] Israel has also been implicated as a U.S. proxy in Africa, South Asia, and South America (in addition to many locales throughout the Arab world). Whatever role the United States plays in fomenting worldwide unrest or the codification of servitude, Israel is a ready tool or proxy, if not directly then certainly as what might be called a satellite surrogate of U.S. foreign policy. The disproportionate modes of dispossession that Indigenous peoples, American Indians particularly, experience because of U.S. and Israeli colonization show that philosophical and spiritual identifications between the United States and Israel have produced numerous material consequences for Indians in addition to the more conspicuous victims, the Palestinians. While Israeli military and strategic assistance to Central American autocrats explicitly harms Indigenous peoples, there is much evidence to suggest that Natives in the United States also are victimized by Israel's close ties to the United States, primarily through neoliberal trade and development that pillage resources and limit economic development to the framework of profit-obsessed capitalism rather than allowing for the practice of legitimate egalitarian principles. Israel profits from neoliberalism at the expense of indigenes.

RESETTLING THE UNSETTLED STATE

The vast majority of Jewish settlers to Palestine until 1967 were from Europe and the Arab world. The movement to settle the West Bank (and at various points the Gaza Strip and Sinai Peninsula) gained momentum in the 1970s and has not slowed, in large part based on U.S. influence—not merely in terms of the financial and political support proffered by the U.S. government, but in terms of the nationality of many of the settlers. In 2011,

WikiLeaks published diplomatic cables from the U.S. consular office in Tel Aviv. The State Department officers "found that the U.S. citizens' reasons for moving to Jewish settlements in the area where Palestinians hope to establish a state were three-fold: social, economic, and ideological."[18]

The social factors include the opportunity to live in a largely isolated community with like-minded neighbors under heavy guard by the Israel Defense Forces. The economic advantages include tax breaks, subsidized loans, charity from evangelical Christians, and easy commutes to the green line on segregated roads. (The settlement of Elkana even provides schoolchildren free busing to ultra-right-wing rallies.) The ideological phenomena are of primary concern, although there is no element of social and economic life in a settlement unaffected by ideology. The diplomatic cables conceptualize ideology in this instance as messianic fervor, of which many settlers are certainly possessed, but we can examine it in broader contexts of discourse, identity, and mythology.

Much of the current West Bank settler discourse emerges from U.S. history and bears hallmarks of North American racialist jurisprudence. It likewise recapitulates the same myths of divine purpose endemic to U.S. self-esteem. In fact, many American settlers to the West Bank, about 15 percent of the total settler population, self-identify as liberal, according to the research of Sara Hirschhorn, who was profiled in the Israeli daily *Ha'aretz:*

> "Jewish-American immigrants [to the territories] were primarily young, single, and highly identified as Jewish or traditional but not necessarily Orthodox in their religious orientation," Hirschhorn said. "They were primarily political liberals in the United States, voted for the Democratic Party and have been active in 1960s radicalism in the United States, participating in the Civil Rights Movement and the struggle against the Vietnam War."[19]

The *Ha'aretz* profile continues,

> Many Americans who moved to the settlements after the Six-Day War see what they're doing in Israel as an extension of their radicalism in the United States, Hirschhorn said. "They would also say that what some of them consider what they're doing in the territories in part as an expression of their own Jewish civil rights.
>
> "In coming to Israel and participating in the settlement movement these American Jews continued in their radicalism," the Massachusetts native said. "While many others from their generation went back to a more conventional lifestyle—becoming soccer mommies and moving to Scarsdale [an affluent New York suburb]—here they moved to a hilltop on the West Bank."

Hirschhorn added that many Americans who move to the West Bank are trying to recapture the pioneering idealism of the state's Zionist founders, while others are driven by a biblical imperative to settle the land.[20]

Hirschhorn, like earlier scholars, concludes that only a small portion of American West Bank settlers are overtly motivated by messianism. The majority of those settlers consider messianism secondary or unrelated to their presence in Palestine.

The term *messianism* requires consideration. Hirschhorn's usage appears to be synonymous with "a biblical imperative to settle the land," which is generally accurate, although the term can also describe any sort of fervor of an intransigent variety. In both senses of the term, the self-identified liberal settlers who supposedly eschew messianism in fact practice it. In some ways they embody it. By settling a foreign land while claiming adherence to humanistic principles, they actually intensify (through the uncompromising assumptions of exclusion) the notion that Palestine is a land belonging to people who are not Palestinian.

It would be easy to theorize a discrepancy between the settlers' stated commitment to civil rights and their messianism, but the two attitudes actually align. Let us focus on the belief that settlement of Palestine is "an expression of their own Jewish civil rights," which is not as ridiculous as it first appears. The liberal discourses of American multiculturalism allow for expression of both colonial desire and communal racism because those discourses are devoted to the modern logic of individualism—the process by which racism is consigned to individualistic failure or ignorance rather than being located in the institutions of the colonial state. Furthermore, it has long been a contention across the Zionist political spectrum that Israel is a national embodiment of Jewish culture. If this is the case (and here I submit that national identity is never a complete representation of organic culture), then rejection or even contestation of Zionism becomes an act of cultural insensitivity, susceptible to charges of anti-Semitism or intolerance.

This rationale not only protects Israel from criticism but also allows the settlers to conceptualize their presence on the West Bank as cultural performance, unburdened by violence or aggression. If Israel is the material outcome of Jewishness, then there is no contradiction in professing support for U.S. minorities and simultaneously effecting Palestinian dispossession, for the Palestinians are merely unfortunate bystanders in a Judeocentric drama of very recent vintage, but one that precedes them in imagination. Being liberal (in the modern U.S. sense of the term) offers a terrific basis for a concerned citizen to evolve into an ideologue with the power to summon for personal use the vast weaponry of a militarized nation-state. Messianic narratives, even when unclaimed, demand that sort of evolution.

American Indians too are an inconvenient impediment to a project much grander than their earthly lives. The West Bank settlers' support of U.S. minorities does not extend to Indigenous self-determination—in U.S. discourses, it rarely does. Everywhere in the United States we see the interplay of liberalism (informed by unacknowledged messianism) with settler colonial values of permanent entitlement (to land, to access, to belonging, to upward mobility—in short, to all the spoils of conquest, without having to assume responsibility for its immorality). Perhaps this phenomenon is nowhere more evident than in the controversies over Devils Tower in Wyoming. Known by Natives as Mato Tupilak and sacred to the Lakota and other nations, Devils Tower is a hot spot for recreational climbers, who pound metal into the rock face and interfere with religious rituals.

Unsuccessful in their bid to outlaw climbing on Devils Tower, Natives have been treated to fantastic displays of liberal colonial logic. Frank Sanders, for example, was deeply concerned with the plight of Indians. "The Native Americans need physical help," he explained to *Climbing* writer Luke Laeser. "We have been working with the clinic at the Porcupine Reservation bringing them very basic supplies (things that you and I take for granted)."[21] In turn, Sanders undertook Project 365 in 2007–8, climbing Devils Tower every day for a year to help raise money for needy Indians. Asserting the sacredness of the site to himself, he later founded www.devilstowersacredtomanypeople .org.[22] In climbing Devils Tower for 365 days in a row, Sanders aimed to end Indian poverty and create an interracial harmony unseen in the region since the first days of European contact. The only thing Natives asked of him was to quit desecrating Mato Tipila.

AGENCY AND APPROPRIATION

Recent work in inter/national analysis has brought forth two important advances. The first is the transformation of Native peoples from complex political subjects into metaphorical objects of decolonial credibility. To put it more simply, Indians have become actors in the rhetorical battlegrounds of the Israel-Palestine conflict. Zionists say, Jews are like the Indians.[23] Palestinians say, Nonsense, we are. Both Zionists and anti-Zionists recognize in Indians a sort of moral authority on the subject of dispossession with which they seek to be associated. I should pause for a moment to note that I find many problems with the formulation. I am identifying it as a phenomenon, common these days, rather than endorsing it.

My main problem with these appeals to Native authority as a way to accrue decolonial legitimacy is simple: neither Zionists nor anti-Zionists need to be correct for anything to change in our understanding of Palestine, not to mention our understanding of America (which gets trivialized and dehistoricized in this type of situation). Indeed, the historical dispossession of Indians has often resembled, and in some instances has more than resembled, the mistreatment of Jews, particularly in Spain on the eve of Columbus's voyage and in eastern Europe after the Industrial Revolution. But these realities do not preclude Palestinian dispossession from also resembling that of Indians. In fact, Palestinian dispossession also often resembles historical Jewish dispossession; that the Palestinians' current oppressors self-identify as Jewish does not diminish this simple fact of history. Thus, the crude comparisons made for the sake of rhetorical expediency stop short of analyzing the historical, economic, and discursive forces that inform the U.S.-Israeli alliance and bind Natives and Palestinians to the same anticolonial polity.

The second thing that comes out of these advances in inter/national analysis is what we learn about the practice of American Indian studies as an academic enterprise that exists beyond the corridors of academe, by which I mean the element of the field, not always consistent but omnipresent, that compels its participants to practice communal engagement and pursue social justice (to use an old-fashioned term, one that might interchange with human rights, sovereignty, self-determination, liberation, and so forth). This ethic, in contradistinction to the traditional notion of scholars as practitioners of an objective vocation, is apparent in the mission statements of several academic departments. The Native American and Indigenous Studies program at the University of Texas, for instance, is "particularly concerned with scholarship and intellectual exchange that contributes to the economic, social, and political advancement of indigenous peoples."[24] Likewise, the American Indian Studies program at the University of Arizona says it explores "issues from American Indian perspectives which place the land, its history, and the people at the center," making clear its emphasis: "American Indian Studies promotes Indian self-determination, self-governance, and strong leadership as defined by Indian nations, tribes, and communities, all of which originated from the enduring beliefs and philosophies of our ancestors."[25] Similar professions of material engagement and commitment to self-determination are common. Such is the case in Palestine studies.

Interest in Palestine among Native scholars is logical. The field, after all, has long offered critique of U.S. empire and imperialism and produced comparative analyses of Indians with other racial and religious minorities. It is not surprising, then, that at least some attention is directed toward an expansionist Israel not only funded by the United States but claiming to be a modern incarnation and proud conserver of American manifest destiny. Israel, we must remember, is often conceptualized by American elites and rank-and-file Christians alike not merely as a worthy recipient of U.S. patronage but as an indivisible component of American cultural identity. Barack Obama made clear this bond in his 2012 American Israel Public Affairs Committee (AIPAC) speech: "The United States and Israel share interests, but we also share those human values that Shimon [Perez] spoke about: a commitment to human dignity. A belief that freedom is a right that is given to all of God's children. An experience that shows us that democracy is the one and only form of government that can truly respond to the aspirations of citizens."[26]

Yet there might be more to the growing importance of Palestine to American Indian studies. I would suggest that interest in Palestine among Native and Indigenous scholars represents at least in part a realization of the field's ideals of decolonial advocacy. I do not raise this point to romanticize American Indian studies or to totalize it. Rather, I suggest that any field with a commitment to the repatriation of the communities it studies will eventually become transnational because the powers against which the dispossessed fight are interrelated. And because of a variety of phenomena, transnationalism in American Indian studies quickly moved to incorporate Palestine.

The comparison of the United States and Israel is particularly germane around the concept of values, a term Obama emphasized in his AIPAC speech. Less than a year after that speech, when former U.S. senator Chuck Hagel faced scrutiny as Obama's choice as secretary of defense because of his supposed hostility to Israel (an accusation with no basis in fact), Hagel responded to criticism by proclaiming, "America's relationship with Israel is one that is fundamentally built on our nations' shared values, common interests and democratic ideals."[27] Values, of course, are unstable things—unreliable, too, because they are invested with so many explicit and implicit demands and coercions. In this case, as Hagel's passage indicates, there is a long-standing discourse of shared values between the United States and

Israel that mutually implicates Natives and Palestinians as premodern and unworthy of liberation.

What are those values? Democracy. Modernity. Industriousness. Freedom. Nobility. Humanity. Compassion. Natives and Palestinians not only lack these qualities but seek to undermine them. American values arise not only from an expansionist capitalism but also from the redemptive mythologies of Israeli colonization, which has led many people in American Indian studies to question the accuracy of Zionism's heroic narratives and to explore how the current situation of Palestinians under military occupation lends understanding to Native reinterpretations of those American values. As Kauanui notes,

> The politics of indigeneity bring much to bear on critical analyses of Israeli exceptionalism, as it is bolstered and bankrolled by an American exceptionalism that denies the colonization of Native North America. Comparative examinations of Israeli settler colonialism in relation to questions of occupation, self-determination and decolonization within the framework of international law demand ethical consideration by Native American and Indigenous Studies scholars.[28]

While the inclusion of Palestine in American Indian studies tells us much about the shifting possibilities of Palestine studies, particularly its uneasy relationship with Middle East studies, it also illuminates (or reinforces) a particular set of commitments in American Indian studies. Such is especially true of the material politics of decolonization and its role in the formation of certain liberationist ethics to which many practitioners of American Indian and Indigenous studies adhere. The analysis of Palestine in American Indian studies forces us to continue exploring the cultures and geographies of indigeneity.

Here the issue of Palestine continues to prove instructive. In the culture wars of Israel-Palestine, there is much chatter about the matter of indigeneity. In fact, it is the central moral basis for claims of geographic and cultural ownership in the so-called Holy Land, a reality illuminated by former Canadian MP Irwin Cotler when he proclaimed, "Israel is the aboriginal homeland of the Jewish people across space and time. Its birth certificate originates in its inception as a First Nation, and not simply, however important, in its United Nations international birth certificate."[29] Cotler's claim is remarkable for several reasons. By appropriating the language of Indigenous peoplehood ("aboriginal," "First Nation"), Cotler positions Israel, against available historical evidence, as a presence dating to antiquity and a beneficiary of exceptional juridical standing based on a specific legal categorization.[30]

Although conceptually Cotler articulates a variant of the Zionist claim of Jewish ownership of Palestine, his language bespeaks an approach outside the commonplaces of Zionist discourse, which has largely focused on historical grievance (particularly European anti-Semitism), promissory narratives (God granted the land to Jews), and the inevitability of ingathering the diaspora (we were here in the past and thus have a right to be here in the present). In Cotler's argument, these commonplaces recede to assumptions as a new form of reasoning emerges, that of Israel as predecessor to the very existence of Palestinians, who become the conquerors, the foreigners, the aliens, the strangers. This argument rejects historical evidence of Palestinian dispossession and instead consigns them to the status of aggressor, stewards of their own suffering. Less obviously, it also disenfranchises Indigenous peoples in North America by subordinating their claims of nationhood into the logic of Western conquest. Cotler offers one example of the ability of Western multicultural practice to appropriate anything at its disposal in order to buttress an imperial power structure, for his pronouncement offers nothing to indicate that he would support a level of autonomy for Indigenous peoples in Canada similar to that enjoyed by the Israeli state.

Indeed, Zionists have consistently employed the language of indigeneity—"*Jews are* indigenous to the land"—to explain the settlement of Palestine throughout the twentieth century or to rationalize the current settlement of the West Bank. Allen Z. Hertz, for instance, declares, "Conceptually, the Jewish people is aboriginal to its ancestral homeland in the same way that the First Nations are aboriginal to their ancestral lands in the Americas."[31] Palestinians in return often rely on the same language of indigeneity to counter Zionist claims or to assert a moral narrative of belonging vis-à-vis the unjustness of foreign settlement. The New England Committee to Defend Palestine describes the Israel-Palestine conflict thus: "It is a conflict between the indigenous Palestinian people and the Europeans who came with guns to steal their land and resources."[32] When Zionists and Palestinians lay claim to indigeneity, they are not merely being technical. The term *Indigenous* is infused with many connotations about access, belonging, biology, culture, jurisdiction, and identity. Indigeneity is not simply a moral entitlement but a legal and political category. To access that category is to be positioned as steward and legatee of a particular territory. Thus, the appropriation of the language of Indians inherently recognizes Indians as the rightful indigenes of North America—a recognition made infrequently by politicians and commentators—and simultaneously appropriates Natives into an extraneous debate whose conduct invalidates their agency.

The debate invalidates Indian agency because rarely does it visualize Natives as living communities engaged in the work of repatriation—or even in the work of survival. When a person says, "Jews are the Indians of the Holy Land," the statement affixes Indians into a specific historical posture that renders them rhetorical but not legal or contemporaneous claimants against colonization. This is so because the claim is fundamentally statist, referencing a particular history to support an argument of the present. The referenced history does not make it into the present. The argument it informs already occupies that space.

Further evidence that this sort of move invalidates Indian agency is available in the rhetoric itself. One need only read major forums of debate—The *New York Times*, the *Washington Post*, *Slate*, the *Huffington Post*, and even social media such as Facebook and Twitter—to notice the extent to which visions of the American past bear on the matter of Palestine. Attenuated notions of Indian dispossession often rationalize Palestinian dispossession. As Laila Al-Marayati observes, "Today, most Americans do not believe that the decimation and expulsion of entire Indian tribes in response to 'terrorist' attacks against wagon trains was justified. But, as one caller to a syndicated radio program suggested, since we're not about to give anything back to the Indians, why should the Israelis be expected to return stolen land to the Palestinians?"[33]

Unlike the Jews-as-Indians argument, this one acknowledges Indian disenfranchisement (again, only in the past), but excludes any possibility of repatriation. Yet, exactly as in the Jews-as-Indians argument, the goal is to justify the original sins of Zionism and the current settlement of the West Bank. This time the Palestinians become Indians, and both communities end up consigned to an unfortunate but inevitable antiquity overwhelmed by the progress of a linear history, another powerful example of how a colonial ethos allows people to own history without being responsible for it. The common wisdom and common sense of this argument arise from a settler logic of divine possession and democratic entitlement whose values—the hegemony of its assumptions—render conquest a permanent feature of modern American consciousness. Zionism has adopted this consciousness in its desire to normatize—that is, to render normative, as opposed to merely normal—garrison settlement and military occupation. For Zionists, colonization is permanent even as it happens—in many ways before it has even taken place, for the ideologies of modernity underlying expansionist worldviews emphasize the progress of a distinct state culture with a neoliberal economy and a militarized infrastructure. The idea of returning land to Indians is crazy, indeed, as crazy as the idea of allowing Palestinians to remain on theirs.

Ha'aretz columnist Ari Shavit offered an example of this phenomenon amid the debates inspired by his 2013 book *My Promised Land,* a compendium of settler dissimulation. In an interview with *New Yorker* editor David Remnick, Shavit professes his refusal to condemn the Israelis who participated in massacres of Palestinians in 1948. "Now I think it's very important to remember," he declares, "I mean, this country [the United States] is based on crimes that are much worse than Lydda, much worse than Lydda."[34] (The 1948 Israeli massacre in and depopulation of Lydda and the neighboring village of Ramle, which Shavit explores at length, displaced as many as seventy thousand Palestinians. Ben-Gurion International Airport sits atop the site of the two villages.) Remnick then asks Shavit about the difference between U.S. and Israeli massacres. "About a hundred years," Shavit replies.

Shavit avers that U.S. colonization is worse than its Israeli counterpart and implies that in the near future, Zionist ethnic cleansing will matter less, in the same way that U.S. ethnic cleansing has been diminished by the passage of time. The implication likewise downplays the seriousness of Zionist ethnic cleansing in the present. I have negligible interest in the first claim, as I see little use in quantifying and then ranking mass suffering according to the peculiar algorithms of colonial guilt. The United States colonized hundreds of distinct nations; Israel colonized a handful, Palestine primarily. Shavit appears to be unaware of, or indifferent to, the multiplicity of conflicts and encounters in America, or of the ongoing struggles to decolonize the continent. Nor were Zionist massacres limited to Lydda and Ramle. There is nothing useful to say about Shavit's apocryphal one-hundred-year gap between U.S. and Israeli colonization; we can merely highlight its spectacular wrongness.

His implications are worth notice, though. Time can heal the past only in specific circumstances—when the oppressive party makes amends, for example, or reverses destructive policies. For Shavit and like-minded commentators, though, time itself can progress beyond the resilience of memory. This conception of the world reinforces the temporal peculiarities of logic motivated by conquest and acquisition. The *nakba* matters less than the triumph of Zionism for no reason other than the triumph of American colonization.

Shavit's argument, like those of similar interlocutors, is no more complex than this non sequitur. It imagines a permanent past because it cannot process complexities of the present. Shavit does not write history from the vantage point of the victor; he writes as a tenuous citizen anxious that victories of the past are only historical. The native, in other words, has not accepted the permanence of the colonizer. If Shavit were to acknowledge that Natives do not adhere to settler timelines, his arguments about Israeli timelessness would be impossible.

The Indian interventions into these debates are of special interest. Much of the scholarly and political opposition to Zionism moves beyond moral displeasure at the behavior of Israel and its American sponsor, concerning itself instead with broader questions of power and meaning. As Stephen P. Gasteyer and Cornelia Butler Flora explain in their comparison of Palestine with Iowa and Patagonia, "The settlement of these areas involved processes of discovery, valuation, settlement, and conquest by outsiders. Part of the last two phases contained elements of equality but restricted equality to the dominant class, the conquerors (Jews in Palestine, later Israel, or European-Americans in the Patagonia and Iowa). Part of the conquest involved a rationale of taming, civilizing, and making more efficient a 'wild' land and 'savage' people."[35]

What, then, does it mean to confront a state whose presence, ipso facto, ensures legal and territorial dominance of its Indigenous communities and its legitimization as a permanent arbiter of its subjects' destinies? In the interrelated narratives of colonial permanence in the United States and Israel, we have a profound set of circumstances within which to explore this question. Answering the question from a perspective that does not take it as a point of fact that the United States and Israel are permanent has an added benefit of delegitimizing the state, but the primary function of the perspective is to imagine a future outside the notion that displacement and disenfranchisement must be permanent simply because they succeeded.

I would emphasize that despite an abundance of American-Israeli interactions—military, economic, diplomatic, cultural, historical, religious—the relationship of the two states is most profound at a level of discourse and ideology. In fact, a manifest Holy Land ethos has played an enormous role in the development of American society, both physically and philosophically. As Tim Giago notes in highlighting the interconnectedness of Natives and Palestinians, "The early settlers believed it was God's will (Manifest Destiny) that the heathens be driven from the land. It was God's will that the land be settled and populated by white Christians. They looked upon the indigenous population as a mere obstacle to be slaughtered or removed."[36] That ethos predates, but also presupposes, the creation of Israel. In this sense, the ancient Israel of the Old Testament was realized not through modern Zionism but in the settlement of North America.

Steven Newcomb explores these phenomena in his book *Pagans in the Promised Land*. He notes that "when dominating forms of reasoning (categorization) found in the Old Testament narrative are unconsciously used to reason about American Indians, Indian lands metaphorically become—from the viewpoint of the United States—the promised land of the chosen people of the United States."[37] Newcomb's analysis is valuable, though I would question the extent to which reasoning about American Indians as biblical Canaanites is unconscious. The teleology of North America as a new promised land is obvious in the early days of European settlement, but even now the inventions of America as a metaphorical Israel, with Indians as a romanticized but ungodly presence, remains common—quite consciously so.

These discursive geographies have traveled continuously between North America and Palestine. In turn, the geographies of American Indian and Indigenous studies have transcended the restrictions inherent to the nation-state, the quintessential entity of colonization. In so doing, the field challenges the probity of the nation-state as a governing authority and progenitor of social organization. As Duane Champagne notes in the introduction to a comparative collection coedited with Palestinian Ismael Abu-Saad examining the future of Indigenous peoples, "Native struggles within nation-state systems are not simply efforts to gain inclusion or access to citizenship. . . . Native peoples wish to preserve land, economic subsistence and means, and political and cultural autonomy. In many cases, nation-states often find the demands of Native communities threatening, at odds with national policies of integration and assimilation."[38]

This passage illuminates one of the central features of inter/national scholarship, its insistence on transnational dialogue extraneous and opposed to the physical and legal parameters of the nation-state.

PERFORMING INTER/NATIONALISM

In closing, I would like to offer a few thoughts about the conditions of performing inter/nationalist scholarship.

In many ways, Palestine has become a test case of one's bona fides in American studies, ethnic studies, and other areas of inquiry—likewise in political and community organizations beyond academe. To be opposed to, say, the Iraq invasion while simultaneously supporting Israel ensures, at least among a considerable demographic, a loss or weakening of credibility. Anti-Zionism as test case of one's trustworthiness represents the ascension of Palestine into the consciousness of the political and academic Left and, more important, into the worldwide collective of Indigenous scholars challenging the structures and mores of academic convention. This ascension of Palestine arises from the recognition, always evident but now common, that Israel is not merely an ally or client of the United States, but a profound component of its imperial practice. To support Israel is to support U.S. empire; thus other professions of resistance to U.S. empire come into conflict with their own values in the presence of Zionism.

Any political or methodological commitment as a litmus test is inherently problematic, for the litmus test can render struggle a fashion responsive to the recital of slogans or coded professions of support. Palestine can become a thin signifier of interpersonal belonging rather than a site of serious reckoning vis-à-vis the multidisciplinary spaces that accommodate its presence. Those inherent problems notwithstanding, the juxtaposition of Natives and Palestinians represents a deterritorialization of traditional disciplinary areas. In many ways, it makes more sense for Palestine studies and Indigenous studies to be in conversation than Palestine studies and Middle East studies, since Middle East studies encompasses vast geographies in which Palestine is but a specialized subset; it has, moreover, traditionally accommodated various incarnations of Zionism and institutionally accepted Israel, in its current ethnocentric form, as a permanent reality.

For scholars serious about better comprehending Palestine's present and working to ensure its future, American Indian studies offers more groundbreaking and germane critique than do the Cold War–era area studies. In Palestine, American Indian studies participants can access a view of history as it has been reinvented in the present, wherein the residue of conquest continues in North America through plutocratic governance and functions in Palestine through the old-fashioned use of soldiers, tanks, tear gas, guns, grenades, and armed settlers, a violent continuation of the U.S. legacy of Holy Land mythmaking and ostensible reclamation.

Conducting this type of work on campus presents challenges, some of them irreconcilable with the ethical commonplaces of American Indian studies. We do much of our teaching and research in public space, in the case of those who work in state institutions, so immediately the task of decolonization extends to the very site of our sustenance. The task of American Indian studies, then, involves constant attention to the seemingly benign iterations of land theft and dispossession. Adding Palestine to the mix intensifies the task, but to our enrichment, and, importantly, to the detriment of those invested in the colonial university.

NOTES

This chapter was first published in Steven Salaita, *Inter/Nationalism: Decolonizing Native America and Palestine* (Minneapolis: Minnesota University Press, 2016), 1–26. Copyright Steven Salaita 2016.

1. Warrior writes at length of his days as Said's student in "Native Critics and the World: Edward Said and Nationalism," in *American Indian Literary Nationalism,* by Jace Weaver, Craig S. Womack, and Robert Warrior (Albuquerque: University of New Mexico Press, 2006), 179–224.

2. I refer to McNickle's sense of tribalism as the cultural orientations that define who is Native. Darcy McNickle, *Native American Tribalism: Indian Survivals and Renewals* (Oxford: Oxford University Press, 2003).

3. Sa'ed Adel Atshan, "Palestinian Trail of Tears: Joy Harjo's Missed Opportunity for Indigenous Solidarity," *Indian Country Today,* December 2011, accessed August 24, 2018, http://usacbi.org/2012/12/palestinian-trail-of-tears-joy-harjos-missed-opportunity-for-indigenous-solidarity/.

4. See the website of the US Campaign for the Academic and Cultural Boycott of Israel: www.usacbi.org.

5. Neferti X. M. Tadiar, "Why the Question of Palestine Is a Feminist Concern," *Social Text,* February 15, 2012, http://www.socialtextjournal.org/blog/2012/02/why-the-question-of-palestine-is-a-feminist-concern.php.

6. J. Kēhaulani Kauanui, "One Occupation," *Social Text,* July 5, 2012, https://socialtextjournal.org/periscope_article/one_occupation/.

7. Perry Miller, *Errand into the Wilderness* (Cambridge, MA: Harvard University Press, 1956); Sacvan Bercovitch, *The Puritan Origins of the American Self* (New Haven, CT: Yale University Press, 2011).

8. Hilton Obenzinger, *American Palestine* (Princeton, NJ: Princeton University Press, 1999).

9. Orly Benjamin, "Roots of the Neoliberal Takeover in Israel," *Challenge,* July/August 2008, http://www.challenge-mag.com/en/article__224/roots_of_the_neoliberal_takeover_in_israel; Adam Jones, *Genocide: A Comprehensive Introduction,* 2nd ed. (London: Routledge, 2010), 147.

10. Jodi Byrd, *The Transit of Empire: Indigenous Critiques of Colonialism* (Minneapolis: University of Minnesota Press, 2011); Jasbir Puar, *Terrorist Assemblages: Homonationalism in Queer Times* (Durham, NC: Duke University

Press, 2007); Scott Lauria Morgensen, *Spaces between Us: Queer Settler Colonialism and Indigenous Colonization* (Minneapolis: University of Minnesota Press, 2011).

11. The New York Police Department, for example, opened a branch in Israel in 2012, ten years after receiving formal training in policing practices from Israel's military-intelligence apparatus. Margaret Hartmann, "NYPD Now Has an Israel Branch," *New York,* September 6, 2012, http://nymag.com/daily/intelligencer /2012/09/nypd-now-has-an-israel-branch.html.

12. Jimmy Johnson and Linda Quiquivix, "Israel and Mexico Swap Notes on Abusing Rights," *Electronic Intifada,* May 21, 2013, http://electronicintifada.net /content/israel-and-mexico-swap-notes-abusing-rights/12475.

13. The line is quoted from a 2009 Marcos speech archived at http:// mywordismyweapon.blogspot.com/2009/01/of-sowing-and-harvests-subcomandante .html.

14. Philip Taubman, "Israel Said to Aid Latin Aims of U.S.," *New York Times,* July 21, 1983, http://www.nytimes.com/1983/07/21/world/israel-said-to-aid-latin-aims-of-us.html.

15. Irin Carmon, "Linked Arms," *Tablet,* February 21, 2012, http://www .tabletmag.com/jewish-news-and-politics/91666/linked-arms.

16. Ibid.

17. Robert Parry, "Ariel Sharon and Israel's Hand in Guatemala's Genocide," *Global Research,* January 17, 2014, http://www.globalresearch.ca/israels-hand-in-guatemalas-genocide/5336243.

18. Justin Elliott, "WikiLeaks' Revealing Information about U.S. Citizens Living in West Bank," *Salon,* August 24, 2011, http://www.salon.com/2011/08/24 /wikileaks_us_citizens_west_bank/.

19. Raphael Ahren, "The American Settler You Don't Know," *Ha'aretz,* October 7, 2011, http://www.haaretz.com/weekend/anglo-file/the-american-settler-you-don-t-know-1.388640.

20. Ibid.

21. Luke Laeser, "Project 365—Climbing Devils Tower Every Day for a Year," *Climbing,* n.d., accessed July 13, 2015, http://www.climbing.com/climber/project -365-climbing-devils-tower-every-day-for-a-year/.

22. As explained in Laeser's article (ibid.), "An annual voluntary climbing ban occurs in June on Devils Tower that many folks comply with. Others, like Frank [Sanders], find the tower to be a sacred place in their own belief system and see that climbing can be a sacred activity as well. Frank hoped to unite the many people who find Devils Tower a sacred place in aiding the Native Americans in the region. As Frank puts it: 'This is not El Cap in 2.5 Hours. It's more like Three Cups of Tea and it is what one soul has been doing for his 57th year on this planet.' His 'not-for-profit' organization is www.devilstower-sacredtomanypeople.org."

23. This narrative played out in a controversial 2010 Columbia University conference sponsored by its Institute for Israel and Jewish Studies and Institute for Religion, Culture and Public Life. "In this conference," organizers announced, "we hope to address some of the rich, timely and thought-provoking connections

between Jews and Native Americans, both discursive and actual." Some Natives and Palestinians criticized the conference for its explicit and implicit Zionist focus.

24. Homepage of the Native American and Indigenous Studies program, University of Texas at Austin, n.d., accessed August 24, 2018, http://www.utexas.edu/cola/inits/nais/.

25. Homepage of the American Indian Studies program, University of Arizona, n.d., https://ais.arizona.edu/american-indian-studies-mission

26. "Remarks by the President at AIPAC Policy Conference," March 4, 2012, https://obamawhitehouse.archives.gov/the-press-office/2012/03/04/remarks-president-aipac-policy-conference-0.

27. Chemi Salev, "Hagel: 'I Intend to Expand the Depth and Breadth of U.S.–Israel Cooperation,'" *Ha'aretz,* January 15, 2013, http://www.haaretz.com/news/diplomacy-defense/hagel-i-intend-to-expand-the-depth-and-breadth-of-u-s-israel-cooperation.premium-1.494075. As a senator, Hagel reliably voted for both pro-Israel and anti-Palestinian legislation. For more information about his voting record and professions of support for Israel, see "J Street Supports Senator Hagel," December 17, 2012, https://jstreet.org/press-releases/j-streets-supports-sen-hagel-rebuts-charges-against-him_1/#.W3mYMJNKhmA.

28. J. Kēhaulani Kuaunai, "Ethical Questions of Boycotting Israel," in *Shifting Borders: America and the Middle East/North Africa,* ed. Alex Lubin (Beirut: American University of Beirut Press, 2014), 322–23.

29. Irwin Cotler, "The Gathering Storm, and Beyond," *Jerusalem Post,* May 14, 2008, http://www.jpost.com/Opinion/Op-EdContributors/Article.aspx?id=101152.

30. A number of scholarly books have shown that Zionism's claims to an ancient Jewish past in Palestine are largely mythological: Shlomo Sand, *The Invention of the Land of Israel: From Holy Land to Homeland,* trans. Geremy Forman (London: Verso, 2012); Keith Whitelam, *The Invention of Ancient Israel: The Silencing of Palestinian History* (London: Routledge, 1997); Eyal Weizman, *Hollow Land: Israel's Architecture of Occupation* (London: Verso, 2012).

31. Allen Z. Hertz, "Aboriginal Rights of the Jewish People," *American Thinker,* October 30, 2011, http://www.americanthinker.com/articles/2011/10/aboriginal_rights_of_the_jewish_people.html.

32. New England Committee to Defend Palestine, *A Short History of the Colonization of Palestine,* pamphlet, accessed July 13, 2015, http://www.onepalestine.org/resources/flyers/MythHistory.pdf.

33. Laila Al-Marayati, "Will Palestinians Go the Way of Native Americans?," *Los Angeles Times,* April 21, 2002, http://articles.latimes.com/2002/apr/21/opinion/op-almarayati.rtf.

34. Quoted in Nathan Thrall, "Feeling Good about Feeling Bad," *London Review of Books,* October 9, 2014.

35. Stephen P. Gasteyer and Cornelia Butler Flora, "Modernizing the Savage: Colonization and Perceptions of Landscape and Lifescape," *Sociologica Ruralis* 40, no. 1 (2000): 134.

36. Tim Giago, "Israel Could Have Learned Much from Native Americans," *Native Times,* August 22, 2005, http://www.nativetimes.com/index.asp?action=di splayarticle&article_id=6881.

37. Steven T. Newcomb, *Pagans in the Promised Land: Decoding the Doctrine of Discovery* (Golden, CO: Fulcrum, 2008), xxii.

38. Duane Champagne and Ismael Abu-Saad, introduction to *Future of Indigenous People: Strategies for Survival and Development,* ed. Duane Champagne and Ismael Abu-Saad (Los Angeles: UCLA American Indian Studies Center, 2003), x.

SIX

Uncle Tom Was an Indian

TRACING THE RED IN BLACK SLAVERY

Tiya Miles

The story of Uncle Tom in Harriet Beecher Stowe's nineteenth-century best-selling novel *Uncle Tom's Cabin* has been read and reread, told and retold, on stages and in classrooms. In it, Uncle Tom, a steadfast and guileless African American slave, remains kindhearted to the end toward the white people who sell and persecute him. As his final and harshest owner, Simon Legree, leans over Tom intending to kill him, Tom whispers, "I'd give ye my heart's blood; and, taking every drop of blood in this poor old body would save your precious soul, I'd give 'em freely, as the Lord gave his for me. Oh, Mas'r! don't bring this great sin on your soul! It will hurt you more than 'twill me!"[1] The Christlike character of Uncle Tom was so compelling for nineteenth-century readers—who, as literary critic Jane Tompkins has argued, were steeped in a culture of Christian sentimentalism—that the book launched a wave of popular antislavery feeling.[2] In the years since the abolition of slavery in the United States, the image of Uncle Tom continues to resonate, though with negative connotations. His character has become symbolic of the institution of American slavery, so that to call a contemporary African American person an "Uncle Tom" is to brand that person with the insult of servile and accommodationist behavior.

Yet Cora Gillam, a former slave who was interviewed in the 1930s as part of the Works Progress Administration (WPA) Federal Writers' Project, offers a very different picture of a man she refers to as "Uncle Tom." In a lengthy statement, Gillam informs her interviewer, "Now I want to tell you about my uncle Tom. Like I said, he was half-Indian. But the Negro part didn't show hardly any. There was something about uncle Tom that made both White and Black people be afraid of him."[3] Though Cora Gillam is speaking of an actual person and Harriet Beecher Stowe of a fictional

FIGURE 6.1. Lucinda Davis, age about 89, Oklahoma, c. 1936–38. https://www.loc.gov/item
/mesnp130053/.

character, I am quoting Gillam here to introduce a competing image—of a
slave called Uncle Tom. In Stowe's imagination, Tom is Black and benevolent, "full glossy Black" with "truly African features."[4] In contrast, Gillam's
Tom is more Indian than Black and is decidedly strong. Considering these
Toms side by side, we see not only two persons but also two versions of the
model American slave: one kind, the other fierce; one Black, the other part
Indian. Gillam's remembrance of a man who was of Black and Native ancestry challenges the familiar version of slavery in which everyone is either Black
or white. Her narrative is a window into a complex understanding of
American slavery, an understanding that includes Native Americans in this
critical national drama (see figure 6.1).

The association between Black people and enslavement in American culture has become instinctive, natural. Consider recent films on the subject,
such as *Amistad* and *Beloved,* that have won large audiences or critical
acclaim. These stories offer no surprises about slavery's main characters: the

slaves are Black or of Black and white ancestry, and the slave owners are white. But as historian James Walvin has argued in his book *Questioning Slavery,* this second-nature correlation of enslavement with Black people is a correlation that rewrites history. It was not always the case in the United States, and the British colonies that preceded it, that enslavement applied only to African Americans and that slavery involved only Blacks and whites. As Walvin observes, "Looking back, the association between black slavery and the Americas seems so natural, so much a part of the historical and economic development of the region, that the two seemed obvious partners. Quite the contrary, it was no such thing."[5]

Walvin goes on to explain that American slavery was birthed out of an intimate triangular relationship between Europe, Africa, and the Americas. Necessarily, Europeans, Africans, and people indigenous to the Americas became enmeshed in the developing phenomenon. The transatlantic slave trade was indiscriminate, catching up anyone and everyone in its net. Still, the popular story of slavery in America, the one told in novels, films, and even high school and college classrooms, is a story without American Indians in it.[6] Worse yet, it is a story that has been reproduced by respected scholars in African American and Native American histories who have painted slavery with a narrow brush. In *Race and History,* John Hope Franklin writes Native people out of the South, ignoring the many Native nations that occupy that region and have contributed to shaping its history. Franklin states, "My field of concentration has been the South, where I have studied intensively the two great racial groups, black and white, the principal actors in the drama of Southern history. (Even before most of them were expelled from the South by Andrew Jackson, Native Americans played only a limited role in the region.)"[7] And in his classic *Custer Died for Your Sins: An Indian Manifesto,* Vine Deloria Jr. says about Native Americans, "It is fortunate that we were never slaves. We gave up land instead of life and labor."[8] The misperceptions in these statements by otherwise erudite scholars reflect many Americans' views. As historian Jack Forbes has urged, "The existence of a large group of 'Red-Black People,' part-American and part-African, has been largely overlooked. . . . Still further, the former existence of comparatively large numbers of Native American slaves has also been ignored generally, with great consequence for both early Native and Afroamerican history."[9] These exclusions and inaccuracies must be addressed if we are ever to stretch ourselves toward a richer understanding of American slavery. Perhaps what we need to move toward this goal is what historian Ronald Takaki has called "a fresh angle, a study of the American past from a comparative perspective."[10] If we look at African American history and Native American history side by side rather than in isolation, we will see the edges where those histories meet, and we will begin to comprehend a fuller and more fascinating picture. At the intersections of Black and Native experiences, we gain greater understanding of the histories of both groups.

This essay is an exploratory contemplation of the multiple and varying experiences as well as the legacy of Native Americans in slavery. I begin with a brief historical overview of Indians as slaves and slave owners, then discuss Black and Native kinship ties grounded in this past. Next, through an account of Black Indian women's experiences in slavery, I consider the potential impact of slave history on scholarship about Native American women. Finally, I delve into the vagaries and contradictions of Black Indian identities that emerge out of the history of Native enslavement.

BACKTRACKING: INDIANS AND SLAVERY

In the New World, Native Americans and imported Africans were the planters' laborers of choice.

IRA BERLIN, *Many Thousands Gone*

If the association between Black people and slavery is by now a natural one, how do we disrupt it to grasp a different reality? One method is to backtrack and revisit the beginnings of slavery in North America. A number of scholars have taken on this task, tracing out the slow and cumbersome development of institutionalized slavery as an economic, cultural, racial, and gendered system that grew out of the European quest for empire. Sociologists Michael Omi and Howard Winant have argued that race as we understand it, with all its concomitant categories, hierarchies, and meanings, began with the European project to colonize the Americas. As European explorers encountered Native American peoples who were unlike themselves, they sought to assess and categorize them. Defining Native people as different, heathen, and inferior meant it was possible for European settlers to treat them poorly, to value territory and wealth over the dignity and rights of the people who occupied the land. Omi and Winant write,

The conquest, therefore, was the first—and given the dramatic nature of the case, perhaps the greatest—racial formation project. Its significance was by no means limited to the Western Hemisphere, for it began the work of constituting Europe as the metropole, the center, of a group of empires which could take, as Marx would later write, "the globe for a theater." It represented this new imperial structure as a struggle between civilization and barbarism, and implicated in this representation all the great European philosophies, literary traditions, and social theories of the modern age.[11]

As momentous as this movement proved to be, it was also far reaching, stretching into Africa to pluck free laborers and pillage natural resources. What followed was a complex and high-stakes system: the movement of capital, products, and persons across continents for national and personal gain.

The single-minded vision of "empire as a way of life" did not discriminate between Black and Red people. Both groups, representing multiple nations and tribes, were seen as ripe for the picking. Indigenous Americans in South America, Central America, North America, and the Caribbean, as well as Africans, were coerced and pressed into labor by the British, Dutch, Spanish, Portuguese, and French. Omi and Winant argue that "the seizure of territories and goods, the introduction of slavery through the *encomienda* and other forms of coerced Native labor, and then through the organization of the African slave trade—not to mention the practice of outright extermination—all presupposed a worldview which distinguished Europeans, as the children of God, full-fledged human beings, etc., from 'Others.'"[12] As this statement intimates, Native Americans were the first slaves in the Americas. With the majority of the Indigenous population in Central and South America decimated by European diseases, the remaining population was weakened and vulnerable. In the Portuguese colony of Brazil, which would become a shining success in its production of sugar and wealth, Indigenous people were the original slaves. In the Spanish-controlled North American Southwest, Native people were also forced into servile labor, carrying Spanish supplies and even Spaniards on their backs like packhorses. In Jamestown, Virginia, the first successful British colony in what would become the United States, Native people were likewise pressed into laboring for European interlopers.

To persevere, Jamestown required more agricultural workers than it had, and this demand only increased with the eventual success of the colony's tobacco crop on the British market. In response to this need, Virginia gentlemen and colonial leaders used white indentured servants, transplanted Africans, and American Indians as a captive and inferior labor force.[13] By 1660, Virginians were so well pleased with the enterprise of African slave labor that they solicited Dutch captains to sell them shiploads of Africans. Soon after, in 1676, Virginia colonists legalized the enslavement of Native people by enacting that "soldiers who had captured Indians should 'reteyne and keepe all such Indian slaves or other Indian goods as they either have taken or hereafter shall take.'"[14] As Africans' and Indians' role as slaves solidified, white indentured servants, who had composed the first work gangs on Virginia plantations, appeared in the fields less and less.[15] This was in part because fewer white servants were choosing to move to the colony and also, importantly, because a rigid color line had begun to emerge. Whiteness became synonymous with freedom and nonwhiteness with slavery. From this point onward, Virginians did not take care to distinguish between Africans and Indians. Indeed, as historian Edmund Morgan notes, "Indians and Negroes were henceforth lumped together in Virginia legislation, and white Virginians treated black, red, and intermediate shades of brown as interchangeable. . . . As Virginians began to expand their slaveholdings, they seem to have had Indians as much in view as Africans."[16] Nonwhite people of any variety were seen as suitable for enslavement because their color was the mark of their difference and, in the view of whites, their inferiority. The British saw Blacks and Indians as equally debased, equally lacking in moral virtue. By the mid-seventeenth century, the project to colonize the Americas had developed into a pervasive ideology and system of white supremacy in which all people of color were viewed as subordinate and suspect.

This system of white supremacy was nourished by an ideology of white superiority that pervaded the rhetoric and writing of the seventeenth-and eighteenth-century English. Historian Winthrop Jordan has written extensively on the image of Africans and Indians in the British mind, arguing that the English saw Africans as "black," a descriptor that, for them, connoted evil, bestiality, and filth. After encountering North American Native Americans— people with brown skin who exhibited "savage" behavior and were known to be enslaved in the West Indies—English colonists associated them with the dark and "uncivilized" Africans. Jordan asserts that "it is easy to see why: whether considered in terms of religion, nationality, savagery, or geographical location Indians seemed more like Negroes than like Englishmen."[17] Seeming "more like Negroes" meant that Native people were located "on the losing side of a crucial dividing line," which, along with Africans, "set them apart for drastic exploitation, oppression, and degradation."[18]

Though European colonists in North America heartily adopted the enslavement of Indians in the late 1600s and early 1700s, they decreased this practice over time. The poor logic of enslaving people in their own homeland soon became clear to Euro-Americans as runaway Indian slaves continually found their way back home. In addition, Native Americans proved highly susceptible to the foreign diseases that had already decimated hundreds of African slaves in the Middle Passage. And Indian slaves, the colonists claimed, were just poor workers. Increasingly, colonists favored and sought African slaves over Native American ones, and the relative value placed on African slaves was evident in their high price.[19] At the same time, Indian people who found themselves displaced from Native communities or who chose to remain close to Black relatives continued to be swept up by slavery. Their presence within slave communities was rarely documented, however. As Blackness became synonymous with bondage, it seemed like common sense for planters to define enslaved persons as Black, regardless of their possibly complicated racial backgrounds. Ira Berlin explains that "the massive influx [of African slaves] overwhelmed the Native-American population, and Indian slaves were swallowed in the tide. . . . Native-American slaves soon vanished from the census enumerations and plantation daybooks, as planters simply categorized their Indian slaves as Africans."[20]

Though absent from the written record, Native American slaves are remembered in the oral testimony of their relatives. Mary Allen Darrows, a former slave from Arkansas, explained that her grandmother was "a little full-blooded Indian girl" who was captured and enslaved by white men in the "Indian Nation" (Alabama)."[21] In another example, Sweetie Ivery Wagoner, a former slave from Oklahoma, reported, "My father was a slave, but he wasn't a Negro. He was a Creek Indian whom the Cherokee Indians stole long years ago and put in slavery just like he was a Negro, and he married with a slave woman and raised a big family."[22] To some historians, Indian enslavement has seemed incidental and unimportant in comparison to more than two centuries of institutionalized Black enslavement in the United States. But as historian J. Leitch Wright has argued, no experience of slavery is insignificant, especially to those who were enslaved. Wright contends, "Readers usually get the impression that this [Indian slavery] was a transitory and not particularly significant phenomenon. The aboriginal perspective was quite different."[23] Slavery as an aspect of Native American history is meaningful, both in what it tells us about the range of Native experiences and in what it signifies for the status of Native people in early America.

Equally important to the story of Native Americans and slavery is the fact that Indians owned slaves in the Southeast and in the western Indian

Territory. Native American acceptance of slavery was slow to develop and continually contested by most Native people. Still, some Indians bought, sold, and worked Black slaves—in several cases, hundreds of them. Practices of slaveholding differed from tribe to tribe; some tribes (like the Seminoles and Creeks) maintained relatively loose and lenient systems, while others (like the Cherokees and Choctaws) developed harsh and controlled systems over time. Native slaveholders hoped and believed that by owning land and Black slaves, they could demonstrate their level of "civilization" to American federal and local powers and thus gain a measure of protection from impending displacement. Despite this and other concessions, however, the Native nations collectively known as the Five Civilized Tribes were forced west in the 1830s to make way for white settlement.[24] Slaveholding in Indian country persisted until the American Civil War.

BLOOD TELLS: THE REVELATIONS OF KINSHIP

If you'll believe it, this [bed] spread took first prize. Look, here's the blue ribbon pinned on yet. What they thought was so wonderful was that I knit every stitch of it without glasses. But that is not so funny, because I have never worn glasses in my life. I guess that is some more of my Indian blood telling.

CORA GILLAM, *WPA interview*

In her interview with a Federal Writers' Project employee, former slave Cora Gillam claims that "blood tells." By this she means that "blood," or Indian ancestry, explains something about her that is otherwise inexplicable. Her prizewinning bedspread appeared to the judges to have been sewn by an African American woman, but Gillam complicates this initial impression by highlighting her Native American heritage and connecting that heritage with the quality of good eyesight. It is, she reveals, her Native "blood," present but unseen, that has facilitated the creation of the beautiful textile. Though clearly essentialist in its attribution of good health to Native ancestry, Gillam's statement points to fruitful directions for inquiry. Following Gillam's lead, what can "blood" tell us? What can we learn by looking at family lineage that would not otherwise be obvious in a study of Native Americans and slavery?

In the Southeast, where most Native Americans and Africans encountered one another, the intricate constellations of Native kinship systems shaped social interactions, political agendas, and crime and punishment within Native communities. For southeastern tribes, kinship was a primary determinant of social and ceremonial relations.[25] A person without kinship ties was hardly a person at all, and a person with kinship ties was an integral part of an extended family, or clan. Information about clan membership determined the trajectory that any encounter or relationship would follow.[26] A person could expect to be received hospitably by a clan member even if that clan member was a personal stranger or lived in a distant town, and a person could be punished or killed for a crime committed by a clan member whom he or she had never met.[27] Kinship was the web that knit Native people together as tribes, and Native people viewed the world through the intricate netting of that web. Given the centrality of kinship to Native definitions of peoplehood, tracing bloodlines across Black and Indian communities seems both a fitting and effective means of locating further dimensions of Native Americans' experience with slavery. In the absence of reliable historical records, cartographies of kinship can serve as a guide to the complex ways that Native people were drawn into slavery's matrix.

Anthropologist Melville Herskovits of Howard University found in studies conducted from 1926 to 1928 that over 25 percent of the African American population reported having Native American ancestry.[28] Even allowing for misrepresentation or imprecise memory, this figure suggests that significant numbers of Black Americans have one or more Native American forebears. Jack Forbes has argued that "by the nineteenth century it seems quite certain that Afroamericans, whether living in Latin America, the Caribbean or in North America, had absorbed considerable amounts of Native American ancestry."[29] In the 1600s, 1700s, and 1800s, when many of these interracial links were forged, the descendants of a Native American and African American would have been defined as Indian by other Indians of their tribe. Native nations in the Southeast tended toward matrilineality and reckoned clan membership through the mother's family line. Within the framework of a matrilineal kinship system, a person was Cherokee, Creek, Seminole, and so on if the person's mother was Cherokee, Creek, or Seminole. Race as we understand it now was not the determining factor in a person's tribal identity or tribal membership. Instead, lineage determined belonging. A person who appeared "Black" and had a Native American mother would have been defined and accepted as Indian. Later, in the early 1800s, as southeastern tribes began to incorporate aspects of the Euro-American patrilineal kinship system, mixed-race descendants of Native mothers or Native fathers could be considered Indian by their Native relatives and associates. The prevailing understanding was consistent: if your relatives were Indian, so were you.[30]

The children and grandchildren of Indian and Black families were considered Native by their Native relatives and Black by their Black relatives. They belonged to dual and overlapping tribal/racial communities and were most likely fluent in the values and cultural practices of both. Because of phenotypical characteristics that marked them as "Black" and because of their location in Black families, children of Native and Black couples were especially vulnerable to enslavement. Whether by birth, trade, or capture, they could easily fall prey to slave dealers and slave owners. Even as Native Americans were enslaved outright in early America, Black Indians, or people of both Black and Native descent, were enslaved in large numbers along with African Americans into the nineteenth century.

Interracial marriage in the slave quarters and in free communities of color meant that the Black population and Indian population were overlapping and expanding and that the slave population included more and more persons of Black and Native descent. Advertisements for runaway slaves in eighteenth-century newspapers indicate the mixed-race heritage of many slaves and also show the ambivalence of white slave owners in describing slaves of Black and Native ancestry. Repeatedly in these advertisements, slaves are defined as "Negro" or "Mulatto" with "claims" of Indianness or the ability to "pass" as Indian, but rarely are slaves designated as "Indian" or both Black and Indian.[31] A survey of advertisements for escaped Black Indian slaves from several newspapers follows:

> A Mulatto slave named David, about twenty-two years of age, five feet eight or nine inches high, a cunning artful Fellow with a sly Look, slim made, a little knock-kneed, says he is of the Indian breed.[32]
>
> A mulatto servant man, named John Newton about 20 years of age, an Indian by birth, about 5 feet 6 inches high, slender made, has a thin visage, sour look, remarkable projected lips, and wears his own black hair tied behind.[33]
>
> A tall thin Mulatto slave, looks very much like an Indian, and will endeavor to pass as such when it suits him.[34]
>
> A Mulatto slave named Dan, much the Colour of an Indian is a lusty fellow about 25 years of age.[35]
>
> A negro man of the name Tom, about 5 feet 6 inches tall, of a yellowish complexion much the appearance of an Indian. . . . His hair is of a

different kind from that of a Negro's, rather more of the Indian's, but partaking of both.[36]

A Mulatto man named Jim who is a slave, but pretends to have a right to his freedom. His father was an Indian. . . . He is a short well fed fellow, about 27 years of age, with long black hair resembling an Indian's.[37]

In these examples, slave owners deflect the right of Black Indians to be Indian by reducing Indianness to a list of "traits" such as hair, attitude, skin color, and known relatives. The authenticity of Black Indians' Indianness is called into question by the circumlocutory language of many of these advertisements.[38] In some cases, slave owners misclassified Black Indians because they were sloppy, in other cases because it made no difference exactly what racial background a colored, enslaved person claimed. In still other cases, persons who were both Black and Indian were misidentified because whites stood to gain at the reduction of the Native American population. "Black" people did not have the rightful claim to American land that Native people had. To define Indians as Black meant there would be fewer "real" Indians with whom land deals and treaties had to be negotiated.[39]

The intricate and even paradoxical means of defining racial categories in the United States has meant that enslaved Black Indians have not been defined as Indian but instead as solely Black. The simplification of mixed-race ancestry and resulting misclassification of people have contributed to the fiction that Native Americans did not play a role in slavery past the eighteenth century. Given the prevailing understanding of racial categories, many of us find the notion of Indians who are also Black difficult to accept. The logic within which we operate when defining Blacks and Indians is governed by the dialect of the "one-drop rule" and blood quantum ratio. The "one-drop rule," which holds that a person who has one drop of Black blood is Black, was devised by Euro-American slave owners. It ensured an ever-growing slave population fattened by the children of Black slaves and white masters, even as it protected white people from "legitimizing mulattoes," "quadroons," and "octoroons" as white. Likewise, the blood quantum ratio method of defining Native Americans was developed by white policy makers in the late nineteenth century. It holds that a person can be Indian only if he or she demonstrates a particular ratio of Native forebears to non-Native forebears.[40] Because it was difficult for some Native people to meet this criterion because of intermarriage in their families, there were fewer Indians whom federal and state officials had to recognize as having rightful claims to their homeland, and to political sovereignty as tribal nations. The one-drop rule ensured that there would be more Black laborers for slavery's human machine, while the blood quantum ratio ensured that there would be more available land for white settlement and development.

For people of both Black and Native descent, these two rules interface in a way that makes it difficult for Black Indians to be considered Indian. Anthropologist Circe Sturm confronts this dilemma, arguing that "the rules of hypodescent played out in such a way that people with any degree of African American blood were usually classified exclusively as Black. . . . Multiracial individuals with Black ancestry were always 'Black.'"[41] Sturm notes that, given this logic, it has been much easier for Indians with white ancestry to be defined as "Indian" than it has been for Indians with Black ancestry. What is important to recognize here is that these means of defining group membership for Blacks and Native Americans originated outside Black and Native communities. Though many African American and Native American people subscribe to these definitions today, during the antebellum period, Blacks and Indians regularly defined the members of their families and tribes in accordance with their own values. Black Indian people were viewed as Indian by Native community members. And just as important, many Black Indian people constructed biracial identities for themselves.

The WPA interviews with Black Indians who were former slaves include self-descriptions that suggest a biracial and bicultural consciousness. I offer these examples of Black Indian slaves' self-descriptions as a means of indicating their self-conceptualizations as Black Indian people. Former slave Sweetie Ivery Wagoner states that her father was an enslaved Creek man who married a Black woman. She also describes her parent's dress as an indicator of their Indian identity: "My folks was part Indian alright; they wore blankets and breeches with fur around the bottoms. My father's own daddy was Randolph Get-a-bout."[42] R. C. Smith, like many Black Indians who were interviewed, traces out his Native lineage: "My father was half Cherokee Indian. His father was bought by an Indian woman and she took him for her husband. . . . My father played with Cornelius Boudinot when he was a child. Cherokee Bill was my second cousin."[43] This gesture of naming Native relatives, common in interviews with Black Indians, might be understood as a habit grounded in Native kinship customs. Alternately, or simultaneously, the gesture could be read as an attempt to authenticate the speaker's Indianness in the face of skepticism, a bicultural characteristic grounded in the particular experience of Black Indians.

Cornelius Neely Nave, a Black-Cherokee man who was the slave of Cherokees, described himself as follows: "I wasn't scared of them Indians for pappa always told me his master, Henry Nave, was his own father; that makes me part Indian and the reason my hair is long, straight and black like a horse mane."[44] As Nave's statement implies, Black Indian slaves owned by Native people experienced their Indianness in complex and contradictory ways, as their relationship to Native cultures would have been filtered through and constrained by the fact that their enslavers were Indians. In a final example, a Black-Creek healer explains his talent as bicultural in nature: "Cross blood means extra knowledge. I can take my cane and blow it twice and do the same thing a Creek full blood doctor does in four times. Two bloods makes two talents. Two bloods has more swifter solid good sense. I is one of them."[45]

Defined on the most literal level of blood ties, Black Indians were Indians as well as Blacks. Additionally, beyond this literal interpretation, Black people could become Indian through adoption. The experience of Molly, a Black slave adopted into a Cherokee clan, points to the ways that racial categories were malleable in Native communities. Molly was purchased in the late 1700s by a white man named Sam Dent who had been an Indian trader in Cherokee territory. Dent gave Molly to the Deer clan as retribution for having beaten to death his Cherokee wife, a Deer clan member. The Deer clan accepted Molly as a family member in place of the deceased woman and gave her the name Chickaua.[46]

Molly lived with her new family as a free woman until her liberty was challenged in 1833 by the white daughter of Sam Dent's associate, who claimed ownership of Molly and her son, Cunestuta (or Isaac Tucker). The Deer clan refused to give Molly and Isaac up to the agents who had been sent to retrieve them. Instead, clan members challenged the white claimant, whose name was Molly Hightower, before the Cherokee Supreme Court. They urged the "Council and authorities of the Cherokee nation" to protect Molly and her son, insisting, "[We] ask and require of our Council and headmen for assistance and for Council to resist this oppression and legal wrong attempted to be practiced on our Brother and Sister by the Hightower in leasing into slavery two of whom have ever been considered native Cherokee [sic]. We feel that the attempt is one of cruel grievance [sic]."[47] In this document, the petitioners refer to Molly and Cunestuta as "brother and sister" and "native Cherokees" and argue that as adoptees into the Deer clan, the former Black slaves were now Cherokee citizens. The Cherokee Supreme Court agreed and protected the mother and son's status as Cherokees. In the words of historian William McLoughlin, the court concluded that "the slave Molly, had become a Cherokee, had always been treated as a Cherokee, and still retained the rights of Cherokee citizenship by virtue of her adoption into the Deer clan, regardless of her race, complexion, or ancestry. By this same right, her son was also a Cherokee citizen."[48]

THE WAY IT IS: BLACK INDIAN WOMEN IN SLAVERY

I was a Cherokee slave and now I am a Cherokee freedwoman, and besides that I am a quarter Cherokee my own self. And this is the way it is.

SARAH WILSON, *WPA interview*

As evidenced by the customs of Native kinship systems, the accounts of Black Indian slaves, and the outcome of a representative Native court case, Black Indians were Indians. When taken as a presupposition, this conclusion opens up new questions in the study of Native American history. Take, for instance, the history of Native women in the United States—a topic that has been neglected in the broader field of Native American studies. Scholars like Bea Medicine, Patricia Albers, Theda Perdue, and Nancy Shoemaker have addressed this absence in their own work on Native women. Anthropologist Patricia Albers points out that attention to the Native American past has focused on men, particularly chiefs and warriors. She argues that "native women rarely appear" in historical writings and are "conspicuous by their absence."[49] Laura Klein and Lillian Ackerman make a similar case, asserting that the textures and meanings of Indian women's lives are left unexplored in ethnographic works: "Silence surrounds the lives of Native North American Women. . . . The wives, sisters, and mothers of Native nations do appear in traditional ethnographies but only where they are expected, and the meanings of their lives are left to the readers' imagination."[50]

In addition to the lack of attention to Native women, there is the equally problematic issue of sparse and compromised sources for research. Historian Nancy Shoemaker explicates the problem of locating reliable sources for Native women's history. Particularly in colonial and early America, records were kept by white men who, if they noticed Native women at all, viewed them through a Eurocentric and masculinist lens that did not allow for clear vision of Native women's experience. Shoemaker explains, "From Columbus's initial descriptions of 'India' up through the twentieth century, most of the available written records have been produced by Euro-American men— explorers, traders, missionaries, and government policymakers. . . . Historical accounts of Indian women usually depict them as 'squaw drudges,' beasts of burden bowed down with overwork and spousal oppression, or as 'Indian princesses,' voluptuous and promiscuous objects of white and Indian men's sexual desire."[51] As Theda Perdue argues, even when white men were intimate and careful observers, they could not accurately describe Native women's lives. Perdue notes that "male European observers had virtually no access to the private lives of women or to women's culture. Even those who married Native women usually had only scant insight into the most basic matters."[52]

The historical experience of Native women has been difficult to unearth, even for scholars who are versed in and committed to the subject. Presupposing that Black Indians are Indians has the potential to reveal new sources of information for this crucial work. A number of Black Indian women lived as slaves in the American colonies and the States. Thus themes and arguments that scholars of Black women's history have explored in their studies of slave women can now be read as intersecting with Native women's history. Topics like sexual abuse, breeding, and physical brutality, key in the experience of Black slave women, now become meaningful and illuminating in the study of Indian women's lives. Moreover, the firsthand experience of Black Indian women as recorded in slave interviews and narratives is an untapped source of primary material for Native women's history. As personal accounts that delve into the everyday happenings and key issues in the lives of a specific set of Native women, these narratives are valuable and rare.

For instance, slave interviews reveal that the threat of rape clouded the lives of Black Indian women, as it did for all enslaved Black women. As scholars of Native women's history address the misrepresentation of Native women's sexuality and the particularities of culturally specific understandings of sex, they might broaden their studies by attending to the issue of sexual abuse in Black Indian women's experience. In one interview, former slave Hannah Travis painfully recounts her mother's abuse. The daughter of a "full blooded Indian" woman and a Black French man, Travis's mother worked in the kitchen of her master and mistress.[53] The inhumane treatment she endured is apparent in the punishment she received if she missed a spot while washing the dishes. Her master would "make her drink the old dirty dishwater [and] whip her if she didn't drink it."[54] In addition, Hannah Travis's mother was raped by her master, Hannah's father. Hannah Travis says of this incident, "I hate my father. He was white. I never did have no use for him.... He was my mother's master.... My mother was just forced. I hate him."[55]

Ellen Cragin, the daughter of a Black woman and Indian man, explains that her father was conceived during a period when her enslaved grandmother had run away: "My father was an Indian. Way back in the dark days, his mother ran away, and when she came up, that's what she come with—a little Indian boy. They called him 'Waw-hoo'che.'" Cragin continues, "They used to call me 'Waw-hoo'che' and 'the Red-Headed Indian Brat.' I got into a fight once with my mistress' daughter on account of that."[56] The "dark days" of slavery were riddled with violence in the experience of this young Black Indian girl. She saw her mother forced to breed for the master and repeatedly witnessed her mother being whipped. While a child, Cragin watched as her pregnant mother was beaten with a technique that was developed to protect the valuable offspring of slave women while brutally punishing the women themselves. The master or overseer would dig a hole for the protection of the woman's extended belly, while leaving her back and hips exposed.[57] Cragin recounts, "One day, Tom Polk [her master] hit my mother. That was before she ran away. He hit her because she didn't pick the required amount of cotton. . . . I don't know how many times he hit her. I was small. . . . I went to see. And they had her down. She was stout, and they had dug a hole in the ground to put her belly in. I never did get over that."[58] Cragin says further of her master, "He would have children by a nigger woman and then have them by her daughter." In an effort to protect her mother, Cragin once took up arms: "I went out one day and got a gun. I don't know whose gun it was. I said to myself 'If you whip my mother today, I am going to shoot you.' I didn't know where the gun belonged. My oldest sister told me to take it and set it by the door, and I did it."[59]

Mamie Thompson, born after Emancipation, described the life of her enslaved mother. Thompson's mother was "mixed with Cherokee Indian and Negro," resulting from her father's status as "a full blood Indian."[60] When she resisted the sexual advances of a white overseer, she was placed on the auction block: "Master Redman had her in the field working. The overseer was a white man. He tried to take her down and carry on with her. . . . He was mad cause he couldn't overpower her. Master Redman got her in the kitchen to whoop her with a cowhide; she told him she would kill him; she got a stick. He let her out and they came to buy her—a Negro trader."[61] Thompson's mother was later recovered and brought home by her mistress.

Sarah Wilson, the woman whose words begin this section of the essay, was a Black Cherokee slave owned by a white-Cherokee family. Her story is both illuminating and compelling in the ways that it details the experience of one

Black Indian girl and indicts that girl's own Cherokee relatives for their cruelty. Sarah Wilson's master, whom she describes as "a devil on this earth," was a white man married to a Cherokee woman.[62] The couple's son was Wilson's father. Though Wilson does not describe the sexual encounter between her African American mother and the master's son, it is probable that her mother was forced. Wilson says of her father, "Young Master Ned was a devil too."[63] She also reports that her master practiced breeding and sold female slaves who did not have babies. Wilson describes her mistress, who was also her grandmother, as being equally harsh: "Old Master wasn't the only hellion either. Old Mistress just as bad, and she took most of her wrath out hitting us children all the time."[64] Wilson reveals that she learned from her Black grandmother the reason for the mistress's venom: "When I was eight years old, Old Mistress died, and Grandmammy told me why Old Mistress picked on me so. She told me about me being half Mister Ned's blood."[65] Clearly, Sarah Wilson's experience adds another dimension to the meaning of blood ties for Black Indians. The depravities and ideologies of slavery, when adopted by Native people, had the potential to warp kinship ties between Indians and Black Indian relatives. Being part Cherokee made Sarah Wilson a threat to her Cherokee grandmother. And Wilson only received minimal protection from her father. In much the same way as white owners who fathered Black babies, he casually defended her against her grandmother's beatings. Wilson reports that on these occasions her father would say, with a laugh, "Let her alone, she got big blood in her."[66]

These accounts and others of sexual abuse and violence reveal the ways that Black Indian women experienced slavery. They were raped, beaten, and threatened, and their children witnessed their vulnerability and violation. Whole families were affected, and sometimes implicated, by the abuse of their relatives and the inhumanity of enslavement. As the experiences of women who were Indian as well as Black, these happenings have a place in the history of Native American women. In the early 1980s, pathbreaking slavery studies began to ask how the particularities of an interrelated gendered and raced experience shaped Black women's lives.[67] With attention to the untapped sources of slave women's interviews and narratives, scholars of Native women's history might now ask, How did Black Indian women experience slavery as *Native Women?* What new issues, if any, arose out of the complex configuration of this specific slave experience? Did Black Indian women understand their enslavement and resistance in ways that were culturally specific? Did they locate their experience within broader tribal and

Native group histories? Did they develop biracial identities and bicultural communities? Historian Nell Irvin Painter has observed in her essay "Soul Murder and Slavery: Toward a Fully Loaded Cost Accounting" that the prevalence of violence and sexual abuse during slavery indelibly stained Black women's lives.[68] Certainly, this history has shaped Black women's ideas about themselves and their sexuality, even in the present day. As historian Paula Giddings has argued, "The issues of gender and sexuality have been made so painful to us in our history that we have largely hidden them from ourselves.... Consequently, they remain largely unresolved."[69] Might similar arguments about sexual abuse and the persistence of historical memory be made for Native women, once this aspect of Black Indian women's experience is taken into account? Or does the distinctive historical shape of Native women's experience, when complicated by Black Indian women's voices, offer fresh paradigms for understanding both Black and Native women's history? These questions and more emerge when we tell a story of slavery with Indians in it and recognize Black Indians as Indians.

BLACK INDIAN IDENTITIES:
CONTRADICTIONS AND CONCLUSIONS

Constructing a history of slavery that includes Native people contributes to a richer picture of the American, Native American, and African American pasts. But a richer picture is at the same time more complicated, characterized by contradictions and contestations of the familiar and comfortable. The narrative of Cora Gillam, the former slave from Mississippi whose description of "Uncle Tom" introduces this essay, exemplifies some of the contradictions inherent in this endeavor. I presented Gillam's words at two junctures in this chapter—at the start to illustrate dual images of Uncle Tom, and in the body to demonstrate the importance of attending to Black and Native kinship networks. However, I deferred until now a discussion of how Gillam's representation of her uncle raises intriguing and challenging questions about her representation of a Black Indian identity.

As Laura Lovett has demonstrated, African Americans' invocation of Native ancestry is a motif in the WPA narratives. Lovett defines these recurring rhetorical moments as attempts on the part of interviewees to resist the hierarchies of segregation by muddying the waters of racial categorization. In other words, interviewees challenged fixed notions of biological Blackness and Black inferiority by highlighting Native American family legacies. Lovett posits that in referencing Native kin, interviewees enacted "genealogical performances" that operated as ideological and political disruptions of the racial status quo.[70] Gillam's "genealogical performance" traces Native heritage to contextualize her own personal strengths. But even as Gillam's narrative challenges fixed racial categories, it privileges Indianness over Blackness, imbuing Indian "blood" with an essentialized array of special qualities. Gillam's account lends specificity to the history of Black Indians in slavery. At the same time, it reveals the contested issues of racial hierarchy and racial prestige with which Black Indian slaves and their descendants have wrestled.

Cora Gillam is a confident and purposeful interviewee. She aims to shape her own story and informs the interviewer of this intent when she interrupts the framework the interviewer has imposed by exclaiming, "Wait a minute lady." Gillam explains that she is the child of a Black-Cherokee woman and white man. The mixed-race aspect of her identity, particularly her Indianness, is central to the story she tells about herself. She explains early in the interview when asked if her father was a slave, "No ma'am, oh no indeedy, my father was not a slave. Can't you tell by me that he was white?" She goes on to explain her racial identity further:

My grandmother—on mother's side, was full blooded Cherokee. She came from North Carolina. In early days my mother and her brother and sisters were stolen from their home in North Carolina and taken to Mississippi and sold for slaves. You know the Indians could follow trails better than other kind of folks, and she tracked her children down and stayed in the south. My mother was only part-Negro; so was her brother, uncle Tom. He seemed all Indian. You know, the Cherokees were peaceable Indians, until you got them mad. Then they was the fiercest fighters of any tribes.[71]

At this point in the narrative, Gillam directs her attention to the valiant story of her uncle Tom, devoting considerable time to chronicling his accomplishments:

Now I want to tell you about my uncle Tom. Like I said, he was half-Indian. But the Negro part didn't show hardly any. There was something about uncle Tom that made both white and black be afraid of him. They say uncle Tom was the best reader, white or black, for miles. That was what got him in trouble. Slaves was not allowed to read. They didn't want them to know that freedom was coming. No ma'am! . . . That Indian in uncle Tom made him not scared of anybody. He had a newspaper with latest war news and gathered a crowd of slaves to read them when peace was coming. White men say it done to get uprising among slaves. A crowd of white gather and take uncle Tom to jail. Twenty of them said they would beat him, each man, till they so tired they can't lay on one more lick. If he still alive, then they hang him. . . . The Indian in uncle Tom rose. Strength—big extra strength seemed to come to him. First man what opened that door, he leaped on him and laid him out. No white man could stand against him in that Indian fighting spirit. They was scared of him. He almost tore that jailhouse down, lady. Yes he did.[72]

Gillam's account of her uncle's bravery is certainly moving. But what does it mean that her uncle "seemed all Indian" and that "the Negro part didn't show hardly any"? Gillam does not describe Tom physically, and it seems that these references reflect Tom's character rather than his phenotype. Gillam's description of the Indian "rising" in Tom when he is forced to defend himself against a lynch mob suggests that she sees her uncle's Indianness as the source and encapsulation of his strength. Like a genie in the bottle of embodied Blackness, Tom's Indianness is invested with a power and magnificence that can be conjured in times of need. Moreover, the strength that Tom derives from his Indianness stands in implicit opposition to his Black heritage, which Gillam never designates as the source of positive or special qualities. Laura Lovett has argued insightfully that WPA interviewees invoked (often stereotyped) Indian characteristics to demonstrate a legacy of resistance in their families. In the case of Gillam and others, however, this rhetorical act of protest can simultaneously be read as an act of negation, coding Black Indian resistance as solely Indian and thereby rendering invisible an accompanying tradition of Black resistance.

This reading of Cora Gillam's narrative challenges more celebratory views of Black Indian historical identities and Black and Native relations. But the project of reimagining the history of slavery in America, of weaving Native experiences into that history, brings with it the responsibility of complicating our findings. Just as the popular version of slavery is incomplete, a version in which Indians and Black Indians appear is likewise unfinished unless we continually push the boundaries of our knowledge and expectations. Constructing a complex story of American slavery, and of Black and Native relations, means exploring what is disconcerting and contradictory, even as we seek what is liberatory and luminous.

This chapter was first published in *Confounding the Color Line: Indian-Black Relations in Multidisciplinary Perspective,* ed. James Brooks (Lincoln: University of Nebraska Press, 2002), 137–60.

1. Harriet Beecher Stowe, *Uncle Tom's Cabin* (1852; repr., New York: Signet, 1966), 440.

2. Jane Tompkins, *Sensational Designs: The Cultural Work of American Fiction, 1790–1860* (New York: Oxford University Press, 1985), chap. 5.

3. Works Progress Administration: Oklahoma Writers Project, *Slave Narratives: A Folk History of Slavery in the United States from Interviews with Former Slaves* (Washington, DC: Government Printing Office, 1932), microfilm, 28. I am grateful to Patrick Minges for compiling and sharing many of the WPA interviews used in this essay. The WPA interviews, structured by specific questions, reveal details of everyday slave life such as diet, housing, work, childbirth and childrearing, methods of punishment, and degree of mobility. While rich as source material, these interviews must be read closely and critically, as many of them are conducted by white workers, creating a dynamic that led some interviewees to mask their actual feelings about slavery. Perhaps the most reliable approach to reconstructing a picture of slave women's experience from these interviews is a comparative analysis that teases out common themes and shared experiences across a range of interviews. This type of reading can glean major aspects of slave women's experience without wholly depending on the complete veracity and forthrightness of single interviewees. For more on the use of WPA materials, see Melvina Johnson Young, "Exploring the WPA Narratives: Finding the Voices of Black Women and Men," in *Theorizing Black Feminisms,* ed. Stanlie James and Abena Busia (New York: Routledge, 1993), 55–74.

4. Stowe, *Uncle Tom,* 32.

5. James Walvin, *Questioning Slavery* (New York: Routledge, 1996), 1.

6. I borrow this phrasing from Colin Calloway, who commonly describes his historical work as "writing American history with Indians in it."

7. John Hope Franklin, *Race and History: Selected Essays 1938–1988* (Baton Rouge: Louisiana State University Press, 1989), 71.

8. Vine Deloria Jr., *Custer Died for Your Sins: An Indian Manifesto* (1969; repr., Norman: University of Oklahoma Press, 1988), 7.

9. Jack Forbes, *Africans and Native Americans: The Language of Race and the Evolution of Red-Black Peoples* (Urbana: University of Illinois Press, 1993), 190.

10. Ronald Takaki, *A Different Mirror: A History of Multicultural America* (Boston: Little, Brown, 1993), 7.

11. Michael Omi and Howard Winant, *Racial Formation in the United States: From the 1960s to the 1990s,* 2nd ed. (New York: Routledge, 1994), 62.

12. Omi and Winant, *Racial Formation,* 62.

13. Edmund Morgan, *American Slavery, American Freedom: The Ordeal of Colonial Virginia* (New York: W. W. Norton, 1974).

14. Quoted in Morgan, *American Slavery,* 329.

15. Morgan, *American Slavery*, 308.

16. Morgan, *American Slavery*, 329.

17. Winthrop Jordan, *The White Man's Burden: Historical Origins of Racism in the United States* (London: Oxford University Press, 1974), 48. See also Winthrop Jordan, *White over Black: American Attitudes toward the Negro, 1550–1812* (New York: W. W. Norton, 1968).

18. Jordan, *White Man's Burden*, 46; Walvin, *Questioning Slavery*, 75.

19. Walvin, *Questioning Slavery*, 4–5, 10.

20. Ira Berlin, *Many Thousands Gone: The First Two Centuries of Slavery in North America* (Cambridge, MA: Harvard University Press, 1998), 145.

21. Interview with Mary Allen Darrows in Works Progress Administration, *Slave Narratives*, 95.

22. Interview with Sweetie Ivery Wagoner in *The WPA Oklahoma Slave Narratives*, ed. T. Lindsay Baker and Julie Baker (Norman: University of Oklahoma Press, 1996), 442.

23. J. Leitch Wright, *The Only Land They Know: American Indians in the Old South* (Lincoln: University of Nebraska Press, 1981), 126.

24. The "Five Civilized Tribes" was a label assigned to Cherokees, Creeks, Choctaws, Chickasaws, and Seminoles by white officials and reformers in the nineteenth century.

25. Charles Hudson, *The Southeastern Indians* (Knoxville: University of Tennessee Press, 1976), 193; Duane Champagne, "Institutional and Cultural Order in the Early Cherokee Society: A Sociological Interpretation," *Journal of Cherokee Studies* 15 (1990): 3–26, 12.

26. William Gilbert, "Eastern Cherokee Social Organization," in *Social Anthropology of North American Tribes,* ed. Fred Eggan (Chicago: University of Chicago Press, 1937), 296.

27. Champagne, "Institutional and Cultural Order," 11; Hudson, *Southeastern Indians,* 192.

28. Melville Herskovits, *The American Negro: A Study in Race Crossing* (New York: Knopf, 1928).

29. Forbes, *Africans and Native Americans,* 270.

30. Slaveholding and a related acceptance of racial hierarchy among tribes of the Southeast meant that this rule of thumb concerning kinship was sometimes challenged. Mixed-race Black-Native people could be legally defined as belonging outside the tribal group. But most Native people ignored exclusionary laws against Blacks and continued to view Black Indian relatives as kin.

31. In *Africans and Native Americans,* Jack Forbes details the terminology that was developed for racial classification.

32. *Virginia Gazette,* July 15, 1773, 3. I am grateful to Alex Bontemps for compiling and sharing his collection of newspaper advertisements describing Black Indian slaves.

33. *Virginia Gazette,* July 19, 1776, 4.

34. *Maryland Gazette,* May 21, 1752, 3.

35. *Maryland Gazette*, February 1, 1749, 3.

36. *Virginia Gazette*, November 11, 1773, 2.

37. *Virginia Gazette*, November 26, 1772, 3.

38. There are examples in which slave owners describe runaway slaves as "half Indian" or "mustee," a term used to designate people of Black and Indian descent; however, the majority of the ads I reviewed did not clearly designate Black Indians. In an example of an advertisement that is clear, the subscriber seeks "a half Indian fellow who calls himself Jack Brown." *Virginia Gazette*, March 10, 1774, 3.

39. Berlin concludes that the danger of recognizing a Black Indian person's Indianness became apparent in the 1790s, when a new Spanish governor of Louisiana showed a measure of support for free people of color. In response to this chink in the institutionalized armor of state oppression of colored people, mixed-race Black Indians sued the colony for their freedom on the grounds that they were descended from legally free Indians. Louisiana planters responded venomously, forcing the governor to abandon his alliance with free people of color. Berlin, *Many Thousands Gone*, 352–53.

40. The Bureau of Indian Affairs generally defines this ratio as one full-blood Native grandparent out of four, though individual tribes have varying ways of determining citizenship.

41. Circe Sturm, "Blood Politics, Racial Classification, and Cherokee National Identity: The Trials and Tribulations of the Cherokee Freedmen," *American Indian Quarterly* 22, no. 1/2 (Winter–Spring 1998): 230–58.

42. Interview with Sweetie Ivery Wagoner in *WPA Oklahoma Slave Narratives*, 443.

43. Interview with R. C. Smith in *WPA Oklahoma Slave Narratives*, 398.

44. Interview with Cornelius Neely Nave in *WPA Oklahoma Slave Narratives*, 398.

45. Quoted in Sigmund Sameth, "Creek Negroes: A Study of Race Relations" (master's thesis, University of Oklahoma, 1940), 62.

46. Cherokee Supreme Court Docket, 1833, Tennessee State Library and Archives. For additional accounts of Molly's case, see William McLoughlin, *Cherokee Renascence in the New Republic* (Princeton, NJ: Princeton University Press, 1986), 347; Rennard Strickland, *Fire and the Spirits: Cherokee Law from Clan to Court* (Norman: University of Oklahoma Press, 1977), 54.

47. Cherokee Supreme Court, 1833.

48. McLoughlin, *Renascence,* 347.

49. Patricia Albers and Bea Medicine, eds., *The Hidden Half: Studies of Plains Indian Women* (New York: University Press of America, 1983), 4.

50. Laura Klein and Lillian Ackerman, eds., *Women and Power in Native North America* (Norman: University of Oklahoma Press, 1995), 3.

51. Nancy Shoemaker, introduction to *Negotiators of Change: Historical Perspectives on Native American Women,* ed. Nancy Shoemaker (New York: Routledge, 1995), 2–3.

52. Theda Perdue, introduction to *Cherokee Women: Gender and Culture Change, 1700–1835* (Lincoln: University of Nebraska Press, 1998), 4.

53. Interview with Hannah Travis in Works Progress Administration, *Slave Narratives*, 350.

54. Interview with Hannah Travis, 351.

55. Interview with Hannah Travis, 352.

56. Interview with Ellen Cragin in Works Progress Administration, *Slave Narratives*, 42, 43.

57. Historian Angela Davis discusses this method of punishment in the first chapter of her book *Women, Race, and Class* (New York: Vintage Books, 1983).

58. Interview with Ellen Cragin, 44–45.

59. Interview with Ellen Cragin, 44–45.

60. Interview with Mamie Thompson in Works Progress Administration, *Slave Narratives*, 319.

61. Interview with Mamie Thompson, 319.

62. Interview with Sarah Wilson, 493.

63. Interview with Sarah Wilson, 495.

64. Interview with Sarah Wilson, 494.

65. Interview with Sarah Wilson, 495.

66. Interview with Sarah Wilson, 495.

67. Studies in the 1980s by Deborah Gray White, Angela Davis, bell hooks, Paula Giddings, Jacqueline Jones, Elizabeth Fox-Genovese, Catherine Clinton, and others were the first to explore major themes that apply widely to the experiences of Black slave women. Deborah Gray White, *Ar'n't I a Woman? Female Slaves in the Plantation South* (New York: W. W. Norton, 1985); Davis, *Women, Race, and Class;* Jacqueline Jones, *Labor of Love, Labor of Sorrow* (New York: Vintage, 1986); bell hooks, *Ain't I a Woman: Black Women and Feminism* (Boston: South End Press, 1981); Elizabeth Fox-Genovese, "Strategies and Forms of Resistance: Focus on Slave Women in the United States," in *Resistance: Studies in African, Caribbean and Afro-American History,* ed. Gary Okihiro (Amherst: University of Massachusetts Press, 1986), 143–60; Elizabeth Fox-Genovese, *Within the Plantation Household* (Chapel Hill: University of North Carolina Press, 1988); Catherine Clinton, *The Plantation Mistress: Woman's World in the Old South* (New York: Pantheon, 1982).

68. Nell Irvin Painter, "Soul Murder and Slavery: Toward a Fully Loaded Cost Accounting," in *U.S. History as Women's History: New Feminist Essays,* ed. Linda Kerber, Alice Kessler-Harris, and Kathryn Sklar (Chapel Hill: University of North Carolina Press, 1995), 125–46.

69. Paula Giddings, "The Last Taboo," in *Race-ing Justice, Engendering Power,* ed. Toni Morrison (New York: Pantheon, 1992), 442.

70. Laura L. Lovett, "'African and Cherokee by Choice': Race and Resistance under Legalized Segregation," *American Indian Quarterly* 22, no. 1/2 (Winter–Spring 1998): 203–29.

71. Interview with Cora Gillam, 27–28.

72. Interview with Cora Gillam, 28.

SEVEN

"The Whatever That Survived"

THINKING RACIALIZED IMMIGRATION THROUGH
BLACKNESS AND THE AFTERLIFE OF SLAVERY

Tiffany Willoughby-Herard

We are in America because our lives meant nothing to those in power in the countries we came from. You've come here to realize that our lives also mean nothing here. Some . . . try to distance ourselves from this reality, thinking that because we are another type of "other" . . . migrants, refugees—this is not our problem. . . . But ultimately we realize . . .

EDWIDGE DANTICAT[1]

We are people who need to have two different talks with our black offspring: one about why we're here and the other about why it's not always a promised land for people who look like us.

EDWIDGE DANTICAT[2]

This essay meditates about citizenship and the nation-state and the history of enslavement in order to enter the necessary and laden conversation about anti-Blackness and the politics of racialized immigration. My toolkit includes creative writing, historiography, and cultural studies approaches.[3] My goal is to invoke a longer spatial-temporal frame in order to consider enslavement and racialized immigration status *together* as a site of thinking race relationally outside of the interest and ethnic competition structure of post–civil rights electoral politics. Elsewhere, I have described why and how to go beyond analogies, substitutions, parallels, and comparisons and instead foreground immigrant rights advocacy that is multi-issue and that refuses the effacement of Black people.[4] My goal is to amplify the voice of that tendency within the immigration rights movement in the United States that is more keenly aware of its relationship to black survival and to "antislavery thought and action," which is its main armature.[5] We can articulate our serious concern for the plight of undocumented workers, deported students, people who can secure citizenship only by serving in American military misadventures, the millions residing in immigrant detention centers, and immigrant laborers—*and* witness and name the violent murder and criminalization of Black people in every arena of social experience through the enduring nature of slavery, lynching, convict lease conditions, and the sexual violence that links them. Literary scholar Saidiya Hartman's concept of the "after-life of slavery,"[6] and sociologist Dale Tomich's concept of "second slavery,"[7] more fully articulate how racial chattel slavery is central to the contemporary struggle for immigration rights and how and why that struggle goes beyond citizenship. Hartman and Tomich share the conclusion that the post-Emancipation period has far more in common with the period of racial chattel slavery than most of us are willing to acknowledge. It is not accidental that the violence used to mobilize hateful anti-(racialized)-immigrant speeches and attacks reminds us of enslavement—because slavery has an enduring afterlife of gratuitous violence at its heart. Hartman and Tomich offer a systematic way to more fully articulate the relationship between slavery and myths about Emancipation, on the one hand, and immigration from currently and formerly colonized places, on the other. This attention to the enduring nature of "juridical and economic instances of symbolic and total racial violence"[8] "exposes the limits of the liberal conception of racial justice—and its underlying logic of exclusion—whether as formal equality in the juridical (right to vote) or substantive equality in the economic (opportunity to compete) sphere."[9] In other words, as these scholars insist on slavery as paradigmatic to racial capitalism's relations of power, we must expect bondage and its social relations to "crash the narrative of racial progress."[10]

For me it is time for some *sankofa,* an Akan (West African) political ethical imperative to *san* (return), *ko* (go back), and *fa* (fetch/retrieve). Sankofa is a symbol and principle that serves to remind us that the past is a "resource" and not merely a "reference." It is ripe with meaning for Africans. One interpretation, among several, is "Go back to the past and recover it." Yet another one is "Return to the source." Similarly, sankofa may be interpreted as an injunction to "learn from the past" and finally as an order to "never forget the past and path you made when moving ahead. The typical visual form is a bird standing or walking forward while reaching back with its head into its feathers."[11] Such work draws from the rebellious wisdom that Blackness often offers racialized citizenship to correct for amnesias, erasures, and historical disappearances. The return to slavery, then, is not a way to sidestep the conversations of the present but to shore them up.

> I could
> Chart the surnames of Border Patrol officers in the southwestern United
>   States or
> spectacularize the story about Haitian-U.S. immigrants fleeing to Canada to
>   meet
> the demand
> *"Convince me that deporting those bodies resonates affectively with Black
>   people!!!!"*
> But I am
> still mourning . . . you . . . them . . . us
>
> It has been so for a very long time, for generations
> we wished it would be safer for you . . .
> we could not make it any safer for you than it has been for us . . .
> this place is a slaughterhouse . . .
> and we are still its prime cuts . . .
> the machinery being used on you was designed for us and for you . . .
> three or four centuries ago . . .
> we are walking around through your and our nightmare . . .
> and we are waking up to watch it day after day after day after day . . .
> this citizenship is not worth the paper it is written on . . .
> and when you are a member . . . when you finally do belong
> they will eat your children . . .
> they are never full enough of our dreams deferred.
>
> This is the afterlife of slavery that I am talking about, not merely shortened
>   lives and a bitter institutional character of freighted social relations but an
>   affective zone of terror—simply legitimized terror. The cage, the trick bag
>   of the nation-state. It will get worse. It has been worse before.
>
> They are not done with this moment of hanging and humiliating and gender-
>   ing us through the scenes of subjecting you
> We who are the remnant . . .
> the "whatever that survived"[12]
> those screaming "Please, take care of my child!" as we lay dying[13]
> knowing that the child is done for
> your child . . . my child . . . us.
>
>   (Tiffany Willoughby-Herard, "Learning from 'The Whatever That Survived'")

One context for thinking relationally about racialized immigrants and Blackness is that in the twenty-first century, as in the past, families are being separated and kinship is being ruptured by the state in order to protect members of a cherished social and epistemological category that is always in the making: the citizen.[14] Such disruption of kinship does not occur because parents failed some test of citizenship; it occurs because these parents and their issue are the ringer for citizenship itself. Punishing migrant families in this fashion is an available policy and can occur, specifically, because racialized citizenship (qua *whitening*, as it is more candidly named in the rest of the racial democracies in the Americas) is a social world that exists forever beyond reach. From the murder of Vincent Chin, to the rape of Abner Louima, to the murder of Amadou Diallo, to the murder of Eleanor Bumpurs, to the murder of Stephon Taylor, to the murder of Korryn Gaines, to the murder of Dorian Harris, *and* to all the others *deported just this week* in California and all the others whose children will be taken into state custody as if they are parentless this month in California,[15] we are all encouraged to watch these horrors as if they were normal and necessary to protect this racialized category of the social, the citizen. These acts, by representatives of state and society, are always based on presumptions that these practices and their meanings and the lessons that they convey are necessary to defend the legal order, a society built on rules, and those who benefit from membership.

Citizenship as a category has nothing to do with racialized bodies other than as a literal wall of exclusion and a prop to myths of temporary inclusion. Our thinking race relationally compels us to tarry with the myriad people/s murdered by vigilantes, by the state, and by people who curry favor for being respectable fathers and pillars of the community, people who in truth don't meet the dictates of respectability or the dictates of masculinist-worthy memory. This thinking race relationally is not about flattening the particularity and social location of these very distinctive losses but about calling for better thinking about the meaning and purpose of multiple social locations as they are imbricated with dispossession and theft of the body, psyche, and land.

Organizing around race relationally is not only an ethical high-water mark; it is an essential praxis for allowing the tools of global Black resistance to fight the intentional and concerted violence of nation building and its liberal schemas of racialized citizenship rights—for those born in the United States and those born everywhere else. For Black internationalists and Black nationalists, Blackness has been the categorical antagonist to white nationalism and colonized racial-state making in the Americas. This understanding of Blackness sits alongside and in mutual constitution with First Nation status as one of the other categorical antagonists of white nationalism.

"Getting it" that multiple sites could and would index themselves as the categorical antagonist to white nationalism is simply a matter of learning to navigate and build together across positionalities and fields of devaluation.

THE NATION PROTECTS: THE PRIZE POSITION
OF CUSTODIAL MINOR OF THE NATION, A.K.A. CITIZEN

There are a number of things "some people know that others do not," to use Victor Bascara's idiom. Those who are protected by the nation and who are its designated beneficiaries have the luxury of believing that the nation guarantees protection, progress, development, forward thinking, artistic innovation, helpful scientific experimentation, and protective national narratives of belonging. Bascara describes these empty promises of the nation and the citizenship that it can bestow as "innocence, victimization, rescue, and recovery."[16] Regardless of the quality of experiences that nationalism puts people through, membership and belonging in the contemporary racialized and colonial nation-state requires that members tell their narratives about their own experiences through whatever will advance the idea of the nation as a just entity, a good community, and an ethical civilization. But as Bascara demonstrates in a study of cultural representations of refugees—one category of *people who know things that others do not*—refugees have intimate knowledge of mass persecution and of the fact that many people cannot be rescued or recovered, because of the nation-state's structural choices. Or, in Bascara's words, "apprehending of the refugee is apprehending of the anomalies of a multiplicity of structures of social and cultural organization."[17] Civilized societies cross the boundary into mass murder as a fundamental part of their "tortured genesis"[18] and the making of sovereignty but rarely if ever have to admit to those crossings. Refugee status and experience is a potent example for thinking race relationally, because—like the forces that tether enslavement, plantation labor, indenture, and lynching—the social category of the refugee is essential to racial-state making. It seems important to consider these vigorously in order to study race relationally and perhaps to discard the struggle for citizenship. Contrary to the stated goal of both mainstream immigrant rights advocacy and mainstream racial politics advocacy (both of which pivot around ethnic group interest politics), there are a number of histories that bear remembering and wish to be recalled. For many of us citizenship is both an impossible and false ideal for the racialized body.

When we engage in certain forms of ethnic group interest politics, we make ourselves innocent of the multiple and interlocking ways that the nation and its discourses produce "categories of abjection"[19] and then encourage our complicity in what Frank Wilderson has called "borrowed institutionality"[20]—what Audre Lorde, before him, called "using the master's tools."[21] The claims of singularity and incommensurability between racialized immigration and slavery, while absolutely true, do not absolve us from knowing and acting on the things that *some people know*. This requires, as Grace Hong and Roderick Ferguson suggest, "highlighting such differentials [of power, value, and social death] ... to attempt to do the vexed work of forging a coalitional politics through these differences."[22] To this end, in my research and activism for nearly two decades, I have pursued an immigration rights agenda that does not disavow slavery or the abolitionist consciousness that has so relentlessly fought the extension and replication of the human relation that is racialized enslavement. *All* of us can temporarily acquire contingent beneficiary status and be awarded the prize position of custodial minor of the nation, a.k.a. citizen.[23] However, an abolitionist consciousness poses questions about the costs of this award—the ever-elusive citizenship—suggesting that each of us is worth far more. Abolitionist consciousness pleads with us. Abolitionist consciousness warns with a cautionary tale, having taken revolutionary steps to listen to the legions of *people who know*—about the cost of racialized citizenship and what it never pays for or protects us from. Bascara would have us wonder about the things that cannot be translated, about belonging and exclusion and proximity to death.

DISCIPLINING RACIALIZED IMMIGRANTS WITH DESCENDANTS OF SLAVES

For over a century, social workers, criminologists, and academics have shared the common concern of writing believable accounts of why the children of racialized immigrants "do well" in the United States.[24] This cottage industry of explanation, to signal and highlight the success of the racialized immigrant, has at times drawn on the so-called failure of the descendants of enslaved Africans in the Americas. The latter represent the past, an uneconomic system of white minority rule over politically immature and incapable people. The racialized immigrants, however, represent futurity, the tensions and shame of the history of enslavement resolved, and the arrival of a pluralist America. The conditions faced by descendants of enslaved Africans today are used to warn and direct the social life of racialized immigrants. Some of the scholarly discourse on racialized immigrants is steeped in a belief extant in the Americas that the United States is the embodiment of postimperial white nation-building and that it constitutes humanity's global future. In the words of an oft-disproved stereotype, racialized immigrants constitute the welcome model minority, easily assimilable and upwardly mobile.

Yet, Black internationalists, one branch of Black radical political thinkers, have offered deeply ambivalent cautions against American nationality after examining the racial labor hierarchy that structured the post-Emancipation economy of the Americas and the making of national identity in Cuba, the Dominican Republic, and Haiti.[25] Scholars of African descent in race and ethnic politics (a subfield in political science) explain that immigrant status does not insulate "Black Ethnics" (one group of racialized immigrants) from institutionalized, structural intersectional violence.[26] In these accounts the descendants of slaves experience confinement spatially, economically, and socially in ways that presage what is actually available for racialized immigrants.[27]

The "afterlife of slavery" in the Americas, then, reflects the processes by which people are racialized into three categories of exclusion: the slave, the racialized immigrant, and the citizen (the custodial minor of the nation). The slave and the racialized immigrant are hounded to death (in ways that are inextricably bound) to extract status, wealth, inclusion, property, and life years so that they can be accumulated and distributed to the citizen, a white or whitened body with short-term and temporary access to the legal rights and protections against state and vigilante violence and entitlements to deploy those forms of violence as part of a recurring loyalty test to the nation. This is the chief conceit of citizenship. The descendants of the enslaved and the racialized immigrant are urged to participate in the struggle for legal rights to secure the coveted status of citizenship and thereby to inherit the flesh-property of the enslaved. But the slave's mere existence as enslaved person serves as a vital reminder that citizenship is not tethered most fundamentally to noncitizenship (which implies belonging in another political and geographic location) but rather to the body of the slave. The history of racial enslavement in the Americas has resulted in a situation whereby the descendants of enslaved Africans as a group largely occupy the same conditions of life and death as their enslaved African ancestors in the Americas. The immigrant, particularly the phenotypically and spatially racialized immigrant, is not only often mistaken for belonging to the category of the slave because citizenship is constantly questioned,[28] but in the Americas most often the racialized immigrant body conjures *associations with the gratuitous violence and natal alienation of enslavement*—because refugee status, territory status, and federal recognition status exist as legal categories that derive specifically from and in mutual constitution with the history of racial slavery, racial expansionism, and racial colonialism. Across the Americas, these bodies are sites of conquest in which acts of systematic barbarity and inhumanity shore up virtuous white humanity and its freedom projects in nation building.[29] It is important to remember these social forces so that we do not forget the relationship between an American Century built on counterfeit treaties with peoples in the Americas and around the world who had achieved their independence only to find their supposed recognition as political communities on the world stage subjected to contractual forms of indenture and entrenched dispossession.

LEARNING FROM ENSLAVEMENT—TODAY

Racial slavery, racial settler colonialism, and white naturalized citizenship are the foundation stones of the white republican nation and its notions of democracy. Racial justice frameworks raise such basic questions about the nature of citizenship as experienced by the inheritors of struggles for citizenship—struggles that produced racial liberalism and did not uproot anti-Black ideologies as powerful social forces.

Citizenship uses a toxic, heteropatriarchal, filial logic to trap people into believing that they belong to the nation. As Saidiya Hartman writes, we were "sold [as] strangers; those outside the web of kin and clan relationships, nonmembers of the polity, foreigners and barbarians at the outskirts of their country, and lawbreakers expelled from society"[30] in order to help us dispense with the familial ties of nation and the familiar meanings of citizenship belonging. Insisting that it is our experience as strangers that matters more than our belonging, Hartman explains, "the routes traveled by strangers were as close to a *mother country* as I would come."[31] Hartman's claim centers the enduring condition of being eternally without belonging, and it holds that both geographic entities—the one from which one came and the one to which one arrived—are constituted by their silences about their common property in enslaved persons.

Hartman[32] and Tomich[33] help us avoid that old canard of modernity that Black political consciousness—remembrance of enslavement, in this case—is too outmoded for contemporary politics. Their shared remembrance of enslavement (and its afterlife in Hartman's case; and its second life in Tomich's case) compels us to go beyond civil rights politics and law and ethnic interest group electoral competition to remember the Black sources[34] of "anti-slavery thought and action,"[35] the sacrifices made and horrors endured by obscured Black family members in creating "li[ves] of dignified struggle" for everyone else.[36]

Both Hartman and Tomich trouble the notion that the post-Emancipation period justifies thinking about slavery as archaic and backward compared to everything else that emerged after its abolition. The material conditions and social meanings associated with slavery help us understand how it was never an archaic form, nor was it the polar opposite of wage labor but was expanded, intensified, and transformed and "increasingly integrated into industrial production."[37] The post-Emancipation process of reintroducing indentured labor, concretizing contract-based and duty-bound labor, and wage labor is deemed the second slavery because the "first slavery" was a "condition for its reproduction."[38]

To be plain, instead of explaining the racialized immigrants working in fields and in households today, criminalized for simply residing in the United States, as racially stigmatized groups who are "like slaves," we can begin to think of their social status and treatment as expected, necessary evidence of slavery's afterlife. Many things shift when we do this. Hartman's concept means that slavery changes but endures. This is why we see this analogy, this comparison, and this substitution: because slavery and the colonial relationship of power that it provokes are still the defining regime of the world economy—both affective and material.[39]

Hartman and Tomich demonstrate the ways in which we have not passed into a "new" or more "modern" expression of bondage in which the antiquated "old" abolitionist thought and practice is no longer relevant for reckoning with the contemporary expressions of power and violence. Tomich provides a sustained critique of the notion that all forms of governance, moral sensibilities, economic activities, labor relations, and groups of laborers are modern, efficient, progressive, advanced, free, inevitable, and the distinctive polar opposite of everything that obtained under racial chattel slavery. Instead, Tomich examines transitions in the nineteenth century "formation and reformation of slave relations within historical processes of the capitalist world economy,"[40] finding that "slavery is imbricated . . . in capitalist develop-ment."[41] Tomich goes further, suggesting that if one wants to think seriously about slavery and Emancipation, it is more important to examine the role of "abolitionist thought and action" as the singular precursor to Emancipation. While Tomich addresses the "spatial redistribution and quantitative increase in the production of tropical products,"[42] Hartman addresses the social and legal relations of bourgeois individualism, meritocracy, kinship, and con-tracts that governed and organized capital and state. Such contract rights constitute an extension of freedom and create greater burdens of citizenship for the formerly enslaved to watch over their rights with greater vigilance; and they obscure the gratuitous violence, natal alienation, and generalized dishonor (everyday brutality) that continue to constitute the existence of the formerly enslaved after Emancipation. Hartman explores the ways in which the post-Emancipation period intensified the internalization of the rhetoric of responsibility and the regime of obligation by the freed people.

THE BLOOD SPORTS MASQUERADING AS
THE TRUMP PRESIDENCY

On January 12, 2018, and on May 16, 2018, President Donald Trump set the tone, again, for the public debate about restricting the immigration of racial-ized populations. I argue that the first set of comments (that Haiti, El Salvador, and all of Africa are "shithole" countries) and the second (that immigrants are "animals") are related. The comments remind hearers not only of the racial colonial history of the Americas but also of the intersection of race and nation that relied on white immigration, restricted immigration for people of African descent, and adopted a whole host of other policies of racial containment.

Trump's comments demonstrate how racist anti-immigrant discourses articulate with and shore up anti-Black ones: both discourses serve

1. to cause premature death through a "constantly shifting relationality [that produces] a dividing line between valued and devalued, which can cut within, as well as across, racial groupings,"[43]

2. to pry racialized people away from the legal guarantees and formal promises of citizenship (whitened though it may paradigmatically be in the Americas),

3. to exacerbate and conceal the ways that persons who are spatially and ontologically racialized through Blackness, indigeneity, and the borderlands[44] cannot count on legal citizenship to stave off state or vigilante violence, and

4. to erase how prevalent these discourses are across the Americas and globally.

Why refer to these particular countries unless racialized immigrant bodies are imbricated and read through their relationship to the devaluation of Black bodies globally and to specific histories of racial colonial and racial slavery political orders? Trump's words introduced to a new generation how racialized immigration and anti-Black racial subjection have historically been viewed together. Such racist and race-baiting comments as Trump's are embedded in U.S. foreign policy. They shore up racist cultural ideologies about citizenship and belonging, and they are neither surprising nor unusual. Indeed, the shape of our domestic racial hierarchy provides a reliable map to the racial categorizations that shape our foreign policy. When Trump exclaimed, "Why do we need more Haitians? *Take them out*," he was invoking a U.S. history of stoking racist vigilante violence and encouraging xenophobic mayhem and murder that gives expression to and is mutually constituted with quotidian and spectacular gendered anti-Black violence. Trump favors a "merit-based" immigration system that views Haitians, Salvadorans, and everyone in the dozens of countries on the African continent as racially unworthy of becoming U.S. citizens. Trump's racism is lethal, but it is an essential ingredient in the making of the nation-state and its concepts of citizenship. His rhetoric has already produced fatalities and beatings and race riots like the infamous August 13, 2017, white supremacist rally in Charlottesville. The current U.S. president has attempted to goad the society into mass sectional violence every day. His rhetoric takes advantage of instigating distraction, chaos, and trauma to blow up the public-policy-making environment and to toxify the struggle for transformational social justice. The conditions of thought that understand the Black body as unfree are inextricably linked to the construction of the idea of the racialized migrant as an nonperson.[45]

· · ·

Working through slavery as the anchoring form of social explanation for the modern state and its practices and policies is not coming from some thinly veiled attempt to elevate Black people to a higher station in the racial hierarchy. Scholars explain contemporary racial violence through slavery in order to undermine utterly and forever this bankrupt and foolish notion that we have achieved or are on a path toward democracy even as we murder everything and everyone in sight.

We are raising the dead. We witness the present and those who "had the extraordinary will and incredible stamina to keep struggling along a corridor of death"[46] by remembering those who did not survive.[47] This is about a debt all of us owe to those people buried alive; dragged away and marched across the African continent; afraid they would be eaten; buried alive in barracoons, buried alive again in the holds of ships, buried in the sea, made to bear the lived experience of being human property. This is about an unrepayable debt—something that we have been made to understand. Certainly, by now all of us must understand these things since our social order has been predicated on erasing those people, in the past and in the present, who have been made into debt.

This is the scale of analysis within which struggles for citizenship for racialized immigrants must be considered. Achieving citizenship operates through a complex racial triangulation that makes racialized citizens complicit and that provides cover for the white nation's story about its racial liberalism. This belonging and its rituals provide innumerable lessons; those pledges of allegiance to places that specialize in dispossessing the social relationships between parents and children; thus creating the conditions for all forms of social violence to be reduced to incidents, and deepening one's own disconnection to the history of enslavement of the Africans in one's own family, village, town, and nation of belonging. That one desires to become human by escaping the project of citizen making and slave making in whatever borough one is born is easy to empathize with. However, the nation is an extortionist trick bag: the national project itself wields enormous power over people's aspirations, desires to rebel, and erotic compulsions, driving those that are other than what they were designated to be to reside elsewhere so that they might survive—haunted and hunted, yet having some semblance of memory. Citizenship promises that such tensions of history can be escaped. But we never escape. And as long as the world is about the business of making slaves out of Black bodies, our escape into citizenship is contingent on either making determined common cause with the enslaved or with becoming slave catchers and proprietors of the business in enslaving.

ACKNOWLEDGMENTS

Thank you to Alpha Balde, Lisa Beard, Maylei Blackwell, Terrence Calhoun, Michael Hames-Garcia, Angie Hopkins, Daniel Martinez HoSang, Sharon Luk, Michelle McKinley, Ernesto J. Martinez, Jeanne Scheper, Jasmine Syedullah, and the LUNAS Research and Writing Group.

NOTES

1. Edwidge Danticat, "Message to My Daughters," in *The Fire This Time: A New Generation Speaks about Race,* ed. Jesmyn Ward (New York: Scribner, 2016), 210.

2. Danticat, "Message to My Daughters," 212.

3. Ndumiso Dladla, "African Philosophical Hermeneutics: The Critique of Eurocentrism and Ubuntu as a Philopraxis for Liberation," in *Here Is a Table: A Philosophical Essay on the History of Race in South Africa,* rev. ed. (Pretoria, South Africa: Bantu Logic, 2008), 62.

4. Tiffany Willoughby-Herard, "More Expendable Than Slaves? Racial Justice and the After-Life of Slavery," *Politics, Groups, and Identities* 2, no. 3 (2014): 506–21. See also Avery Gordon and Christopher Newfield, eds., *Mapping Multiculturalism* (Minneapolis: University of Minnesota Press, 1997); Frank B. Wilderson III, *Red, White, and Black: Cinema and the Structure of U.S. Antagonisms* (Durham, NC: Duke University Press, 2010); Tryon Woods, "The Fact of Anti-Blackness: Decolonization in Chiapas and the Niger River Delta," *Human Architecture: Journal of the Sociology of Self-Knowledge* 5, no. 3 (2007): 319–30, http://scholarworks .umb.edu/humanarchitecture/vol5/iss3/29.

5. Dale Tomich, "The 'Second Slavery': Bonded Labor and the Transformation of the Nineteenth-Century World," in *Through the Prism of Slavery: Labor, Capital, and World Economy* (Lanham, MD: Rowman and Littlefield, 2003), 56. From political posters that I made and distributed as a member of a queer people of color formation organizing against anti-Black violence and the English-only movement in 1994–95 to singing songs like Susana Baca's "El Mayoral" (The Slave Driver) at mass immigration rights marches and invoking the Fugitive Slave Act in speeches at these same marches, situating the relationship between enslavement and the present has been a long-held preoccupation of remembrance.

6. Saidiya Hartman, *Scenes of Subjection: Terror, Slavery, and Self-Making in Nineteenth Century America* (New York: Oxford University Press, 1997); Saidiya Hartman, *Lose Your Mother: A Journey along the Atlantic Slave Route* (New York: Farrar, Strauss and Giroux, 2008).

7. Tomich, "'Second Slavery,'" 56–71.

8. Denise Da Silva, "Extraordinary Times: A Preface," *Cultural Dynamics* 26, no.1 (2014): 5.

9. Da Silva, "Extraordinary Times," 4.

10. Da Silva, "Extraordinary Times," 5.

11. Kbonsura A. Wilson, "Sankofa, Concept," in *The Encyclopedia of African Religion,* ed. Molefi Kete Asante and Ama Mazama (Thousand Oaks, CA: Sage, 2009), 587.

12. Dladla, "African Philosophical Hermeneutics," 62.

13. Sindiwe Magona, *Chasing after the Tails of My Father's Cattle* (Johannesburg: Seriti sa Sechaba, 2015). In several poignant moments in the text, the novel's protagonist, who dies in childbirth after suffering the loss of nearly a dozen children in their toddler years, makes this exclamation. The last words of the dying mother are "Take care of my child," words that hail a life of pro-feminist choices by the father of the one daughter who survives.

14. I am referencing three senses of ruptured kinship—Christina Sharpe's, Dorothy Roberts's, and that of the Women in Dialogue and Every Mother Is a Working Mother Network. All are useful to sense my meaning here. Christina Sharpe, "Gayl Jones's *Corregidora* and Reading the 'Days That Were Pages of Hysteria,'" in *Monstrous Intimacies: Making Post-slavery Subjects* (Durham, NC: Duke University Press, 2010), 27–66; Dorothy Roberts, *Shattered Bonds: The Color of Child Welfare* (New York: Basic Books, 2002); *DHS: Give Us Back Our Children* (Philadelphia: Every Mother Is a Working Mother Network and Scribe Video Center, 2010), DVD. Sharpe's meaning focuses on dispossession of enslaved Africans being made into property; Roberts's meaning of ruptured kinship talks about public policy organized around natal alienation and trauma through adoption policies. That both scholars and the documentary film echo *criada* in Brazil is haunting and upends notions that gendered racial subjection belongs to particular national systems and their distinctive antipoverty public policy around family dissolution and "child protection." Nick Miroff and Paul Sonne, "Trump Administration Preparing to Shelter Migrant Children on Military Bases," *Washington Post,* May 15, 2018, https://www.washingtonpost.com/world/national-security/trump-administration-preparing-to-shelter-migrant-children-on-military-bases/2018/05/15/f8103356–584e-11e8-b656-a5f8c2a9295d_story.html. After a 2014 Obama administration policy that housed children in Oklahoma and Texas and other states, the Trump administration plans to compel action by migrant parents in detention by taking their children into custody and placing them under the supervision of the same agencies and offices that break the boundaries of Black families by remanding migrant minors to state detention.

15. Jazmine Ulloa, "ICE Is Increasing Presence in California Because of 'Sanctuary State' Law, Says Trump Immigration Chief," *Los Angeles Times,* January 3, 2018, http://www.latimes.com/politics/essential/la-pol-ca-essential-politics-updates-ice-is-increasing-presence-in-california-1514999654-htmlstory.html.

16. Victor Bascara, "'In the Middle': The Miseducation of a Refugee," in *Strange Affinities: The Gender and Sexual Politics of Comparative Racialization,* ed. Grace Kyungwon Hong and Roderick A. Ferguson (Durham, NC: Duke University Press, 2011), 198.

17. Bascara, "'In the Middle,'" 198.

18. Bascara, "'In the Middle,'" 196.

19. Bascara, "'In the Middle,'" 198.

20. Wilderson, *Red, White, and Black*, 30n10.

21. Audre Lorde, "The Master's Tools Will Never Dismantle the Master's House," in *Sister Outsider: Essays and Speeches* (1984; repr., Berkeley, CA: Crossing Press, 2007), 110–14.

22. Grace Kyungwon Hong and Roderick A. Ferguson, introduction to *Strange Affinities: The Gender and Sexual Politics of Comparative Racialization,* ed. Grace Kyungwon Hong and Roderick A. Ferguson (Durham, NC: Duke University Press, 2011), 9.

23. Lauren Berlant's notion of the "innocence/illiteracy" of the "infantile citizen" offers something for reflection here. Lauren Berlant, "The Theory of Infantile Citizenship," *Public Culture* 5, no. 3 (1993): 395–410.

24. Arthur Schlesinger, "E Pluribus Unum?," in *The Disuniting of America: Reflections on a Multicultural Society* (New York: Norton, 1992), 11–13; Percy C. Hintzen and Jean Muteba Rahier, eds., *Problematizing Blackness: Self-Ethnographies by Black Immigrants to the United States* (New York: Routledge, 2003).

25. Brenda Gayle Plummer finds that the immigration path to assimilation is permanently blocked for persons of African descent and that this prods their skepticism of the national project, having compelled them toward internationalist and transnational organizing from the 1700s to the present. Brenda G. Plummer, *Rising Wind: Black Americans and U.S. Foreign Affairs, 1935–1960* (Chapel Hill: University of North Carolina Press, 1996); Gerald Horne, *The Deepest South: The United States, Brazil, and the African Slave Trade* (New York: New York University Press, 2007); Gerald Horne, *White Pacific: US Imperialism and Black Slavery in the South Seas after the Civil War* (Honolulu: University of Hawai'i Press, 2007). Noteworthy is Pedro Noguera's "Anything but Black: Bringing Politics Back to the Study of Race," in *Problematizing Blackness: Self-Ethnographies by Black Immigrants to the United States,* ed. Percy C. Hintzen and Jean Muteba Rahier (New York: Routledge, 2003), 193–200.

26. Sharon D. Wright Austin, *The Caribbeanization of Black Politics: Race, Group Consciousness, and Political Participation in America* (Albany: State University of New York Press, 2018); Sharon D. Wright Austin, ed., "The Caribbeanization of Black Politics," special issue, *National Political Science Review* 19, no. 1 (2018).

27. Near daily accounts show up in local and national news coverage in the United States of Black, Muslim, and Latino people being hounded out of their places of work, leisure; being publicly humiliated, detained by the police, and murdered for golfing, sleeping, buying prom clothes, pushing their babies, barbecuing in public, driving, walking, dancing, sitting in classrooms. There is a linked fate that has been set in motion by the tenor and operations of enslavement.

28. Associated Press, "Border Agent Questions 2 Women for Speaking Spanish," May 22, 2018, http://wjla.com/news/nation-world/border-agent-questions-2-women-for-speaking-spanish-05-21-2018-214258605; Ariel Zilber and Rory Tingle, "REVEALED: Racist Lawyer Who Threatened to Call ICE on Workers

Speaking Spanish in a Manhattan Restaurant Is a Trump Supporter Who Was Filmed Shouting 'You Are Not a Jew' at a Rabbi during a NYC Protest," *Daily Mail,* May 22, 2018, http://www.dailymail.co.uk/news/article-5737433/Racist-lawyer-threatens-call-ICE-workers-speaking-Spanish.html.

29. Marilyn Lake and Henry Reynolds, eds., *Drawing the Global Colour Line: White Men's Countries and the International Challenge of Racial Equality* (Cambridge: Cambridge University Press, 2008); Matthew Frye Jacobson, *Barbarian Virtues: The United States Encounters Foreign Peoples at Home and Abroad, 1876–1917* (New York: Hill and Wang, 2000); Horne, *White Pacific;* Penny Von Eschen, *Race against Empire: Black Americans and Anti-colonialism, 1937–1957,* rev. ed. (Ithaca, NY: Cornell University Press, 1997).

30. Hartman, *Lose Your Mother,* 5.

31. Hartman, *Lose Your Mother,* 9.

32. Hartman, *Scenes of Subjection;* Hartman, *Lose Your Mother.*

33. Tomich, "'Second Slavery.'"

34. Noguera, "Anything but Black."

35. Tomich, "'Second Slavery,'" 56. Thus, Tomich dispenses with the two prominent explanations of the emancipation of enslaved Africans: that slavery was ended by (1) internal contradictions of republican political movements in emergent nations and (2) Great Britain's abolition of the slave trade.

36. Rinku Sen, "Are Immigrants and Refugees People of Color?" *Color Lines: The National Newsmagazine on Race and Politics* 39 (July/August 2007), 3. Marta Cruz-Jansen makes this link more explicit by identifying proverbs and jokes in Spanish that mark how whitening erases African forebears and ancestors as a family "advances." Marta Cruz-Jansen, "Latinegras: Desired Women—Undesirable, Mothers, Sisters, Wives," *Frontiers: A Journal of Women Studies* 22, no. 3 (2001): 168–83.

37. Tomich, "'Second Slavery,'" 63.

38. Tomich, "'Second Slavery,'" 63.

39. Tomich, "'Second Slavery,'" 63.

40. Tomich, "'Second Slavery,'" 57.

41. Tomich, "'Second Slavery,'" 58.

42. Tomich, "'Second Slavery,'" 58.

43. Hong and Ferguson, introduction, 10–11.

44. Maylei Blackwell, "Translenguas: Mapping the Possibilities and Challenges of Transnational Women's Organizing across Geographies of Difference," in *Translocalities/Translocalidades: Feminist Politics of Translation in the Latin/a Americas,* ed. Sonia Alvarez, Claudia de Lima Costa, Veronica Feliu, Rebecca Hester, Norma Klahn, and Millie Thayer (Durham, NC: Duke University Press, 2014), 299–320; Maylei Blackwell, "Geographies of Difference: Mapping Multiple Feminist Insurgencies and Transnational Public Cultures in the Americas" (PhD diss., University of California, Santa Cruz, 2000).

45. Emboldened by his ability to use hate speech in public without sanction or censure, Trump referred to immigrants who fall into the rhetorical arenas where undocumented, deported, and criminal overlap "animals" and offended the larger

community across the hemisphere concerned about the ongoing race-baiting and racism of his immigration policies. Jade Magnus Ogunnaike et al., "'Sh*&hole Countries.' 'Animals.' Trump's Xenophobia Cannot Be the New Normal,'" Color of Change mailing list, March 23, 2018. In yet another polarizing controversy over what Trump actually said, in both instances some attendees deny any vulgarity or inappropriateness. Given Trump's prior racist and misogynist and xenophobic and anti-African comments, as well as the transcripts that have been released, it is rational to conclude that he definitely made such comments. Ali Vitali, Kasie Hunt, and Frank Thorp V, "Trump Referred to Haiti and African Nations as 'Shithole' Countries," NBC News, January 12, 2018, https://www.nbcnews.com/politics /white-house/trump-referred-haiti-african-countries-shithole-nations-n836946; Josh Dawsey, "Trump Derides Protections for Immigrants from 'Shithole' Countries," *Washington Post,* January 12, 2018, https://www.washingtonpost.com /politics/trump-attacks-protections-for-immigrants-from-shithole-countries-in- oval-office-meeting/2018/01/11/bfc0725c-f711-11e7-91af-31ac729add94_story.html.

46. John Annerino, *Dead in Their Tracks: Crossing America's Desert Borderlands in the New Era* (New York: Basic Books, 1999), 103–4.

47. William Andrews and Nellie McKay, eds., *Toni Morrison's "Beloved": A Casebook* (New York: Oxford University Press, 1999); Mae Henderson, "Toni Morrison's *Beloved:* Re-membering the Body as Historical Text," in *Comparative American Identities: Race, Sex, and Nationalities in the Modern Text,* ed. Hortense Spillers (New York: Routledge, 1991), 62–86; Toni Morrison, *Beloved* (New York: Alfred Knopf, 1987); Toni Morrison, "The Site of Memory," in *Inventing the Truth: The Art and Craft of Memoir,* 2nd ed., ed. William Zinsser (Boston: Houghton Mifflin, 1995), 83–102.

PART THREE

———

Historical Frameworks

The essays in this section examine relational formations of race across time, foregrounding the ways that particular historical forces and events contest and transform racial meanings, identities, and power through relational frameworks. The essays in this section disrupt relatively well-known histories of racialized groups by reading them against histories of other racialized groups or of groups operating under a different racial regime: Puerto Rican colonials at an Indian school, for instance, or Japanese American soldiers from Hawai'i stationed in the Jim Crow South in the months after Pearl Harbor. The authors also demonstrate innovative use of archival and primary sources, placing resources dealing with different groups into generative dialogue. In the process, the authors show how adopting a relational approach can quickly and starkly reveal how uneven the process of racial construction can be.

Catherine Ramírez's essay, "Indians and Negroes in Spite of Themselves: Puerto Rican Students at the Carlisle Indian Industrial School," looks at how a relational perspective on race complicates and exposes the limits of the dominant conceptualizations of assimilation. The essay approaches assimilation as a relational process by studying the experiences of Puerto Ricans who attended the Carlisle Indian Industrial School from 1898 to 1918. Drawing from school records, letters, testimonies, and newspaper stories, Ramírez examines the Puerto Rican students' assimilation as colonized and racialized subjects and the ways they contested their induction into a racially stratified society. Their case shows that assimilation is more than the process whereby the boundary between mainstream and margin blurs or disappears; assimilation is also, paradoxically, the process whereby that boundary is reinforced. As Ramírez insightfully asks, "What did these other colonials learn about their place in an expanding empire, a nation of burgeoning immigration, and

163

a hardening racial hierarchy defined increasingly by the so-called vanishing Indian and one-drop rule for African Americans? How did 'our Porto Ricans,' as they were known, fit into or frustrate that hierarchy?" Ramírez shows us that relational racialization can also shed light on Devon Carbado's concept of "racial naturalization": the "social practice wherein all of us are Americanized and made socially intelligible via racial categorization." For Puerto Ricans at the Carlisle school, such "assimilation" and "naturalization" meant being more closely aligned with Native Americans, which meant being incorporated into the lowest rungs of the U.S. racial hierarchy.

While Ramírez's essay complicates traditional models of assimilation by demonstrating what happens when colonial subjects are the subject of such projects in relation to Native Americans, Jeffrey Yamashita's essay, "Becoming 'Hawaiian': A Relational Racialization of Japanese American Soldiers from Hawai'i during World War II in the U.S. South," looks at how U.S. military mobilization in World War II brought multiple racial systems, white supremacy, and settler colonialism in the Jim Crow South into new conversation. The Japanese attack on Pearl Harbor propelled already brewing anti-Japanese racism in Hawai'i and on the West Coast to a more national audience, which later led to the forcible removal and incarceration of all Japanese and Japanese Americans on the West Coast and some in Hawai'i at the same time. African American GIs were being subjected to Jim Crow norms. Yamashita examines the relational racialization among Japanese American soldiers from Hawai'i during their mobilization to and training at Camp Shelby, Mississippi, tracing the interconnections among different nonwhite and Indigenous groups in relation to whiteness and white supremacy. His essay demonstrates how their move to Mississippi allowed Japanese Americans from Hawai'i to become "Hawaiian"—a racialization that was founded on the operations of anti-Japanese racism on the U.S. mainland, haole desires to prove Hawai'i worthy for statehood, and the soldiers' own desire to distance themselves from associations with anti-Black racism. Yamashita demonstrates how American soldiers of Japanese descent used "essentialism as a strategic survival mechanism" that provided them "a shield against anti-Japanese racism on the U.S. mainland and especially the U.S. South."

The next two essays in this section are explicit enjoinders to think about place as a category of analysis when examining overlapping systems of racial ideologies. Perla M. Guerrero's essay, "Vietnamese Refugees and Mexican Immigrants: Southern Regional Racialization in the Late Twentieth Century," examines the experiences of Vietnamese refugees resettled by the federal government in northwest Arkansas in 1975. The settlement of Vietnamese refugees in a southern state added new complexity to the U.S. racial order and its multiple racial projects. Guerrero shows how the prevailing terrain of Black racialization shaped the conditions under which such refugees were incorporated into the polity. In particular, she shows how the anti-Black terror at the turn of the twentieth century led to the near complete expulsion of African Americans from northwest Arkansas, shaping the conditions that faced Asian and Latino/a immigrants decades later. As Guerrero notes, "Studying the region can elucidate how anti-Black racism shapes the lives of refugees and immigrants and reveal the anti-Black structures that continue to exist across the United States."

Raoul Liévanos's essay, "Green, Blue, Yellow, and Red: The Relational Racialization of Space in the Stockton Metropolitan Area," focuses on "the production of space as a racial project in which the making of physical spaces for human habitation and commerce is intricately interconnected with the extension of racial categories to space for the purposes of distributing resources along racial lines." Through a close examination of Stockton, California, across the twentieth century, he examines the housing policies—including loan appraisal systems, redlining, and racial covenants—that over decades hardened local lines of racial segregation. Liévanos's scholarship demonstrates not only that the presence or absence of racialized groups has been central to determining a property's value—determining which areas are "hazardous" and which are safe investments—but also that these estimations have long relied on relational logics and assumptions.

—————

EIGHT

Indians and Negroes in Spite of Themselves

PUERTO RICAN STUDENTS AT THE CARLISLE INDIAN INDUSTRIAL SCHOOL

Catherine S. Ramírez

On September 5, 1899, fifteen-year-old Vicente Figueroa of Guayama, Puerto Rico, enrolled in the Carlisle Indian Industrial School in Carlisle, Pennsylvania. He spent five years at the boarding school for Native Americans, where he, like many of his classmates, learned English and a trade. After leaving the school in 1904, Figueroa remained in Pennsylvania. He worked for several years in Philadelphia, Bethlehem, and Pittsburgh. Then, in 1911, he applied for a position with the Indian Service in Denver. In a letter to Charles Dagenette, supervisor of Indian employment in Denver and a Carlisle alumnus, Carlisle superintendent Moses Friedman identified Figueroa as a machinist and concrete finisher. "He is good at the latter occupation and finds steady work in a good season," Friedman observed. He also noted that Figueroa was "a Porto Rican, mostly Negro." Figueroa did not get the job with the Indian Service but still expressed gratitude to what he and many other former students called "Dear Old Carlisle." "I always speak highly of the school," he wrote in a July 31, 1912, letter to Friedman, "and I thank . . . the school for what I am."[1]

Figueroa was one of about sixty Puerto Rican youths who attended the Carlisle Indian Industrial School from 1898—the year Spain ceded Puerto Rico, along with Cuba and the Philippines, to the United States—to 1918, the year the school closed (see figure 8.1).[2] The pupils ranged in age from eleven to nineteen years.[3] Roughly thirty-eight were male and twenty-one were female.[4] The former learned farming or a trade, while the latter were trained to cook, sew, do laundry, and care for children. Carlisle aimed to produce a particular kind of worker—manual laborers and domestic

FIGURE 8.1. Puerto Rican students at the Carlisle Indian Industrial School, published in *The Red Man and Helper*, July 31, 1903. Reproduced by permission of the Cumberland County Historical Society.

servants—and normative men and women. Above all, it sought to transform Indigenous youth into Americans. So what happened to its Puerto Rican students? In addition to learning English and a trade, what did these other colonials learn about their place in an expanding empire, a nation of burgeoning immigration, and a hardening racial hierarchy defined increasingly by the so-called vanishing Indian and one-drop rule for African Americans? How did "our Porto Ricans," as they were known, fit into or frustrate that hierarchy?[5]

To address these questions, I look to the history of assimilation in the United States. Assimilation is widely seen as an outcome of immigration and as the price or reward of the American dream. Often, assimilation is defined against racialization, the process whereby racial categories are produced and understood as part of a racial hierarchy. Yet what happens when we decouple immigration and assimilation and approach assimilation *as* racialization? Instead of framing assimilation in relation to immigration and against racialization, I look at efforts to "civilize" Native Americans, African Africans, and Puerto Ricans in the wake of the Indian, Civil, and Spanish American Wars, moments when regimes of difference, to use Patrick Wolfe's terms, were being challenged and consolidated in the United States.[6] Then, I examine the case of the Puerto Ricans at Carlisle. Using school records, letters, testimonies, and newspaper stories, I show how these students were incorporated into a stratified society as racialized and colonized subjects and how they resisted that incorporation.

By juxtaposing efforts to civilize Native Americans, Blacks, and Puerto Ricans, I also draw attention to assimilation as a "mutually constitutive process" and "process of categorization"—in other words, as a relational process.[7] Since the 1990s, sociologists have highlighted its relational nature by theorizing what they term "segmented assimilation": "a theoretical framework for understanding the process by which the new second generation—the children of contemporary immigrants—becomes incorporated into the system of stratification in the host society and the different outcomes of this process."[8] But as shown by the experiences of so-called backward races at Carlisle and its predecessor, the Hampton Normal and Agricultural Institute, segmented assimilation predates its emergence as a framework for study; that is, segmented assimilation existed long before scholars came up with a term for it.[9] Nor have the children of immigrants been the only group to undergo segmented assimilation. Indeed, as long as there have been tiered societies, including and especially societies founded on the expropriation of land and labor, social groups have been incorporated unequally into one segment or another. If we approach assimilation as a relational process, one organized around ranking, entering, and being situated in a regime of difference, then we see that assimilation is often one and the same as subordination, marginalization, or even, paradoxically, exclusion (differential inclusion, in other words).[10] By studying the experiences of African Americans, Native Americans, and Puerto Ricans at Carlisle and Hampton in relation to one another, I offer a glimpse of assimilation's prehistory and show that assimilation is more than the process whereby the boundary between mainstream and margin blurs or disappears; it is also the process whereby that boundary is, paradoxically, reinforced.

THE CARLISLE INDIAN INDUSTRIAL SCHOOL AND HAMPTON NORMAL AND AGRICULTURAL INSTITUTE

Established in 1879 at a former garrison, Carlisle was the first federally funded, coeducational, off-reservation boarding school for Native Americans in the United States. Like the Dawes Act of 1887, the school's goal, in the words of founder Richard Henry Pratt, was to civilize, "citizenize," and absorb Indigenous youth by removing them from their homes and families.[11]

Where the Dawes Act sought to break up tribes and to convert Native Americans into individual owners of private property, Carlisle endeavored to tear Indigenous families apart and to turn young Native Americans into docile, low-skilled workers.

In 1904, Pratt resigned as school superintendent, a consequence of having locked horns repeatedly and very publicly with the Bureau of Indian Affairs. Ten years later, Carlisle was under investigation by Congress for mismanagement of funds. There were also complaints about draconian disciplinary measures and lax supervision of students both on and off campus. In 1918 the school closed, and the army repossessed the grounds for use as a hospital for World War I veterans.

In its thirty-nine years, about 8,000 students passed through Carlisle.[12] In addition to learning English, if they did not already know it, and basic academic skills, students received vocational training and participated in the school's "outing program," a hallmark of its curriculum. Dubbed the "supreme Americanizer," the outing program aspired to bring Indigenous youth closer to whites and to augment their vocational training by placing them in white homes and workplaces throughout the northeastern United States.[13]

Another Carlisle hallmark was the before-and-after portrait. Newly arrived students were photographed in a studio or on campus wearing either traditional regalia, such as feather headdresses and breastplates, or the disheveled clothes that they had worn on the journey from their homes to Carlisle. Then they were photographed after they had been given a bath, had their hair shorn, and had been issued the school's stiff, military-like uniform. Both the before and the after photos were staged, and many were sold as cabinet, boudoir, or stereoview cards and postcards. Pratt was keenly aware of their value and used them to convince lawmakers, government bureaucrats, potential donors, and "friends of the Indian" of Carlisle's "civilizing effects."[14] And while he claimed to detest Wild West shows for encouraging Native Americans "to remain Indians,"[15] the more barbaric the Indian appeared in the "before" image, the better. The juxtaposition of the "before" and the "after" photos purported to testify to Carlisle's success in converting what one teacher called "blanket Indians" into "civilized" men and women.[16]

At a time when many Americans subscribed to the maxim that the only good Indian was a dead one, Pratt maintained that the so-called Indian problem could be solved by "killing the Indian and saving the man."[17] Through the end of the nineteenth century, he and other self-professed "friends of the Indian" insisted that Native Americans were malleable enough to be civilized.

"It is a great mistake to think that the Indian is born an inevitable savage," Carlisle's founder contended. "He is born a blank, like all the rest of us. Left in the surroundings of savagery, he grows to possess a savage language, superstition, and life.... Transfer the savage-born infant to the surroundings of civilization and he will grow to possess a civilized language and habit."[18] By the same token, these "friends of the Indian" feared that Native Americans could easily revert to "Indian ways."[19] "To civilize the Indians, get them into civilization," Pratt advised. "To keep them civilized, let them stay."[20]

In 1875, Pratt was presented with the opportunity to get a group of Indians into civilization. After the Red River Wars in Oklahoma and Texas, he was charged with transporting seventy-two captive Kiowa, Comanche, Cheyenne, Arapaho, and Caddo—many of whom were leaders of their respective nations—to Fort Marion in St. Augustine, Florida. Once they arrived at the fortress, Pratt proceeded to turn "his prison into a school for teaching civilization to the Indians."[21] His ability to "tame" Native Americans, some of whom were reputed to be among the most incorrigible of their time, garnered positive attention from philanthropists, clergymen, lawmakers, and scholars.[22] In 1877, after the War Department determined that the Fort Marion prisoners could be released, Pratt arranged to send a group to the Hampton Normal and Agricultural Institute in Hampton, Virginia.

Hampton was established in 1868 "to train selected Negro youths who should go out and teach and lead their people," in the words of its founder, Samuel Chapman Armstrong.[23] Yet from 1877 to 1923, the school also admitted over 1,300 Native American students from sixty-five tribes.[24] During this period, it claimed to be "devoted to the Negro and Indian Races."[25] In fact, Hampton was compensated by the federal government for the Indigenous pupils it received; Black students were expected to "earn ... their own way through school."[26] Its Indian program came to an end after Congress withdrew funding for it.[27] Today, Hampton University is a historically Black university.

Both Armstrong and Pratt were Civil War veterans who reinvented themselves as educators in the wake of the Civil and Indian Wars. Armstrong led colored troops in the Union Army during the former war, while Pratt commanded an African American regiment, the famous Buffalo Soldiers, during the latter. And just as Pratt held that Native Americans could be civilized under the right circumstances, Armstrong maintained that "blacks had emerged from slavery culturally and morally inferior to whites and only under the benevolent tutelage of whites could they hope to make genuine racial progress."[28]

Similarities notwithstanding, there were stark differences between the two men and the institutions they led, in great part because they saw distinct and disparate destinies for their respective students. Where Armstrong understood that African Americans had a clear and fixed place in an increasingly segregated society, Pratt endeavored to uproot Native Americans and to scatter them among whites. Detribalization, acculturation, proselytization, and miscegenation would make Indians disappear; assimilation was tantamount to vanishing. Meanwhile, African Americans would remain a conspicuously separate but putatively equal faction under Jim Crow, a regime that prohibited their "detribalization" and mingling with whites.[29] Armstrong rationalized racial segregation on the grounds that "[b]eing kept out of white men's societies of all kinds create[d] independent, healthy organizations" for the southern Negro. And although he longed to see more of his Black pupils travel to Africa as missionaries, he dismissed the colonization movement—proposals to remove Blacks from the United States—as a "stupid" and "outrageous" pipe dream.[30]

ASSIMILATION AS RACIAL AND CULTURAL RANKING

On April 13, 1878, Pratt arrived at Hampton with sixty-two Native Americans in tow.[31] He had misgivings about educating them in isolation from whites and openly fretted about the school's "remoteness from the observations of our best people."[32] More to the point, he was worried about educating Native Americans alongside African Americans. After only one year at Hampton, he moved what he considered his Indians to Carlisle because, as he put it, he did not want "to further the segregating and reservating process."[33] That Native Americans would be further segregated and "reserved" at an *all*-Indian school was no hindrance to him.

For decades, the "co-education of Negroes and Indians at the Hampton Institute [was] watched with interest," despite measures to keep the two groups of students apart, with separate curricula, classrooms, dormitories, dining halls, and social activities.[34] "[S]ocial intercourse between the races of opposite sexes [was also] limited and guarded. Trouble might come of it," Hampton teacher Helen Ludlow acknowledged, quickly adding, "None ever has."[35] Meanwhile, heterosexual relations between Native Americans and whites ensued, with two of Ludlow's star female Indigenous students marrying white men and two white female teachers marrying Indigenous men.[36]

In the final years of Hampton's Indian program, after congressional funding for Native American students and their number—in particular, the number of Native American males—had dwindled, rumors that "Indian girls flirted so with the colored boys" continued to besiege the school.[37] While "friends of the Indian" worried about and attempted to prevent the union of Native Americans and Blacks, they expected and even welcomed "amalgamation" between Native Americans and whites. As Wolfe has eloquently shown, from the point of view of the colonizer, miscegenation between whites and Indians would hasten the Indigenous people's inevitable extinction and bolster the settler's "rights to the soil."[38] In contrast, the one-drop rule dictated that Black-Indian unions would only produce more blacks or "mongrels."

Still, Pratt and some of his contemporaries saw value in Native Americans' relationship with and to African Americans. Black students at Hampton were not only charged with orienting newly arrived Native Americans; they were upheld as exemplars of assimilation. Not unlike Carlisle's outing program, slavery was deemed a "supreme Americanizer," for it brought Blacks into "close contact . . . with the white's civilization, language, labor, and religion."[39] Pratt saw Blacks' interaction with whites not only as a "tremendous advantage"[40] for the former group, but as "the greatest blessing that ever came to the Negro race."[41] "[B]rought from the Torrid Zone across a great ocean in vast numbers"[42] and "[t]ransferred into . . . new surroundings and experiences," African slaves "became English-speaking and civilized, because forced into association with English-speaking and civilized people; became healthy and multiplied, because they were property; and industrious, because industry, which brings contentment and health, was a necessary quality to increase their value."[43]

By being deracinated and forced into contact with their white masters, African slaves and their New World descendants had lost their "aboriginal habits" and "old languages"[44] and underwent what Pratt termed, quite baldly, "assimilation under duress."[45] They were better off for it, he insisted, and Native Americans would be, too, if he had his way. His contradictory views of the African American as both pariah and model point to assimilation's contradictions and underscore its violence as a process that can involve not only displacement and the eradication of culture and language, but an enforced jockeying among groups as they scramble to get close to the powerful and to distance themselves from the less powerful or powerless. In other words, assimilation is a process of what Aihwa Ong terms "racial and cultural ranking."[46] To bring that ranking into relief, let us turn to the Puerto Rican students at the Carlisle Indian Industrial School.

INDIOS PUERTORRIQUEÑOS

Carlisle's first Puerto Rican student, Juan Santano, enrolled on November 23, 1898, six months after the U.S. Navy invaded San Juan. He remained a student at the Indian school until April 24, 1904.[47] According to Pratt, "soldiers returning from serving in that island" brought the boy, who was around sixteen years old and spoke no English, to the mainland.[48] Nearly sixty Puerto Ricans followed, and the majority arrived from 1900 to 1910.[49]

The United States wasted little time in attempting to Americanize the island's inhabitants, strategically setting its sights on children. As early as 1898, a U.S.-style public school system was already in place in Puerto Rico. A normal school, modeled after normal schools for Indians and Blacks in the United States, followed in 1900, and the University of Puerto Rico was founded in 1903. At all levels of education, English was the primary language of instruction, a policy that would last until the 1940s. In addition, from 1898 to 1903, Congress set aside money for scholarships that would bring Puerto Rican youths to the mainland for study. Carlisle was one of several educational institutions to tap that scholarship fund.[50] Puerto Ricans, particularly Afro–Puerto Ricans, also enrolled at Hampton and the Tuskegee Institute, which was founded by Hampton alumnus Booker T. Washington.[51]

Like Pratt and Armstrong, John Eaton, Puerto Rico's first education minister, had served in the Union Army during the Civil War, in which he oversaw the establishment of schools for newly freed slaves. As U.S. commissioner of education from 1870 to 1886, he visited the Carlisle Indian Industrial School many times.[52] His successor in Puerto Rico, Martin Grove Brumbaugh, targeted the children of elite families—"lo mejorcito que tiene Puerto Rico," in the words of one alumna—for enrollment at Carlisle, much in the same way that Pratt worked to enroll the children of tribal leaders at his school.[53] Their privileged status notwithstanding, the Puerto Ricans who landed at Carlisle would find themselves in a bedeviling racial hierarchy, one in which they were rendered "Indians" and "Negroes."

For evidence of enunciations of this racial hierarchy, we may look to Carlisle's long, albeit incomplete, paper trail. To obtain federal funds, school documents often required students to avow their "Indianness" and to state their tribal affiliation. Many of the Puerto Ricans' forms are marked with cross-outs and added text. For example, in the application for enrollment for Emilio de Arce Pagán, an eighteen-year-old who arrived at Carlisle on February 7, 1911, "Indian" is crossed out and replaced with "Porto Rican."[54] Likewise, "Tribe" is crossed out on José Gonzalo's July 23, 1912, application for enrollment and replaced with "Spain," while "Spaniard" and "Porto Rican" substitute for "Indian."[55] Vicente Figueroa and Delores Nieves were identified in school records as "Negroes." Like many of their compatriots, however, Nieves wrote "Porto-Rican" after "Tribe" on a postcard the school sent to check up on former students,[56] and Figueroa self-identified on forms as "Porto Rican" and "Spanish."[57] José Prado plainly stated, "I am not an Indian," on a May 5, 1915, form.[58] And in a January 20, 1914, letter to the school's superintendent, former student Adela Barrelli noted, "I always like to hear from [the] school although I am not an Indian."[59] These cross-outs, added text, and explanations point to the expanding empire's effort to incorporate its newly conquered subjects in an intelligible way (see figure 8.2), as well as to Puerto Ricans' refusal to be classified as Indian, an inferior racial category throughout Latin America.

A number of the Puerto Ricans who attended Carlisle were dismayed, if not horrified, to find themselves grouped with and as Indians. Some reiterated racist stereotypes about Native Americans in their recollections about the school. In a June 16, 1911, letter to Superintendent Friedman, Providencia Martínez of Ponce, Puerto Rico, reported that she was shocked to encounter Native Americans when she arrived at Carlisle on November 8, 1901. "Really, we did not know that the school was a regular school for Indians when we went there," she recalled. "We thought that there were [A]mericans[,] as well as [P]orto [R]icans [there]." In the three years she spent at Carlisle, she "lernt [sic] to like the Indians very much. That is some of the refine one [sic]. They were very nice to the [P]orto [R]ican[s,] although at first they hated us." Martinez's father was less sanguine about his daughter's stint at the Indian school. "[H]e used to cry thinking that that place was not a place where we could be happy," she told Friedman. "You can imagine why he thought so. Down here we do not know anything about good [I]ndians but of those you read in books that are regular animals."[60]

Angela Rivera Tudó, Martinez's classmate, arrived at Carlisle in November 1901 harboring many of the same racist suspicions about Native Americans. In an article that appeared in *La Correspondencia de Puerto Rico* on January 3, 1931, she remembered her first night at the boarding school as "una pesa-

FIGURE 8.2. Emanuel Ruiz Rexach and another student published in *The Red Man and Helper,* April 17, 1903, with the caption "Indian and Puerto Rican studying together at Carlisle Indian School." Reproduced by permission of the Cumberland County Historical Society.

dilla" (a nightmare). She was so scared that her Native American roommates would scalp her that she clutched her head through the night to ensure that it remained intact ("Me agarraba la cabeza para ver si todavía estaba en su puesto"). Where some former students, like Figueroa, expressed fondness for "Dear Old Carlisle," Tudó charged that the school had abused Puerto Ricans by equating them with "savages" ("poniéndonos al nivel de unos salvajes"). She was glad she learned English while living on the mainland and even went on to pen *Idioms and Other Expressions in English and Spanish.*[61] Thirty years later, however, she was still smarting for having been reduced to an "indio puertorriqueño" by the island's new, patently ignorant masters. "Nos tomó por Indios puesto que Puerto Rico es parte del grupo de islas los americanos llaman West Indies" (They mistook us for Indians simply because Puerto Rico is part of the West Indies), she bemoaned.[62] "To ... remember those 'good' times" at Carlisle, she noted with more than a hint of sarcasm, she invited her former classmates, fellow "'Indios' Puertorriqueños," to a reunion to be held at her house in San Juan on January 5, 1931.[63]

The following year, Juan José Osuna published "An Indian in Spite of Myself," an autobiographical essay about his experience at Carlisle. In 1901, at the age of fifteen, he left his widowed mother and eight siblings in Caguas and set out with a group of Puerto Rican youths for "that half-mythical land of promise, the United States of America ... to study, master a profession, and return to serve our native land." The apprentice bookkeeper and future dean of the College of Education at the University of Puerto Rico aspired to be a lawyer and believed he was heading to a school that would set him on the appropriate path. He was stunned by what and whom he encountered when he arrived at Carlisle:

> We looked at the windows of the buildings, and very peculiar-looking faces peered out at us. We had never seen such people before. The buildings seemed full of them. Behold, we had arrived at the Carlisle Indian School! The United States of America, our new rulers, thought that the people of Puerto Rico were Indians; hence they should be sent to an Indian school, and Carlisle happened to be the nearest. Our lives as Indians began May 2nd, 1901, at six o'clock in the morning.[64]

Reminiscent of Frantz Fanon's celebrated essay, "The Fact of Blackness," "An Indian in Spite of Myself" points to a process of racialization, or, more precisely, to what Devon Carbado has termed "racial naturalization": the "social practice wherein all of us are Americanized and made socially intelligible via racial categorization."[65] Whereas the Martinican Fanon became a "Negro," a fabrication of a white supremacist empire, when he arrived in France, Osuna became an "Indian," a fabrication of yet another white supremacist empire, when he arrived at Carlisle. Meanwhile, his compatriots, Figueroa and Nieves, became (or perhaps remained) "Negroes," a subordinate category traversing multiple imperial racial hierarchies, French, Spanish, and U.S. alike, despite their self-identification as Puerto Rican and/or Spanish. Whether classified as "Negro" or "Indian," the Puerto Rican youths who landed at Carlisle found themselves "objects in the midst of other objects," as Fanon writes.[66]

As future laborers, Carlisle's Puerto Rican students were inducted into a regime of difference that was not only raced but also classed, as evinced by the work they were required and trained to do. "All the large boys had to choose a trade, while we smaller ones were assigned all sorts of duties from house-cleaning to serving as orderly to General Pratts [sic]," Osuna recounted.[67] One of his first tasks after arriving at Carlisle was to weed a large onion field. "We were strung out in a long line with taskmaster Bennett, the farmer, keeping the line of progress as straight as he could by the aid of a whip," he recalled. "[T]his type of education was not exactly in keeping with my preconceived ideas of the 'land of promise.'"[68] Some students took umbrage at having to do manual and domestic labor, perhaps because they hailed from well-to-do families and were unaccustomed to such work. For instance, José Prado grumbled that he should not have to do kitchen work since his father was paying his tuition. His parents also sent the school extra money for his violin lessons.[69] The students' complaints reached Luis Muñoz Rivera, editor of the *Puerto Rico Herald,* who took it upon himself to visit Carlisle in August 1901. His report, titled "Una visita a Indian School," concluded that Carlisle was a first-rate school for vocational training, but no place for "la abstracción mental de estudios" (academics, in other words).[70]

Coincidentally, Puerto Ricans arrived at Carlisle at a moment when questions were being raised about the Dawes Act and the "Indian question" was being revised. Whereas policy makers and "friends of the Indian," like Pratt, had maintained through the nineteenth century that Native Americans could and would be absorbed into the mainstream, by the turn of the century, a growing number of government bureaucrats had concluded that Native Americans "were destined to live on the fringes of civilization."[71] For example, Francis Leupp, commissioner of Indian Affairs from 1904 to 1909, recommended in his first *Annual Report* that the assimilation program lower its sights from transforming Native Americans to merely improving them, for, as he put it, the Indian would "always remain an Indian."[72] Meanwhile, Estelle Reel, superintendent of Indian schools from 1898 to 1910, revamped the Indian Office's curriculum so that it emphasized basic manual and domestic labor, like fixing tools and doing light chores.[73] Likewise, the Hampton publication, *Southern Workman,* dismissed efforts to educate Native Americans among whites at institutions like Harvard, Dartmouth, and William and Mary as "a dismal failure" and lamented the return of one "Indian girl" to her "rude Indian home with a knowledge of French and music but without any instruction in cooking, sewing, or the care of the home."[74] Expectations of Indigenous people as simple manual and domestic workers may have been deemed practical to some. Yet those expectations not only reflected ideas about the limited and subordinate role Native Americans should play in society; they also produced that very role. By the start of the twentieth century, "[a]ssimilation was no longer an optimistic enterprise born of idealism or faith in universal human progress," Frederick Hoxie has noted. "The term now referred to the process by which 'primitive' people were brought into regular contact with an 'advanced' society."[75]

In keeping with contemporary policies regarding Native American education and assimilation, Osuna was issued his "working outfit" on his second day at Carlisle: "overalls, checkered shirt . . . and heavy shoes."[76] In 1902, he was sent to work on the farm of Dr. J. P. Welsh in Orangeville, Pennsylvania, as part of the school's outing program. Welsh was the principal of the Bloomsburg State Normal School in nearby Bloomsburg, Pennsylvania. Instead of returning to Carlisle, Osuna remained with his employer and attended school in Orangeville. Then he enrolled at the Bloomsburg State Normal School. "I did not want to return to Carlisle," Osuna admitted. "Frankly, I did not like the place. I never thought it was the school for me. I was not an Indian; I was a Puerto Rican of Spanish descent."[77] Despite being away from Carlisle for three years, he was invited to participate in the school's commencement ceremony and was issued a diploma in 1905. Of the roughly sixty Puerto Ricans who attended Carlisle, he and Tudó were two of only seven to graduate.[78] "I am an alumnus of the Carlisle Indian Industrial School," Osuna reminded his reader, and perhaps himself, at the end of his essay. "I am an Indian in spite of myself."[79]

Just as Carlisle helped foster a sense of pan-Indianism among some of its Native American pupils, it reinforced its Puerto Rican students' Puerto Ricanness.[80] It prompted more than a few to disavow Puerto Rico's own Indigenous past and present, as evinced by some students' assertions that they had never seen Indigenous people before arriving at Carlisle, that they were lumped with Native Americans because of Yankee ignorance and/or a geographical error, or that they simply were not Indians. As the students and their guardians reiterated, the students were Puerto Ricans "of Spanish descent," as opposed to Puerto Ricans of Taino, African, or mixed origin. Ultimately, Carlisle's Puerto Ricans made a familiar assimilationist move, one taken by more than a handful of other groups in the United States, from the Irish in the nineteenth century to Mexican Americans in the twentieth and twenty-first: they asserted their claim to whiteness.

THE PARADOX OF ASSIMILATION

For Pratt, civilization was not only a way of being or a condition, but a place. To learn how to be civilized, Native Americans needed to be brought to civilization, whether they wanted to or not. To remain civilized, they needed to stay in civilization. Similarly, Armstrong reminded his contemporaries who concocted plans to rid the United States of Black people by shipping them overseas that the "Afro-American is here to stay."[81] Yet the place—physical and otherwise—of African Americans and Native Americans in society following the Civil and Indian Wars would not be the same as that of white Americans. Jim Crow mandated that Blacks be excluded from the mainstream (white society, in other words). In contrast, Native Americans were to be absorbed and disappeared by that mainstream. Meanwhile, Puerto Ricans' puzzling status as outsiders on the inside would be articulated via the infamous and inherently contradictory statement that the island was "foreign to the United States in a domestic sense."[82] Differences notwithstanding, these seemingly different responses to the so-called Negro and Indian problems and the debate over the status of Puerto Rico in the expanding empire brought into relief the perceived inferiority of racialized and colonized peoples. Above all, they shed light on assimilation as a process that is often violent and unequal and always relational.

ACKNOWLEDGMENTS

I am grateful to Ramón Gutiérrez, Daniel Martinez HoSang, Natalia Molina, and the other participants in the 2016 "Studying Race Relationally" workshop at the University of Chicago for their feedback and support. I also thank the University of California Institute for Mexico and the United States and the Committee on Research at the University of California, Santa Cruz, for underwriting my research. Special thanks to Kirsten Silva Gruesz and Amy Lonetree for reading early drafts of this essay. All errors and oversights are solely mine.

NOTES

1. Group 75, box 29, folder 1374, Records of the Carlisle Indian Industrial School, National Archives and Records Administration, Washington, DC (hereafter cited as RCIIS).

2. The precise number of Puerto Rican students who passed through Carlisle is not entirely clear. Genevieve Bell tallies 59–60; Pablo Navarro-Rivera, 60; and Barbara Landis, 62. Genevieve Bell, "Telling Stories out of School: Remembering

the Carlisle Indian Industrial School, 1879–1918" (PhD diss., Stanford University, 1998), vii, 290, 369, 397; Pablo Navarro-Rivera, "Acculturation under Duress: The Puerto Rican Experience at the Carlisle Indian Industrial School, 1898–1918," *Centro Journal* 18, no. 1 (2006): 239; Pablo Navarro-Rivera, "The Imperial Enterprise and Educational Policies in Colonial Puerto Rico," in *Colonial Crucible: Empire in the Making of the Modern American State,* ed. Alfred W. McCoy and Francisco A. Scarano (Madison: University of Wisconsin Press, 2009), 163–74; Barbara Landis, "Carlisle Indian Industrial School (1879–1918), Tribal Enrollment Tally," accessed August 10, 2018, https://home.epix.net/~landis/tally.html. Records for 50 Puerto Rican students are available via the Carlisle Indian Digital Resource Center, accessed June 30, 2016, http://carlisleindian.dickinson.edu/.

3. Navarro-Rivera, "Acculturation under Duress," 238.

4. Bell, "Telling Stories out of School," 397.

5. "Our Porto Ricans" is from the Carlisle student newspaper, *The Arrow* 1, no. 1 (August 25, 1904): 3, series III, box 20, folder 771, Richard Henry Pratt Papers (WA MSS S-1174), Beinecke Rare Book and Manuscript Library, Yale University Library, New Haven, CT (hereafter cited as Pratt Papers).

6. Patrick Wolfe, "Land, Labor, and Difference: Elementary Structures of Race," *American Historical Review* 106, no. 3 (2001): 866–905.

7. I take my understanding of the relational and comparative from Natalia Molina, "Examining Chicana/o History through a Relational Lens," *Pacific Historical Review* 82, no. 4 (2013): 520–41; and Ania Loomba, "Race and the Possibilities of Comparative Critique," *New Literary History* 40, no. 3 (2009): 501–22.

8. Min Zhou, "Segmented Assimilation: Issues, Controversies, and Recent Research on the New Second Generation," *International Migration Review* 31, no. 4 (1997): 975.

9. "Backward races" is from chap. 1 of Robert Francis Engs, *Educating the Disenfranchised and Disinherited: Samuel Chapman Armstrong and Hampton Institute, 1839–1893* (Knoxville: University of Tennessee Press, 1999).

10. Sandro Mezzadra et al., "Differential Inclusion/Exclusion," in "New Keywords: Migration and Borders," ed. Nicholas De Genova, Sandro Mezzadra, and John Pickles, special issue, *Cultural Studies* 29, no. 1 (2015): 25–26. See also Lisa Marie Cacho's concept of "differential devaluation" in *Social Death: Racialized Rightlessness and the Criminalization of the Unprotected* (New York: New York University Press, 2012), 18.

11. Series III, box 19, folder 659, Pratt Papers. For the full text of the Dawes Act (also known as the General Allotment Act), see "An Act to Provide for the Allotment of Lands in Severalty to Indians on the Various Reservations, and to Extend the Protection of the Laws of the United States and the Territories over the Indians, and for Other Purposes," accessed August 10, 2018, http://avalon.law.yale.edu/19th_century/dawes.asp.

12. There were 8,000 to 8,500 students from seventy-five nations who attended Carlisle, according to Bell, "Telling Stories out of School," vi; and the dust jacket of

Linda F. Witmer, *The Indian Industrial School, Carlisle, Pennsylvania, 1879–1918* (Carlisle, PA: Cumberland County Historical Society, 1993).

13. Witmer, *Indian Industrial School*, 35.

14. Ibid., 114.

15. Series III, box 19, folder 659, Pratt Papers.

16. Helen Ludlow, *Ten Years' Work for Indians at the Hampton Normal and Agricultural Institute at Hampton, Virginia, 1878–1888* (Hampton, VA: Hampton Normal and Agricultural Institute, 1888), 45. For an astute analysis of Carlisle's before-and-after portraits of Native American pupils, see Hayes Peter Mauro, *The Art of Americanization at the Carlisle Indian School* (Albuquerque: University of New Mexico Press, 2011).

17. Richard Henry Pratt, "The Advantages of Mingling Indians with Whites," in *Americanizing the American Indians: Writings by the "Friends of the Indian," 1880–1900*, ed. Francis Paul Prucha (Cambridge, MA: Harvard University Press, 1973), 261. A version of this text may also be found in series III, box 19, folder 653, Pratt Papers.

18. Pratt, "Advantages of Mingling Indians with Whites," 268.

19. Ludlow, *Ten Years' Work*, 44.

20. Series III, box 19, folder 659, Pratt Papers.

21. David Wallace Adams, *Education for Extinction: American Indians and the Boarding School Experience, 1875–1928* (Lawrence: University of Kansas Press, 1995), 39.

22. Ibid., 45.

23. Quoted in Edith Armstrong Talbot, *Samuel Chapman Armstrong: A Biographical Study* (New York: Negro Universities Press, 1969), 157.

24. Jeanne Zeidler, foreword to *To Lead and to Serve: American Indian Education at Hampton Institute, 1878–1923*, ed. Mary Lou Hultgren and Paulette Fairbanks Molin (Virginia Beach: Virginia Foundation for the Humanities and Public Policy, 1989), 6.

25. Ludlow, *Ten Years' Work*, iv–v.

26. "Co-education of Races," *Southern Workman* 28, no. 1 (January 1899): 2, Publications Collection, Hampton University Archives.

27. Hampton received $167 per Native American student per year from the federal government when it began its Indian program, according to Engs, *Educating the Disenfranchised*, 118. See also Donald F. Lindsey, *Indians at Hampton Institute, 1877–1923* (Urbana: University of Illinois Press, 1995), 247–71.

28. Adams, *Education for Extinction*, 45.

29. Jim Crow was the de jure and de facto system of racial segregation in the United States from the late nineteenth century until 1965, when the Voting Rights Act ended legally sanctioned state barriers to voting in federal, state, and local elections.

30. Series I, box 1, folder 36, Samuel Chapman Armstrong Collection, Sawyer Library, Williams College, Williamstown, MA (hereafter cited as Armstrong Collection).

31. Adams, *Education for Extinction*, 46.

32. Series III, box 20, folder 696, Pratt Papers.

33. Ibid.

34. "Co-education of Races," 2.

35. Ludlow, *Ten Years' Work*, 14.

36. Helen W. Ludlow, "Hampton's Indian Students at Home," in *Hampton Institute, 1868 to 1885: Its Work for Two Races*, ed. M. F. Armstrong, Helen W. Ludlow, and Elaine Goodale (Hampton, VA: Normal School Press Print, 1885), 15–19.

37. This quote is from Hampton teacher Caroline Andrus's September 6, 1923, letter to former student Addie Stevens Bouchier, as quoted in Lindsey, *Indians at Hampton Institute*, 261.

38. Wolfe, "Land, Labor, and Difference," 884. As Wolfe explains, "Territorial expropriation was foundational to the colonial formations into which Europeans incorporated" Native Americans, while "blacks' relationship with their colonizers—from the colonizers' point of view at least—centered on labor. In this light, the varying miscegenation policies make immediate sense, since assimilation reduces an indigenous population with rival claims to the land, while an exclusive strategy enlarges an enslaved labor force." Ibid., 867.

39. "Co-education of Races," 2.

40. Series III, box 19, folder 669, Pratt Papers.

41. Pratt, "Advantages of Mingling Indians with Whites," 263.

42. Series III, box 19, folder 669, Pratt Papers.

43. Pratt, "Advantages of Mingling Indians with Whites," 263.

44. Series III, box 19, folder 669, Pratt Papers.

45. Quoted in Lindsey, *Indians at Hampton Institute*, 25.

46. Aihwa Ong, "Cultural Citizenship as Subject-Making: Immigrants Negotiate Racial and Cultural Boundaries in the United States," *Current Anthropology* 37, no. 5 (1996): 740. See also David R. Roediger, *The Wages of Whiteness: Race and the Making of the American Working Class* (New York: Verso, 1999).

47. Juan Santano Student File, Carlisle Indian Digital Resource Center, accessed November 17, 2015, http://carlisleindian.dickinson.edu/student_files/juan-santano-student-file.

48. Richard Henry Pratt to Dr. M. G. Brumbaugh, October 8, 1900, group 75, box 1, folder 1323, RCIIS. See also Navarro-Rivera, "Acculturation under Duress," 238.

49. Bell, "Telling Stories out of School," 369.

50. Navarro-Rivera, "Imperial Enterprise and Educational Policies," 164–69. See also Navarro-Rivera, "Acculturation under Duress"; Sonia Migdalia Rosa, "Puerto Ricans at Carlisle Indian School," in *The Praeger Handbook of Latino Education in the U.S.*, vol. 2, ed. Lourdes Díaz Soto (Westport, CT: Praeger, 2007), 387–88. Congress ended funding for Puerto Ricans to attend Carlisle in 1903; Frederick Hoxie, *A Final Promise: The Campaign to Assimilate the Indians, 1880–1920* (Lincoln: University of Nebraska Press, 1984), 192.

51. Navarro-Rivera, "The Imperial Enterprise and Educational Policies in Colonial Puerto Rico," 164–69. On Cubans at Tuskegee, see Frank Andre Guridy, *Forging Diaspora: Afro-Cubans and African Americans in a World of Empire and Jim Crow* (Chapel Hill: University of North Carolina Press, 2010), especially chap. 1.

52. Rosa, "Puerto Ricans at Carlisle Indian School," 388.

53. Angela Rivera Tudó, "Los 'Indios' de Puerto Rico," *La Correspondencia de Puerto Rico,* January 3, 1931, 4. Regarding the elite status of many of Carlisle's Puerto Rican students, see Rosa, "Puerto Ricans at Carlisle Indian School."

54. Emilio de Arce Pagán Student File, Carlisle Indian Digital Resource Center, accessed November 17, 2015, http://carlisleindian.dickinson.edu/student_files/emilio-de-arce-pagan-student-file.

55. Group 75, box 113, folder 4676, RCIIS.

56. Delores Nieves Student File, Carlisle Indian Digital Resource Center, accessed December 16, 2015, http://carlisleindian.dickinson.edu/student_files/delores-nieves-student-file.

57. Group 75, box 29, folder 1374, RCIIS.

58. Group 75, box 124, folder 4962, RCIIS.

59. Adela Barrelli Student File, Carlisle Indian Digital Resource Center, accessed December 15, 2015, http://carlisleindian.dickinson.edu/student_files/adela-barrelli-student-file.

60. Providencia Martinez Student File, Carlisle Indian Digital Resource Center, accessed November 17, 2015, http://carlisleindian.dickinson.edu/student_files/providencia-martinez-student-file.

61. Angela Rivera de Tudó, *Idioms and Other Expressions in English and Spanish, and Their Use with a University Supplement, and about 500 Proverbs in English and Spanish, and a List of Homophonous Words* (San Juan, PR: Casa Baldrich, 1940).

62. Tudó, "Los 'Indios' de Puerto Rico," 4.

63. Ibid.

64. Juan José Osuna, "An Indian in Spite of Myself," *Summer School Review* 10, no. 5 (1932): 2.

65. Devon W. Carbado, "Racial Naturalization," *American Quarterly* 57, no. 3 (2005): 633.

66. Frantz Fanon, "The Fact of Blackness," in *Black Skin, White Masks,* trans. Charles Lam Markmann (New York: Grove Press, 1967), 109.

67. Osuna, "An Indian in Spite of Myself," 3.

68. Ibid.

69. Regarding Prado's complaint about having to work in a kitchen, see the January 3, 1917, letter from Father Feeser of St. Patrick's Rectory in Carlisle, Pennsylvania, in Group 75, box 124, folder 4962, RCIIS.

70. Luis Muñoz Rivera, "Una visita a Indian School," *Puerto Rico Herald* 1, no. 10 (September 14, 1901).

71. Hoxie, *A Final Promise,* 96.

72. Ibid., 163, 199.

73. Ibid., 196. See also K. Tsianina Lomawaima and T. Tsianina Lomawaima, "Estelle Reel, Superintendent of Indian Schools, 1898–1910: Politics, Curriculum, and Land," *Journal of American Indian Education* 35, no. 3 (1996): 5–31.

74. "Co-education of Races," 3.

75. Hoxie, *A Final Promise,* 187.

76. Osuna, "An Indian in Spite of Myself," 3.

77. Ibid., 4.

78. Navarro-Rivera, "Acculturation under Duress," 243. Bell estimates that of the some 8,500 students who attended Carlisle, only 600 graduated; Bell, "Telling Stories out of School," vii.

79. Osuna, "An Indian in Spite of Myself," 4.

80. On Carlisle's role as a wellspring for what would come to be known as pan-Indianism, see Hazel W. Hertzberg, *The Search for an American Indian Identity: Modern Pan-Indian Movements* (Syracuse, NY: Syracuse University Press, 1971).

81. Series I, box 1, folder 36, Armstrong Collection.

82. "Foreign to the United States in a domestic sense" is from *Downes v. Bidwell,* the 1901 case in which the U.S. Supreme Court ruled on the status of Puerto Rico, Guam, and the Philippines as "'unincorporated territories,' belonging to—but not part of—the United States." Christina Duffy Burnett and Burke Marshall, "Between the Foreign and the Domestic: The Doctrine of Territorial Incorporation, Invented and Reinvented," in *Foreign in a Domestic Sense: Puerto Rico, American Expansion, and the Constitution,* ed. Christina Duffy Burnett and Burke Marshall (Durham, NC: Duke University Press, 2001), 1.

NINE

Becoming "Hawaiian"

A RELATIONAL RACIALIZATION
OF JAPANESE AMERICAN SOLDIERS FROM HAWAI'I
DURING WORLD WAR II IN THE U.S. SOUTH

Jeffrey T. Yamashita

While recounting his experiences participating in the 100th/442nd Regimental Combat Team (RCT), the famous segregated Japanese American military unit that fought in the European campaign during World War II, Senator Daniel Inouye (D-HI) described the divisions between the Japanese American soldiers from Hawai'i and those from the U.S. mainland. He did so in terms of differences between *buddhaheads* (Japanese Americans from Hawai'i) and *kotonks* (Japanese Americans from the U.S. mainland, primarily the West Coast). The nickname *buddhahead* was a play on the word *buta*, Japanese for "pig," and *kotonk* referred to the sound of one's head hitting the ground in a fight. While there were some cultural differences between the groups, both *buddhaheads* and *kotonks* were second-generation Japanese Americans, or Nisei.[1] However, media coverage identified the *buddhahead* soldiers from Hawai'i as Americans of Japanese ancestry (AJA) and labeled the *kotonk* soldiers as Nisei. Historians such as Robert Asahina, Lyn Crost, and Bill Yenne have illustrated the tensions, fights, and misunderstandings that erupted between these two groups of men during basic training at Camp Shelby, Mississippi. On the other hand, Inouye's rendition of the historical episode hinged on a crystallization of an imagined military fraternity and community that spanned thousands of miles from Honolulu to the incarceration camps in Arkansas.[2]

According to Inouye, the turning point that brought the two groups of men together occurred when some of the AJA soldiers stationed at Camp Shelby were invited to attend a social at the Rohwer incarceration camp in Arkansas. When the men initially saw the barbed wires and desolate-looking barracks at Rohwer, Inouye recalled, everyone was silent. At that moment, according to Inouye, the AJA soldiers began to better understand and empathize with the psychological, emotional, and physical losses experienced by the Nisei soldiers and their families. Inouye declared that the significance of the moment solidified the bonds between the two groups and gave them a renewed desire to demonstrate Japanese American military heroism and patriotism, not only for their communities in Hawai'i and the U.S. mainland but also for the larger Japanese American Community.[3] This romantic narrative of a shared relationship between the communities in Hawai'i and the U.S. mainland did not begin or end with the men of the 100th/442nd RCT during basic training at Camp Shelby; it merely papered over the blurred lines of the Japanese America Community between Hawai'i and the U.S. mainland with a grand narrative of Japanese American military heroism and participation.[4] For the AJA soldiers, however, the journey from Hawai'i to Camp Shelby led them to be relationally racialized as Hawaiian rather than as Japanese American.

As the AJA soldiers of the 100th Battalion and 442nd RCT traveled to Camp Shelby, they began to experience a blending of racial understandings that muddied the lines between Japanese American and Hawaiian. The AJA soldiers were not particularly "Japanese" like the Nisei soldiers from the U.S. mainland. To the AJA soldiers, the Japanese Americans from the U.S. mainland were socially and culturally different, even though the two groups shared similar ethnic affiliations. During World War II, the Japanese and Japanese American population in Hawai'i was 157,905 (37.9 percent of the population), and on the U.S. West Coast, the Japanese and Japanese Americans numbered as high as 120,000, constituting less than 1 percent of the population.[5] Researcher Yukiko Kimura observed during the war that "Hawaii-Japanese may be more backward than the California-Japanese" and argued that "less aggressive ones stayed here [in Hawai'i], while more ambitious ones moved to California." Kimura noted that "Hawaii-Japanese" were referred to as "Hawaii-gaeri" (or "Hawai'i bumpkins") because they came from primitive islands, while the California-Japanese were "from real America and represent[ed] the higher level of civilization." Kimura also remarked that "Hawaii-gaeri" came to refer to someone who "is dressed in an ill-shaped foreign dress even if he or she has never been to Hawaii."[6] Researcher Charles Kikuchi, a Nisei from the mainland, wrote in his diary that "I found these Hawaiian boys rather uninteresting. They seem to be unsophisticated country boys from Hawaii and that's all. . . . The boys speak very lowly and their English is poor so that it was difficult to understand them."[7] Kimura and Kikuchi picked up on a cultural difference that created a binary between the Americanized, assimilated Nisei on the U.S. mainland with the less Americanized AJA. In contrast to the Japanese American culture on the U.S. mainland, the AJA soldiers grew up in a culture that was called Local identity in Hawaiʻi.

Sociologist Harry Kitano described this "Local" culture of Japanese Americans from Hawaiʻi in *Japanese Americans: The Evolution of a Subculture*, arguing that they were distinct from Japanese from Japan and Japanese Americans raised on the American continent. Kitano explained that

> a Hawaiian culture has developed that is a blend of the Pacific Islands, the Asian, the native, and the haole [white American]. The proportions of the blend are open to conjecture and probably depend on group identification and position. But even though the influences of the blend may differ, permanent residents of the islands refer to this culture as "local." Although there are ethnocentric connotations to the term, it is also a recognition that the local— whether of Asian, islander, European, or American ancestry—has developed a way of looking at the world that is different from his countrymen across the oceans.[8]

Many of the AJA soldiers performed and projected Local identity during mobilization, training, deployment, and battle. But U.S. mainland audiences misinterpreted Local identity as Hawaiian culture. While traveling to and stationed at Camp Shelby, the AJA soldiers were labeled by newspapers from Hawaiʻi to Mississippi as deeply associated with Hawaiʻi. The blending of different identities—from Hawaiians of Japanese ancestry, Hawaiians, Hawaiian Japanese, or Japanese Hawaiian[9]—gave the AJA soldiers the opportunity to use essentialism as a strategic survival mechanism by allowing them to perform a racialized identity that was read as Hawaiian. This provided a shield against anti-Japanese racism on the U.S. mainland and especially the U.S. South—where, the commanding officer of the 442nd RCT remarked, the American public "is not familiar with Japanese-Americans, their problems and difficulties and their unwavering patriotism."[10] In addition, the American public did not fully comprehend the relationship between the AJA soldiers from Hawaiʻi and the incarcerated Japanese Americans. Throughout their travels from Hawaiʻi to Camp Shelby, the AJA GIs performed Hawaiian music and danced the hula for audiences from California to Mississippi.[11] On their stop in Louisville, the welcoming crew of two hundred residents coaxed the AJA soldiers to sing "some native songs," and "thirteen carloads of Hawaiian melody was the result. Many of [the soldiers] hauled out steel guitars, ukuleles, and mandolins for accompaniment."[12]

Another factor that allowed the AJA men in the 442nd RCT to be misidentified as Hawaiian was the initial successful mobilization of the 100th Battalion, initially composed of AJA soldiers. By 1942 the U.S. government was committed to fighting a racial war with Japan, and the opportunity for military participation had been extended to Japanese Americans. The U.S. government, attempting to mitigate public claims of racial discrimination, allowed Japanese Americans to serve in the U.S. Army, which formerly barred them because of their perceived connection with the Japanese enemy. As positive coverage of the 100th Battalion rolled in, President Franklin D. Roosevelt announced on February 1, 1943, that another Japanese American military unit would be organized: the 442nd RCT (in 1944, the 100th Battalion and the 442nd RCT became one fighting unit—100th/442nd RCT—in the European campaign).[13] The initial plan was to enlist fifteen hundred men from the Hawaiian Islands and three thousand men from the U.S. mainland, primarily from the incarceration camps.[14] Secretary of War Henry L. Stimson believed that offering Japanese Americans a chance to fight in the U.S. military provided them an opportunity to demonstrate that "loyalty to the country is the voice that must be heard." He went on to note that he was "glad that I now am able to give active proof that this basic American belief is not a war casualty" and that "the situation in Hawaii was an important factor in the army's decision" to admit Japanese Americans into military service.[15] Following Mr. Stimson's address, AJA men in Hawai'i began to volunteer for service, which was met with much support and appreciation from political and military power brokers in the Islands.

The U.S. military mobilization in response to military conflicts in both Europe and the Pacific moved millions of people from all corners of the nation. The Japanese attack on Pearl Harbor propelled already brewing anti-Japanese racism in Hawai'i and the West Coast to a more national audience, which then led to the forcible removal of all Japanese and Japanese Americans on the West Coast and some in Hawai'i to incarceration camps across the United States. In this chapter, I will examine relational racialization among AJA soldiers from Hawai'i to reveal a process by which the men "became" Hawaiian during their migration to and training at Camp Shelby, Mississippi. This analysis builds on Natalia Molina's call for a relational understanding of racialization—one that expands beyond binaries and comparative analyses

and that reveals new understandings of the makings, impacts, and consequences of racial formation by examining interconnections among different
nonwhite and Indigenous groups in relation to whiteness and white supremacy.[16] This chapter will show how the movement of these two units, the 100th
Battalion and the 442nd RCT, to Mississippi allowed Local Japanese from
Hawai'i to "become" Hawaiian—a racialization that was founded on the
distancing from associations with anti-Black racism, the desire to prove
Hawai'i as worthy for statehood, and the navigations of anti-Japanese racism
on the U.S. mainland. By employing a relational racialization model, my
historical analysis of the racialization of the AJA soldier from Hawai'i while
in the U.S. South shows how two different but interconnected racial structures (a white-Asian-Hawaiian racial dynamic in Hawai'i and a white-Black
racial binary in the U.S. South) intersected and were mutually influenced.
Understanding the racialization of the AJA soldiers from Hawai'i relationally reveals the importance of understanding the geographical heterogeneity
of the 100th/442nd RCT, which had a profound impact on the AJAs' racialization as Hawaiian.

THE AJA SOLDIERS AT CAMP SHELBY:
RELATIONAL RACIALIZATION AS HAWAIIAN

The coverage of the AJA GIs held a deep significance for not only Riley Allen,
the editor of the *Honolulu Star-Bulletin,* one of the prominent newspapers
in the Islands, but also for many other Hawai'i residents. In a letter to
Colonel C. W. Pence, the commanding officer of the 442nd RCT, Riley
Allen wrote, "To us the situation at Camp Shelby is a *[sic]* more than of local
importance. It is of national, indeed of international, significance."[17] In the
hearts and minds of the residents of Hawai'i and especially the Japanese community, Camp Shelby served as not only a space where AJA GIs could prove
their loyalty or seek an adventure but also an imagined place where the home
front in Hawai'i had a vested interest in their success. Representative J. R.
Farrington also viewed the experiences and accomplishments of the AJA
men as a vital component during the war. Farrington wrote voluminous cor-
respondence to both Riley Allen and John Terry, a member of the *Honolulu
Star-Bulletin's* Washington bureau, about the AJA men and the Local
Japanese in Hawai'i. Farrington explicitly highlighted the strategic need to
portray the AJA men as heroes. In a letter to John Terry, Farrington

responded to the news that AJA men were being deployed to the Pacific theater as interpreters to fight the Japanese. "The record of the Americans of Japanese ancestry," he wrote, "is developing into a most interesting one and still offers a great source of interesting material for magazine publication."[18] He saw publications as a way to combat anti-Japanese sentiments while propelling the image of the AJA war hero into the national consciousness. Terry informed Farrington that he was in close contact with other editors from national media outlets and presses that could potentially write a war book chronicling the experiences of the AJA soldiers, and he met with the editors of the *New York Times,* Knopf, and Appleton-Century to solicit materials on "AJA stuff." Although Terry explains that "war books aren't worth the effort of writing them (Clark Lee's book sold only 20,000 copies)," the letter reveals that these influential white men—Terry, Farrington, and Allen—used their resources through the press, whether in Hawai'i or nationally, to advance an agenda of making visible the contributions, experiences, and heroic actions of the AJA soldiers.[19]

Two years before the 442nd RCT's move to Camp Shelby in 1943, African American soldiers had voiced their vehement complaints in a front-page article in the *Baltimore Afro-American,* with the headline "Miss. Camp Dixie's Worst." While their white GI counterparts enjoyed guesthouses, a library, movie theater, recreational hall, and baseball field, African American GIs had none of these amenities.[20] Hattiesburg, the closest town to Camp Shelby, provided "too few pleasure spots for whites" and refused to entertain the African American GIs altogether. While training in Camp Shelby, African American soldiers were relegated to service units, which was basically manual labor. Ollie Stewart of the *Baltimore Afro-American* reported, "They do a lot of manual labor, but they are combat troops. Their tasks, it was explained to me, often make them the first to draw enemy fire in an engagement, and they often bear the brunt of rear guard action."[21] Even while AJA soldiers were stationed at Camp Shelby in June 1943, the Black press and prominent African Americans like Judge Hastie, the civilian aide to the secretary of war, vigorously voiced their concerns about the differential treatment: "At Camp Shelby, Mississippi, two Negro soldiers lie in hospital, wounded in an affray with highway patrolmen. The environs of Camp Shelby are more than familiar to the military authorities."[22] This condition of anti-Black racism did not reach the shores of Hawai'i.

John Terry wrote to Riley Allen in August 1943, just several months after the arrival of the AJA men to Camp Shelby,

I have just seen an issue of the Star-B which contains the report of an army investigation about fights involving AJA's here [in Honolulu]. I had not realized that there had been rumors current in the islands to the effect that there had been large-scale disorders or riots. There certainly has been nothing in the nature of "race riots" in Mississippi. In the series of three articles I wrote from here on the combat team, I mention fights. I trust there will be no misunderstanding on that point. Those were individual affairs, or involving limited numbers of soldiers rather than soldiers and civilians. Col. Turner told me emphatically that there had never been anything in the nature of race riots.[23]

In this exchange, both Terry and Allen were attempting to comprehend the AJA situation both in Hawai'i and in Camp Shelby. Yet, rather than exploring the rumors of "race riots" or reading the Black press's coverage of Camp Shelby, these influential men at the *Honolulu Star-Bulletin* downplayed stories of racial discrimination and Jim Crow policies that affected not only African American GIs but also the AJA men at the military camp. Instead of reporting the anti-Black racism in the South and the impact that racial tensions may have had on the AJA men, Terry deemed only two types of tension significant—one being tension between the AJA men from Hawai'i and the Nisei men from the U.S. mainland and the other being the heat. Terry concluded that there was friction between the two groups of men because the Japanese Americans from the mainland were given preferential treatment in receiving noncommissioned ranks, even though they were a minority within the segregated combat team. In his entire report, Terry's only reservation about the AJA men was the friction within the combat group.

Racism directed toward African Americans in the United States and the Hawaiian Islands deeply influenced every aspect of life, from leisure activities to community politics. At local shops and restaurants across the Hawaiian Islands, Jim Crow ideologies influenced the reception of African American GIs by local residents. African Americans were barred from Waikiki restaurants and nightclubs because local business owners desired to appease the white servicemen from the Deep South.[24] During the same period that the AJAs were heading to Camp Shelby, a contingent of African American soldiers was transferred to Kahuku, Oahu, on the north shore, where there was a large settlement of Japanese and Filipinos who worked for the Kahuku Plantation Company. These African American soldiers, all from the U.S. South, were met with suspicion, fear, and curiosity by the people of Kahuku, and the locals' perceptions were fueled by "previous reports, rumors, and transferred mainland prejudices."[25]

The local newspapers in Hawai'i played an immense role in portraying African American GIs in a way that further perpetuated fear and suspicion. The *Honolulu Star-Bulletin* and *Honolulu Advertiser* both extended the racist practices of large mainland newspapers. If a crime was committed by an African American, the word "Negro" would always be included in the description, which according to Judy Kubo "plays upon the psychology of the people who read the papers and plays a great role in stamping upon the minds of the readers the crimes committed by 'Negroes.'"[26] On the other hand, if a criminal perpetrator was not African American, the local newspaper would refer to the person as a "serviceman, a soldier, a sailor, or a marine." Riley Allen, the editor of the *Honolulu Star-Bulletin,* had the habit of distinguishing the subtle difference between "soldier" and "Negro soldier" that left the impression that the latter was responsible for the racial strife plaguing the "racial paradise" of Hawai'i. Allen, a prominent member of the haole elite, even believed wholeheartedly that the Negro presence in the Hawaiian Islands hurt the racial makeup of the Islands and threatened their racial harmony.[27]

Terry may have believed that "intolerance based on ignorance and prejudice exists, and will continue to exist, on a wide scale, but it does not seem to be taking any very active form in Hattiesburg."[28] However, the Black press, several months before, had reported extreme incidents of anti-Black racism. In May 1943, the *Pittsburgh Courier* reprinted a pointed editorial, "Failure at Hattiesburg," from the *Saint Louis Star-Times* and described it as "the strongest editorial to come out of the South-Central States and we congratulate the *Star-Times* on its forthright stand." The editorial derided the local court in Hattiesburg for acquitting three defendants accused of lynching an African American and believed that "the debacle at Hattiesburg is a sign of the enormous distance we still must travel before the theoretical values of our democracy are made a reality." The Black press covered not only anti-Black racism in Hattiesburg but also the many transgressions committed against African Americans in Mississippi as a whole.[29] With this historical juxtaposition, it is interesting that there was no mention of these race riots and AJA soldiers' experiences with anti-Black racism in the local newspapers in Hawai'i.

Besides the haole elites in Hawai'i navigating anti-Black racism, AJA soldiers in Camp Shelby also understood the legitimacy of anti-Black racism in the South. A local Chinese college student wrote in her student journal for a sociology course at the University of Hawai'i about the letters she received from former classmates. Her remarks speak to the way Blackness was censored at Camp Shelby:

Received 3 letters from former classmates now in Camp Shelby, Mississippi. Claude wrote about the "(censored) situation" down there. I am guessing that the censored word is "negro" because the context of the rest of the paragraph points toward a situation like that, and because while browsing through Holmes' *The Negro's Struggle for Survival* the other day, I noticed the negro population, as shown on the 1930 census map of the U.S. to be most dense in Mississippi. The letter in part read as follows: "I must tell you about the (censored) situation down here. We, who came from the islands, haven't thought about (censored) matters too seriously—at least not like down here. We have been specifically instructed to keep away from them. Have nothing to do with them what-so-ever. Don't even talk to them. Keep away from places where they congregate. I was (censored) when I heard all these things. It seems that for over a hundred years the (censored) have maintained this (censored) and if we ever did do anything that would be against this custom, they would look down upon us. It's pretty tough for us, but if that's the law around these parts we'll have to play accordingly."[30]

Distancing themselves from the racial "situation" and embracing U.S. norms by "playing accordingly" let the AJA soldiers be portrayed as patriotic by the local press in Camp Shelby. The *Hattiesburg American* reported that "by voluntarily enlisting for service in the combat team, these soldiers already have taken the first steps to demonstrate their patriotism," and it highlighted that the AJA men organized an "I am an American Day."[31] While recognizing the fact that the AJA soldiers had volunteered to fight, both the *Hattiesburg American* and *Honolulu Star-Bulletin* failed to mention that many African Americans were barred from the armed forces.[32] The *Hattiesburg American*'s support of the AJA soldiers came from its editor, Andrew Harmon. Terry reported that "officers in the war department who are interested in the success of the 442nd should be gratified to know that a man of Mr. Harmon's caliber occupies a strategic position in the community, and is heart and soul behind the combat team."[33] In addition, wealthy proprietor Earl Finch of Hattiesburg also offered significant resources to the AJA soldiers. The U.S. army even banned the circulation of the Black press's reports on racial discrimination against African American GIs until September 1941.[34] Even when juxtaposing the willingness to volunteer in the U.S. Army, in December 1942 the *Baltimore Afro-American* reported that Lewis B. Hershey, director of the Selective Service System, revealed that there were more "colored troops" than white volunteers;[35] however, this information was never released to the public in Hawai'i, possibly to conceal any similarities or prevent comparisons between the African American volunteer soldiers and AJA volunteer soldiers. Since the newspapers made no explicit links between the struggles of these two groups of volunteers, the image of the AJA soldiers was not associated with the racial hostilities directed toward African American GIs.

This desire to protect the image of AJA soldiers from anti-Black racism and elevate them as Hawaiian was directed by the haole elites in the tourist and plantation industries. Ethnic studies scholar Adria Imada has argued that the U.S. mainland perception of Hawai'i in the decade preceding World War II was based on a touristic fantasy that erased Asians from the imagined space of Hawai'i. In the years leading up to World War II, promoters erased Asians from tourism literature and portraits of Hawai'i. They no longer mentioned the Local Asian populations—Japanese, Okinawans, Chinese, Koreans, and Filipinos. Historian Christine Skwiot demonstrates that haole elites in Hawai'i sought statehood for Hawai'i in the decades preceding World War II not only to protect their exports but also to respond to the threat of U.S. military rule stemming from the infamous Massie case, in which several Local Asian and Native Hawaiian men were accused of sexually assaulting the wife of a Navy officer. In response to this case, which received national coverage, haole elites sought to burnish their tarnished image and advocated for statehood through the propagation of favorable tourism to Hawai'i. Many of their claims promoted Hawai'i as a "South Sea populated paradise solely by caring whites and carefree natives or just by whites acting out fantasies of native culture."[36] During the war, haole elites advanced the "worthiness" of the Territory of Hawai'i for statehood by emphasizing coverage that presented AJA soldiers as Hawaiian. Broadcasting Hawaiian music became the most popular and influential medium through which Hawai'i as paradise traveled to the ears of the U.S. continent. *Life* magazine reported that "since Pearl Harbor, U.S. interest in Hawaiian customs and culture has tripled, according to the Hawaiian Federation of America. Uncounted acres of grass skirts have been mailed home to girl friends by servicemen in the Pacific. Hence uncounted American girls are now learning the hula."[37] For the AJA soldiers en route to Camp Shelby, performing Hawaiian music for local residents along the way only added to the solidification of their misidentification as Hawaiian.

During the enlistment drives, the military brass and haole elites in Hawai'i associated themselves with the AJA soldiers preparing to ship out by providing an initial narrative of patriotism, freedom, and democracy—all in hopes of solidifying Hawai'i's relationship with the larger United States. On the island of Maui, Brigadier General R. E. Mittelstaedt, Maui district commander, mentioned that "before coming here I served with the army in California," and "among the men under me were many Americans of Japanese ancestry, and I want to say they were among the best soldiers we had."[38] On the Big Island at a recruitment drive attended by more than a thousand AJA, C. T. Tong, commander of Hilo Post No. 3 of the American Legion, exhorted the AJA men that "the eyes of our government and of the entire nation are focused on you and your conduct as soldiers of the American army."[39] The University of Hawai'i at Manoa (UH) also provided support for the AJA men volunteering to fight for the United States against the Axis powers. Gregg M. Sinclair, president of UH, implored the Japanese American students to take up arms and be a part of the plan to enlist fifteen hundred Japanese Americans. In addition, Sinclair, understanding the larger political implications of Japanese American involvement in the U.S. military, said that "we feel that the enlistment of our American students of Japanese ancestry is another opportunity for the university and its personnel to take its rightful place in the American community."[40] To Sinclair, the AJA soldiers held the potential to shine a positive light on Hawai'i while elevating not only the university but also the territory in the eyes of the nation.

While at Camp Shelby, the AJA soldiers' performance of Local culture provided a way for them to be accepted by white southerners in Mississippi. A month after the acquittals of alleged white lynchers in Hattiesburg, an unidentified AJA soldier wrote home that "I have made quite a bit of acquaintances in Hattiesburg but they are all nice girls and we are friends, merely because we have found interest in each others history, background and behavior."[41] This "history, background and behavior" suggests a type of "acceptable" culture perhaps along the lines of AJA soldiers misidentified as Hawaiian. A prime example of this interest in the AJA soldiers is reflected in a letter from Private Tomochika Uyeda to Leslie Eichelberger of the Honolulu YMCA. Uyeda recalled that

> so far, the officers and other "haole" [white] soldiers have been very helpful and kind to us. They like to hear about Hawaii and its people and wonder how the people get along so fine. You know, since we came here, we sounded as though we were from the Hawaiian Tourist Bureau selling ideas of Hawaii. It is fun when we get to know the other soldiers stationed here. There are some soldiers who call us names such as Tojo, Jap and other disgusting names but we do not pay any attention to them.[42]

Uyeda's reference to the Hawaiian Tourist Bureau acknowledges that some of the AJA soldiers were willingly spreading an image of Hawai'i that was attached to their Japanese (American) faces. Sergeant Masaichi Goto, a member of the 100th/442nd RCT, believed that "the boys did more for Hawaii than the Tourist Bureau in forty years" and that "it was astonishing to find the vague ideas many Americans had about the islands. Very many said to us, 'Certainly, when the war should be over, they would visit Hawaii.'"[43] In addition, the letter shows that for AJA soldiers, being identified as Hawaiian only went so far. The white GIs still directed anti-Japanese racial slurs at them: "There are some soldiers who call us names such as Tojo, Jap and other disgusting names but we do not pay any attention to them." Mentioning these disgusting names that relied on anti-Japanese racism speaks to a larger sentiment that was hidden by the misidentification of AJAs as Hawaiian. This statement also speaks to the deep divisions between the AJA and Nisei soldiers. Chiyo Suzuki, who worked at the USO at the Jerome incarceration camp in Arkansas, also befriended many of the AJA soldiers from Hawai'i at Camp Shelby. After interviewing her at the Jerome camp, researcher Charles Kikuchi observed that "it gripes her when some of the Nisei in the 442nd say they are Hawaiian when people ask them because she feels that they should say they are Japanese Americans in order to help the Nisei here."[44]

AJA soldiers came to understand that even though there was anti-Japanese racism in Hawai'i, they could claim a Hawaiian identity that afforded some protections from anti-Japanese racism on the mainland. Historians of anti-Japanese racism in the United States have largely treated the anti-Japanese racism in Hawai'i and the U.S. mainland as two separate but connected phenomena. Gary Okihiro in *Cane Fires* contends that the racial discrimination against AJAs in Hawai'i paralleled the oppression of Japanese Americans on the West Coast.[45] But the AJA soldiers' experiences with anti-Japanese racism on the U.S. mainland, equipped with their perspective and knowledge of anti-Japanese racism in Hawai'i, allowed them to navigate anti-Japanese racism on the U.S. mainland. These experiences left a bitter taste and led many to identify with Hawai'i rather than Japanese America, incarcerated and relocated, on the U.S. mainland. An AJA soldier who went by the name Bobcat explained to Kikuchi in 1944 that

> we were just considered Hawaiians and nobody ever talked about evacuation. We came to the mainland in June 1942 and I noticed the funny attitudes the haoles had just as soon as we got into Oakland. . . . They didn't take us as Japanese. Whenever anyone asked us we just said we were from Hawaii and

we didn't mention that we were Japanese at all. I found out how the haoles treated the Japanese when I read about the evacuation and all about sabotage in the papers. Then people began to mistrust us. It wasn't as bad in Wisconsin as it was in Mississippi. . . . But it wasn't until I came to the mainland and saw just how the haoles looked down on the Japanese. All I see out here is haole faces and I get lonesome for the islands. I've done my share in this war and I want to head home where people are more friendlier. . . . There are too many haoles out here and they will never accept the Nihonjin [Japanese] as equals like in Hawaii.[46]

Some of the AJA soldiers began to understand the predicament that many of the Japanese Americans were experiencing on the U.S. mainland. Those AJA soldiers who recognized the parallels between anti-Japanese racism in Hawai'i and that found on the U.S. mainland expressed the need for solidarity to combat it. Chaplain Masao Yamada of the 100th Battalion conveyed his dismay to a Japanese American from the mainland that "the boys in Hawai'i must make up for all the California errors. The only certainty regarding loyalty of the Japanese is from Hawai'i . . . [and] Hawai'i can hold its own, but you must help the minority win their place on the mainland."[47] In response to the need for solidarity, Staff Sergeant Joseph Itagaki wrote to Representative Farrington and communicated his desire that the Territory of Hawai'i support the incarcerated Japanese Americans. Farrington, however, responded that he talked to other political leaders in Hawai'i and that "most of them felt that we should concentrate on our own problems, and not be drawn into those of people elsewhere."[48] To the haole elites, AJA soldiers' social capital was more vital to the campaign for Hawai'i's statehood, a concern for Hawai'i's civil rights, than the civil rights of the incarcerated Japanese Americans.

· · ·

This misidentification of the AJA soldiers as Hawaiian came at a time when Indigenous Hawaiians were viewed as a vanishing people. The Black press intimated that they were perceived as the "last vanishing American," and that while Hawai'i's many racial groups and institutions enhanced the experience there, that very diversity was playing a part in this disappearance. The *Baltimore Afro-American* reported that the authorities in Hawai'i were "striving to preserve some of the aspects of Hawaiian culture for posterity" because they believed that "we may well look upon our Hawaiian brother as the 'last vanishing American.'"[49] In addition, in 1943 one of the local newspapers in Hawai'i published a series entitled "Hawaiians—a Forgotten Race?," which documented the various ways the Indigenous population was unfit to return to their native ways.[50] While Indigenous Hawaiians were seen as a "vanishing" population, AJA soldiers in Camp Shelby "became" Hawaiian to the media and larger U.S. society through their portrayal of a heroism congruent with the U.S. empire. Within this dynamic, Andrea Smith has argued, "the appropriation of Native identity by even people of color or Third World subjects cannot be easily distinguished from a logic of genocide or a logic of biopower whereby Natives must die so that postmodern subjects can live."[51] With this insight, the discursive formation of AJA soldiers in the U.S. South was based on Indigenous genocide that made them representatives of "Hawaiian-ness"—a process that was influenced by anti-Black racism, anti-Japanese racism, and the desire for Hawaiian statehood.

The Local Japanese soldiers from Hawai'i navigated different racial structures in Hawai'i and the U.S. South by presenting their Local identity as Hawaiian during a period of intense anti-Japanese racism. By focusing on the relational racialization of the AJA soldier during World War II, this chapter reveals how transcending the analytic of Japanese-white relations that has dominated Japanese American historiography can offer a new understanding of the heterogeneity and power dynamics behind the construction and racialization of AJA soldiers as Hawaiian.

NOTES

1. Most Japanese American soldiers from Hawai'i considered themselves Americans of Japanese ancestry (AJA) or Local Japanese, and the Japanese Americans from the mainland identified as Nisei or Japanese American. In the rest of the chapter, I refer to the Japanese Americans from Hawai'i as AJA and Japanese Americans from the mainland as Nisei. Andrew Lind, *Hawaii's Japanese: An Experiment in Democracy* (Princeton, NJ: Princeton University Press, 1946); Roland Kotani, *The Japanese in Hawaii: A Century of Struggle* (Honolulu: Hochi, 1985).

2. Holly Allen, "The Citizen-Soldier and the Citizen-Internee: Military Fraternity, Race, and American Nationhood, 1942–46," in *Race and the Production of Modern American Nationalism,* ed. Reynolds J. Scott-Childress (New York: Garland, 1999), 314; Robert Asahina, *Just Americans: How Japanese Americans Won a War at Home and Abroad—the Story of the 100th Battalion/442nd Regimental Combat Team in World War II* (New York: Gotham, 2006), 60, 73; Lyn Crost, *Honor by Fire: Japanese Americans at War in Europe and the Pacific* (Novato, CA: Presidio, 1994), 67; Bill Yenne, *Rising Sons: The Japanese American GIs Who Fought*

for the United States in World War II (New York: Thomas Dunne Books, 2007), 67–76.

3. Tom Ikeda and Beverly Kashino, "Daniel Inouye Interview," Densho Visual Collection (A-M), June 30, 1998, accessed May 28, 2015, http://archive.densho.org /main.aspx; Dan Nakaso, "442nd RCT," *Honolulu Advertiser* (hereafter cited as *HA*), August 16, 2009; Jason Ripper, *American Stories: Living American History, Volume II: From 1865* (Armonk, NY: M. E. Sharpe, 2008), 189.

4. I capitalize "Community" because it is, to borrow Benedict Anderson's term, an imagined community composed of many different communities, ranging from the Local Japanese community in Hawai'i to the Japanese American communities in the incarceration camps on the U.S. continent.

5. Eleanor C. Nordyke and Y. Scott Matsumoto, "The Japanese in Hawaii: A Historical and Demographic Perspective," *Hawaiian Journal of History* 11 (1977): 162–74.

6. Yukiko Kimura to Galen M. Fisher, August 2, 1943, box 1, folder "Japanese," War Research Laboratory Records, Hamilton Library, University of Hawai'i at Manoa, Honolulu (hereafter cited as WRLR); Yukiko Kimura, "A Comparative Study of Collective Adjustment of the Issei, the First Generation Japanese, in Hawaii and in the Mainland United States Since Pearl Harbor" (PhD diss., University of Chicago, 1952), 317–44; Yukiko Kimura, *Issei: Japanese Immigrants in Hawaii* (Honolulu: University of Hawai'i Press, 1988), 52.

7. Charles Kikuchi, *Charles Kikuchi Diary,* September 19, 1944, box 15, vol. 14, Charles Kikuchi Papers, Charles E. Young Research Library, University of California, Los Angeles (hereafter cited as CKP).

8. Harry Kitano, *Japanese Americans: The Evolution of a Subculture* (Englewood Cliffs, NJ: Prentice-Hall, 1969), 185–86.

9. Masayo Duus, one of the leading scholars on the 100th/442nd RCT, referred to the AJA soldiers as Hawaiians. Others have confusingly mixed up the different identities of these AJA soldiers, which can be seen through the countless articles that charted the experiences and heroic actions of the 100th/442nd RCT.

10. "AJAs Are Given Official Welcome," *Honolulu Star-Bulletin* (hereafter cited as *HSB*), April 16, 1943; "Hawai'i Volunteer Soldiers Officially Welcomed at Shelby: Called Symbol of Loyalty by Pence," *HA,* April 16, 1943.

11. "Shelby Briefs," *Hattiesburg American,* June 2, 1943.

12. "Loyal U.S. Japs Arrive at Shelby: 2500 from Hawaii Prepare to Fight for America," *Times Picayune,* April 15, 1943.

13. Takashi Fujitani, *Race for Empire: Koreans as Japanese and Japanese as Americans during World War II* (Berkeley: University of California Press, 2011), 117–21; Masayo Duus, *Unlikely Liberators: The Men of the 100th and 442nd* (Honolulu: University of Hawaii Press, 1987), 58.

14. For the history of the formation of the AJA contingent within the 442nd Regimental Combat Team, see Duus, *Unlikely Liberators;* Thomas Daniel Murphy, *Ambassadors in Arms: The Story of Hawaii's 100th Battalion* (Honolulu: University of Hawaii Press, 1955); Asahina, *Just Americans;* Franklin Odo, *No Sword to Bury:*

Japanese Americans in Hawai'i during World War II (Philadelphia: Temple University Press, 2004).

15. "Program Announced by War Secretary," *HA,* January 29, 1943; "Emmons Reveals Plan to Enlist 1,500 Japanese-Americans Here: Volunteers Will Go Into Combat Units," *HA,* January 30, 1943; "Volunteer AJ Units to Train in Mississippi: Isle Group to Total 1,500 with 3,000 from Mainland," *HSB,* February 1, 1943.

16. Natalia Molina, "Examining Chicana/o History through a Relational Lens," *Pacific Historical Review* 82, no. 4 (2013): 520–41.

17. Riley Allen to Colonel C. W. Pence, August 23, 1943, folder 819, Joseph Farrington Congressional Papers, Hawai'i State Archives, Honolulu (hereafter cited as JFCP).

18. J. R. Farrington to John Terry, November 30, 1943, folder 818, JFCP. Folder 818 contains many letters between Farrington, Terry, and Allen about how to properly manage the image of the AJA soldiers at Camp Shelby and the Japanese in Hawai'i.

19. John Terry to J. R. Farrington, November 15, 1943, folder 818, JFCP.

20. "Miss. Camp Dixie's Worst," *Baltimore Afro-American* (hereafter cited as *BAA*), August 2, 1941; "Shelby Men Want to Be Transferred—Lack of Recreation, Hostilities of Police Cited; Many Have Been Beaten," *BAA,* August 2, 1941.

21. Ollie Stewart, "Making Soldiers of Backwoodsmen—Camp Shelby's 2000 Recruits Made Up of Many Who Have Had Only 3 Years of Schooling; Chaplain's Biggest Job Is to Write Letters Home," *BAA,* August 2, 1941.

22. Memorandum, Major James S. Tatman, acting chief of the Analysis Branch, to the director of the Office of War Information, June 14, 1943, Office of War Information, National Archives Record Group 208, in Phillip McGuire's *Taps for a Jim Crow Army: Letters from Black Soldiers in World War II* (Santa Barbara, CA: ABC-Clio, 1983), 187; "Shelby Men Want to Be Transferred," *BAA,* August 2, 1941; "Four Negro Units Stationed at Camp Shelby," *Pittsburgh Courier* (hereafter cited as *PC*), August 2, 1941; "Race Soldiers at Camp Shelby Volunteer Many Complaints," *PC,* August 2, 1941.

23. John Terry to Riley H. Allen, August 26, 1943, folder 819, JFCP.

24. Jeff-Phyllis Kon Cooke, "Post-war Trends in the Island Attitude toward the Negro," *Social Process in Hawaii* 11 (May 1947): 100; "Anecdotes on Feeling regarding Negroes in Hawaii," June 1944, box 16, folder 24, Confidential Research Files, 1942–1959, Romanzo Adams Social Research Laboratory, Hamilton Library, University of Hawai'i at Manoa, Honolulu (hereafter cited as RASRL).

25. Judy Kubo, "The Negro Soldier in Kahuku," *Social Process in Hawaii* 9–10 (July 1945): 28.

26. Judy Kubo, "The Negro Soldier in Kahuku," *Social Process in Hawaii* 9–10 (July 1945): 32.

27. John William Siddall, ed., *Men of Hawaii: Being a Biographical Reference Library, Complete and Authentic, of the Men of Note and Substantial Achievement in the Hawaiian Islands,* vol. 1 (Territory of Hawaii: Honolulu Star-Bulletin, 1917), 18; Gerald Horne, *Fighting in Paradise: Labor Unions, Racism, and Communists in the*

Making of Modern Hawaii (Honolulu: University of Hawai'i Press, 2011), 59; Kubo, "Negro Soldier," 31–32.

28. John Terry to Colonel William P. Scobey, August 26, 1943, folder 819, JFCP.

29. "Failure at Hattiesburg," *PC,* May 8, 1943; "Mississippi Tense as Trial Begins," *PC,* April 24, 1943; "Investigate Mississippi Bus Trouble," *PC,* May 29, 1943; "Un-Americanism in Mississippi," *PC,* May 1, 1943; "Race Riots Sweep Nation: 16 Dead, Over 300 Hurt in Michigan, Texas, Mississippi," *PC,* June 26 1943; "Investigates Peonage Case in Mississippi," *PC,* June 19, 1943.

30. "June 28—Monday," box 3, folder "Student Journals 41–60," Student Papers, RASRL.

31. "Americans," *Hattiesburg American,* June 1943; "Shelby Briefs," *Hattiesburg American,* June 2, 1943.

32. "War Dep't Bans Volunteers after Ruling on Negroes," *PC,* December 27, 1941.

33. John Terry to William P. Scobey, August 1943, folder 819, JRFCP.

34. "Army Ban on Afro Lifted: Expose of M.P. Abuse Caused Ban," *BAA,* September 20, 1941.

35. "More Colored than Whites Volunteer for Army: Hershey's Report Reveals That Very Few Seek Deferment," *BAA,* December 5, 1942.

36. Adria Imada, *Aloha America: Hula Circuits through the U.S. Empire* (Durham, NC: Duke University Press), 186–88; Christine Skwiot, *Purposes of Paradise: U.S. Tourism and Empire in Cuba and Hawai'i* (Philadelphia: University of Pennsylvania Press, 2010), 140–42; DeSoto Brown, "Beautiful Romantic Hawaii: How the Fantasy Image Came to Be," *Journal of Decorative and Propaganda Arts* 20 (1994): 252–71.

37. "The Classic Hula: American Girls Are Now Learning Ancient Native Dance of Hawaii," *Life,* March 6, 1944.

38. "Maui Commander Pays Tribute to AJA Volunteers," *HSB,* February 5, 1943.

39. "Hilo Citizens Told of Their Obligations," *HA,* February 9, 1943.

40. "U.H. Students Eager to Enlist, Says Sinclair," *HA,* January 29, 1943; "Enlistment Plan Wins Support: Japanese-Americans Pleased by Recognition," *HA,* January 29, 1943.

41. AJA soldier to Chinese girl, June 28, 1943, box 1, folder 5, Confidential Research Files, RASRL.

42. Private Tomichika Uyeda to Mr. Leslie E. Eichelberger, May 3, 1943, box 1, folder 5, Confidential Research Files, RASRL.

43. Grace E. Wills, "Soldier, Shake!," October 1944, box 3, book 5, Hawaii War Records Depository, Hamilton Library, University of Hawai'i at Manoa, Honolulu; Grace E. Wills, "Soldier, Shake!," *Asia and the Americas* 45, no. 4 (April 1945): 211–12.

44. Kikuchi, *Diary,* August 10, 1944.

45. Gary Okihiro, *Cane Fires: The Anti-Japanese Movement in Hawaii, 1865–1945* (Philadelphia: Temple University Press, 1991). See also Roger Daniels, *The Politics of Prejudice: The Anti-Japanese Movement in California and the Struggle for*

Japanese Exclusion (Berkeley: University of California Press, 1977); Yuji Ichioka, *Issei: The World of the First Generation Japanese Immigrants, 1885–1924* (New York: Free Press, 1990).

46. Kikuchi, *Diary,* September 19, 1944.

47. Masao Yamada to M. Katagiri, July 2, 1943, box 1, folder "Japanese," WRLR; Miles E. Cary, "Problems of the Mainland Japanese and Their Possible Meanings for Hawaii," July 20, 1944, ibid.

48. Joseph Itagaki to Joseph Farrington, September 26, 1944, box 19, folder 764, JFCP; Joseph Farrington to Joseph Itagaki, September 28, 1944, ibid.

49. Richard A. Herron, "Hawaiian Looked upon as 'Last Vanishing American,'" *BAA,* July 10, 1943.

50. Dorothy Benyas, "Hawaiians Unfitted to Return to Native Ways, Says Scientist," *Honolulu Advertiser,* April 23, 1934; Stevan Lee, "The Hawaiians: A Forgotten Race?" April 7, 1943, box 5, folder "Hawaiians and the War," Bernhard L. Hormann Student Papers, RASRL.

51. Andrea Smith, "Queer Theory and Native Studies: The Heteronormativity of Settler Colonialism," *GLQ: A Journal of Lesbian and Gay Studies* 16, no. 1 (2010): 54.

TEN

Vietnamese Refugees and Mexican Immigrants

SOUTHERN REGIONAL RACIALIZATION IN THE LATE TWENTIETH CENTURY

Perla M. Guerrero

Dr. Lam Van Thatch, the informal leader of the group, wore a brown tailored suit as he led seventy exhausted Vietnamese refugees from the airplane on May 2, 1975.[1] About four hundred people, including church leaders and members, Girl Scouts, and, arguably, one white supremacist, welcomed them to Fort Smith. The Vietnamese arrivals stood in the rainy, fifty-five-degree weather—some without coats—at the municipal airport as Mayor Jack Freeze and Governor David Pryor welcomed them to Arkansas and the United States.[2] There were genial signs in English and Vietnamese. Unfriendly signs were largely absent except for one, with a Star of David and a swastika in the background, that read "RESCUE USA from REDS FIRST!!! WHiTE MAN UNiTE!!! AND FigHT!!"[3] As the governor gave his speech, the man with the racist sign repeatedly yelled that the refugee presence was a Zionist conspiracy. In turn, others in attendance attempted to drown him out by shouting, "Welcome, welcome!" At one point a woman tried to tear down the Nazi sign, but a minister intervened. A scuffle ensued as members of the welcoming group struggled to prevent national news photographers from taking the man's picture and capturing his response to the Vietnamese refugees.[4]

Amid this chaos, forty-one-year-old Governor Pryor, a Democrat just past his third month in office, explained to the refugees through an interpreter that the people of the United States, particularly Arkansans, understood their situation: "We hope that you realize that we share the agony, pain and sorrow you have experienced."[5] Citing the benevolent nature of people across the country as they gathered provisions such as clothing and toys, he emphasized

Arkansans' Christian rectitude: "Let me assure you, if I may, that the people of Arkansas are an open and friendly people. We have a long history and tradition of sharing what we have with others and using our best attempts to subscribe to the Biblical admonition, 'Do unto others as you would have them do unto you.' . . . This is the spirit and the nature of our people."[6] Despite attempting to paint the situation in a good light, Pryor could not ignore those dissenters who objected—sometimes vehemently—to the arrival of Vietnamese refugees on U.S. shores and particularly to their placement in Arkansas.

Unlike Little Rock, in the state's central region, or counties in its southeast, northwest Arkansas was overwhelmingly white—a consequence, at least in part, of anti-Black terror at the turn of the twentieth century. In this context, the arrival of twenty-six thousand nonwhite people constituted a huge demographic shift, even if most Vietnamese refugees would be there only temporarily. The scarcity of African Americans in the region made the backgrounds of Southeast Asians that much more important as Arkansans dealt with racial difference.

Situated at the intersection of Asian American studies and southern history, this chapter examines the racialization of Vietnamese refugees in Arkansas in 1975, when the federal government selected Fort Chaffee as a refugee-processing center. The settlement of Vietnamese refugees in a southern state added new complexity to the U.S. racial order and its multiple racial projects. I center on the experiences of the Vietnamese in Arkansas to analyze processes of racialization as well as to elucidate the legacies of southern history. In other words, this chapter focuses on the experiences of Vietnamese refugees in order to delineate racialization processes in a particular kind of southern place and examine how those processes are shaped by a place's histories, including those of racial violence and the removal of Black communities. By grounding this study in local history with long-lasting consequences for understandings of race, we can begin to analyze deeply the regional racial formations of the South.

As Wendy Cheng has demonstrated, the region is an important unit of analysis, since race is not constructed or experienced uniformly. Cheng defines "regional racial formation" as "place-specific processes of racial formation, in which locally accepted racial orders and hierarchies complicate and sometimes challenge hegemonic ideologies and facile notions of race."[7] This chapter centers place and race in order to unpack the racialization of Vietnamese refugees in 1975 and to understand how their racialization changed over a period of months.

The South has frequently been studied as a racial binary, as if it had only Black and white people, but scholars have been gradually complicating such an understanding.[8] Nevertheless, much painstaking research remains to be done in order to uncover the nuances in the region and even the different kinds of places that comprise it. Scholars have discussed the Souths that are rural or urban, those housing both Black and white communities, and now those places where Latinas/os have lived for decades. Northwest Arkansas is a South at the intersection of these axes. It was overwhelmingly white for most of the twentieth century and now has more Latinas/os than African Americans, Native Americans, or Asian Americans. In these ways, it differs significantly from other parts of the state, and its social relations reflect those specificities.[9]

This study helps explain the elasticity of racialization, as a single group can be defined in shifting and competing ways. In the popular imagination, the Vietnamese went from victims needing rescue (as long as they met certain criteria proving that they were not too different from idealized white Arkansans) to the "yellow peril" (feared for being too different and unassimilable, partly because of their multigenerational family units) to "model minorities" (in contrast to other newcomers such as Cuban refugees and Mexican immigrants).[10] Cuban refugees arrived in 1980 amid national and international accusations that Fidel Castro's government had unleashed criminals, prostitutes, and the mentally ill. Given these discourses, and the fact that this cohort of Cubans was largely working class and of African descent and had a substantial number of gay people, Arkansans and their politicians constructed them as deviant criminals and mobilized to remove them from the state.[11] Arkansans were unaware that in order to leave the island, Cubans had to apply for an exit permit and obtain a *carta de escoria* ("dreg" letter) in which they publicly confessed to crimes they supposedly committed, and some people claimed their gay identities or presented themselves as gay in order to get their permit.[12] At the time, a government report about Fort Chaffee noted that gay men self-segregated into certain barracks, giving them a high level of visibility that in turn drew media coverage; a later report estimated that twenty-five hundred gay men arrived in Arkansas.[13] In the 1990s, Mexican migrants and other Latin American immigrants arrived during a significant regional economic reorganization that provided many of them with low-wage work, especially in the poultry industry. At the turn of the twenty-first century, Latinas/os were increasingly racialized as "illegal aliens" but were praised by the governor at the time, Mike Huckabee, for their devotion to God and family.[14]

Indeed, one of Arkansans' idiosyncrasies was drawing on Christianity to advocate for accepting Vietnamese who would suffer if sent back to live under Communism and, later, Mexican immigrants, while often denying such acceptance to African Americans as well as Cuban refugees who also fled Communism. Northwest Arkansas can also illustrate how whiteness and Blackness operate in a place that had been racially homogenous. More importantly, studying the region can elucidate how anti-Black racism shapes the lives of refugees and immigrants and reveal the anti-Black structures that continue to exist across the United States.

The responses of the state of Arkansas and Arkansans to the presence of unprecedented numbers of Vietnamese people reflected national factors such as controversy over the Vietnam War, fear of competition in the labor market, and long-standing nationalist, anti-Asian sentiments. These dynamics intersected with Christian beliefs, including the rise of the Moral Majority with its racial overtones; states' rights; and racial mores grounded in local history. Particularly significant for social relations was the history of anti-Black racial terror, which resulted in the removal and displacement of Black communities from the area in the early 1900s. Consequently, northwest Arkansas was nearly 99 percent white for most of the twentieth century, making Vietnamese and other Southeast Asian refugees a significant and startling demographic presence.

The ideas of Christian charity and duty to refugees helped Arkansans frame the arrival of Vietnamese men and women in the state, but the politics of race—as they undergirded antipathy to the federal government and deployed rhetoric that drew on "yellow peril" ideas—restricted and channeled the lives and labor of Vietnamese refugees.[15] Northwestern Arkansans' whiteness shaped their encounters with refugees; they frequently referenced the racial and ethnic backgrounds of Vietnamese people as reasons to shun them. Some individuals feared competition during a difficult economic moment, yet others saw opportunities for a more willing and exploitable labor force.

This is not to suggest that Blackness and Black people were not important to Arkansans' racial mores, but rather to show that tens of thousands of Vietnamese arrivals presented a dramatic shift in a place that had maintained a white regional identity for nearly a century. In short, this history of terror had repercussions for dealing with racial and ethnic difference that would affect Asians and Latinas/os into the late twentieth century. This study offers an entry point to think about how a field of racial positions or a racial hierarchy works, is reified, or is altered by showing how white Arkansans offered a modicum of conditional acceptance to (some) Vietnamese refugees while denying the same to communities already present, such as African Americans.[16] It also allows us to understand the formation of a racial concept that is anchored in place, material realities, and social relations and how it is altered over time in relation to the new "others" who arrive.[17]

REGIONAL HISTORY, RACE, AND RACIAL ANXIETIES

Northwest Arkansas became overwhelmingly white through racial-cleansing campaigns that included two vicious episodes in Harrison, Arkansas, in 1905 and 1909. These events were part of a larger pattern of state-sanctioned anti-Black violence that perpetrated the murder, displacement, and removal of African Americans from vast expanses of land in Arkansas, Georgia, Mississippi, Oklahoma, Illinois, and Missouri. White people perpetuated the expulsion of Blacks from communities in northwest Arkansas through racist practices such as creating "sundown towns," where African Americans could not be present after daylight hours for fear of being beaten, murdered, or lynched.[18]

When more than twenty-five thousand Vietnamese refugees arrived in Fort Chaffee, they were numerically comparable to the entire population of Crawford County in 1970. Northwest Arkansans had limited exposure to people from other places and virtually none to Asian people, since Japanese American internment camps—which housed some seventeen thousand people from 1942 to 1944 in Arkansas—had been in the state's southeast, but they were privy to and participated in the racialization of Vietnamese people at the national scale. The Vietnam War was well covered by the media, and when veterans returned, they contributed their stories and perspectives to ongoing discourse.

These decades were a period of great change, most of which was indeed imposed by the federal government. The so-called Second Reconstruction during the long civil rights era embodied federal intervention in U.S. southern society as it attempted to get the region to accept national changes around issues of equality for African Americans.[19] Many of the transformations were the result of legal challenges taken to courts or mandated through federal legislation, including the *Brown* decisions, the Civil Rights Act, and the Voting Rights Act. Despite massive resistance and episodes of brutal violence, change once again came to the region.[20] Many of the white people who could afford to do so moved from the urban centers to the suburbs in order to maintain their way of life, their segregated social spheres, and their all-white schools.[21]

Vietnamese refugees were only the latest Asians to enter the nation and face U.S. Americans' anxieties about them as allegedly forever foreign and unassimilable. In the case of Arkansas, this confrontation occurred in an area that had been maintained by both custom and coercion as a majority-white region. Although Arkansans' ideas of Christian charity and duty to refugees helped bring about the Vietnamese arrival in the state, their "yellow peril" racialization ideas drew on anti-Asian sentiments. Religion, the received understanding of the war, and regional historical legacies also restricted the kind of welcome the refugees were offered.

STATES' RIGHTS, THE WAR, AND CHRISTIANITY

When Fort Chaffee opened as a refugee-processing center, state officials and Arkansans expressed resentment toward the federal government for imposing on the state and its people. The underlying tension was centered on questions of autonomy and states' rights. During World War II, this tension arose with regard to Japanese American internment in southeast Arkansas. The question had also come up in the state during the integration of Central High School in 1957, as the world watched Governor Faubus deny entry to nine Black students. Although the arrival of Vietnamese refugees in 1975 took place under different circumstances than the establishment of World War II camps and the desegregation of Central High School, at the center of each situation was the issue of states' rights and the presence or containment of nonwhite people.

On April 25, 1975, the *Arkansas Gazette* reported that Fort Chaffee was going to be used as a refugee center, yet among many people in the state the news was treated as a preposterous rumor. The story was likely not given much weight for three reasons: the news came through "unnamed" sources, state officials and congressmen contacted did not know of any such move, and army officers at the fort had heard nothing. Senator John L. McClellan, a Democrat, told the newspaper that Chaffee was not being immediately considered because he was "assured by the State Department that no such decision ha[d] been made concerning Fort Chaffee and that it w[ould] not be made without further consultation" with him.[22] The next day, Pentagon officials declared that Fort Chaffee was being considered as a site; state officials were not quoted about the matter.[23] On April 28 the Pentagon announced that it had chosen Fort Chaffee as well as Eglin Air Force Base in Florida, Fort Indiantown Gap in Pennsylvania, and Camp Pendleton in California as processing centers. The centers were chosen to disperse the refugee population, an attempt to preemptively halt the formation of ethnic enclaves. The camps would house up to twenty thousand refugees indefinitely, though the Pentagon hoped to relocate their populations within two weeks.[24] Despite not having been consulted, Arkansas government officials publicly encouraged Arkansans to support the relocation effort. Arkansans' responses, however, varied as they drew on myriad concepts, from moral duty to respect for former loyal allies to good Christian behavior.

Some Arkansans drew on their Christian beliefs to welcome the Vietnamese newcomers and wrote Governor Pryor to commend him for his actions. Caroline L. Brendel's letter is representative of many the governor received: "Please permit me to express my commendation of your Christian charity and kindness in personally welcoming refugees. God will richly bless you and your family for what you have done for 'the least of these etc.'" [25] To the letter writers who supported his actions, Pryor often replied with a form letter that read in part, "It pleases me to learn of your support of federal and state efforts to assist in providing humanitarian aid to Vietnamese evacuees. Arkansas is a community of people whose spirit and heart offer friendship and aid to all persons who seek our help."[26] Since Arkansas is part of the Bible Belt, it is hardly surprising that many people's comments to the governor reflected Christian beliefs. These sentiments were expressed in editorials written throughout the state.

Other Arkansans believed the United States had a moral duty to the Vietnamese people. According to the *Dumas Clarion* in southeast Arkansas, "The United States ought to find room for the new refugees, to whom this nation owes an obligation" because many of them were relatives of U.S. citizens or worked for the U.S. government.[27] The *Yell County Record* from Danville in the lower northwest put it to readers in the following manner: "What it really gets down to is strictly humane—is it morally right or not for America to bring back the Vietnamese who helped us during the past 10 years? . . . Maybe it's not the right time to bring a 100,000 [sic] refugees and over, to America because of our unemployment and our slow economy, but it's hard to say that it is not our 'moral' obligation." The *Yell County Record* editors invoked the United States' moral obligation as emblematic of the country: "Hopefully, we as Americans can retain this value as a people and nation."[28]

Arkansans' Christian values, even if they did not explicitly mention religion, shaped the framework of morality and duty through which they understood their responsibilities as Americans. The Moral Majority was on the upswing and on its way to becoming the Christian Right with a focus on "traditional values" and fighting the "moral breakdown of America."[29] Because the decision to use the camp was made without any input from local and state officials, Arkansans saw it as an infringement of their rights and as an imposition on the state. But when the decision was made and the people were already there, the situation put many of their beliefs to the test. The moral obligation—the Christian course of action—was to sponsor a refugee or family because it was the right thing to do.

Indeed, many of the groups that fled Vietnam immediately after the fall of Saigon were professionals: doctors, lawyers, and teachers. Three weeks after Fort Chaffee opened, the camp's population of about 26,500 represented a relatively narrow range of Vietnamese society. Whereas Vietnam as a whole was 80 percent Buddhist and 10 percent Catholic, the camp's residents were 47 percent Buddhist, 38 percent Catholic, 6 percent Protestant, and 5 percent Confucian or Cao-Dai, with 4 percent who did not express a religious preference. The majority of the refugees had some mastery of English. Thirty percent rated their English as excellent, while 40 percent claimed that they spoke the language "fairly well." The refugees arrived from Guam, where 28 percent already had secured U.S. sponsors. This was remarkable, because the first cohort of refugees to arrive in Fort Chaffee recounted that they were in Guam for only twenty-four hours, suggesting they fled Vietnam with a strong idea of who might sponsor them. Thirty-four percent had relatives in the states; only 10 percent had no ties to their new country of arrival.[30] The overrepresentation of Catholics, the English-language abilities of the refugees, and their connections to the United States through sponsors and family members strongly indicate that this cohort belonged to the middle and upper classes in their native country. Pointing out the desirable qualifications of these new arrivals served to alleviate anxieties that refugees were going to be a burden on the United States. Notably, this argument was not based on humanitarianism or moral obligation; rather, it was a much more pragmatic approach that acknowledged there was a price to pay for the United States' (failed) intervention in Vietnam.

The editors, however, could not resist invoking the Statue of Liberty and, by extension, its meaning for so many: freedom. They asked, "Or would the opponents, in the final analysis, have us dismantle the statue and send it back to France with a brief note of thanks?" The question was meant to disquiet readers, forcing them to consider the ramifications of their actions. If the U.S. populace, Arkansans in particular, turned their backs on Vietnamese refugees, the paper suggested, they might as well put a tombstone on everything the United States purportedly represented.[31]

At the end of the year, Arkansans in various communities sponsored 2,061 Vietnamese newcomers, 1,840 of whom came from Fort Chaffee.[32] The 1980 census shows that from 1975 to 1980, 1,577 Vietnamese people arrived in the state, along with 863 "other Asia[ns]." The latter likely represented other Southeast Asians, such as Laotians, who arrived during the refugee resettlement.[33] The more than two thousand Vietnamese residents in Arkansas were sponsored by citizens in cities throughout the state. The largest concentrations were in Fort Smith, with 416; Little Rock, with 200; and Grannis, with 221.[34] In the meantime, however, many Arkansans panicked over fears that Fort Chaffee's use as a refugee-processing center could hurt them and that having this number of Vietnamese neighbors in their midst would damage their lives.

YELLOW PERIL: RACIALIZED FEARS AND ECONOMIC OPPORTUNITIES

Some Arkansans drew on the yellow peril trope to racialize Vietnamese refugees as threatening and unassimilable. As a group, the refugees were seen as menacing outsiders who would at best change the culture and at worst corrupt it. Vietnamese people in Arkansas were thought to be incompatible with U.S. norms in their language, dress, and hygiene, or were viewed as competitors in the labor sphere. Arkansans believed that changes in racial makeup and culture were detrimental to the nation and more immediately to their community, and that competition from foreigners for jobs and benefits was unfair because jobs should be reserved solely for native-born workers, Black and white.[35] These different reactions were also based on class hierarchies. While Vietnamese professionals and military personnel, who had the English-language proficiency and grooming habits desired by Arkansans, were welcomed to a degree, their rural and poor compatriots were not.

To some Arkansans, the Vietnamese had appeal as a more willing and exploitable workforce than poor whites or Blacks. In April 1975 the unemployment rate in Arkansas was 9.6 percent, higher than the national rate of

8.8 percent.[36] Nevertheless, business owners throughout the state quickly asked for Vietnamese laborers. A manufacturer from the northeast town of Jonesboro asked for fifty workers to begin immediately; two car dealers needed mechanics; others asked for shoemakers and tailors.[37] Officials in some cities requested doctors and dentists: Winslow, Arkansas, asked for a doctor and his wife as well as for a nurse and her husband. Phil Matthews of the Arkansas Hospital Association sought to find workers with medical training or who were in health-related fields.[38] Frolic Footwear requested two hundred workers because the company's plant had been unable to recruit Arkansans. Leland Harland, the director of personnel, said, "We feel the main reason is that people are making more on unemployment compensation than they would if they were working."[39] According to Harland, many unemployed workers received $84 a week tax free, plus $150 a month in food stamps. "There's no way to get people off unemployment with that kind of money," he said. Since Frolic Footwear's wages averaged $2.75 an hour, a forty-hour workweek would, after taxes, yield $110.[40] The offers for work were not necessarily benevolent, however. A man with a 164-acre farm wanted a boy or girl, or possibly a woman and child, to help him full-time with a "salary to be paid at some future date if arrangement is working out." He was also willing to split up a family because he knew of a farm ten miles away that also needed help.[41] One man was direct when he wrote that the Vietnamese workers he was seeking "must be agile and willing to please."[42]

Other Arkansans had xenophobic fears about Vietnamese refugees ruining the state and the national culture. Gim Shek, a NASA engineer, made the following assessment:

> Our involvement and loss in Vietnam to shame us; the influx of thousands of foreigners to smother our economic growth; [the refugee situation] is making a sucker out of us. Those foreigners coming here are not bringing their hearts. They will eventually bring over more of their kind, and won't be satisfied until they have brought over part of the "Country." . . . We think poor management [in Washington] is going to put us out of business as a nation of might.[43]

Shek's concern was that Vietnamese refugees would eventually take over the country by bringing more relatives. His xenophobia was such that he feared they could even bring down the "mighty" United States. Shek saw the Vietnamese not as refugees fleeing a country wrecked by a U.S.-backed war and all the concomitant terrors such as hunger, displacement, homelessness, and death, but rather as invaders seeking to transfer part of Vietnam to the United States. In short, he understood Vietnamese identity through the trope of yellow peril.

The arguments Shek and other Arkansans presented contain two crucial components. On the one hand, their fears were personal, as they worried for themselves and their children's economic and educational well-being. They saw the government's investment in refugees as unfair given the harsh circumstances they lived with every day. On the other hand, they were concerned about the nation and its culture, viewing the refugees as a horde that would inevitably destroy everything they loved about their towns and their country.

The cultural arguments against Vietnamese refugees were premised on the idea that the group was a blight on society because of their supposedly high birth rates and levels of disease, along with their presumed refusal to assimilate. All these tropes have a long history in the United States. They have been serially and strategically deployed against many communities of color, including people seen as Black, Brown, Yellow, and Red—whether native, immigrant, or refugee. In response, the federal government has tried to control the various racial and ethnic communities at different historical moments of crisis. The primary aim of prohibiting Asians from entering the United States was to curtail or halt the growth of those communities altogether. Americans with nativist sentiments have historically advocated those kinds of restrictions; such attitudes have loomed particularly large during economic downturns and during U.S. wars with Asia. During the Vietnam era, nativism and economic anxiety coalesced as the nation was in the midst of a severe recession. U.S. workers wanted to have jobs and saw Vietnamese people as competitors. Nevertheless, many of the objections were not expressed as fear of competition; instead, they revolved around cultural and racial arguments. Vietnamese people were racialized through negative ascriptions about disease and prostitution, yet they also suffered from positive ascriptions that saw them as potentially successful competitors for resources. Both positive and negative ascriptions were deployed to predict the wholesale destruction of the United States and its identity.

THE FIRST COHORT OF VIETNAMESE REFUGEES AT FORT CHAFFEE

Many of the people brought to Fort Chaffee were highly educated professionals: doctors, lawyers, and former military personnel who were anti-Communists.

FIGURE 10.1. A class for Vietnamese refugees at Fort Chaffee, Arkansas, 1975. Picture #6 (group photo), Sondra Lamar Collection. Courtesy of the Pebley Center, Boreham Library, University of Arkansas–Fort Smith.

The following section draws directly from the testimony of Vietnamese people who were in Fort Chaffee in the summer of 1975 (see figure 10.1). These are the voices of the first Vietnamese refugees who were able to leave their native country. They represent people with resources—economic, political, social, or military—who therefore had the information, connections, and means to escape a few days before or after the fall of Saigon.[44]

Hoa Thi Kim Tran, a twenty-two-year-old who fled Vietnam with eight family members, shared her story with Jerry Turner, her advanced English teacher.

> When I was in Saigon, I never imagined the day I would stop my studies and should leave my country for ever.... Like most Vietnamese refugees, the reason why I left Viet Nam is that I love Freedom. I wept bitterly the day I left my country. But I must choose the best way: the Liberty.... I dare say that the days of evacuation we spent were the most terrible days. We escaped from Viet Nam in an awful panic. But, arriving at United States, we were consoled

by the American volunteers who helped all the refugees with an unceasing smile. On behalf of all Vietnamese, I want to say "many thanks for your help" to the staff, nurses, doctors and especially to the teachers (who always help us to improve our English) who are working in this camp.[45]

Not all Vietnamese students wrote about their escape or their feelings, but those who did shared Tran's sentiments and gratitude. She also knew that difficulties awaited her family:

> The problem for us is we are afraid that we cannot adapt ourselves to the american life. According to me, one of many differences between american and Vietnamese people is that Vietnamese like to live together in the same house with grand parents, parents, children, relatives while most americans live alone, think themselves when they become major and when they begin to earn their living. In Viet Nam, although sons and daughters are married, the Father (even who is very old) behaves like the leader of the family until his death.[46]

Hong Thi Cam Trinh, twenty-four, left Saigon on April 27 with her sixty-year-old parents, who left properties behind. Their departure interrupted her medical studies, and in Fort Chaffee she worked in the dispensary until a doctor introduced her to the obstetrics/gynecology ward, where she volunteered as an interpreter because it reminded her of her time in Vietnamese hospitals.

> Where will be resettled? I don't know. How is our future? I don't know. How is about my education, my medical training? I don't have any sure answer. "It is very difficult to get in a medical school in the U.S." They always repeat when I ask to. But I think "Aide-toi, le ciel t'aidera," then I will try and try more and more and try to keep my hope, my mind.

In her essay she described the phrase as a French proverb and translated it as "Help yourself, God will help you after."[47]

Trinh was the kind of person whom nativist and xenophobic Arkansans could not imagine. But she and others like her—medical personnel—quickly came to Governor Pryor's attention. He appointed a special committee to determine the possibility of licensing them along with some advanced medical students as certified physicians under Arkansas law because of a "critical need for trained medical personnel in many of Arkansas' rural counties."[48] By early August the governor's office estimated that 130 doctors remained in

Fort Chaffee; however, they were being sponsored at a rate of four per day, making it "imperative that [a] training program should be initiated as soon as practicable." The special committee determined that there were about five senior medical students and fifteen physicians interested in becoming certified to practice medicine in Arkansas. To be licensed, however, they had to pass the Educational Council for Foreign Medical Graduates (ECFMG) exam and serve a one-year internship in an approved medical facility. The University of Arkansas Medical Center (UAMS) would prepare the candidates for the exam, which was scheduled for July 1976 at a cost of about $10,000 per person. On August 15, Pryor released a statement authorizing the expenditure of $165,000 from the state's emergency fund—$100,000 for stipends and direct expenses, $42,000 for housing and maintenance, and $23,000 for education expenses incurred by UAMS.[49]

Several constituents wrote to Pryor to warn him about the dangers of the Vietnamese presence in Arkansas, citing the threat of yellow peril. Their letters argued that Vietnamese refugees were not entitled to valuable resources offered by the state and federal governments—and the governor and his office agreed.[50] On July 30, 1975, Rick Osborne, a staff member in Pryor's office, reported that Colonel Morris, director of both the Arkansas Student Loan Program and the Guaranteed Student Loan Foundation, called to inquire whether any Vietnamese refugees would be interested in a loan. Osborne told Morris "to discreetly check and not alert them of existence of the funds more than necessary in keeping with the Governor's policy of not encouraging the refugees to stay any longer than necessary. State loans—federal funds, but Arkansans *need* the money too."[51] Thus the governor and his office agreed with the logic and goals of many Arkansas residents in wishing the Vietnamese refugees' stay in Arkansas to be as short as possible. Pryor's efforts to facilitate the stay of twenty doctors and advanced medical students were in sharp contrast to this stance. That program, however, provided benefits to the state and to Arkansans as well as to the Vietnamese. It was in the state's best interests to send qualified medical personnel to rural areas, while participating in the program provided the sponsorship refugees needed to leave the camp. This situation, however, was an exception, because for the most part neither Arkansans nor the state government wanted Vietnamese refugees to stay in the state. These sentiments fell in line with research demonstrating that although many U.S. citizens said they did not object to Vietnamese refugees in the United States, they greatly disapproved of intermarriage with their own families and said they would refuse to have refugees as guests in their homes.[52] In short, most people in the United States did not want them too close by.

. . .

The approaches to the two groups of students demonstrate some of the contradictions in the response to Vietnamese refugees. In the case of medical students and doctors, Governor Pryor ignored constituents' objections and secured funds for their training for the ECFMG. In the other case, he impeded students from finding out that they might be eligible for state monies. Arguably, both groups of students would contribute to the state, though advanced medical students and doctors would presumably do so more quickly. But the note from the governor's office shows that the objection was not solely to the use of state or federal funds: Governor Pryor did not want to encourage Vietnamese refugees to stay in the state, even if they were pursuing higher education. The governor's efforts to keep racial "others" from settling in Arkansas mirror the legacy of anti-Black racism. That history helped construct regional identity around the rewards and presumptions of whiteness, and it also meant that Vietnamese refugees could count on fewer potential allies in communities of color, which, while hardly immune to anti-Asian racism, might at least have been open to a more diverse demography.

In the case of the doctors, Pryor went against his policy of not encouraging Vietnamese refugees to live in Arkansas because he saw them as a valuable resource that filled a critical gap in his constituents' needs. Like their less educated compatriots, the Vietnamese doctors were potentially a more willing and exploitable labor force than native Arkansans. Their legal situation necessitated a remedy that could be resolved only through finding a sponsor. By facilitating the links that let Vietnamese doctors leave Chaffee, Arkansas secured a more controllable workforce: medical personnel were dependent on the resources the state provided in order to pass the ECFMG exam and presumably to receive their first jobs in the country. More importantly, the group of medical practitioners consisted of a handful of individuals as opposed to hundreds or thousands of people. The refusal to advertise available funds to other students reveals the governor's intention of limiting the Vietnamese stay in Arkansas, perhaps because Arkansans feared an Asian horde that would destroy the United States.

However, Vietnamese refugees also benefited from anti-Black structural forces. Although some Arkansans did not want them to be processed at Fort

Chaffee, they begrudgingly accepted them. Even when the racializing discourse shifted to that of yellow peril, Arkansans and state government officials did not mobilize to remove the Vietnamese completely or to shut down Fort Chaffee. In contrast, Arkansans did not offer this begrudging acceptance to Cubans in 1980. The case of the Cubans, who were largely of African descent, demonstrates how quickly the state and its people would mobilize against a Black community. The rumors that the Cubans were gay and Communist also fed negative feelings.

The Cuban refugees were primarily single males, a factor that also shaped processes of racialization and affected the welcome that was offered. More work is necessary to further study the role of family in immigration discourses, especially the power of the trope of the traditional nuclear family, which can serve to make some immigrants more legible and desirable to communities. For example, in 1975, yellow peril notions represented Vietnamese and other Southeast Asian refugees as having too many children, while their multigenerational family units—grandparents, parents, siblings, and children—were considered nonnormative and too odd for Arkansas. In contrast, Mexican immigrants in the 1990s benefited from having families who mirrored the idealized nuclear family unit—mom, dad, and children. At the beginning of a substantial Latina/o migration, largely Mexican, to Arkansas, the supposed Latina/o family unit served to cast these migrants in a positive light. Their nuclear families were emblematic of the so-called traditional family values that many southerners embraced. Such an understanding even facilitated the interpretation of Latina/o teen pregnancies as positive:

> It seemed that the Hispanic family unit was very sound, that [they had a] respect and love of children, and they had a family cohesiveness which was admirable. . . . Of course we were very aware that [with] the wave of Hispanic[s] coming in, that the girls were getting pregnant very early, having lots of babies but it did not seem to be, um, as in the Black population, where there are a lot of out-of-wedlock births, it seemed that in the Hispanic population that the girls were married, these pregnancies were welcomed and planned.[53]

In those instances, Latinas/os benefited from anti-Black racism that understood Black teenage pregnancies as emblematic of a larger racialized notion—the Black broken family.

Yet in the twenty-first century, white Arkansans often compare Mexicans unfavorably to the Vietnamese. Some Arkansans, in passing or as an indictment, have lamented, "We never had to put signs up in Vietnamese for Asians; they just learned English. I don't know why Mexicans can't do the same."[54] Such a statement draws from a sanitized version of past experiences with the Vietnamese to mark Latinas/os as inferior in a racialized hierarchy or field of racial positions for their supposed inability or unwillingness to learn English. It also conceals the fact that multiple agencies and organizations funded and coordinated efforts to process Southeast Asian refugees, providing English interpreters and translators when necessary. It also ignores the English-language abilities already present in at least the first cohort of refugees that was sent to Fort Chaffee.

The shift in the way Vietnamese were understood, from victims to yellow peril to model minorities, exemplifies the elasticity of racialization. More importantly, the racial formation of Vietnamese refugees—an Asiatic racial form—is being remade in relation to other groups of people, including other Southeast Asians, and to the material conditions on the ground. Elsewhere, I have written about how in the 1990s Vietnamese students were positioned in relationship to Laotians—the former were cast as reserved but respectful while the latter were cast as difficult, especially the girls. That racialization, however, happened in relationship to Latina/o, Black, and white students.[55] The racial logics used to racialize and categorize Vietnamese in particular ways can help scholars understand how racial forms that are anchored in place are not simply derivatives, third terms, or additives to social structures. They are, rather, formations on their own terms.

NOTES

This chapter was first published as Perla M. Guerrero, "Yellow Peril in Arkansas: War, Christianity, and the Regional Racialization of Vietnamese Refugees," *Kalfou: A Journal of Comparative and Relational Ethnic Studies* 3, no. 2 (2016): 230–52. Used by permission of Temple University Press. © 2016 by Regents of the University of California. All rights reserved.

1. Mike Trimble, "Last, Sad Effort Gets Underway in First Welcome," *Arkansas Gazette* (Little Rock), May 3, 1975.

2. Peggy Robertson, "Governor Greets First 71 Refugees," *Arkansas Gazette,* May 3, 1975.

3. *Arkansas Gazette,* "Arkansas: A Temporary Home," May 3, 1975. Capitalization as in original placard.

4. Trimble, "Last, Sad Effort."

5. "A Welcome to the Refugees," editorial, *Arkansas Gazette,* May 3, 1975.

6. Robertson, "Governor Greets First 71 Refugees."

7. Wendy Cheng, *The Changs Next Door to the Díazes: Remapping Race in Suburban California* (Minneapolis: University of Minnesota Press, 2013), 10.

8. James W. Loewen, *The Mississippi Chinese: Between Black and White* (Long Grove, IL: Waveland Press, 1971); Malinda Mayor Lowery, *Lumbee Indians in the Jim Crow South: Race, Identity, and the Making of a Nation* (Chapel Hill: University of North Carolina, 2010); Helen B. Marrow, *New Destination Dreaming: Immigration, Race, and Legal Status in the Rural American South* (Stanford, CA: Stanford University Press, 2011); Helen B. Marrow, "New Immigrant Destinations and the American Colour Line," *Ethnic and Racial Studies* 32, no. 6 (2009): 1037–57; Khyati Y. Joshi and Jigna Desai, *Asian Americans in Dixie: Race and Migration in the South* (Urbana: University of Illinois, 2013); Irene Browne and Mary Odem, "'Juan Crow' in the Nuevo South? Racialization of Guatemalan and Dominican Immigrants in the Atlanta Metro Area," *Du Bois Review: Social Science Research on Race* 9, no. 2 (2012): 321–37; Perla M. Guerrero, "A Tenuous Welcome for Latinas/os and Asians: States' Rights Discourse in Late Twentieth-Century Arkansas," in *Race and Ethnicity in Arkansas: New Perspectives*, ed. John Kirk (Fayetteville: University of Arkansas Press, 2014), 141–51.

9. Leslie Bow and John Howard have each written nuanced histories about Asians in other parts of Arkansas. Leslie Bow, *Partly Colored: Asian Americans and Racial Anomaly in the Segregated South* (New York: New York University, 2010); John Howard, *Concentration Camps on the Home Front: Japanese Americans in the House of Jim Crow* (Chicago: University of Chicago, 2008).

10. Fear of Asian people within economic and cultural spheres has a history in the United States that dates back to the late nineteenth century, while the racialization of Asians as physically and intellectually different from white people and the intersection of anti-Asian fears and nativism predominate during economic downturns. Although "yellow peril" is Asian-specific, similar tropes have been strategically deployed against African Americans, Native Americans, and Latinas/os. For more on yellow peril, see Colleen Lye, *America's Asia: Racial Form and American Literature, 1893–1945* (Princeton, NJ: Princeton University Press, 2005); Lisa Lowe, *Immigrant Acts: On Asian American Cultural Politics* (Durham, NC: Duke University Press, 1996). For discussions of the ways in which Asians have been racialized across space and time, see Nayan Shah, *Contagious Divides: Epidemics and Race in San Francisco's Chinatown* (Berkeley: University of California Press, 2001); Roger Daniels, *Prisoners without Trial: Japanese Americans in World War II* (New York: Hill and Wang, 1993).

11. "Two Decades Later, Mariel Boat Lift Refugees Still Feel Effects of Riot," *Los Angeles Times*, May 5, 2001.

12. B.E. Aguirre, "Cuban Mass Migration and the Social Construction of Deviants," *Bulletin of Latin American Research* 13, no. 2 (1994): 155–83; Susana Peña, *¡Oye Loca! From the Mariel Boatlift to Gay Cuban Miami* (Minneapolis: University of Minnesota Press, 2013); Julio Capó Jr., "Queering Mariel: Mediating Cold War Foreign Policy and U.S. Citizenship among Cuba's Homosexual Exile Community, 1978–1994," *Journal of American Ethnic History* 29, no. 4 (2010): 78–106.

13. "Problem Population—Gays," in *Chaffee—Resettlement, Consolidation, December* 3, 1980, p. 58, box 2, folder 7 ("C/HTF: Office Papers, Nov. 25, 1980—July 29, 1981"), MC 870, Alina Fernandez Papers, Special Collections Department, University of Arkansas Libraries, Fayetteville, AR (hereafter cited as AFP); Warren Brown, "Cuban Boatlift Drew Thousands of Homosexuals," *Washington Post,* July 7, 1980, sec. A.; Wilford J. Forbush, director, Cuban/Haitian Task Force, to Jack Svahn, memo, "Fort Chaffee Resettlement Plan," March 10, 1981, p. 4, box 1, folder 5 ("C/HTF: March 3, 1981–March 31, 1981"), AFP. For an analysis of race, class, sexual orientation, and Communism for Mariel Cubans in Arkansas, see Perla M. Guerrero, *Nuevo South: Latinas/os, Asians, and Remaking of Place* (Austin: University of Texas Press, 2017), chap. 3.

14. Jennifer Stump, "Huckabee Announces Hispanic Program at LR Festival," *Arkansas Democrat-Gazette* (Little Rock), May 8, 2000.

15. Ideas of Christian duty after military intervention also shaped the adoption of Asian children. Arissa H. Oh, *To Save the Children of Korea: The Cold War Origins of International Adoption* (Palo Alto, CA: Stanford University Press, 2015).

16. Claire Jean Kim, "The Racial Triangulation of Asian Americans," *Politics and Society* 27, no. 1 (1999): 105–38.

17. Colleen Lye, "The Afro-Asian Analogy," *PMLA* 123, no. 5 (2008): 1732–36.

18. For more information about sundown towns in the United States, see James W. Loewen, *Sundown Towns: A Hidden Dimension of American Racism* (New York: Touchstone, 2005); for the case of Harrison, see Jacqueline Froelich and David Zimmermann, "Total Eclipse: The Destruction of the African American Community of Harrison, Arkansas in 1905 and 1909," *Arkansas Historical Quarterly* 58, no. 2 (1999): 131–59.

19. Manning Marable, *Race, Reform, and Rebellion: The Second Reconstruction and Beyond in Black America, 1945–2006,* 3rd ed. (Jackson: University Press of Mississippi, 2007); Clive Webb, ed., *Massive Resistance: Southern Opposition to the Second Reconstruction* (New York: Oxford University Press, 2005).

20. Numan V. Bartley, *The Rise of Massive Resistance: Race and Politics in the South during the 1950s* (Baton Rouge: Louisiana State University Press, 1999); George Lewis, *Massive Resistance: The White Response to the Civil Rights Movement* (London: Hodder Arnold, 2006); Francis M. Wilhoit, *The Politics of Massive Resistance* (New York: G. Braziller, 1973).

21. Kevin M. Kruse, *White Flight: Atlanta and the Making of Modern Conservatism* (Princeton, NJ: Princeton University Press, 2005); Matthew D. Lassiter, *The Silent Majority: Suburban Politics in the Sunbelt South* (Princeton, NJ: Princeton University Press, 2006).

22. "Plan Reported to Use Chaffee," *Arkansas Gazette,* April 25, 1975.

23. "Fort Chaffee Just One Possibility as Refugee Camp, Pentagon Says," *Arkansas Gazette,* April 26, 1975.

24. Roy Bode, "Use of Fort Chaffee Confirmed," *Arkansas Gazette,* April 29, 1975.

25. Caroline L. Brendel to David Pryor, May 3, 1975, box 67, folder 29 ("Vietnamese Refugee Program—Favorable"), MC 336, David Hampton Pryor

Papers, Special Collections Department, University of Arkansas Libraries, Fayetteville, AR (hereafter cited as DHPP). For letters that express similar sentiments, see this folder.

26. David Pryor to constituents supportive of Vietnamese refugees in Arkansas, 1975, box 67, folder 29, DHPP.

27. *Dumas (AR) Clarion,* quoted in "The Arkansas Press: Those Vietnamese Refugees at Fort Chaffee," *Arkansas Gazette,* May 11, 1975.

28. *Yell County Record* (Danville, AR), quoted in ibid.

29. Donald T. Critchlow, *The Conservative Ascendancy: How the GOP Right Made Political History* (Cambridge, MA: Harvard University Press, 2007), 176.

30. "Procedures Set Up for Relief Agencies to Route Refugees," *Arkansas Gazette,* May 28, 1975.

31. Ibid. A close look at U.S. history demonstrates that freedom and liberty have been the rights of only a small percentage of the nation's population. For two excellent analyses, see Evelyn Nakano Glenn, *Unequal Freedom: How Race and Gender Shaped American Citizenship and Labor* (Cambridge, MA: Harvard University Press, 2002); Mae M. Ngai, *Impossible Subjects: Illegal Aliens and the Making of Modern America* (Princeton, NJ: Princeton University Press, 2004).

32. "Exhibit A: Refugees Resettled into Society as of December 20, 1975," in a proposal from Reverend Tom Adkinson, associate minister at Lakeside United Methodist Church, Pine Bluff, Arkansas, February 26, 1976, box 92, folder 19 ("Vietnamese/English Education Proposal, 1976"), DHPP.

33. U.S. Census Bureau, *1980 Census of Population, Chapter D, Detailed Population Characteristics, Part 5, Arkansas* (Washington, DC: Department of Commerce, November 1983), 8, table 195. These numbers do not include foreign-born persons from China, Hong Kong, India, Iran, Israel, Japan, Korea, Lebanon, the Philippines, Thailand, or Turkey.

34. "Exhibit B / Printout Dated 31 Dec. 1975 and Released through Governor's Office," in Adkinson proposal, February 26, 1976, DHPP.

35. I did not find that white Arkansans thought it was unfair for African Americans to receive unemployment, food stamps, or other benefits. Several, however, brought up other people of color whom they perceived as foreigners to the nation without regard to citizenship status, such as ethnic Puerto Ricans, Cubans, and Mexicans.

36. Ernest Dumas, "Chaffee to Provide Transitory Housing, Bumpers, Pryor Say," *Arkansas Gazette,* April 30, 1975; "Labor Force Statistics from the Current Population Survey—Unemployment Rate," Bureau of Labor Statistics, U.S. Department of Labor, accessed July 28, 2016, http://data.bls.gov/pdq/SurveyOutputServlet.

37. Carol Griffee, "Aid for Refugees: Good Intentions Outshine Spite," *Arkansas Gazette,* May 16, 1975.

38. Notes RE: Phil Matthews, box 68, folder 7 ("Vietnamese Refugee Program—Sponsorship M-R") and folder 8 ("Vietnamese Refugee Program—Sponsorship S-Z"), DHPP.

39. "Shoe Firm Wants to Hire 150 Refugees," *Arkansas Gazette,* May 17, 1975.

40. Ibid.

41. Griffee, "Aid for Refugees."

42. May 1975, box 68, folders 1–8, DHPP.

43. Gim Shek to David Pryor, May 5, 1975, box 67, folder 30 ("Vietnamese Refugee Program—Unfavorable"), DHPP.

44. Mrs. [Do Van Thuan], "A Painful Trip," August 20, 1975, Southeast Asia Relocation Collection, Artwork/Photographs, Pebley Center, Boreham Library, University of Arkansas, Fort Smith (hereafter cited as SEARC).

45. Tran Thi Kim Hoa, writing assignment for "Advanced Class, 4:30–6," Fort Chaffee, Arkansas, August 19, 1975, SEARC. Refugees signed in to their English class according to Vietnamese custom: surname, middle name(s), given name; their names in the essay reflect the U.S. custom of given name, middle name(s), surname. The footnotes, however, reflect how they signed in to class or wrote their names on the assignment and what is found in the archive.

46. Ibid.

47. Trinh Thi Cam Hong, August 19, 1975, SEARC.

48. David Pryor to John Miller, August 7, 1975, box 68, folder 4 ("Vietnamese Refugee Program—Special Assistance"), DHPP.

49. Statement by David Pryor, August 15, 1975, box 68, folder 4 ("Vietnamese Refugee Program—Special Assistance"), DHPP.

50. "That Golden Door," *Southwest Times Record* (Fort Smith, AR), August 23, 1975, attached to letter from A. DeGroff to the *Southwest Times Record* and carbon copied to Governor David Pryor and John Eisenhower, August 23, 1975, box 67, folder 33 ("Vietnamese Refugee Program—Assistance Offered [3 of 3]"), DHPP.

51. Note from Rick Osborne, Office of the Governor, July 30, 1975, box 68, folder 9 ("Vietnamese Refugee Program—Suggestions and Ideas"), DHPP.

52. Alden E. Roberts, "Racism Sent and Received: Americans and Vietnamese View One Another," *Research in Race and Ethnic Relations* 5 (1988): 75–97.

53. Anna (pseudonym) worked in local public schools for most of her career; personal interview, September 9, 2005.

54. I overheard comments like these in public during the various times that I conducted field research in 2004, 2005, 2008, and 2012, and several interviewees said they had heard similar remarks or that other Arkansans confided these observations to them as one white person to another.

55. Guerrero, *Nuevo South,* chap. 4.

ELEVEN

Green, Blue, Yellow, and Red

THE RELATIONAL RACIALIZATION OF SPACE
IN THE STOCKTON METROPOLITAN AREA

Raoul S. Liévanos

Relational approaches to studying race have illuminated the nuanced character of racial hierarchies beyond the binary Black-white paradigm of earlier racial scholarship.[1] Similarly, scholars working at the intersection of race and urban studies demonstrate that racial hierarchies define residential settlements in the United States, whereby residential proximity to whites and Asians is generally preferred among real estate consumers over proximity to Latinxs and Blacks.[2] Historical and qualitative research demonstrates that the racialization of people and places is a fundamental process in the creation of racially stratified residential settlements.[3] Racialization refers to the "extension of racial meaning to a previously racially unclassified relationship, social practice, or group."[4] This process is understood relationally, whereby "the status and meanings associated with one group are contingent upon those of another."[5] Racial projects link relational racialization to material conditions of society because they are "simultaneously an interpretation, representation, or explanation of racial dynamics, and an effort to reorganize and redistribute resources along particular racial lines."[6]

This chapter contributes to previous research by advancing our understanding of the relationship between racial and spatial hierarchies. Specifically, it uncovers the historical and relational use of racial categories that in the 1930s contributed to the formation of racially stratified residential settlements and urban-industrial development in the metropolitan area of Stockton, California. As others scholars have found, the West Coast of the United States in general, and California in particular, have been characterized throughout their history by elevated levels of immigration, racial-ethnic diversity, and racial hierarchies alongside white, European American dominance.[7] Such contexts facilitate the study of race relationally beyond the traditional Black-white racial dichotomy.

The Stockton case is especially useful for examining the role of racial projects in organizing race and space in qualitative and hierarchical terms. The Stockton metropolis, synonymous with San Joaquin County, California, has had concentrations of immigrants that exceed those found throughout the United States in every year from 1850 to 2000. Before 1965, most immigrants to the metropolis came from Europe, were categorized as white, and rose to powerful political, economic, and spatial positions that they have sustained.[8] Resembling national patterns, most immigrants to the Stockton metropolitan area from 1970 to 2000 have been Asian and Latinx.[9] Most Latinx immigration to the metropolis has historically been from Mexico. Early Asian immigration was predominantly from China and Japan, but since 1970 it has consistently been from other Asian countries.

By the year 2000, the metropolis was ranked in the top six of the one hundred largest U.S. metropolitan areas for its high levels of spatial segregation between whites and Asians.[10] This high level of segregation occurred in the context of the metropolis's population mostly self-identifying as white (58 percent), Asian (11 percent; 0.56 percent Japanese; 0.98 percent Chinese; 3.86 percent Filipinx, and 5.6 percent other Asian), Black or African American (7 percent), American Indian or Alaska Native (1 percent), and Latinx of any racial group (31 percent). Local journalists take for granted the state of segregated neighborhoods in the city of Stockton, the locus of the metropolis's racial-ethnic diversity:

> Authoritatively telling us what we already know, Census 2000 says Stocktonians live in racially segregated neighborhoods. Despite decades in the so-called melting pot, Stockton's north side is mostly white. The south side is mostly Latino and black. Southeast Asians live clumped in ethnic enclaves. Martin Luther King had a dream. It wasn't Stockton.[11]

My objective in this chapter is to examine a historical racial project rooted in New Deal federal housing policy that sought to stabilize neighborhood foreclosure rates after the Great Depression. The specific racial project was reflected in the nationwide system of neighborhood residential appraisals conducted by the Home Owners' Loan Corporation (HOLC) in Stockton and 238 other U.S. cities in the 1930s.[12] These appraisals graded neighborhoods' investment risk, ranging from green (first, A, or "best"), blue (second, B, or "still desirable"), yellow (third, C, or "declining"), and red (fourth, D, or "hazardous") based on neighborhood racial composition and a number of other factors. My analysis of this state-sponsored racial project follows Michael Omi and Howard Winant, as well as Kevin Fox Gotham, by focusing on the centrality of a specific state institution in shaping the relational racialization process that institutionalized the qualitative and hierarchical ordering of racial settlement patterns and urban-industrial development in the United States.

In addition, this chapter fills a gap in previous research by moving beyond merely acknowledging the existence of this racially hierarchical grading system.[13] It does so by advancing our understanding of the explicit ways the HOLC grading system unfolded in *relationally* racialized ways. This chapter also contributes to research on how relational racialized processes unfolded in the era before the civil rights movement and before the 1965 immigration reform, an era defined in part by open and explicit efforts by white elites to organize racial hierarchies in the United States.[14] Ultimately, this chapter demonstrates the instrumental role of the state—supported by the real estate industry, "national racial narratives," and academic theories—in establishing durable hierarchies of race and space that inform contemporary racial settlement patterns in Stockton and likely other major U.S. metropolitan areas.[15] Below, I outline the sociospatial approach and research strategy I take to the study of relational racialization before presenting my analysis of the HOLC racial project and its continuing significance for shaping Stockton's racialized residential settlement and urban-industrial development. I conclude by discussing this chapter's contributions to the relational study of race and space and its future research implications.

SOCIOSPATIAL APPROACH

Previous research has produced valuable insights into the mutual constitution of various axes of social division and the relational racialization of different social groups. For example, Laura Pulido links the differential racialization of African, Mexican, and Japanese American groups in Los Angeles to their predominant class positions and their divergent trajectories of leftist activism from 1968 to 1978.[16] Tomás Almaguer's historical-comparative analysis situates the origins of white supremacy for European Americans in California in relation to "the dispossession of Indians and Mexicans and the economic restrictions imposed on black, Chinese, and Japanese immigrant workers."[17] Claire Jean Kim extends these insights by focusing specifically on how Asian Americans were "racially triangulated" in California and elsewhere in the United States by white "opinionmakers" (i.e., elected officials, journalists, scholars, community leaders, and business elites) into an intermediary status between white dominance and Black subordination. A key mechanism of triangulation was the valorization of Asians over Blacks amid the exclusion of Asians as "immutably foreign" and ineligible for citizenship. This triangulation dynamic for Asian Americans—rooted in the anti-Chinese movement that resulted in the 1882 Chinese Exclusion Act and rearticulated subsequently for Japanese, Koreans, and other Asians—is a central "normative blueprint for who should get what" in the field of racial positions that ultimately seeks to uphold white racial power.[18]

Similar racial triangulation processes have applied to Latinxs. For example, Mexicans were classified as white and were thus eligible for citizenship in 1848, provided they lived on land ceded to the United States after the U.S.-Mexico War. Mexican-origin workers were, however, increasingly criminalized if they entered the United States without "authorization" in the 1920s, classified as a separate "Mexican" race by 1930, and perceived as economic threats during the Great Depression, from 1929 to 1939. Natalia Molina demonstrates how Mexicans' contradictory and long-lasting position as citizens who were "legally white but racially other" was shaped by recycled "racial scripts" of nonwhite inferiority and foreignness previously applied to American Indians, Blacks, and Asians.[19] These clashed with the "racial scripts" equating whiteness to perceived European, Anglo-Saxon virtues of reason, civilization, and spiritual purity.[20]

Research has produced incredible insights into the relational character of race, but the explicit role of space in the relational racialization process has received relatively little systematic attention. Clement Lai's analysis of urban renewal in the Fillmore District of San Francisco is one exception, as it elaborates on Kim's racial triangulation model with an eye toward understanding the spatial dimensions of racial formation at multiple scales.[21] Specifically, Lai develops a "racial triangulation of space" model in which racial triangulation is "a spatial process where spatial relations inform racial positioning, and triangulation likewise helps produce space and reproduce spatial relations."[22] The lengthy Fillmore District redevelopment project finally ended in the late 2000s but had commenced in the 1950s along with other post–World War II urban renewal efforts in the United States. Spatialized racial triangulation processes characterized this redevelopment project: Japanese American and

African American people and spaces around Fillmore were differently positioned in the representations and political-economic processes associated with the district's redevelopment. This dynamic intertwined discourses of blight and Cold War Orientalism. The former discourse was predominantly marshaled at African American spaces to justify their demolition while "the latter discourse elid[ed] differences between Japanese American spaces and Japan and result[ed] in the construction of a Japanese Cultural and Trade Center."[23]

Lai's model overlaps to some extent with the sociospatial approach within urban sociology, which also informs my analysis. The sociospatial approach uses a multiscale lens, ranging from local to broader spatial contexts, to understand the influence of cultural factors such as the symbolic meanings of social groups and physical spaces, as well as political-economic dynamics of capital investment and state policy, on the production of space as "at once *work* and *product*—a materialization of 'social being.'"[24] From this standpoint, pro-growth coalitions are seen as key drivers of uneven development and racial segregation.[25] These coalitions include public and private actors that coalesce around local zoning, infrastructure development, and growth agendas in pursuit of profits from land use intensification.[26] Accordingly, these coalitions often feature the "white opinonmakers," that is, the same economic, political, and media elite that have been historically central in shaping the discourse and materiality of racial hierarchies in the United States.[27]

Using this sociospatial lens, I focus my analysis on the production of space as a racial project in which the making of physical spaces for human habitation and commerce is intricately interconnected with the extension of racial categories to space for the purposes of distributing resources along racial lines.[28] Building on the work of Kim and Lai, I focus particularly on the *relational racialization of space,* which I define as the relational deployment of racial meanings by institutional actors and processes that organize residential settlements and the physical environment according to the perceived physical characteristics, behavioral traits, and social value of hierarchically ordered social groups. My approach, however, deviates from that of Kim and Lai. Specifically, it reveals the central role that sociospatial dynamics—the configurations of knowledge systems (e.g., social scientific theory), segregationist worldviews, state policies, and real estate industry practice—play in racial projects that articulate and rearticulate spatialized racial hierarchies through a broader array of racialized bodies outside of the white-Asian-Black triangular model in the Stockton metropolitan area.[29]

Lastly, my sociospatial approach incorporates key insights from previous studies that seriously consider the physical environment in shaping racial and spatial hierarchies. For example, my analysis is informed by Mario Luis Small's poignant observation that fixed physical boundaries are important tools in socially differentiating and stratifying residential settlements.[30] My analysis also builds on key insights from the environmental justice literature. Specifically, I advance Lisa Sun-Hee Park and David N. Pellow's understanding of the centrality of racialized discourses in justifying the subjugation of nonwhites and immigrants into hazardous residential spaces and in contributing to the formation of environmental inequality (i.e., the unequal distribution of power, resources, and environmental benefits and burdens in U.S. society).[31] Further, my explicit focus on the relational construction of racial hierarchies between and within the white-nonwhite binary and in relation to urban-industrial development advances Pulido's analysis of the role that state policies, such as those involving the HOLC, and the real estate sector play in relegating various nonwhite groups to the comparably environmentally hazardous urban-industrial environment while upholding white privilege and enabling whites to secure "relatively cleaner environments by moving away from older industrial cores via suburbanization."[32]

RESEARCH STRATEGY

I used a multitude of data sources in my analysis. My understanding of the early racial and ethnic geography and urban-industrial development in the metropolis is informed by secondary sources dating back to before the founding of Stockton and California in 1850.[33] I also conducted spatial analysis of Sanborn fire insurance survey maps for fourteen towns and cities in the Stockton metropolitan area dating back to the 1880s. Sanborn maps contain detailed information about the location of industrial facilities and other fire hazards, as well as the street addresses and locations of racially and ethnically defined churches, schools, businesses, and even dwellings.[34] I found racially and ethnically defined establishments in the twelve cities and communities shown in figure 11.1. In this chapter, I present Sanborn data on racial-ethnic establishments from the 1917 Stockton map survey to provide greater social and spatial context to the map and survey developed by the HOLC in its 1938 "residential security survey" of Stockton.

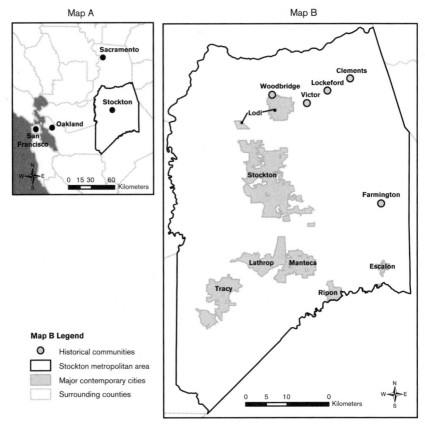

Map A   Map B

Map B Legend
○   Historical communities
▢   Stockton metropolitan area
▨   Major contemporary cities
▢   Surrounding counties

FIGURE 11.1. Map A: Northern California and the Stockton metropolitan area. Map B: Contemporary cities and historical communities in the Stockton metropolitan area. Maps by the author.

I downloaded the 1938 HOLC Stockton survey report, supporting documents, and map from a digital archive.[35] I subjected the texts and maps to coordinated content and spatial analyses to understand how the relational racialization of space was being institutionalized in the real estate sector and in government policy. Following the lead of previous nuanced analyses of the HOLC survey maps for select cities (e.g., that of Amy Hillier), I analyze how the HOLC Stockton survey reflected how the agency relationally constructed their racialized notions of "detrimental influences" and neighborhood investment risk with that found in prominent national narratives, academic theories, government policy, and the real estate industry. I determined how the HOLC's relational grading system was of continuing significance for contemporary settlement patterns and urban-industrial development in the metropolis with additional secondary sources (including studies by Dawn Bohulano Mabalon and John U. Ogbu), and neighborhood-level (i.e., census tract-level) data on population and housing patterns from the 2000 U.S. Census and industrial zoning designations as of 2004 from the California Spatial Information Library's general plan database.[36]

THE RELATIONAL RACIALIZATION OF SPACE IN STOCKTON

The Stockton metropolitan area was once populated predominantly by the Miwok and Yokut tribes of California's Central Valley.[37] The lands and lives of many of the area's tribal members were taken, however, by the Spanish conquest; American Indian relocation to missions in the San Francisco Bay area; trading, ranching, and trapping operations under Mexican rule; and a series of epidemics. Some survived to witness German immigrant Charles M. Weber lead the development of the city of Stockton on the Campo de los Franceses land grant after his participation in the U.S.-Mexico War. Stockton's namesake, Commodore Robert F. Stockton, was a U.S. naval officer who rescued Weber from Mexican captivity during the war.[38]

Stockton became a supply base for the gold rush after the gold was discovered in the "southern mines" of the Sierra Nevada foothills east and southeast of Stockton. Being close to major navigable waterways, Stockton was connected to the San Joaquin and Sacramento Rivers and San Francisco Bay. Stockton soon became an important immigrant gateway because of its developing infrastructure and proximity to San Francisco and the gold mines. The local business and political elite comprising the city's early growth coalition was racialized as white and predominantly of northern and western European descent. They settled in Stockton, obtained much of the land, and incorporated the city in July 1850.[39] Chinese immigrants and Black laborers, both free and enslaved, were early nonwhite arrivals to the Stockton area amid the gold rush. After mining went bust for these groups, or they were forcibly removed from the mines through white exclusionary actions, many of them settled in Stockton and found alternative means of low- or sometimes middle-class employment.[40]

Stockton soon became an administrative and industrial center, while local white elites and growth coalition members aimed to make it California's "manufacturing city." From 1850 to 1860, the city produced goods primarily for the mining industry (i.e., food and kindred products, metalwork, and transportation equipment), but from 1860 to 1890 this focus transitioned to flour milling and manufacturing equipment for the growing agricultural sector (particularly wheat farming). Manufacturing agricultural implements, canning, and shipbuilding were dominant industrial activities from 1890 to 1950.[41] Historical census records indicate that the Stockton metropolitan area experienced similar patterns of manufacturing growth and decline as seen throughout the United States: the number of manufacturing establishments operating in the area increased from zero in 1850 to 352 in 1900, followed by a decline in manufacturing to 207 establishments by 1940.[42] According to James Roberts, and as suggested by the Sanborn maps, most of the Stockton metropolitan area's manufacturing was concentrated in Stockton.

HOLC's 1938 Stockton Survey: Institutionalizing Neighborhood Racial Hierarchies

The decline in Stockton's manufacturing sector coincided with the Great Depression. New Deal federal housing programs of the 1930s were one policy response aimed at helping those who were adversely affected by the newly destabilized housing markets around the country. The Home Owners' Loan Act of 1933 was a piece of the New Deal housing program. The legislation established the HOLC, which was charged with standardizing residential appraisal methods through its confidential residential survey surveys (RSSs). In its RSSs, the HOLC ordered neighborhood desirability by four grades: "first" was given to the "best" green areas, "second" to "still desirable" blue areas, "third" to "declining" yellow areas, and "fourth" to the "hazardous" red areas. Early historical research argued that the HOLC was responsible for initiating the practice of redlining through its RSSs, which would subsequently inform its lending of over one million mortgages during the Great Depression, as well as the loans given by the Federal Housing Administration (FHA), which became a far more prominent mortgage lender during this period.[43] Redlining generally refers to "lending (or insurance) discrimination that bases credit decisions on the location of the property to the exclusion of characteristics of the borrower or the property."[44] The racial composition of neighborhoods encompassing the property has historically been a key factor in shaping redlining patterns.[45]

Hillier argues that a more careful reading of history shows that the HOLC was not entirely complicit in redlining, but that it was instrumental in institutionalizing racialized real estate practices. That is, the HOLC made loans in redlined areas, lenders were already avoiding neighborhoods they perceived as high risk before the HOLC RSSs, the HOLC was directed under the policy of its umbrella organization (the Federal Home Loan Bank Board) to restrict access to the HOLC maps for other regulatory agencies, and many of these other agencies—like the FHA (created in 1934), and private lenders not given access to HOLC maps—were already conducting their own (and sometimes more detailed) residential appraisals.[46] Indeed, by the 1920s, racially restrictive covenants, a type of land use control, were widely used by U.S. real estate firms and community builders to "regulate the distribution of the population, direct investment into certain geographical areas and away from others, and shape the development of entire subdivisions and neighborhoods."[47] It was the underwriting manual and policies of the FHA that mandated the use of racially restrictive covenants and residential mortgage loan redlining to exclude nonwhites and other "detrimental influences" from predominantly white and elite neighborhoods.[48]

Thus, redlining and racially restrictive covenants were in place before the HOLC was created. Those practices and much of the real estate industry of the 1930s were undergirded by a segregationist ideology and popular academic theories—especially the "ecological theory" used by Homer Hoyt, the University of Chicago economist and federal housing program adviser—that held that neighborhood social and physical disorder and decay would occur if "incompatible" racial groups were allowed to enter white neighborhoods.[49] Given this history, it is perhaps best to understand the HOLC as playing an important role in institutionalizing racist real estate actions, academic theory, and segregationist ideologies through its neighborhood appraisals.

There are three additional points regarding the HOLC that are particularly important for understanding its role in relationally racializing space in Stockton. First, the HOLC reported that by 1938 it held only 7 percent of the mortgages and 8 percent of real estate in Stockton. Second, the HOLC's Stockton RSS suggests the agency's neighborhood appraisals reconciled locally prominent real estate industry practices at the time with many of the logics characteristic of a "white spatial imaginary": broader segregationist ideologies, academic theory, and federal policy espousing the desirability of socially homogeneous residential space and controlled environments amid the recovery from the Great Depression.[50] Third, the HOLC's Stockton RSS reflected how it accomplished such reconciliation while incorporating into its grading system the broader "national racial narrative" at the time, punctuated by the paramount racial threat posed by Black residents to the social stability and investment worthiness of a neighborhood, as well as the conflation of that perceived racial threat with proximity to urban-industrial environments and other red or hazardous areas.[51]

Qualitative comments contained within the HOLC's Stockton RSS illustrate how their graded areas were understood relationally. The summary of their first-grade/A/green areas, and second-grade/B/blue areas on the Stockton RSS map (see figure 11.2) did not explicitly mention race. The first-grade areas were generally framed as new, well-planned, "homogeneous," "hot spots" for future growth and investment, and desirable in "good times" or "bad." The second areas were not new, nor were they necessarily homogeneous, but lenders still made loans with favorable terms in those areas. These second-tier areas were routinely described as "like a 1935 automobile—still good, but not what the people are buying today who can afford a new one."[52]

The lower two grades were discussed with reference to their representativeness as sites of decline in the infrastructure to maintain racial exclusivity or they had already succumbed to "decay" and the "infiltration of subversive races." Specifically, the third grade/C areas are yellow on the original HOLC map. The color signals drivers to be cautious or to slow down when approaching an intersection; here, it signals that one is approaching a hazardous space, usually one that has expiring deed restrictions (i.e., racially restrictive covenants) that are used to guard against the "infiltration of lower grade populations" and maintain neighborhood "homogeneity." The fourth grade/D areas represented with red in the original HOLC map were generally explained as having "detrimental influences in a pronounced degree, undesirable population or infiltration of it." Furthermore, these lowest-grade areas were "broader than the so-called slum districts. Some mortgage lenders may refuse to make loans in these neighborhoods and others will lend only on a conservative basis."[53]

Neighborhood population composition, along with other housing and market factors, were used to signify neighborhood investment risk in the HOLC RSS of Stockton. Additional material included in the HOLC's Stockton RSS illuminates how the "hazardous" fourth grade or red spaces were conflated with Blacks, other nonwhites, and other neighborhood attributes:

A study of . . . 1930 census figures indicates that as a whole the city's population is a homogenous one. In 1930 there were only 433 negroes in the city and the other colored races numbered but 4800. *Generally speaking these and*

*other than white racial elements are very generally confined to the "red areas"
shown upon the Security Area Map and to the commercial and industrial areas
which surround them* [emphasis added]. The danger of infiltration of these
racial elements is, therefore, minimized.[54]

An important sentiment conveyed in this quote was that the city's urban-
industrial boundaries help contain the "infiltration" of nonwhites into the
predominantly white (89.07 percent) population of Stockton. The quote,
however, specifically singles out Blacks while obscuring the other racialized
groups then present in Stockton. According to the 1930 race and nativity
census figures referenced in this quote, the 433 Blacks were only 0.90 percent
of the 47,963 people living in Stockton, while the 4,808 "other colored races"
represented 10.02 percent of that population. Within the other category, the
predominant group was Mexicans (4.13 percent), followed by Japanese (2.89
percent), Chinese (2.07 percent), Filipinxs, Hawaiians, and other racialized
groups (0.82 percent), and American Indians (0.11 percent). Foreign-born
whites were 14.40 percent of the total population, with Italians comprising
the largest share at 29.38 percent. The primary nonwhite category highlighted
in the federal census and by the HOLC at the time was thus the very small
minority of Black residents living in Stockton as of 1930. Black presence was
seen as the biggest racial threat despite (1) the history of racial animosity
expressed both locally, regionally, and nationwide at Asians, especially
Chinese, from the late 1800s through 1924 immigration reform and the
Great Depression; and (2) the more prevalent Mexican population that was
classified as a prominent racial threat by 1930.[55]

Figure 11.2 displays Stockton's forty-three RSS areas and the grades applied
to them by the HOLC after their field visits and interviews with local real
estate interests and mortgage lenders. The industrial and commercial areas
and parks shown in the figure were also derived from the RSS map. The figure displays the HOLC RSS data in relation to Stockton's racial and ethnic
establishments from Stockton's 1917 Sanborn map to give additional context
to the relationally ordered spaces of Stockton during this period. There are a
couple of noteworthy patterns reflected in the Sanborn map data. First, the
Mexican, Spanish, Black, and majority of "Oriental," Chinese, Japanese, and
Korean establishments were clustered together near the urban-industrial core
of Stockton, which dates back to the 1850s.[56] Second, establishments associated with Italians, the primary white immigrants from southern Europe,
were nearer to the urban-industrial core and more distant from the western

European establishments (i.e., French laundries and German religious institutions). This distribution suggests some physical distances between these ethnically demarcated "white" establishments during this period. Lastly, two other religious institutions representing racialized populations are shown in figure 11.2: Jewish temples/synagogues north of Weber Avenue and the oldest Sikh temple in the United States, which was established by Sikhs of Punjabi descent in far south Stockton in the Homestead ("D11") neighborhood south of Charter Way.[57]

Figure 11.2 also shows the University of the Pacific (UOP), between Alpine Avenue and Calaveras River and Pershing and Pacific Avenue. UOP was relocated to its initial 0.16-square-kilometer site in the desirable, suburban, north-central section of Stockton in the early 1920s from its mid-1800s location in the Santa Clara–San Jose area. Stockton's population base, the absence of higher education institutions, a land gift from the J. C. Smith Company, and "energetic support" from the Stockton Chamber of Commerce—historically a key growth coalition member in Stockton—were all factors that reportedly contributed to UOP's relocation to the city.[58] A wide range of accounts suggest that the UOP has historically been known for being a socially desirable alternative driver of urban development to the previous gold rush and manufacturing-dominated legacy of the city's past. For example, the HOLC Stockton field report includes UOP in its list of factors that helped Stockton's "more or less remarkable recovery" from the Great Depression, and the reports include proximity to UOP as one of its "favorable influences."[59] In addition, recent public histories claim that UOP contributes "considerably to the cultural richness and the economic health of the city of Stockton."[60]

The description of the Westmoor ("A1") and Oxford Manor–Avondale–Lake Park ("A2") neighborhoods near UOP (see figure 11.2) suggest the links between proximity to UOP and other socially desirable attributes typically associated with the green, first-grade spaces of north Stockton. Their descriptions also emphasize they "have ample" or were "fully" deed restricted. Figure 11.2 outlines all eighteen RSS areas that were entirely or partially deed-restricted by 1938, according to the HOLC reports. Those deed restrictions include racially restrictive covenants discussed above, which were already in place throughout the country by the 1920s. Westmoor and Oxford Manor–Avondale–Lake Park included no foreign-born families, and their residents' occupations were "professional & business men, retired capitalists, etc." These two neighborhoods thus accord with the model of "green" spaces that was

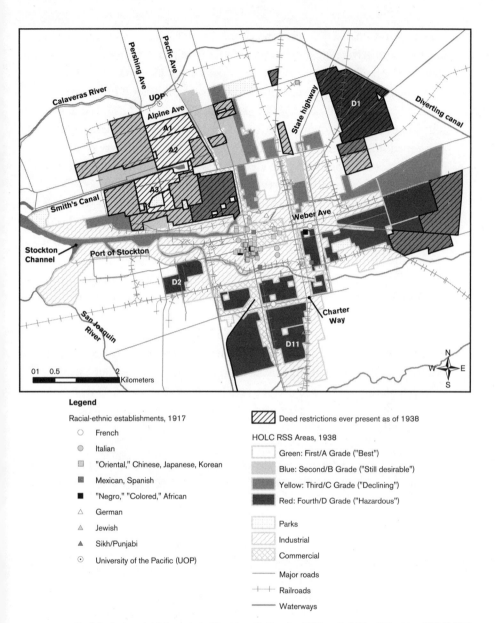

Legend

Racial-ethnic establishments, 1917

○ French

◉ Italian

▨ "Oriental," Chinese, Japanese, Korean

▩ Mexican, Spanish

■ "Negro," "Colored," African

△ German

△ Jewish

▲ Sikh/Punjabi

⊙ University of the Pacific (UOP)

▨ Deed restrictions ever present as of 1938

HOLC RSS Areas, 1938

☐ Green: First/A Grade ("Best")

▨ Blue: Second/B Grade ("Still desirable")

▨ Yellow: Third/C Grade ("Declining")

▨ Red: Fourth/D Grade ("Hazardous")

▨ Parks

▨ Industrial

▨ Commercial

— Major roads

┼┼┼ Railroads

— Waterways

FIGURE 11.2. Racial-ethnic establishments in Stockton, California, 1917, and digitized Stockton HOLC RSS map, 1938. Map by the author.

being institutionalized around the country at this time under state policy and local and private implementation of that policy to reinforce racial exclusivity.[61] The final "green" space was the Lake View–Lake Park–Park Terrace ("A3") neighborhood. The description of this neighborhood links environmental amenities with racial (and class) exclusivity—and thus social desirability—of the neighborhood: "This is a highly deed restricted area which is also zoned single family residential; and is one of the community's best residential districts. . . . Streets facing Victory Park and those bordering Yosemite Lake and Smith's Canal are deserving of a high green grade."[62]

On the other side of the continuum, we see the Boggs Tract–Yosemite Subdivision ("D2") in southwest Stockton. Attending to this space helps us understand how racial meanings are extended relationally to the social groups and physical space constituting this industrial neighborhood near the Port of Stockton. In the HOLC RSS, this neighborhood's favorable influences include "convenience to industrial employment, schools, and trading center." Its detrimental influences include "heterogeneous improvements and population." Its occupational makeup included "farm laborers, factory workers, common labor, etc," and it apparently had 40 percent foreign-born families from Italy, Japan, China, Mexico, and the Philippines. About 3 percent of its population was African American. The report elaborated on its rationale for assigning the lowest-possible fourth grade and "hazardous" label to the neighborhood:

> Zoned for light industry, but none exists at present time. Area is wholly a 1-family working man's district. The western portion known as Boggs Tract is outside the city limits and from a racial standpoint, is a better grade than the eastern part. Construction is largely of a single type and in many cases, borders upon a "shack" variety. Very little pride of occupancy is exhibited and when the area becomes more densely occupied, it bids fair to become a slum district. It is accorded a very low red grade.[63]

Table 11.1 presents attributes that were consistently referenced for neighborhoods in the HOLC RSS of Stockton. The table illuminates how population and housing conditions, mortgage financing, deed restrictions, and various developmental contexts were relationally and unequally distributed by HOLC ratings of green (first/A), blue (second/B), yellow (third/C), and red (fourth/D). Specifically, the lowest ratings were associated with areas composed of racialized nonwhite populations, including "Negroes," "Orientals," Japanese, Chinese, Filipinxs, and Mexicans. Consistent with previous

TABLE 11.1. Select 1938 HOLC RSS area attributes by HOLC rating

	1938 HOLC rating			
HOLC RSS area attributes	Green (First/A)	Blue (Second/B)	Yellow (Third/C)	Red (Fourth/D)
Population and housing conditions				
"Negro" presence	0	0	0	10
"Oriental" presence	0	1	0	7
Japanese presence	0	1	0	5
Chinese presence	0	0	0	5
Filipinx presence	0	0	0	4
Mexican presence	0	0	0	5
Italian presence	0	0	3	2
Immigrant presence	0	9	13	11
Below-average, lowest-estimated annual family income (<$1,397.30, 1938 dollars)	0	0	12	11
Professional inhabitants	2	7	2	0
"Heterogeneous populations and improvements" present	0	0	1	10
N (total $N = 37$)	2	11	13	11
Mortgage financing availability				
"Ample" availability of mortgage funds for home purchase or building	2	12	3	0
N (total $N = 38$)	2	12	13	11
Deed restrictive and developmental context				
Deed restrictions ever present	3	9	5	1
Average kilometers to nearest industry boundary	1.53	1.04	0.67	0.43
Presence of city flood protection service	3	7	1	0
Average kilometers to UOP	1.18	2.15	3.86	5.32
Average kilometers to green (first grade) areas	0.64	1.76	3.51	4.53
Average kilometers to blue (second grade) areas	1.76	2.06	3.15	4.13
Average kilometers to yellow (third grade) areas	3.51	3.15	2.77	3.51
Average kilometers to red (fourth grade) areas	4.53	4.13	3.51	2.58
N (total $N = 43$)	3	15	14	11

SOURCE: 1938 HOLC Stockton, CA, Residential Security Survey.

research, the presence of "Negroes" or Blacks in an RSS area was used as the primary racial indicator of neighborhood undesirability by real estate actors in Stockton.[64] Additionally, the presence of "heterogeneous populations and improvements," often understood in racial terms by local and national real estate actors and regulators, was used to signify a threat to the supposed stabilizing force and investment worthiness of homogeneous, white neighborhoods. These population and housing conditions were reinforced with the concentration of "ample" mortgage financing and racially prohibitive deed restrictions mostly in green- and blue-graded areas to reinforce their relative racial exclusivity. The Sheltered Oaks/City Farms ("D1") neighborhood is one exception to the spatial pattern of deed restrictions. According to the Stockton RSS, the northwest Sheltered Oaks portion of the neighborhood was "deed protected against Orientals and Negroes," but the remaining City Farms portion was without zoning or deed restrictions.[65] Despite this exception, spaces categorized by the HOLC as red, fourth/D grade, and hazardous were those where many lenders were extremely cautious lending out of a heightened sense of "moral risk," given the areas' racial composition and other population and housing conditions.

The developmental context of the HOLC-graded RSS areas reveals the relative inscription of racial hierarchies in the physical spaces of the metropolis and the infrastructure in place to protect them from environmental threats. That is, the highest grades were consistently reserved for areas closer to the green, white, elite, UOP-campus neighborhoods farther from industrial land uses and protected from Stockton's frequent floods by a city pumping plant. The lowest ratings were applied to areas closer to the potential health hazards of industrial zones without the city flood service, and closer to the most stigmatized, nonwhite, red, fourth/D-graded residential settlements in Stockton. The blue- and yellow-graded areas served as the intermediate racial and spatial buffers between elite and white green spaces of north Stockton and the subjugated and Black-containing neighborhoods of south and west Stockton.

The Continuing Significance of the HOLC's Neighborhood Racial Hierarchies

To what extent is the Stockton metropolitan area still shaped by the racial project of the HOLC's neighborhood appraisals and of allied efforts through the local real estate sector and New Deal federal housing policy? Tables 11.2

TABLE 11.2. 1938 HOLC grade status for neighborhoods by mean

(Racial-ethnic and immigrant composition, 2000s)

Neighborhood variable	Majority neighborhood assigned 1938 HOLC grade				
	Green (First/A)	Blue (Second/B)	Yellow (Third/C)	Red (Fourth/D)	Not graded
Racial-ethnic composition, 2000					
Percent of population					
White	73.84	64.73	44.31	33.01	65.35
Black	3.17	6.29	6.54	12.17	6.89
American Indian or Alaska Native	0.00	1.38	1.71	1.73	1.02
Asian	15.98	13.00	12.68	12.01	12.95
Multiracial	8.18	8.47	6.89	6.59	5.98
Asian/multiracial specifying ancestry					
Chinese	2.91	1.06	0.92	1.07	1.18
Japanese	1.47	0.88	0.25	0.34	0.95
Filipinx	3.19	4.62	4.23	6.19	4.74
Latinx, any race	14.62	32.17	53.31	64.06	25.83
Mexican origin	11.67	27.50	46.14	57.16	21.19
With ancestry specified					
English	14.66	7.17	2.65	1.43	8.79
French	4.02	2.21	1.46	1.17	2.58
German	17.92	13.88	6.42	2.82	15.22
Irish	18.33	9.39	4.67	2.40	9.60
Italian	12.84	6.61	2.71	1.87	6.90
Immigrant composition, 2000					
Percent of population: foreign born	6.62	14.29	31.76	33.96	17.03
Percent of foreign born					
Italian	6.43	1.74	0.15	0.22	1.08
Chinese	15.55	2.98	1.41	1.66	3.72
Japanese	5.09	1.76	0.68	0.04	1.01
Filipinx	5.90	5.55	7.10	7.60	12.76
Mexican	14.75	54.20	74.89	79.90	43.44
N (total N = 121)	1	6	7	10	97

SOURCE: 1938 HOLC Stockton, CA, Residential Security Survey; 2000 U.S. Census.

	Majority neighborhood assigned 1938 HOLC grade				
Neighborhood variable	Green (First/A)	Blue (Second/B)	Yellow (Third/C)	Red (Fourth/D)	Not graded
Economic status, 2000					
Median household income (1999 dollars, thousands)	51.49	34.15	20.63	24.92	46.35
Housing values and age, 2000					
Percent owner-occupied housing units	69.19	53.33	32.83	44.29	61.42
Median value of specified owner-occupied housing units (2000 dollars, thousands)	142.50	97.70	84.63	75.23	154.16
Median year housing units built	1944.00	1949.67	1956.29	1957.60	1975.55
Industrial land use, 2004					
Percent zoned industrial, 2004	0	4.04	22.44	32.22	5.74
N (total N = 121)	1	6	7	10	97

SOURCE: 1938 HOLC Stockton, CA, Residential Security Survey; 2000 U.S. Census; California Spatial Information Library.

and 11.3 summarize the results from my analysis of select average racial-ethnic, immigrant, economic, housing, and land use characteristics by the 2000s for the 121 neighborhoods (i.e., census tracts) within the Stockton metropolitan area by HOLC grade status. Figure 11.3 shows the same 121 neighborhoods by HOLC grade status. The six second/B/blue-graded neighborhoods cluster around the first/A/green-graded UOP neighborhood shown in lightest gray in figure 11.3. The seven third/C/yellow-graded neighborhoods are shown above the Crosstown Freeway and straddling Highway 99. The ten fourth/D/red-graded neighborhoods are found south of the Crosstown Freeway and in the August area of east Stockton. The other ninety-seven neighborhoods not graded by the HOLC throughout the metropolis are shown in white in figure 11.3.

There is a clear relationship between HOLC grade and contemporary neighborhood economic status. Of the neighborhoods having a majority of

Map A   Map B

Legend

⊙ University of the Pacific (UOP)

─ Crosstown Freeway

━ Other major roads

Neighborhoods by 1938 HOLC grade

☐ Not graded

▨ Green: First/A Grade ("Best")

▨ Blue: Second/B Grade ("Still desirable")

■ Yellow: Third/C Grade ("Declining")

■ Red: Fourth/D Grade ("Hazardous")

FIGURE 11.3. Map A: Present-day Stockton, California. Map B: Neighborhoods in the Stockton metropolitan area by 1938 HOLC grade. Maps by the author.

their area graded by the HOLC, the distribution of median household income and median housing values followed the HOLC neighborhood hierarchy, ranging from highest in the UOP neighborhood to lowest in the ten red-graded neighborhoods. The average median household income in the ninety-seven neighborhoods not graded by the HOLC was between that of the green- and blue-graded neighborhoods, while the average median housing value of ungraded neighborhoods was the highest in the metropolis. Furthermore, homeownership was highest in the UOP neighborhood, the ungraded neighborhoods, and the blue-graded neighborhoods, and lowest in the red- and yellow-graded neighborhoods.

The neighborhoods' stratified economic status maps on well to the relationship between the HOLC grade and Stockton's contemporary racially segregated settlement patterns of a predominantly white north side, Black and Latinx south side, and distributed Asian enclaves. Racialized white groups were predominant in the historically affluent, racially restricted, and homogeneously white neighborhoods, with higher rates of homeownership in north Stockton, as well as in those ungraded neighborhoods outside Stockton.[66] This linear relationship between HOLC grade and white composition was reflected in the white immigrant populations distributed across HOLC-graded neighborhoods. Those of northern and western European ancestry (English, Irish, German, and French) were concentrated in the green- and blue-graded neighborhoods. Akin to the broader historical pattern in which "whiteness" in the United States came to include southern Europeans, these exclusive white enclaves, especially near Calaveras River, incorporated the Italian-origin population frequently noted in pejorative terms in the HOLC RSS of Stockton.[67] Some attributed this type of "spatial assimilation" to Italian-origin people's gaining access to higher-paying occupations in the predominantly white-owned and locally powerful agricultural sector in the metropolis, including the successful network of cherry growers.[68]

As in the broader racial hierarchy of contemporary U.S. residential settlements, Stockton's Asian populations are thought to collectively represent the second racial tier after whites, and they are relatively equally distributed across the HOLC-graded neighborhoods.[69] The UOP neighborhood had the highest percentage of Asians, while the blue-, yellow-, red-, and ungraded neighborhoods were basically equal in their share of Asian population. But there are important racial and spatial hierarchies within Stockton's Asian population. While representing a small minority, Chinese and Japanese Americans tend to predominate in the green- and blue-graded neighborhoods relative to neighborhoods receiving majority yellow or red grades. The distribution of Chinese and Japanese immigrants by HOLC neighborhood grade reflects an inverse relationship with that of the broader immigrant community.[70] In contrast, Filipinx Americans are most prominent in the red-graded neighborhoods and least represented in the UOP neighborhood. The distribution of Filipinx immigrants contrasts with that of the Chinese and Japanese immigrants, but it approaches that of the broader immigrant community with the exception that Filipinx immigrants are more concentrated in the ninety-seven ungraded neighborhoods throughout the metropolis.

The distribution of Blacks and Latinxs, particularly of Mexican origin, by HOLC neighborhood grade is inverse to the relationship between whites, economic status, and the HOLC neighborhood grades in the metropolis. Blacks and Mexican-origin people are concentrated at comparable levels, respectively, in ungraded and blue- and yellow-graded neighborhoods, but they are least prevalent in the UOP neighborhood and most prevalent in the red, hazardous spaces of Stockton. Such patterns suggest the influence of the broader structural forces that continue to place Latinxs and Blacks at the bottom of the racial and spatial hierarchy of the U.S. metropolis, with Blacks relegated to the disinvested, segregated ghettos and Mexican-origin people to the similarly isolated *barrios* of Stockton.[71]

Other structural and historical forces may tie the spatial location of Blacks and Mexicans to that of the Filipinxs vis-à-vis Chinese, Japanese, and Italians who were able to gain relatively more access to higher-status Stockton neighborhoods. By the late 1960s, the Chinese and Japanese population had shifted from south Stockton to north Stockton residences and elsewhere throughout the metropolis. Ogbu attributes the change in residence for the Chinese and the Japanese to both groups' having more economic success than Mexicans or Blacks, and to the expiration of racially restrictive covenants against the Chinese and Japanese living in the north side since the late 1950s.[72] The settlement patterns of Japanese and Filipinxs must be put into further historical context. After Japan's attack on Pearl Harbor and the Philippines, and President Roosevelt's Executive Order 9066 in 1942, Japanese in the metropolis were demonized, interned, and dispossessed. Filipinxs were treated more favorably during this war period, especially by Stockton's white elites, and they took over many businesses and homes previously held by Japanese in the metropolis and the south Stockton area known as Little Manila. Many Filipinxs also left farmwork—replaced by Mexican labor—for higher-paying jobs afforded by eased restrictions on their participation in the armed forces and in the booming defense-related industries of Stockton during this period.[73] Yet racial discrimination and limited job opportunities outside farmwork characterized the Filipinx experience in Stockton in the postwar period, which placed them in similar economically and politically disadvantaged racialized positions as those of Blacks and the Mexican-origin population in Stockton.[74]

Postwar urban renewal efforts further contributed to the racial marginalization of Blacks, Mexicans, and Filipinxs and to their concentration in south Stockton. Aided by federal legislation and funding, local growth coalition members implemented "slum clearance" in Stockton's "infested" downtown and West End (i.e., Boggs Tract) area, in part through the construction of the Crosstown Freeway, which would connect Interstate 5 to State Route 99. Clearance efforts developed intensely from 1960 to 1970. In the summer of 1962, Stockton's Redevelopment Agency filed condemnation suits against property owners in the West End to clear the area. Demolition took place from 1964 to 1966, reportedly displacing forty-four businesses, fifty-nine single residents, and nine families from the West Side, and it continued eastward toward State Route 99.[75] The Crosstown Freeway was finally finished in the 1990s, but it had already considerably changed downtown Stockton and the West Side by 1972. The development destroyed Little Manila; devastated many of Stockton's low-income, nonwhite, immigrant, and red-graded neighborhoods by the HOLC; and pushed Black, Mexican, and Filipinx residents further into the devalued and industrialized spaces of south Stockton.

The distribution of housing stock and industrial zoning throughout the metropolis demonstrates the continuing significance of racialized settlement patterns that were shaped by the open era of relational racialization and discrimination reflected in the HOLC grading system and associated 1930s real estate activity and state policy.[76] As shown in table 11.3, the variation in the average median year that housing units were built by HOLC neighborhood grade indicates that most houses built in the exclusive UOP neighborhood and the second-tier blue-graded neighborhoods occurred before or shortly after the U.S. Supreme Court declared in *Shelley v. Kraemer* (1948) that racially restrictive covenants blocking nonwhite access to these type of white and elite neighborhoods were unenforceable.[77] Meanwhile, racially unrestricted housing developments peaked in the yellow- and red-graded areas in the mid-1950s, and the newest housing developments peaking in the 1970s were mostly found in the ninety-seven neighborhoods ungraded by the HOLC, which would become majority white in the growing satellite cities elsewhere throughout the metropolis.

The percentage of neighborhoods zoned as industrial by 2004 was highest in the predominantly Black, Mexican, and Filipinx red-graded neighborhoods, followed by the yellow-graded, ungraded, and blue-graded neighborhoods. The exclusive, white, elite, and green UOP neighborhood had no industrial land uses. Read alongside the racially and economically skewed residential development patterns summarized above, the trajectory of industrial development in Stockton and throughout the metropolis suggest that the red-graded and some yellow-graded neighborhoods of Stockton were surrounded by industrial land uses that industrialized further in later years alongside unequally high rates of low-income populations and Blacks, Mexicans, and Filipinxs. These developments further suggest industrial environments may have played a consistent and durable role as physical "boundary markers" for producing and maintaining relationally racialized "hazardous" space in Stockton.[78]

. . .

This chapter reveals how the historical racial project of relationally racializing Stockton neighborhoods by the HOLC and allied segregationist ideologies and academic theory, along with the real estate industry and federal policy, inscribed racial hierarchies into residential settlement space of the Stockton metropolitan area. Furthermore, it demonstrates the extent to which the historical relational racialization of space in Stockton has provided the sociospatial foundations of contemporary racially segregated settlement patterns and urban-industrial development of the metropolis. I now take stock of the broader implications of this chapter's relational approach to race and space and outline directions for future research.

Previous research illuminates the important roles that land ownership, labor market positions, class dynamics, legal and political systems, and citizenship status play in the relational construction of racial hierarchies.[79] This study builds on the literatures at the intersection of relational approaches to race and the sociospatial approach in urban sociology (such as that articulated by Mark Gottdiener and Ray Hutchison) in a manner that extends Lai's racial triangulation of space model and George Lipsitz's understanding of "how racism takes place." While noting that "racial projects are flexible, fluid, and relational," Lipsitz cogently argues that examining the racialization of Black spaces and anti-Black spaces "reveals the particular dynamics that have been central to the construction of racialized space for everyone."[80]

This chapter supports Lipsitz's claim regarding the importance of attending to the spatial relations of Black subjugation to glean important insights into how racism and "the possessive investment in whiteness" occurs historically and in physical space.[81] Indeed, the Stockton case suggests the racialization of space in the neighborhood appraisals standardized by the HOLC in the 1930s essentially used the presence of Black residents as another form of the "one-drop rule" in demarcating the highest neighborhood investment risk, but that is only part of the racial story.[82] The combined *relational* and sociospatial approach used in this chapter reveals that we cannot fully understand the racialization of Black (and white) spaces without taking seriously how the deployment of racial meanings to physical space is conditioned by the mutually constituted statuses and multiscalar discourse about a broader cross-section of racialized groups throughout the metropolis.[83]

In addition, Stockton's historical development suggests the HOLC redgraded areas have been produced over time as subjugated Black, Mexican, *and* Filipinx spaces. These spaces exist in a racial and spatial hierarchy that is "equilibrated" by the racial and spatial positions of the white and elite UOP neighborhood and the intermediary racialized spaces of neighborhoods graded as blue or yellow in the 1930s and the predominantly white neighborhoods in satellite cities that grew rapidly in the latter half of the twentieth century throughout the Stockton metropolitan area.[84] Furthermore, building on the work of Park and Pellow, Pulido, and Small, this chapter demonstrates how the urban-industrial environment is an important tool in the relational racialization process, giving both racial and environmental weight behind the notion of "hazardous" space in Stockton. Such insight is obscured when the physical environment of relationally racialized spaces is neglected.

This chapter has research implications for understanding the relational racialization of space within and beyond the Stockton case. First, comparative and historical research between Stockton and the other 238 cities surveyed by the HOLC in the 1930s, situated within their respective metropolitan contexts, may glean important insights into the general dynamic of how racial hierarchies unfold over time at the regional scale.[85] When and under what conditions are various nonwhite groups, especially Blacks, demarcated as racial threats and constitutive of "hazardous" space in the HOLC appraisals?

In addition, this chapter outlines in broad temporal strokes the links between the relational racialization of space of Stockton in the 1930s and contemporary racial settlement and urban-industrial development patterns from the postwar period to the 2000s. What other sociospatial mechanisms condition these links? Are they found in 1970s-era redlining observed in nearby Sacramento?[86] What role is played by more contemporary disparate mortgage approval and denial patterns for variously racialized *individuals* vis-à-vis their prospective host *neighborhoods* in patterns of stability and change in the racial and spatial hierarchies of the Stockton metropolitan area?[87]

Lastly, this chapter has implications for pressing issues of environmental inequality and planning. We know that environmental inequalities are formed through the mutual exploitation of people of color, immigrants, and the environment through segregation and industrial development.[88] How and under what conditions do the industrial environments that contribute to the relational racialization process in Stockton also present environmental health hazards for the racially subordinated residents segregated near them?

NOTES

1. Tomás Almaguer, *Racial Fault Lines: The Historical Origins of White Supremacy* (Berkeley: University of California Press, 1994); Claire Jean Kim, "The Racial Triangulation of Asian Americans," *Politics and Society* 27, no. 1 (1999): 105–38; Natalia Molina, *How Race Is Made in America: Immigration, Citizenship, and the Historical Power of Racial Scripts* (Berkeley: University of California Press, 2014); Laura Pulido, *Black, Brown, Yellow, and Left: Radical Activism in Los Angeles* (Berkeley: University of California Press, 2006).

2. Camille Zubrinsky Charles, *Won't You Be My Neighbor? Race, Class, and Residence in Los Angeles* (New York: Russell Sage Foundation, 2006).

3. Kevin Fox Gotham, *Race, Real Estate, and Uneven Development: The Kansas City Experience, 1900–2000* (Albany: State University of New York Press, 2002); Bruce D. Haynes and Ray Hutchinson, "The *Ghetto*: Origins, History, Discourse," *City & Community* 29, no. 4 (2008): 347–352; Jesus Hernandez, "Redlining Revisited: Mortgage Lending Patterns in Sacramento 1930–2004," *International Journal of Urban and Regional Research* 33, no. 2 (2009): 291–313; Clement Lai, "The Racial Triangulation of Space: The Case of Urban Renewal in San Francisco's Fillmore District," *Annals of the Association of American Geographers* 102, no. 1 (2012): 151–70; George Lipsitz, *How Racism Takes Place* (Philadelphia: Temple University Press, 2011).

4. Michael Omi and Howard Winant, *Racial Formation in the United States: From the 1960s to the 1990s,* 2nd ed. (New York: Routledge, 1994), 61–62.

5. Pulido, *Black, Brown, Yellow, and Left,* 4.

6. Omi and Winant, *Racial Formation,* 56.

7. Almaguer, *Racial Fault Lines;* Kim, "Racial Triangulation"; Lai, "Racial Triangulation of Space"; Molina, *How Race Is Made;* Lisa Sun-Hee Park and David N. Pellow, "Racial Formation, Environmental Racism, and the Emergence of Silicon Valley," *Ethnicities* 4, no. 3 (2004): 403–24; Pulido, *Black, Brown, Yellow, and Left.*

8. Clive Davis, *Stockton: Sunrise Port on the San Joaquin* (Sun Valley, CA: American Historical Press, 1998); Rudolph M. Lapp, *Blacks in Gold Rush California* (New Haven, CT: Yale University Press, 1977); Dawn Bohulano Mabalon, *Little Manila Is in the Heart: The Making of the Filipina/o American Community in Stockton, California* (Durham, NC: Duke University Press, 2013); Sylvia Sun Minnick, *Samfow: The San Joaquin Chinese Legacy* (Fresno, CA: Panorama, 1988).

9. John R. Logan and Charles Zhang, "Global Neighborhoods: New Pathways to Diversity and Separation," *American Journal of Sociology* 115, no. 4 (2010): 1069–109.

10. Barrett A. Lee, Sean F. Reardon, Chad R. Farrell, Stephen A. Matthews, and David O'Sullivan, "Beyond the Census Tract: Patterns and Determinants of Racial Segregation at Multiple Geographic Scales," *American Sociological Review* 73, no. 5 (2008): 766–91.

11. Michael Fitzgerald, "Deep Roots of Stockton Segregation," *The Record* (Stockton, CA), April 27, 2001.

12. Amy E. Hillier, "Redlining and the Home Owners' Loan Corporation," *Journal of Urban History* 29, no. 4 (2003): 394–420.

13. Gotham, *Race, Real Estate, and Uneven Development;* Hillier, "Redlining"; Amy E. Hillier, "Residential Security Maps and Neighborhood Appraisals: The Home Owner's Loan Corporation and the Case of Philadelphia," *Social Science History* 29, no. 2 (2005): 207–33; Kenneth T. Jackson, *Crabgrass Frontier: The Suburbanization of the United States* (New York: Oxford University Press, 1985).

14. Kim, "Racial Triangulation"; Omi and Winant, *Racial Formation.*

15. Pulido, *Black, Brown, Yellow, and Left.*

16. Pulido, *Black, Brown, Yellow, and Left.*

17. Almaguer, *Racial Fault Lines,* 6.

18. Kim, "Racial Triangulation," 107.

19. Molina, *How Race Is Made.*

20. Almaguer, *Racial Fault Lines,* 22.

21. Kim, "Racial Triangulation"; Lai, "Racial Triangulation of Space"; Pulido, *Black, Brown, Yellow, and Left.*

22. Lai, "Racial Triangulation of Space," 167.

23. Lai, "Racial Triangulation of Space," 151.

24. Henri Lefebvre, *The Production of Space* (1974; repr., Oxford: Blackwell, 1991), 101–2.

25. Mark Gottdiener and Ray Hutchinson, *The New Urban Sociology* (Boulder, CO: Westview Press, 2006).

26. John Logan and Harvey Molotch, *Urban Fortunes: The Political Economy of Place* (1987; repr., Berkeley: University of California Press, 2007).

27. Kim, "Racial Triangulation"; Lai, "Racial Triangulation of Space."

28. Gotham, *Race, Real Estate, and Uneven Development;* Omi and Winant, *Racial Formation.*

29. See Gotham, *Race, Real Estate, and Uneven Development;* Colleen Lye, "The Afro-Asian Analogy," *PMLA* 123, no. 5 (2008): 1732–36.

30. Mario Luis Small, *Villa Victoria: The Transformation of Social Capital in a Boston Barrio* (Chicago: University of Chicago Press, 2004).

31. Park and Pellow, "Racial Formation."

32. Laura Pulido, "Rethinking Environmental Racism: White Privilege and Urban Development in Southern California," *Annals of the Association of American Geographers* 90, no. 1 (2000), 12.

33. Frances Baltich, *Search for Safety: The Founding of Stockton's Black Community* (Sacramento, CA: Artprint Press, 1982); Davis, *Stockton;* Lapp, *Blacks in Gold Rush California;* Mabalon, *Little Manila;* Minnick, *Samfow;* James Arthur Roberts, "Stockton's Manufacturing: The Development, Effects, and Future of Manufacturing in Stockton, California" (PhD diss., University of California, Los Angeles, 1963).

34. Russell A. Kazal, "The Interwar Origins of the White Ethnic," *Journal of American Ethnic History* 23, no. 4 (2004): 78–131; James R. Curtis, "Mexicali's Chinatown," *Geographic Review* 85, no. 3 (1995): 335–48.

35. Richard Marciano, David T. Goldberg, and Chien Y. Hou, "T-RACES: A Testbed for the Redlining Archives of California's Exclusionary Spaces," accessed July 20, 2010, http://salt.unc.edu/T-Races.

36. California Spatial Information Library, "California General Plans," accessed August 31, 2009, http://gforge.casil.ucdavis.edu/frs/download.php/498/genplans. shp.xml; Mabalon, *Little Manila;* John U. Ogbu, *The Next Generation: An Ethnography of Education in an Urban Neighborhood* (New York: Academic Press, 1974).

37. Minnick, *Samfow.*

38. Davis, *Stockton.*

39. Davis, *Stockton;* Minnick, *Samfow.*

40. Almaguer, *Racial Fault Lines;* Minnick, *Samfow;* Lapp, *Blacks in Gold Rush California.*

41. Roberts, "Stockton's Manufacturing."

42. These figures are based on my analyses of historical census data from the Minnesota Population Center, *National Historical Geographic Information System: Pre-release Version 0.1,* University of Minnesota, Minneapolis, 2004.

43. Jackson, *Crabgrass Frontier.*

44. Hillier, "Redlining," 395.

45. Hernandez, "Redlining Revisited"; Meghan Kuebler, "Lending in the Modern Era: Does Racial Composition of Neighborhoods Matter When Individuals Seek Home Financing? A Pilot Study in New England," *City & Community* 11, no. 1 (2012): 31–50.

46. Hillier, "Redlining."

47. Gotham, *Race, Real Estate, and Uneven Development,* 246.

48. Gotham, *Race, Real Estate, and Uneven Development;* Hernandez, "Redlining Revisited"; Jackson, *Crabgrass Frontier;* Marciano, Goldberg, and Hou, "T-RACES"; Pulido, "Rethinking Environmental Racism."

49. Gotham, *Race, Real Estate, and Uneven Development;* Hernandez, "Redlining Revisited"; Hillier, "Redlining"; Hillier, "Residential Security Maps"; Jackson, *Crabgrass Frontier.*

50. Lipsitz, *How Racism Takes Place.*

51. Gotham, *Race, Real Estate, and Uneven Development;* Jackson, *Crabgrass Frontier;* Lipsitz, *How Racism Takes Place;* Pulido, *Black, Brown, Yellow, and Left.*

52. Marciano, Goldberg, and Hou, "T-RACES."

53. Marciano, Goldberg, and Hou, "T-RACES."

54. Marciano, Goldberg, and Hou, "T-RACES."

55. Almaguer, *Racial Fault Lines;* Mabalon, *Little Manila;* Minnick, *Samfow;* Molina, *How Race Is Made in America.*

56. Roberts, "Stockton's Manufacturing."

57. "Sikh Parade Set to Roll in Stockton," *The Record,* April 11, 2013. The relative location of these institutions along the HOLC neighborhood appraisal gradient may have contributed to their racialization in subsequent years, but their presence did not appear to be an influential racial marker in the HOLC reports. Accordingly, their location is not considered in the remainder of the analysis in this section.

58. Coke R. Wood and Leonard Covello, *Stockton Memories: A Pictorial History of Stockton, California* (Fresno, CA: Valley Publishers, 1977), 100.

59. Marciano, Goldberg, and Hou., "T-RACES."

60. Davis, *Stockton,* 108.

61. Gotham, *Race, Real Estate, and Uneven Development;* Jackson, *Crabgrass Frontier.*

62. Marciano, Goldberg, and Hou, "T-RACES."

63. Marciano, Goldberg, and Hou, "T-RACES."

64. Gotham, *Race, Real Estate, and Uneven Development;* Jackson, *Crabgrass Frontier;* Lipsitz, *How Racism Takes Place.*

65. Marciano, Goldberg, and Hou, "T-RACES."

66. Reflecting the historical exclusion of American Indians from elite white settlements in California, no American Indians reside in the elite green-graded UOP neighborhood, and they averaged about 1 percent in all other neighborhoods in the metropolis.

67. Cybelle Fox and Thomas A. Guglielmo, "Defining America's Racial Boundaries: Blacks, Mexicans, and European Immigrants, 1890–1945," *American Journal of Sociology* 118, no. 2 (2012): 327–79.

68. Charles, *Won't You Be My Neighbor?;* Davis, *Stockton;* Howard Lewis, "A Historical Prospective of the San Joaquin Cherry Growers," *San Joaquin Historian* 11, no. 4 (1997): 2–13.

69. Charles, *Won't You Be My Neighbor?;* Logan and Zhang, "Global Neighborhoods."

70. Immigrants were mostly represented in the red-graded areas, followed by the yellow-graded, ungraded, blue-graded, and green-graded neighborhoods.

71. Charles, *Won't You Be My Neighbor?;* Haynes and Hutchison, "The Ghetto"; Lipsitz, *How Racism Takes Place;* Peter Marcuse, "The Enclave, the Citadel, and the Ghetto: What Has Changed in the Post-Fordist U.S. City," *Urban Affairs Review* 33, no. 2 (1997): 228–64; Diego Vigil, "Barrio Genealogy," *City & Community* 7, no. 4 (2008): 366–71; Loïc Wacquant, *Urban Outcasts: A Comparative Sociology of Advanced Marginality* (Malden, MA: Polity Press, 2008).

72. Ogbu, *Next Generation.*

73. Mabalon, *Little Manila.*

74. Davis, *Stockton;* Mabalon, *Little Manila;* Ogbu, *Next Generation.*

75. Mabalon, *Little Manila.*

76. Kim, "Racial Triangulation."

77. Gotham, *Race, Real Estate, and Uneven Development;* Lipsitz, *How Racism Takes Place.*

78. Small, *Villa Victoria.*

79. Almaguer, *Racial Fault Lines;* Kim, "Racial Triangulation"; Molina, *How Race Is Made;* Pulido, *Black, Brown, Yellow, and Left.*

80. Lipsitz, *How Racism Takes Place,* 12–13.

81. Lipsitz, *How Racism Takes Place;* George Lipsitz, *The Possessive Investment in Whiteness: How White People Profit from Identity Politics* (Philadelphia: Temple University Press, 2006).

82. Nikki Khanna, "'If You're Half Black, You're Just Black': Reflected Appraisals and the Persistence of the One-Drop Rule," *Sociological Quarterly* 51, no. 1 (2010): 96–121.

83. Cf. Lai, "Racial Triangulation of Space"; Lye, "Afro-Asian Analogy."

84. Kim, "Racial Triangulation."

85. Pulido, *Black, Brown, Yellow, and Left.*

86. Hernandez, "Redlining Revisited."

87. Kuebler, "Lending in the Modern Era."

88. Park and Pellow, "Racial Formation"; Pulido, "Rethinking Environmental Racism."

PART FOUR

Relational Frameworks
in Contemporary Policy

The essays in this section are rooted in social scientific frameworks that examine racial formations in contemporary settings, foregrounding the ways in which a relational framework produces new optics on group power. The essays also demonstrate the ways such a framework can be brought to bear on different qualitative methodologies within the social sciences, including content analysis, interviews, and studies of racial group formation.

Laura E. Enriquez's essay, "Border-Hopping Mexicans, Law-Abiding Asians, and Racialized Illegality: Analyzing Undocumented College Students' Experiences through a Relational Lens," reveals the ways the category of "undocumented" has been constructed within racialized and nativist discourses. Drawing on fifty-seven in-depth interviews with undocumented college students, she demonstrates how the category "undocumented" serves to make Latina/o immigrants hypervisible while obscuring or ignoring undocumented Asian Pacific Islander (API) immigrants. This racialized illegality leads to divergent forms of inclusionary and exclusionary experiences for Latina/o and API undocumented college students—a dynamic that is especially manifest in their interpersonal interactions and their ability to access educational resources and support structures.

Whereas in Enriquez's study we see that the hypervisibility of one group can eclipse another group, in Michael Rodríguez-Muñiz' essay, "Racial Arithmetic: Ethnoracial Politics in a Relational Key," we see the ways in which groups deploy histories of racial exclusion to argue for the redistribution of resources to their group, sometimes at the expense of another. Rodríguez-Muñiz demonstrates that these arguments consistently evaluate the needs of one group to the benefit or exclusion of others—in other words, they are always relational. Yet they are rarely studied as such.

Rodríguez-Muñiz demonstrates the benefits of an explicitly relational analysis through his study of Chicago's 2011 aldermanic redistricting. During the redistricting, elected officials made competing claims for the ethnoracial composition of the City Council based on the ubiquitous juxtaposition of "Latino" and "Black" demographics in the 2010 census. But by casting Black and Latino political power as a zero-sum game, the redistricters' racial arithmetic allowed long-standing white overrepresentation on the City Council to escape public scrutiny. Rodríguez-Muñiz's study shows how "statistical races are relational entities whose meaning and numerical significance are forged in relation and reference to statistics about other ethnoracial populations. In this way, racial arithmetic cannot but be a relational enterprise."

Both Enriquez and Rodríguez-Muñiz use a relational understanding of race to illuminate existing racial categories, however heterogeneous or tactical in their formation. By contrast, Julie Lee Merseth's essay, "The Relational Positioning of Arab and Muslim Americans in Post-9/11 Racial Politics," reveals the ways that relational logics of racialization have been used to construct new racial categories in response to changing political conditions. Merseth's study shows how Arab American and Muslim American racialization takes place in relation to other groups, specifically Asian Americans and African Americans. Drawing on a content analysis of more than sixty thousand newspaper articles over a span of fifteen years, Merseth examines the frames through which Arabs and Muslims have been racialized, exploring the conflation of these categories and observing framing differences in comparison to Asian Americans and African Americans. Merseth's study demonstrates how the post-9/11 racialization of Arabs and Muslims in the United States has helped to advance the formation of a new racial(ized) group, an emergent political construction relationally positioned in twenty-first-century racial politics.

TWELVE

Border-Hopping Mexicans, Law-Abiding Asians, and Racialized Illegality

ANALYZING UNDOCUMENTED COLLEGE STUDENTS' EXPERIENCES THROUGH A RELATIONAL LENS

Laura E. Enriquez

> People don't realize there are a lot of undocumented immigrants from Asia. When you think undocumented, you think of Mexico and Latin America. I think it would be easier to pass as documented if I were another race.
>
> **ESPERANZA VARGAS**

Reflecting on how race shapes her experiences as an undocumented college student, Esperanza explained that popular misconceptions conflate undocumented immigrants with Latinas/os.[1] Of the eleven million undocumented immigrants living in the United States, 77 percent are of Latin American origin. Thus, almost a quarter of undocumented immigrants are not Latina/o, with about 14 percent coming from Asia, 4 percent from Europe/Canada/Oceana, 3 percent from Africa, and 2 percent from the Caribbean. Furthermore, the Asian undocumented population has grown to about 1.5 million, increasing 385 percent from 1990 to 2013; approximately one in eight Asian immigrants is undocumented.[2] Yet media depictions and anti-immigrant rhetoric obscure these demographic realities with pervasive images linking Mexico and Latin America with undocumented immigration.[3] Indeed, a 2012 national survey found that the majority of respondents believed that Latinas/os are "illegal immigrants" and that undocumented immigrants compose a larger share of the immigrant population than they really do.[4] Thus, Esperanza and other undocumented college students find themselves navigating a social context filled with racialized stereotypes about undocumented immigrants. This chapter studies race relationally to investigate the consequences of this racialized illegality for Latina/o and Asian Pacific Islander (API) undocumented college students in Southern California.

The concept of *immigrant illegality* centers how laws and policies have created and sustained an undocumented immigrant category and how immigration status has become a source of social stratification.[5] Recent scholarship has begun to explore the intersection of race and illegality within the Latina/o population and to compare the experiences of undocumented immigrants from different racial groups.[6] Building on this work, I develop the concept of *racialized illegality* to capture how undocumented immigrants experience illegality differently based on how they are racialized in the United States. Drawing on fifty-seven in-depth interviews with undocumented college students, I first explore how racial and immigrant stereotypes contribute to the construction of a racialized illegality that conflates Latina/o with undocumented status. I then examine how racialized illegality structures and differentiates the instances of inclusion and exclusion that undocumented Latina/o and API students face in interpersonal interactions, including when they access educational resources and support structures. I argue that the construction and experience of illegality are deeply racialized and that they produce both inclusion and exclusion in undocumented students' everyday lives.

Unlike other contributors to this volume, I consider myself primarily a scholar of immigration, not race.[7] My research mostly focuses on the consequences of undocumented immigration status, but I often situate immigration status in relation to other structural inequalities.[8] I found my way to a relational study of race not by moving from racialized subject to question, as Natalia Molina recounts in chapter 2, but because of the questions I was asking about the role of race in the lives of undocumented immigrants. Most of the literature on undocumented youth focuses on Latinas/os and the structural limitations created by their immigration status; few discuss how intersecting social locations, like race, differentiate experiences of illegality.[9] To fill this gap, I sought to assess how race emerges to structure and differentiate the experiences of Latina/o and API undocumented students. I found that a relational framework was a productive tool for imagining the dynamic and multifaceted production of racialized illegality.

About 2.1 million, or one fifth of the undocumented immigrants in the United States, are 1.5-generation young adults who arrived before the age of fifteen and are under the age of thirty-five.[10] They are guaranteed access to K–12 educational institutions by the 1982 U.S. Supreme Court ruling in *Plyler v. Doe*.[11] This legal context and their young age insulate most undocumented youth from the limitations associated with their undocumented status until they leave high school and transition to adulthood.[12] At this point they begin to perceive barriers to their higher education, legal employment, and upward mobility. Indeed, only an estimated 44 percent of undocumented youth who entered the United States before the age of fourteen attend college, and their completion rates are likely much lower.[13]

Despite legal barriers, several state laws and policies support the educational attainment of undocumented youth. At the time of writing, seventeen states, university systems in four other states, and Washington, DC, have tuition equity policies that allow undocumented students to access more affordable in-state college tuition rates, compared to much higher rates for out-of-state residents or international students.[14] These policies have decreased undocumented students' high school dropout rates and increased their college enrollment rates.[15] But financial barriers still disrupt educational pathways by forcing undocumented students to sacrifice study time to work, enroll in less expensive community colleges instead of four-year universities, take time off when they cannot afford tuition, or stop out of college altogether.[16] Seeking to address this, ten states enacted laws that provide access to state, institutional, and/or privately funded financial aid.[17] California, where this study was conducted, has one of the most established and supportive legal contexts for undocumented students; in 2001 it was the second state to enact a tuition equity law, and it has offered access to privately and institutionally funded forms of financial aid since 2011 and state-funded financial aid since 2013.

Research on undocumented 1.5-generation youth has elucidated how immigration status structures educational pathways. Studies of high school experiences show that undocumented youth struggle to access information about supportive educational policies.[18] Work on college experiences explores how undocumented status contributes to stopping out and can lower educational aspirations by creating financial barriers, feelings of institutional neglect, and uncertainty about life after college.[19] This work has drawn conclusions based primarily on the experiences of Latina/o undocumented students. This is problematic, considering that race plays a key role in differentiating the educational opportunities and achievements of Latina/o and API students.[20] To address this gap, I examine the experiences of Latina/o and API undocumented students to assess how racial stereotypes structure and differentiate their experiences of illegality and educational access.

RACE AS A SOURCE OF EXCLUSION AND INCLUSION

Social science researchers argue that Asian Americans and Latinas/os are racial groups because of their phenotypic differences, socioeconomic marginalization, historical discrimination, and perceptions of their inferiority.[21] One strand of this research demonstrates that racial stereotypes are a significant source of exclusion because they have a meaningful impact on people's experiences. On the other hand, the literature on immigrant incorporation suggests that race and ethnicity can be a source of inclusion. I contend that race may shape both the inclusionary and exclusionary experiences of undocumented students.

Race can function as a source of exclusion when racial stereotypes are used to mark individuals as social outsiders. These representations are incorporated into social discourse, shape individuals' interpersonal experiences, and can lead to prejudice.[22] One of the most pervasive stereotypes for both Asian Americans and Latinos/as is that they are foreign. For Asian Americans this takes the form of a "perpetual foreigner" stereotype wherein people of Asian origin are presumed to be recent immigrants.[23] For Latinas/os, the "illegal alien" stereotype marks them as suspected undocumented immigrants.[24] Although both are stereotyped as foreign, the nature of the (il)legality associated with their foreignness differs.

Race can also promote social integration by providing access to resources. Segmented assimilation theorists maintain that the immigrant incorporation process is largely structured by the context of reception—governmental policies, societal reception, and coethnic communities—available to different national-origin groups.[25] Relevant here is that coethnic communities facilitate inclusion by mediating interactions with the receiving society and increasing economic and educational opportunities. Applying this to the undocumented population suggests that the larger and more established

Latina/o undocumented population may drive the racialization of support structures that provide resources and social support to undocumented immigrants.

DATA AND METHODOLOGY

This chapter draws on in-depth, semistructured interviews with fifty-seven undocumented college students in Southern California. Participants are primarily from two racial groups—twenty-five Latinas/os and twenty-six Asian Pacific Islanders. Almost all Latinas/os are of Mexican origin, with one from Colombia and one from Peru. The API sample is more diverse, with fifteen from Korea, five from the Philippines, three from Pakistan, and one each from China, Fiji, and Mongolia. Additionally, there is one participant from eastern Europe and five from South America who identified as having mixed racial backgrounds—two Afro-Latinas from Belize, one biracial Asian-Latina from Peru, one Korean from Argentina, and one Japanese from Peru. Participants in this study deployed a number of racial, ethnic, and national-origin categories to identify themselves and other groups; I have subsumed these into the categories of Latina/o and API because they allow me to categorize and contextualize how contemporary racial frameworks shape their experiences.[26] Given the overrepresentation of Mexican-origin and Korean-origin participants, I avoid overgeneralizing by exploring national-origin variations when they emerge.

Interviews were conducted over a three-year period from October 2010 to February 2014. Participants were recruited by myself and undergraduate research assistants through personal contacts and snowball sampling at ten college campuses—three University of California campuses, four California State University campuses, and three community colleges. Interviews lasted an average of one to two hours and were semistructured to allow for a broad conversation about how undocumented status and race has affected their experiences. Participants answered specific questions about racial and undocumented immigrant stereotypes and also recounted detailed educational histories. All participants were assigned pseudonyms to protect confidentiality.

I analyzed the interview transcripts using Hyperresearch, a qualitative data analysis program. Open coding revealed key themes around how race differentiates everyday experiences of illegality, including stereotypes, assumptions of illegality, access to resources, access to social support, and openness about immigration status. These themes were systematically coded and analyzed by comparing the number of occurrences and the details of each coded text within and across national-origin and racial groups. I then moved into a relational analysis by considering how the forms of racialization and racialized illegality in one racial group had implications for the experiences of those in the other group.

RACIALIZED ILLEGALITY:
LINKING RACIAL AND IMMIGRANT STEREOTYPES
OF CRIMINALITY AND ILLEGALITY

Popular stereotypes equate undocumented immigration with Mexican and other Latina/o people. The concept of racialized illegality articulated here captures how the conflation of racial and immigrant stereotypes differentiates undocumented immigrants' experience of illegality. To understand the connections between race and undocumented status, I asked participants a series of questions about the stereotypes of their racial group, immigrants in their racial group, and undocumented immigrants. Though a number of stereotypes were reported, I trace the development of criminal/illegal and law-abiding narratives across the stereotypes to reveal a racialized illegality that marks Latinas/os as undocumented.

Racial stereotypes pave the way for racialized illegality by labeling Latinas/os as criminal and APIs as law abiding. Describing racial stereotypes, five Latinas/os mentioned aspects of criminality, referencing gang affiliations or suspicions of criminal activity, and four additional Latinas/os mentioned criminalized perceptions of undocumented status. Juan Hernandez listed Latino stereotypes as "beaners, wetbacks, border hoppers, invaders. . . . They think we're inferior to them. . . . They're like, 'Oh you're Mexican, go back to Mexico. I bet you don't even have papers.'" APIs, on the other hand, did not mention criminality or illegality when discussing their racial stereotypes. Instead, four APIs, including Lili Chen, noted connections to obedience and law abidingness: "They think you are not going to cause trouble. You are only going to be a good student, you are going to be smart, and you are going to be obedient." The only APIs who noted any racial associations with criminality were two Pakistani participants; they referred to terrorist stereotypes. Wasim

Marwat explained, "I'm from [the] Middle East and first of all, when 9/11 happened ... there is the pressure of the terrorist." Yet, for the most part, Latinas/os and APIs face racial stereotypes that position them on opposite ends of the spectrum of criminality, setting up different suspicions of illegality.

The racial gap in criminalizing stereotypes and perceived illegality widens when focusing on the stereotypes of immigrants from each racial group. Again, a handful of Latina/o participants and no API participants mentioned illegality. Isla Ayala reflected, "I guess people say that [Latina/o or Mexican] immigrants are criminals because they crossed the border." Further, six Latinas/os identified stereotypes that reflected criminalizing anti-immigrant narratives about undocumented immigrants stealing jobs and resources. Alvaro Barillas recited common ones: "They come to take jobs. . . . They come to take advantage of the benefits that this government offers. . . . That they are scandalous, that they are very noisy. That the Latino areas have more crime." Alternatively, most API participants struggled to identify specific stereotypes about immigrants in their racial groups and focused on their limited acculturation; only three Filipino participants quickly identified associations with nursing professions. The only potentially criminal association was noted by Joyce Jung: "When I was a kid, a lot of the [Korean] immigrants were called runaways. They ran away from their previous country, Korea, because they did something wrong."

Finally, when asked about the stereotypes of undocumented immigrants, most Latina/o and API participants spoke about its connection to Mexican, Latina/o, Hispanic, and/or "brown" people. Take Miriam Delgado and Zeus Yun's examples:

MIRIAM: I think most of the time when they think of undocumented, they mostly think of Hispanics, of Mexicans. They don't see the Asian community or other ethnic groups. They see Hispanic students as not as focused, just troublemakers.

ZEUS: Stereotypical undocumented immigrants are these crazy, brown-skin, short, gangbanging, and migrants, staying in the fields, stealing from people. It's this screwed up image and this individual that is obviously from Mexico.

Highlighting the role of race in the stereotypes of undocumented immigrants, both referred to racial markers, including country of origin and phenotype, and referenced the perceived criminality of Latinas/os in general.

These stereotypes of criminalized Latinas/os and illegalized undocumented immigrants allow for a seamless connection that easily links these two groups in the social consciousness while undocumented APIs fade into the background.

CONSEQUENCES OF RACIALIZED ILLEGALITY: DIVERGING EXPERIENCES OF INCLUSION AND EXCLUSION

Racialized illegality produces divergent experiences within the undocumented student community. Latinas/os are more likely to experience exclusionary interpersonal interactions because of their suspect immigration status, while APIs are more likely to be included because they are not assumed to be undocumented. Yet, Latinas/os experience inclusion when accessing resources and support spaces for undocumented students because they are the majority of this marginalized group. APIs are more likely to feel excluded from these same spaces. Studying race relationally helps reveal these diverging experiences of inclusion and exclusion.

Racialized Assumptions about Illegality in Everyday Interactions

Given the racialized stereotypes of illegality, Latina/o participants felt excluded and vulnerable to being identified as undocumented while API participants experienced a sense of inclusion from easily passing as documented. None of the API participants reported that people assumed they were undocumented, while almost half the Latina/o participants felt that people assumed they were undocumented. Additional Latina/o participants believed that their immigration status could quickly become suspect. Both groups believed that their ability to pass as documented depended on whether their self-presentation reflected racialized stereotypes of illegality.

Eleven of the twenty-five Latina/o participants believed that others assumed they were undocumented, and nine of these thought that this was because of their race. Sonya Alvarez explained, "Just because I'm dark skinned or I am a Mexican they may think, 'Oh yeah that's an undocumented person.' . . . People look at a Mexican person and assume automatically—that person is undocumented." Sonya and most of the Latina/o participants who believed others assumed them to be undocumented thought this was because of their Mexican or Latina/o origin.

None of the twenty-six API participants believed that they had been assumed to be undocumented, and twenty-two credited this to their race. AJ Bongolan, a Filipino student, explained, "Let's say that I'm walking on the street. [Would] people think I'm undocumented? ... No. Because ... if they hear 'undocumented,' the first thing that would come to their mind is Mexican." AJ asserted that racialized illegality insulates him, and other non-Latinas/os, from suspicion that they may be undocumented. Edith Oh, a Korean student, noted, "They would probably think you're legal here and you followed all the laws." When asked why people thought that, she cited common stereotypes about Asians: "I guess just [because] Asians are obedient. Since they were little they listen to their parents. And they follow the laws [and] regulations." Edith maintained that popular stereotypes about Asians as obedient and law abiding are so incompatible with the criminalized image of undocumented immigrants that most people would never connect the two. These racial stereotypes effectively protect API undocumented students from suspicions about their immigration status.

Further exemplifying the significance of cognitive dissonance between racialized illegality and self-presentation, five of the fourteen Latina/o participants who believed that they were not assumed to be undocumented thought this was because their lighter phenotype did not reflect common stereotypes of dark-skinned, mestizo Latinas/os. Compare the experiences of Isla Ayala, a lighter-skinned Latina with Pablo Ortiz, a darker-skinned Latino:

ISLA: They say, "You don't look the part [of an undocumented immigrant]." I really haven't had anything against me because I look lighter than most Mexicans.

PABLO: It's hard for me being dark skinned. . . . My skin color gives the assumption that I'm undocumented.

Phenotype effectively distances lighter-skinned Latinas/os from undocumented immigrant stereotypes and made them feel that they could pass as documented.

Acculturation also distanced both Latina/o and API undocumented students from immigrant and undocumented stereotypes. Of the fourteen Latinas/os who thought they passed as documented, nine reasoned this was because of their high levels of acculturation. Iliana Guzman explained, "People don't assume I'm undocumented because I'm a student and I speak English. Being able to be raised here since I was five years old, and know English, and speak it without an accent." As with lighter phenotype, Iliana's English language fluency, lack of an accent, and student status distances her from stereotypes of unacculturated immigrants and allows her to pass as U.S.-born and thus not potentially undocumented. Others mentioned their style of dress as signaling their acculturation. Similarly, eight of the API participants believed their acculturation further insulated them from assumptions of undocumented status.

For those participants who did not display markers of acculturation, API participants were much less likely than Latinas/os to be presumed undocumented. Anna Kwon, who arrived at the age of ten, explained, "They assume that I'm Korean American since I speak [English] fluently. So it's like, they don't assume that I'm undocumented." Following up, I asked if she would be assumed to be undocumented if she didn't speak English well or if she had a more noticeable accent. She slowly responded, "Maybe." Unconvinced, she quickly added, "Or they would think I'm an international student. Yeah." While linguistic markers may associate APIs with an immigrant status, stereotypes of API immigrants still prevent assumptions of illegality. Indeed, while the API participants were much more likely to have entered the United States at older ages (an average of 9.26 years old compared to 6.73 for Latina/o participants), none mentioned their slight or even heavy accents as markers of potential undocumented status. The opposite was true for the few Latina/o participants with heavier accents. They believed that this contributed to assumptions about their immigration status. Pablo Ortiz, who arrived at age eleven, noted, "My English pronunciation is not great. It's just a luggage that I carry on my back that they're going to recognize my accent, point me out, and say, 'You're undocumented.'"

Given the interrelated assumptions about race, immigrant status, and illegality, Latinas/os' ability to pass as documented is easily compromised if they give any hint that they might be an immigrant or undocumented. Ricky Gomez noted, "Most people that I come into contact [with] don't suspect that I am illegal because I speak pretty good English. I dress differently. I like to dress preppy and everything. It's a lot different than what most people think [of] an illegal undocumented immigrant." Ricky believed that his acculturated self-presentation—English-language competence and clothing choices—distanced him from undocumented stereotypes and allowed him to pass as a citizen despite being Latino. But he also recognized that his level of acculturation did not fully protect him, because "just being Latino makes people second-guess your legality that you're here."

TJ Salazar and Allan Choi provided examples of how APIs are less likely than Latinas/os to have their immigration status questioned, despite similarly signaling their undocumented status:

TJ: People don't really assume that I am undocumented because I am more Spanish looking [light-skinned]. They don't really think about it. But when I tell them that I don't have an ID, it kind of raises a red flag, or when they tell me to sign up for financial aid [and I say I can't].

ALLAN: People don't assume that [being undocumented] about you when you can't drive or when you can't work. When you're, like, at an airport, no one's gonna [be] like, "Oh, you're from Korea. We should double-check you."

Although TJ and Allan can both pass as documented in initial interactions, TJ's experiences show how this can be easily disrupted for Latinas/os when they do anything that might associate them with undocumented status. In his case, his immigration status became suspect when he was unable to obtain a state-issued ID and access financial aid, both of which were unavailable to undocumented immigrants in California at the time of his interview. Alternatively, Allan's Korean background allowed him to avoid these suspicions despite lacking similar identification documents.

Given that it was relatively unlikely that API participants would be suspected of being undocumented, they could hide in plain sight. Daniel Kim recounted a recent incident in which he believed being Korean prevented immigration authorities from questioning him:

I went to San Diego . . . and when we were coming back, they were asking for IDs on the train. . . . When the officer came around, I just showed him my [Korean] passport. And he looked at it, and he saw that it wasn't expired, and he said, "Oh, this is OK." . . . I thought about what happened and I asked myself, what if I were Latino, you know? Would he have scrutinized my passport? Would he have questioned me? Where I was from? How long have I been here? What are you doing here on this train?

San Diego, because it is near the U.S.-Mexican border, is a site of heightened internal immigration enforcement, including identification checks at transportation hubs. Daniel firmly believed that not being Latino led his identification to be less rigorously scrutinized and possibly prevented his detention for not having a valid visa stamp in his passport. Similarly, Karl Song explained, "I don't think there's anything [about me] that says [I am undocumented]. Unless I'm wearing my 'I'm Undocumented' T-shirt. But then people still think, 'Oh, you're just an ally, right?'" Even when wearing a T-shirt that boldly declares his undocumented status as part of a social movement strategy of "coming out as undocumented and unafraid," Karl is unable to trigger suspicion because of the cognitive dissonance created by racialized illegality stereotypes.[27]

These stereotypes operate in the larger multiracial context of Southern California, where whites and Blacks are not assumed to be recent immigrants and thus above suspicion. Luca Popescu, a white undocumented student, suggested that being placed at the top of the racial hierarchy insulated him from discrimination: "When I've told [people], 'Hey, I'm undocumented,' I'm sure that they've given me a lot more credit just because I'm tall and white and a guy." Blackness fades even further into the background, as Dalia Martin, an African American–identified undocumented student from Belize, explained that African Americans are assumed to have a "master category of experiences," presumably being descendants of slaves, low income, less educated, and criminal. Although distance from an immigrant experience protected her from undocumented stereotypes, she faced other forms of racial discrimination. While whites and Blacks may emerge as key reference groups in other contexts in which they compose a larger part of the immigrant population, the pervasive racialization of illegality as a Latina/o issue suggests that APIs, Blacks, and whites are all insulated from suspicion and can more easily pass as documented immigrants or citizens.

Racialized Access to Undocumented Student Resources and Support Structures

Although stereotypes put Latinas/os at risk of negative interpersonal interactions when they are assumed to be undocumented, they also lead them to be identified as needing undocumented student resources and support. Dennis Min characterized this as the "double-edged sword" of racialized illegality: "[Undocumented student resources are] so specific to Hispanic populations. . . . I think the proponents for undocumented immigrants . . . they are also targeting Latino communities . . . [just like] people who are backlashing against illegal immigration." As Dennis suggests, educators and community organizers mainly target Latinas/os when providing undocumented-specific resources and support. This effectively leads Latina/o undocumented students to experience some institutionalized inclusion, while API undocumented students struggle to access resources, social support, and empowerment opportunities.

Reflecting on the consequences of being of another racial origin, participants often focused on how this would affect their access to resources.

Compare the musings of Reina Espino, a Mexican student, and Edith Oh, a Korean student:

> REINA: If I was Asian and undocumented, I think I would hold back a lot because maybe there's not a lot of support in that community. Or maybe there's a lack of information for that community, and so maybe I'd be a little more scared. . . . So, yeah, I think it would be more difficult.
>
> EDITH: I guess they [Latinas/os] feel more comfortable saying it [their immigration status] and more comfortable in seeking help or resources. . . . Like, when you're Asian and being undocumented, it's kind of hard to say, and then you don't know where to go.

Reina, Edith, and others proposed that API communities are less likely than Latina/o communities to provide resources and support for undocumented students. They concluded that this may lead APIs to feel more confused, scared, and uncomfortable when trying to access resources. Indeed, API participants confirmed these feelings.

API participants found that community-based workshops and campaigns on undocumented student resources tended to target Latina/o communities. AJ Bongolan shared,

> It kind of is alienating because most of the programs . . . [are] in Spanish. . . . I went to a workshop . . . and, I mean, they speak English, but the paper that I had to sign was in Spanish, and I don't know what it means. And to me I kind of felt alienated because I don't understand it.

Undocumented student information sessions and resources tend to be offered by Latina/o organizations, heavily advertised to the Latina/o community, and made accessible through materials in Spanish. Although these methods have successfully raised resource awareness among the Latina/o undocumented population, similar resources are less available in API communities. Isaiah Park concurred, saying, "For Asian-Americans, it's like there's a lot of undocumented [people], but there's no place to go to for us." Although many echoed his point, a few Korean participants did point to the Korean Resource Center, a local community organization that helped them access information and resources. Community organizations and events are key spaces for accessing undocumented student resources; however, the larger Latina/o undocumented population and extensive web of Latina/o community organizations made it more likely that Latina/o undocumented students accessed vital educational resources.

Undocumented student organizations on college campuses also function as critical instrumental and emotional support structures. These organizations and their meeting spaces are also racialized, populated mostly by Latinas/os, which has implications for how both Latina/o and API undocumented students experience them. Compare the feelings of Sylvia Muñoz, a Mexican undocumented student, and Ravi Lal, a Pacific Islander undocumented student:

SYLVIA: When I came here to the [undocumented student organization's office] and I met people ... they were welcoming, and I was seen as another family [member]. Because I spend time here, it's becoming my other house. [It's] where I can rely on people.

RAVI: During undergrad, I was very lonely in terms of, like, my experience and sort of understanding who I am as a [undocumented] person. So I started connecting with the AB540 [undocumented student] group on campus. When I entered their space, I was not acknowledged. I stood there for a while, I said hello to a couple of people, but people were just removed from me.

Like other Latina/o participants, Sylvia felt a sense of instant belonging when she met other undocumented Latina/o students in her campus's undocumented student organization. Alternatively, like Ravi, many of the API participants felt like marginal members. Though it is difficult to be new to any organization, barriers to belonging are heightened for API undocumented students who see few or no members with whom they can culturally and ethnically identify.

Because of these experiences, several API participants were members of API-specific undocumented student spaces that fostered a stronger sense of belonging than they found in Latina/o-dominated undocumented student organizations. Lili Chen explained,

I guess cause it's so racialized, like this issue of being undocumented, that if you don't find someone who is within your race, it's really difficult to [pause]. I guess it's not difficult to relate, but it's difficult because there are things that come from your race that you won't find in common with other people who aren't within your race.... It was just really good to go [to the API undocumented organization] because ... these people understand. You don't have to explain anything to them.

Highlighting the racialized nature of the undocumented experience, Lili explained that race and ethnicity create such divergent experiences that they disrupt the sense of understanding that undocumented students can immediately form with one another. API-specific organizational spaces allow undocumented API students to have supportive experiences in which they can take their racialized experiences as a given and develop shared understandings and feelings of belonging.

Feeling comfortable and participating in undocumented student organizations is important because they are key gateways to accessing information about campus resources meant to facilitate the academic success and retention of undocumented students. Reflecting on the consequences of not joining her campus's undocumented student organization, Ana Kwon commented, "I think if I joined, I would know more information about getting benefits. Like, I didn't know about the meal voucher program." Avoiding the undocumented student organization, Ana did not learn about resources that could have eased her struggles as an undocumented student. While she mentioned the meal voucher program, meant to address food insecurity, other key resources include scholarships, low-cost campus housing, commuter vanpools, employment opportunities, and other resources that facilitate academic retention and success.

Finally, undocumented student organizations function as a space of empowerment and personal growth. Daniel Kim reflected on the power of seeing other undocumented students who are comfortable with their immigration status:

> I didn't want to tell others about my status until I got involved with [an undocumented student organization]. . . . They were very comfortable about their statuses. They were out there at marches, [and] rallies. They were giving speeches in public. And so when I saw them, I thought, Oh, maybe I can do it too. I shouldn't be ashamed of my status. This is who I am, and I should accept it and embrace it and come out. And so ever since then, I started speaking out in public.

As Daniel noted, organizations are key to helping undocumented students come to terms with their immigration status and, if they desire, to become active in the immigrant youth movement. This sense of self-acceptance, pride, and empowerment from one's immigration status helps counteract the fear that undocumented youth may have.

CONCLUSION

Previous research has illustrated that undocumented youth and students experience inclusionary exclusion. Yet relatively little work has accounted for how the inclusion and exclusion associated with illegality may vary because of intersecting structural inequalities, like race. Studying race relationally, this chapter demonstrates that racialization significantly differentiates how undocumented Latina/o and API college students experience their illegality. I show that racial and immigrant stereotypes contribute to the construction of a racialized illegality that conflates Latina/o with undocumented status. This racialized illegality led undocumented Latina/o students to be more likely to experience interpersonal exclusion because of their suspect immigration status while undocumented API students were more likely to experience structural exclusion from undocumented student support structures.

Artist Boonyarit Daraphant captures this feeling in a piece entitled *Targeted or Overlooked* (see figure 12.1). He captures how two friends, one Asian American and one Latino, experience racialized illegality. The Latino student is targeted not only by Immigration and Customs Enforcement (ICE) but also by immigrant activists, while the Asian American student is overlooked, undetected by immigration enforcement officials but isolated and presumed to be a citizen ally. This image aptly summarizes how racialized illegality produces unique forms of inclusion and exclusion in undocumented students' everyday experiences.

My findings demonstrate that scholars cannot simply study undocumented status in isolation but must account for how other power dynamics dictate its production and experience. A growing segment of research on undocumented immigrants advances illegality as a *master status,* in which undocumented status overshadows the impact of other social locations.[28] Counter to this, I develop the concept of *racialized illegality* to capture how the construction and experience of illegality are deeply tied to racial power dynamics. This reflects a growing body of work that has documented how laws produce racialized illegality and explored how race shapes the everyday experiences of undocumented and documented individuals.[29] Having a theoretical concept to capture the racialization of illegality is necessary to push scholars to explore how race, as a structural inequality and intersectional social location, is constructing and differentiating experiences of illegality. Future work should also consider how other social categories, such as gender and class, differentiate the construction and experience of illegality.[30]

My findings also demonstrate that taking additional social categories into account is key to understanding the complex and dynamic production of inequality through inclusion and exclusion. In this case, exploring immigration status or race on its own would have obscured the dynamic and

FIGURE 12.1. *Targeted or Overlooked* (2018), a reflection on racialized illegality by Boonyarit Daraphant.

multifaceted production of racialized illegality. Instead, I adopted a relational framework to capture this phenomenon. I suggest that scholars should not only study race relationally but also study power dynamics relationally by taking other forms of inequality into account. Natalia Molina directs us to study race relationally by "zooming out" to "ask who else is (or was) present in or near the communities we study—and what difference these groups' presence makes (or made)." Adapting this directive, I contend that we also need to zoom out of our focus on race to ask: What other social categories and power dynamics are present or intersect with racialization? What difference does the presence of other power structures make? In my case, studying race and illegality relationally allowed me to explore them as intersecting power structures and show how they work together to produce unique forms of marginalization. Similar intersectional constructions of race can be seen in both historical examples (such as the gendered and sexualized racialization of Chinese immigrant men and women in the 1800s) and contemporary ones (like the classed and gendered racialization of African American mothers as "welfare queens.")[31] I urge scholars who are studying race relationally to not only take other racial groups into account but also to explore additional power dynamics that may be present and shaping the racialization process.

ACKNOWLEDGMENTS

Special thanks to all research participants who shared their stories. Funding was provided by the UCLA Institute for Research on Labor and Employment and the UCLA Institute for American Cultures. Research assistance was provided by Carlos Salinas Velasco, Trisha Mazumder, and students in the fall 2010 "Immigrant Rights, Labor, and Higher Education" course at the University of California, Los Angeles.

NOTES

1. I conceptualize Latinas/os as a racial group, rather than as an ethnic group, because of their structural exclusion, historical discrimination, and perceptions of their perpetual inferiority. See José A. Cobas, Jorge Duany, and Joe R. Feagin, eds., *How the United States Racializes Latinos: White Hegemony and Its Consequences* (Boulder, CO: Paradigm, 2009); Julie A. Dowling, *Mexican-Americans and the Question of Race* (Austin: University of Texas Press, 2014); Laura Gómez, *Manifest Destinies: The Making of the Mexican American Race* (New York: New York University Press, 2007); Celia Lacayo, "Perpetual Inferiority: Whites' Racial Ideology toward Latinos," *Sociology of Race and Ethnicity* 3, no. 4 (2017): 566–79; Martha Menchaca, *The Mexican Outsiders: A Community History of Marginalization and Discrimination in California* (Austin: University of Texas Press, 1995); Edward

E. Telles and Vilma Ortiz, *Generations of Exclusion: Mexican Americans, Assimilation, and Race* (New York: Russell Sage Foundation, 2008).

2. Marc R. Rosenblum and Ariel G. Ruiz Soto, *An Analysis of Unauthorized Immigrants in the United States by Country and Region of Birth* (Washington, DC: Migration Policy Institute, 2015).

3. Leo Chavez, *The Latino Threat: Constructing Immigrants, Citizens, and the Nation* (Stanford, CA: Stanford University Press, 2008).

4. Matt A. Barreto, Sylvia Manzano, and Gary Segura, *The Impact of Media Stereotypes on Opinions and Attitudes towards Latinos* (Pasadena, CA: National Hispanic Media Coalition, 2012).

5. Joanna Dreby, *Everyday Illegal: When Policies Undermine Immigrant Families* (Berkeley: University of California Press, 2015); Josiah M. Heyman, "The Study of Illegality and Legality: Which Way Forward?," *PoLAR* 36, no. 2 (2013): 304–7; Douglas S. Massey, *Categorically Unequal: The American Stratification System* (New York: Russell Sage, 2008); Cecilia Menjívar and Daniel Kanstroom, eds., *Constructing Immigrant "Illegality": Critiques, Experiences, and Responses* (New York: Cambridge University Press, 2014); Mae N. Ngai, *Impossible Subjects: Illegal Aliens and the Making of Modern America* (Princeton, NJ: Princeton University Press, 2004).

6. Esther Yoona Cho, "Revisiting Ethnic Niches: A Comparative Analysis of the Labor Market Experiences of Asian and Latino Undocumented Young Adults," *RSF: The Russell Sage Foundation Journal of the Social Sciences* 3, no. 4 (2017): 97–115; San Juanita García, "Racializing 'Illegality': An Intersectional Approach to Understanding How Mexican-Origin Women Navigate an Anti-immigrant Climate," *Sociology of Race and Ethnicity* 3, no. 4 (2017): 474–90; Juan Herrera, "Racialized Illegality: The Regulation of Informal Labor and Space," *Latino Studies* 14, no. 3 (2016): 320–43.

7. I recognize that immigration and race are intimately intertwined. Indeed, historical and contemporary immigration policy has been shaped by race and racism.

8. For examples see Laura E. Enriquez, "A 'Master Status' or the 'Final Straw'? Assessing the Role of Immigration Status in Latino Undocumented Youths' Pathways out of School," *Journal of Ethnic and Migration Studies* 43, no. 9 (2017): 1526–43; Laura E. Enriquez, "Gendering Illegality: Undocumented Young Adults' Negotiation of the Family Formation Process," *American Behavioral Scientist* 61, no. 10 (2017): 1153–71; Laura E. Enriquez, Daisy Vazquez Vera, and S. Karthick Ramakrishnan, "On the Road to Opportunity: Racial Disparities in Obtaining AB-60 Driver Licenses," *Boom California*, November 28, 2017, https://boomcalifornia.com/2017/11/28/on-the-road-to-opportunity/.

9. For exceptions, see Leisy J. Abrego, "Latino Immigrants' Diverse Experiences of 'Illegality,'" in *Constructing Immigrant "Illegality": Critiques, Experiences, and Responses,* ed. Cecilia Menjívar and Daniel Kanstroom (New York: Cambridge University Press, 2014), 139–60; Nicholas De Genova, "The Legal Production of Mexican/Migrant 'Illegality,'" *Latino Studies* 2, no. 2 (2004): 160–85.

10. Jeanne Batalova and Margie McHugh, *Dream vs. Reality: An Analysis of Potential DREAM Act Beneficiaries* (Washington, DC: Migration Policy Institute, 2010).

11. Michael A. Olivas, *No Undocumented Child Left Behind: Plyler V. Doe and the Education of Undocumented Schoolchildren* (New York: New York University Press, 2012).

12. Roberto G. Gonzales, *Lives in Limbo: Undocumented and Coming of Age in America* (Berkeley: University of California Press, 2016).

13. Jeffrey S. Passel and D'Vera Cohn, *A Portrait of the Unauthorized Immigrants in the United States* (Washington, DC: Pew Hispanic Center, 2009).

14. Seventeen states provide in-state tuition: California, Colorado, Connecticut, Florida, Illinois, Kansas, Maryland, Minnesota, Nebraska, New Jersey, New Mexico, New York, Oklahoma, Oregon, Texas, Utah, and Washington. University systems in Hawai'i, Kentucky, Michigan, and Rhode Island have similar tuition equity policies. "Table: Laws & Policies Improving Access to Higher Education for Immigrants," National Immigration Law Center, updated June 2018, https://www.nilc.org/issues/education/eduaccesstoolkit2a/#tables.

15. Stephanie Potochnick, "How States Can Reduce the Dropout Rate for Undocumented Immigrant Youth: The Effects of In-State Resident Tuition Policies," *Social Science Research* 45 (2014): 18–32.

16. Leisy J. Abrego and Roberto G. Gonzales, "Blocked Paths, Uncertain Futures: The Postsecondary Education and Labor Market Prospects of Undocumented Latino Youth," *Journal of Education for Students Placed at Risk* 15, no. 1–2 (2010): 144–57; Daysi Diaz-Strong et al., "Purged: Undocumented Students, Financial Aid Policies, and Access to Higher Education," *Journal of Hispanic Higher Education* 10, no. 2 (2011): 107–19; Lindsay Perez Huber and Maria C. Malagon, "Silenced Struggles: The Experiences of Latina and Latino Undocumented College Students in California," *Nevada Law Journal* 7 (2007): 841–61; Veronica Terriquez, "Dreams Delayed: Barriers to Degree Completion among Undocumented Community College Students," *Journal of Ethnic and Migration Studies* 41, no. 8 (2015): 1302–23.

17. Eight states provide access to state-funded financial aid: California, Hawai'i, New Mexico, Minnesota, Oregon, Oklahoma, Texas, and Washington. Four states provide access to institutional aid or scholarships: California, Illinois, Minnesota, and Utah. NILC, "Laws & Policies Improving Access to Higher Education."

18. Laura E. Enriquez, "'Because We Feel the Pressure and We Also Feel the Support': Examining the Educational Success of Undocumented Immigrant Latina/o Students," *Harvard Educational Review* 81, no. 3 (2011): 476–500; Roberto G. Gonzales, "On the Wrong Side of the Tracks: Understanding the Effects of School Structure and Social Capital in the Educational Pursuits of Undocumented Immigrant Students," *Peabody Journal of Education* 85, no. 4 (2010): 469–85.

19. Leisy J. Abrego, "'I Can't Go to College Because I Don't Have Papers': Incorporation Patterns of Latino Undocumented Youth," *Latino Studies* 4, no. 3 (2006): 212–31; Gonzales, *Lives in Limbo;* Perez Huber and Malagon, "Silenced Struggles"; Terriquez, "Dreams Delayed."

20. Gilda L. Ochoa, *Academic Profiling: Latinos, Asian Americans, and the Achievement Gap* (Minneapolis: University of Minnesota Press, 2013).

21. Tomás Almaguer, *Racial Fault Lines: The Historical Origins of White Supremacy in California* (Berkeley: University of California Press, 1994); Michael Omi and Howard Winant, *Racial Formation in the United States*, 3rd ed. (New York: Routledge, 2015).

22. Hugh Mehan, "The Discourse of the Illegal Immigration Debate: A Case Study in the Politics of Representation," *Discourse Society* 8, no. 2 (1997): 249–70; Walter G. Stephan, "On the Relationship between Stereotypes and Prejudice: An International Study," *Personality and Social Psychology Bulletin* 20, no. 3 (1994): 277–84.

23. Lisa Lowe, *Immigrant Acts: On Asian American Cultural Politics* (Durham, NC: Duke University Press, 1996); Mia Tuan, *Forever Foreigners or Honorary Whites? The Asian Ethnic Experience Today* (New Brunswick, NJ: Rutgers University Press, 1998).

24. Chavez, *Latino Threat*.

25. Alejandro Portes and Min Zhou, "The New Second Generation: Segmented Assimilation and Its Variants," *Annals of the American Academy of Political and Social Science* 530, no. 1 (1993): 74–96.

26. "Latina/o" and "Asian Pacific Islander" are historically situated, socially constructed categories that can unite groups that face similar forces of racial domination but also risk obscuring key group differences. G. Cristina Mora, *Making Hispanics: How Activists, Bureaucrats, and Media Constructed a New American* (Chicago: University of Chicago Press, 2014); Anthony Ocampo, *The Latinos of Asia: How Filipino Americans Break the Rules of Race* (Stanford, CA: Stanford University Press, 2016).

27. For more on this social movement strategy, see Laura E. Enriquez and Abigail C. Saguy, "Coming Out of the Shadows: Structural and Cultural Opportunities for Undocumented Student Mobilization," *American Journal of Cultural Sociology* 4, no. 1 (2016): 107–30.

28. For example, see Gonzales, *Lives in Limbo;* Shannon Gleeson and Roberto G. Gonzales, "When Do Papers Matter? An Institutional Analysis of Undocumented Life in the United States," *International Migration* 50, no. 4 (2012): 1–19; Terriquez, "Dreams Delayed."

29. For example, see Cho, "Revisiting Ethnic Niches"; De Genova, "Legal Production of Mexican/Migrant 'Illegality'"; Enriquez, Vasquez Vera, and Ramakrishnan, "On the Road to Opportunity"; García, "Racializing 'Illegality'"; Herrera, "Racialized Illegality."

30. For an example of gendering illegality, see Enriquez, "Gendering Illegality."

31. Floyd Cheung, "Anxious and Ambivalent Representations: Nineteenth-Century Images of Chinese American Men," *Journal of American Culture* 30, no. 3 (2007): 293–309; Carly Hayden Foster, "The Welfare Queen: Race, Gender, Class, and Public Opinion," *Race, Gender & Class* 15, no. 3/4 (2008): 162–79; George Anthony Peffer, *If They Don't Bring Their Women Here: Chinese Female Immigration before Exclusion* (Urbana: University of Illinois Press, 1999).

THIRTEEN

Racial Arithmetic

ETHNORACIAL POLITICS IN A RELATIONAL KEY

Michael Rodríguez-Muñiz

Over the past two hundred years, the ever-intensifying quantification of racial categories has shaped politics in profound ways. This chapter focuses on one way: *racial arithmetic*.[1] This concept refers to the use of ethnoracial statistics in political argumentation and decision-making. In other words, it names situations in which such knowledge is invoked by political actors to determine or justify the distribution of resources and rights.

U.S. history offers many examples of racial arithmetic. This practice is visible in the infamous 1790 Three-Fifths Compromise that rendered enslaved Blacks three-fifths of a person for purposes of apportionment, as well as in the work of eugenicist movements in the early twentieth century to establish racial quotas for immigration.[2] In both these examples, as in most cases before the civil rights era, ethnoracial statistics were almost exclusively used to institute and legitimize white supremacy. Since then, racial arithmetic has also become central to political and legal efforts to address ethnoracial exclusion and inequality.[3] For instance, Black, Latino, and Asian American civil rights organizations have long relied on data to advocate for greater political representation.[4] A more recent example is the Department of Justice's use of ethnoracial statistics to prove the existence of "racial bias" in the Ferguson, Missouri, police department.[5] In short, political entities and projects have used racial arithmetic to both entrench and upend white power.

While there is no shortage of past or contemporary examples, scholars have had little to say about racial arithmetic and the role of statistics in ethnoracial politics more generally. Research on racial categorization and censuses provides a starting point, but this work tends to focus on the production of data rather than on the ways that this knowledge is used in political contests. The objective of this chapter, therefore, is to turn attention to the practice and politics of racial arithmetic.

In the pages to follow, I pursue this objective in two interlinked steps. First, I argue that the study of racial arithmetic demands a *relational* approach. In contrast to more common group-centric or comparative analyses, this approach treats race as "a mutually constitutive process and thus attends to how, when, and to what extent groups intersect."[6] This orientation makes it possible to recognize that racial arithmetic is an inherently relational practice. Second, I illustrate this point with an empirical analysis of a recent case of racial arithmetic. Drawing primarily on media coverage, I examine Chicago's 2011 aldermanic redistricting and narrate how elected officials mobilized census data to make competing claims about the ethnoracial composition of the City Council. This particular case of racial arithmetic, I argue, rested on the ubiquitous juxtaposition of "Latino" and "Black" demographics, as captured in the 2010 census. Casting Black and Latino[7] political interests as a zero-sum game, this juxtaposition helped long-standing white overrepresentation escape public scrutiny.

RACE, RELATIONALITY, AND STATISTICAL KNOWLEDGE

Racial arithmetic and the broader topic of ethnoracial politics can be studied via several analytic approaches. The major approaches are *group-centric, comparative,* and *relational.* The limitations of the first two have led me to adopt the third.

The historical and social scientific study of ethnoracial politics remains largely bound to a group-centric approach. This approach has produced rich analyses of the histories and politics of specific ethnoracial groups and communities. It is, however, not without limitation. The focus on individual groups encourages a conception of ethnoracial politics composed of isolated and autonomous constituencies. Group-centric analyses are often rooted in a "substantialist" ontology that treats social phenomena as intrinsic and bounded.[8] As sociologist Matthew Desmond argues, this ontology "imposes static and atomistic categories onto a world made up of bunches of intertwining interconnections."[9]

Growing awareness of the limitations of group-centered analyses has led some scholars of race to adopt a "methodology of comparativism."[10] While this approach has produced important insights, comparative analyses still treat ethnoracial identities and movements in isolation. As a result, they too are unable to capture intersections and exchanges between different ethnoracial formations. Recovering these intersections requires a relational analytic.

A relational approach to social analysis gives "ontological primacy, not to groups or places, but to configurations of relations."[11] It does not presume the existence of independent, already formed groups. For research on race, this analytic approach holds that ethnoracial boundaries, identities, and political affiliations do not precede but rather are the *effects* of these relations. Thus, rather than operating in a vacuum, racial projects, to use the language of Michael Omi and Howard Winant, are entangled and enmeshed within a wider field of political activity.[12]

This approach is indispensable for the study of racial arithmetic for two reasons. First, it orients analysis toward the interface between different ethnoracial constituencies. Racial arithmetic, or the use of ethnoracial statistics to make political claims, is undertaken by political actors to advance their agendas over or in alignment with the agendas of others. It thus presupposes more than a single ethnoracial project or constituency.

Second, the approach allows us to capture the intrinsic relationality of ethnoracial statistics. Ethnoracial statistics, or what political scientist Kenneth Prewitt has aptly called "statistical races," are political abstractions that represent a way of thinking and enacting "race" in numerical, aggregate terms.[13] Prewitt reminds us that "there is no such thing as a 'race' without a classification scheme with more than one race category."[14] In other words, there is no singular statistical race; there are only statistical *races*.

Linked to a classificatory scheme and a quantitative ratio, ethnoracial statistics enable interested parties—politicians, marketers, journalists, activists, and the general public—to imagine and talk about, for example, "African American" and "Asian American" populations, as well as to compare "how fast their numbers are growing, how many have jobs, graduated from high school, are in prison, serve in the military, are obese or smoke, own their own homes, or marry each other."[15] As such, statistical races are relational entities whose meaning and numerical significance are forged in relation and reference to statistics about other ethnoracial populations. In this way, racial arithmetic cannot but be a relational enterprise.

Equipped with a relational orientation, I devote the remainder of this chapter to a recent case of racial arithmetic. I will examine the political negotiations and struggles over how to redraw the boundaries of Chicago's fifty aldermanic wards. Redistricting, as I show, provides a clear example of racial arithmetic, as political leaders anchor claims on the statistical races produced by the decennial census.

REDISTRICTING CHICAGO

In Chicago and elsewhere in the country, race and racial interests have historically overdetermined the process and politics of redistricting. As a site of racial arithmetic, redrawing ward boundaries literally divides the metropolis racially. This act, informed technically and rhetorically by ethnoracial statistics, can weaken or strengthen existing racial distributions of political influence and determine the life span of incumbents. White machine politics have long used redistricting to diminish and dilute the electoral power of non-dominant ethnoracial populations. Against this, in Chicago, Black and Latino[16] leaders have fought over the past several decades to increase their respective presence in the City Council.

In 2011, after data from the 2010 census were released, the Chicago City Council once again undertook redistricting. In contrast to the 2001 redistricting, which was lauded as relatively harmonious, many observers believed that the process would be racially conflictive this time around. Indeed, months before negotiations began or a single map was proposed, journalists and elected officials expected a fight. By all accounts, the conflict centered on the demographic portrait painted by the census. Writing for the *Chicago Tribune,* the city's largest daily, journalists John Byrne and Hal Dardick put the problem in the following terms: "Two of the biggest challenges involve race: The city's African American population dropped by more than 181,000, while the city's Latino population grew by about 25,000 according to last year's federal census."[17] For the next several months, this juxtaposition would become ubiquitous in media coverage of negotiations. For some elected officials, these statistics were interpreted and deployed as warrant for more "Latino" wards. Conversely, for many, census data pointed toward the seemingly *inevitable* loss of local African American political power.

With a focus on the politics and practices of racial arithmetic, the next several sections narrate, in a roughly chronological manner, how redistricting unfolded in the Chicago City Council. This account, however, requires beginning just before negotiations began, when the results of the 2010 census first became objects of local and national media coverage.

New census data became publicly available in the early months of 2011. Beginning in February, the press began to report on the results of the census in Chicago. The major story told by the media was population loss. The *Sun-Times,* for example, led its census coverage with the headline "Shrinking Chicago."[18] Its accompanying text opened with the sentence "Chicago's population plunged by 200,418 people—a 6.9 percent decline from 2000, according to the official census count released Tuesday." Its competitor, the *Tribune,* used similar language and statistics.[19] Media coverage of the city's demographic decline was not limited to local outlets. The topic was also covered in the *New York Times,* the *Wall Street Journal, USA Today,* and the *Huffington Post,* among others.

In local and national media, Chicago's demographics were described and discussed in relation to many issues, such as the economic and political impact of demographic decline. Yet few—if any—of these issues rivaled the attention directed at the city's loss of African American residents. According to the census, there was a significant drop in Chicago's Black population and that of other "traditional Black strongholds" like Atlanta, Detroit, and Washington, DC.[20] Monica Davey of the *New York Times* wrote, "As Chicagoans prepare to vote next week for their first new mayor in decades, the city itself looks different from how it did during much of the era of Mayor Richard M. Daley, who is retiring: it has shrunk, and black people in particular have left."[21]

Similar narratives appeared in both of Chicago's major newspapers. Presenting census data, a *Sun-Times* article stated, "Chicago's black population fell the most, nearly 17 percent. Today, Blacks make up only 33 percent of the city's population, down from 36 percent 10 years ago."[22] Black population loss was represented visually in various ways, from photos of boarded-up businesses to infographics pregnant with statistics. For example, the *Tribune* produced a map of community areas to illustrate neighborhood population loss. The map's caption described the city's overall loss as "fueled in part by a decrease in [its] black population." The Black population was also a major theme of editorials and commentaries.[23]

Given that ethnoracial statistics are relational entities, news of Black population loss was often discussed in reference to other ethnoracial populations. In particular, it was consistently contrasted with the population growth of the Latinx population. Whereas media discourse on national trends ubiquitously juxtaposed "white" and "Latino" demographics, press coverage of urban contexts often focused on "Black" and "Latino" demographics. *USA Today,* for instance, published an article in April 2011 with the headline "Census: Hispanics Surpass Blacks in Most U.S. Metros."[24] The opening line of the article stressed the political implications of this trend: "Hispanics now outnumber African-Americans for the first time in most U.S. metropolitan areas, shifting the political and racial dynamics in cities once dominated by whites and blacks." Media outlets made note of local Latinx population growth, and they increasingly positioned it in relation to the African American population.

As redistricting drew near, the juxtaposition of these populations intensified and became politically charged. For example, in August 2011, just as redistricting negotiations were set to begin, the *Huffington Post* ran an article that described Latinx population growth as a "notable counterweight to the black exodus."[25] The article focused primarily on Chicago's Black population but noted that "Latinos are increasing their share of Chicago's population, and there are 25,000 more Latinos in the city now than in 2000." Quoting a *Sun-Times* article, it framed these divergent demographic trends—the respective growth and decline of the city's two largest "minority" populations—as a major reason that the coming redistricting would likely be "among the most contentious in recent history."

THE PROBLEM OF ETHNORACIAL PROPORTIONALITY

As members of the City Council began preparing for redistricting, most council members agreed that one of the major challenges would be how to reconcile Black and Latinx demographics. There were, to be sure, other potential sources of conflict, but the debate about the City Council's ethnoracial composition was arguably the most intense. This debate pivoted, often explicitly, on the notion of ethnoracial proportionality, an idea that is intrinsically relational. As a form of racial arithmetic, this notion stipulates that the ethnoracial composition of an elected body, like the City Council, should correspond to the ethnoracial demographics of its jurisdiction. This idea, Prewitt notes, emerged in the 1960s as a "new way of thinking about racial fairness."[26]

To my knowledge, no calls were made for complete ethnoracial proportionality. Instead, mapmakers seemed to share an aspiration for a *more* proportional map than had been quietly achieved in the previous decade. For some, greater proportionality would help the map survive legal challenges and prevent the city from becoming embroiled in expensive and protracted lawsuits, such as those that marked local redistricting in the 1980s and 1990s. Others sought greater proportionality in the name of making the City Council better reflect the city's residents. Even so, enthusiasm for this aspiration was not universal, because increasing proportionality could also create a more fractious council for the mayor, challenge the political careers of some incumbents, and even severely threaten the existing concentration of political influence and power, whether of longtime white council members or of the Black Caucus. The "new" map had to be different from the "old map," but, as one alderman cautioned, the "devil is in the details."[27]

The major detail then was determining *how* proportional to make the City Council. This question was taken up in the *Tribune* about a month before official negotiations began. In July 2011, journalists Hal Dardick and Kristen Mack described what complete ethnoracial proportionality would look in light of the 2010 census. "If the ethnic and racial makeup of the city mirrored its population, the council would have 16 whites, 16 blacks, 15 Latinos and three Asians." This makeup, they acknowledged, was not politically feasible, but perhaps neither was the current configuration. "The council now has 22 white members, 19 African Americans, eight Latinos and one alderman of Indian descent—a combination well out of sync with the makeup of Chicago following the 2000 census."[28]

According to the analysis of Dardick and Mack, whites were overrepresented by six positions and Blacks overrepresented by three, while Latinos were underrepresented by seven seats and Asian Americans by two. As the press often noted, four "Latino" wards—wards with a Latinx demographic majority—were represented by influential white aldermen. Although white council members had the greatest overrepresentation, media coverage rarely mentioned them, nor did it take much notice of Asian underrepresentation.

Attention usually focused on the comparative representation of Blacks and Latinos in the City Council. Although Dardick and Mack, in the article cited above, mentioned that increases to Latino seats on the council would come at the "expense" of whites, they stressed that this would "especially" be the case for African Americans.[29] These journalists were far from alone in making this assertion. For example, a December 2011 *Sun-Times* article stated, "Last week, a majority of aldermen appeared to be uniting behind a map that would give Hispanics three more super-majority wards as a reward for their 25,218-person population gain at the expense of blacks, who would lose two seats."[30] Even when the word *expense* was not used, it was communicated nonetheless. A September 2011 *Sun-Times* article discussed efforts to "maximize an ever-shrinking African-American population and accommodate a growing but often low voting Hispanic population."[31] Accordingly, the Latinx population was often described as deserving greater representation; the *Sun-Times,* for instance, consistently framed potential increases to the number of "Latino" wards as a demographic "reward."

Arguments about Black expense and Latino gain helped elide the historical overrepresentation of white aldermen. These claims restricted ethnoracial representation narrowly to the results of the 2010 census—the operative logic being that the population that had suffered the greatest population loss should suffer, as a consequence, the greatest political loss. Conversely, the population with the greatest demographic gain should gain the most politically. This represented a kind of selective ethnoracial proportionality, which posited that Black and Latino political outcomes were locked in a zero-sum game.

In the next section, I explore how members of the Black Caucus and the Latino Caucus responded and engaged in racial arithmetic for political representation. As I show, both caucuses were hesitant to embrace this zero-sum logic but were nonetheless committed to mobilizing census statistics to advance, at least to some extent, their competing aims.

BLACK AND LATINO CAUCUSES RESPOND

Months before the official start of negotiations on August 1, the nineteen-member Black Caucus made public the hire of attorney and former South Side alderwoman Freddenna Lyle. Until her razor-thin loss just months before, Lyle had served in the City Council for thirteen years. News of Lyle's selection was the subject of a *Sun-Times* article headlined "Dispute over Boundaries Could Get Ugly." In the article, the chair of the Black Caucus, Alderman Howard Brookins of the 21st Ward, was quoted explaining the group's selection. "She went through it 10 years ago. She's an attorney. And she has an idea as to how City Council works and specific expertise with respect to drawing maps."[32] The Black Caucus publicly stated its commitment to preserving Black wards. As *Sun-Times* journalist Fran Spielman narrated, "Lyle will go to war for her former colleagues in the high-stakes battle to hold on to the 19 City Council seats and 20 majority black wards they have, despite a dramatic decline in Chicago's black population."[33] In May, when Brookins became chair after the controversial resignation of his predecessor, he told reporters that preserving African American–majority wards was his top priority.[34]

To preserve wards, the Black Caucus practiced racial arithmetic. A key aspect of its practice involved using ethnoracial statistics to contest the thesis of Black "expense." Leveraging alternative interpretations of the census results, the Black Caucus argued that the city's demographic composition did not warrant *substantial* change to the number of "Black" wards. Lyle told the press, "As opposed to having 19 wards with 80 or 90 percent black population, you may have some wards that have 65, 70 or 80 percent. But we're going into the process anticipating that we will retain the same number of African-American wards." While acknowledging overall population loss, she claimed that, whereas the Latinx population was "more spread out," the Black population largely continued to live in "compact, single race neighborhoods." Lyle also challenged the idea that Latinx demographic growth should be charged to African American members. "If there is to be an increase in Latino wards, it should come at the expense of wards represented by white aldermen." Lyle's comment was one of the few public statements about white overrepresentation. The attorney justified her position, noting that the 2010 census found nearly fifty-three thousand fewer white residents than enumerated in the previous census.[35] Although they did so less prominently than one might expect, the Black Caucus and its supporters also claimed that the Black population had declined but remained the largest demographic in the city. For instance, as narrated by *Sun-Times* columnist Mark Brown, former alderwoman Dorothy Tillman "complain[ed] that all the ward remap stories were citing the 181,453 decrease in the black population without mentioning that blacks still comprise the largest single population group in Chicago."[36] While the Black Caucus did not publicly call into question the results of the census, they did contest the dominant narrative built on them, namely that African American political loss should follow population loss. But their attempts to preserve "Black" wards met against the racial arithmetic of the Latino Caucus.

In early September, a month after Lyle was hired, members of the Latino Caucus gathered in City Hall to express their desire and resolve to increase the number of "Latino" wards. Standing before cameras and reporters, Latino aldermen drew on census data to make a demographic case for adding new wards. As widely reported in the local press, the 2010 census found twenty-five thousand more Latinx residents than enumerated in the previous census. Emboldened by this statistic, 25th Ward alderman Danny Solis, the chairman of the caucus, told the press, "We're looking to increase our representation. Right now we just know the numbers speak for themselves." Another alderman, Ray Suarez from the 31st Ward, echoed Solis: "We're looking at the numbers, and working with the numbers, to make sure the Latino community has proper representation." By "proper" representation, these aldermen and their attorneys meant proportional representation—a conviction that undergirded a question posed by 22nd Ward alderman Ricardo Muñoz. "If Latinos are one-third of the city, why are they one-fifth of the City Council?"[37]

Although they did not specify a number at the press conference, the Latino Caucus members made clear their belief that demographics mandated an increase in wards. Months before, beginning in July, they had begun articulating that the Latinx population had grown across the city and accounted for nearly a third of its residents. These officials also pushed back against some of the interpretations advanced by the Black Caucus and other members of the council. When the influential white alderman Richard Mell, who oversaw redistricting, described the Latinx population as "diffuse," Alderman Muñoz shot back, "So is the white population. We no longer have the days of concentrated neighborhoods. There's ways of cutting different wards for different purposes. It depends on what the political will is."[38] These claims and counterclaims rested on census data and the conviction that statistics were transparent, needing no translators. As anthropologist Jacqueline Urla has argued, "Rhetorically, numbers function as pure description or inescapable 'facts.'"[39] Indeed, the Latino Caucus maintained, as Alderman Roberto Maldonado of the 26th Ward once put it, that "the numbers now speak louder than ever."[40]

While advancing their respective agendas, both caucuses publicly affirmed their willingness to dialogue and compromise as legally "protected classes." Black Caucus members admitted that the number of "Latino" wards should increase, and the Latino Caucus affirmed that it was not targeting Black political power. Weeks before the Black Caucus made its first map public, Victor Reyes, the former leader of the controversy-ridden Hispanic Democratic Organization, mused, "Maybe there's a solution that doesn't require there to be losers."[41] Yet the juxtaposition of Black and Latinx demographics made finding such a solution difficult. It was precisely at this moment that Chicago's redistricting entered its most conflictual phase: mapmaking.

In September, after weeks of preparation and preliminary negotiations, members of the City Council began to propose maps. Until then, demands for more "Latino" wards, appeals for boundaries to reflect demographic changes, and refusals to surrender "Black" wards had been abstract. To become concrete, these claims had to be inscribed into a map—for, ultimately, this was the object that elected officials and interested parties were struggling over and for. While most of the mapmaking happens behind closed doors in Chicago, the maps' public display and the press coverage they received provide further insight into the practice of racial arithmetic in redistricting. Without claiming to present a comprehensive account, this final section employs a relational perspective to trace the cascade of "dueling maps" that consumed the City Council. Of particular relevance here is how mapmaking hinges on the manufacture of ethnoracial majorities. This is accomplished by shuffling existing boundaries to capture or expel certain populations, a process that homogenizes as much as it fragments.[42]

The Black Caucus introduced the first map. It was unveiled in late September, almost three months before the City Council's self-imposed December 1 deadline for map selection. The Black Caucus's map conceded one majority "Black" ward and added two majority "Latino" wards. A *Chicago Tribune* article described it as a "politically easy" proposal for the caucus, since its main concession—the 2nd Ward in the city's South Loop— had already lost its majority Black population and was represented by a white alderman.[43] Press accounts of the map—and all subsequent maps—were saturated with data on the 2010 census, particularly data on Black demographic loss and Latino population gain. Structured by the pervasive juxtaposition of Black and Latinx demographics, the media also recorded public responses from members of the Latino Caucus. Caucus chair Solis stated, "We're at least 29 percent of the city, almost a third, and that's more than the 13 wards they presented."[44] Another Latino alderman, speaking anonymously, charged that the map had little "parity," given that "blacks have a little bit more population than Hispanics."[45]

The Latino Caucus proposed a map in mid-November, after two public hearings in Latino-dominant wards. Like the Black Caucus map, its map was publicly floated but not officially filed. The Latino Caucus map would create four new "super-majority" Latino wards and two "influence" wards. In super-majority wards, the Latinx population would be at least 65 percent of the overall population. Influence wards would set the demographic threshold at between 35 and 55 percent. Creating these wards required pulling together "Latino" residents and moving out other populations. For instance, this map would transform Alderwoman Toni Foulkes's 15th Ward from predominately African American to majority Latino.[46] It would have a similar effect on a majority-white ward on the North Side. Most controversially, the Latino Caucus map would decrease the number of "Black" wards by two, rather by than the single ward proposed by the Black Caucus.

In early December, Alderman Mell and the Finance and Rules Committee shared a draft map. This map generated the most tension during redistricting. Like the Latino Caucus map, the committee map would decrease "Black" wards by two. It would also decrease "white" wards by five and add three supermajority "Latino" wards and three additional influence wards.[47] In response, Black Caucus attorney Lyle cited a legislative motion that would prevent the map from securing enough votes. "If a map is passed that has 17 African-American wards, there will be another map introduced by ten African-American aldermen."[48] A "flashpoint" of contention became the prospect of creating a supermajority "Latino" ward in the Back of the Yards neighborhood, which was split into five South Side wards. As stated in the *Tribune,* members of the Latino Caucus made a demographic argument in favor of consolidation: "Latino aldermen point to demographics. Back of the Yards is now about 59 percent Hispanic, up from 51 percent in 2000. It's about 31 percent black, down from 36 percent a decade ago."[49] The article went on to note that the Black Caucus chair, Alderman Brookins, "pointed out that only around 43,000 people live in Back of the Yards, so forming a ward that approaches the population standard of roughly 53,000 residents per ward for the new map would require slicing off pieces of surrounding neighborhoods." One African American alderman called the prospective "Latino" supermajority ward in the Back of the Yards a "racial gerrymander."

On December 15, the Latino Caucus filed a revised map. To signal its legal fortitude over the Black Caucus map, the map was titled "The Taxpayer Protection Map." Unlike its original proposal, this map reduced the addition of "Latino" wards from four to three, but it still decreased "Black" wards by two. Alderman Solis told the press, "Now we have a map—that we believe will pass muster, so to speak—a map that represents every ethnic and racial group in the city of Chicago in a fair way."[50] The map received support from eight members of the Latino Caucus and eight white council members, but no support from African American members. At about the same time, a coalition of thirty-two council members introduced the "Map for a Better Chicago." The map was spearheaded by the Black Caucus and Alderman Mell, who shifted his support away from the Latino Caucus proposal. The map included eighteen "Black" wards and thirteen "Latino" wards. This composition required, however, that several North Side wards, largely composed of whites, would have larger populations than many heavily African American South Side wards. Detractors argued that this "deviation" opened room for legal challenges, since it could violate the notion of "one person, one vote."

Both the Black Caucus and the Latino Caucus maps fell short of the forty-one votes needed to approve the map. With negotiations halted, the City Council departed for winter recess without a compromise. In a somewhat tongue-in-cheek fashion, the *Chicago Tribune* editorial board urged the introduction of a "doomsday" map to resolve the impasse. Rather than divide the map to protect incumbents and secure ethnoracial representation, this map "simply divides the city into squares. Ward boundaries don't meander all over the place to sort voters into predictable majorities."[51] Groups calling for an end to ethnoracial gerrymandering promoted similar maps. With negotiations stalled, Mayor Rahm Emanuel threatened to introduce what the press called a "nuclear option"—a ballot question in the next election that would give voters an opportunity to decide whether the City Council should be reduced to twenty-five members.[52]

In early January 2012, the Mexican American Legal Defense and Educational Fund, a national civil rights litigator, submitted its own "Equity" map. The map created fourteen "Latino"-majority wards, one more than the Latino Caucus map, and included the same number of "Black" wards present in the Black Caucus map. In addition, the map placed much of the Back of the Yards into a single ward and even did the same for splintered Chinatown. But no council members endorsed the map because, as one article noted, it ignored "the most important factor in redistricting: protecting incumbents."[53] As this map entered circulation, Mell and members of the Black and Latino Caucuses resumed negotiations.

On January 19, the City Council passed a slightly modified version of the "Map for a Better Chicago" map. As described in the *Tribune*, "Less than two hours after putting the finishing touches on a new map of the city's 50 wards, the Chicago City Council approved it over the vehement objections of some council members whose political futures are imperiled by the redrawn boundaries."[54] Rather than prolong the process and intensify contention and public scrutiny, behind-the-scenes negotiations built sufficient support for the map. It passed with a 41–8 vote, the bare minimum of votes needed. Living up to the city's reputation, the vote made it possible to circumvent public hearings. The compromise between the Black and Latino Caucuses was key. The new map contains eighteen "Black" wards, one short of the prior map, and thirteen majority "Latino" wards, a gain of three.[55] Although white overrepresentation had not emerged as a major point of discussion, several "white" wards were sacrificed, at least in part, to offset these preservations and additions.

. . .

The preceding sections present a relational account of Chicago's most recent experience of redistricting. Long before negotiations began, elected officials and journalists shared in the premonition that the process would be a "racially charged political storm," as one newspaper put it.[56] In a sense, this premonition was correct. But, in part, this was because of how these same actors interpreted the results of the 2010 census and engaged in racial arithmetic. Particular choices led to the focus on Black and Latinx demographics rather than on the historically cemented overrepresentation of whites in the City Council. Eventually, after intense and at times openly conflictual negotiations, the majority of the council agreed to a new map, one deemed more proportionally representative than its predecessor. As I have detailed, competing practices of racial arithmetic sought to configure wards in ways that either preserved or augmented the number of seats for particular ethnoracial populations.

A departure from the dominant approaches in the study of race enabled this account. I have sought neither to highlight a single population nor stage a comparison between two or more projects. Instead, I have employed a relational orientation that, as David Theo Goldberg writes, pursues the "(re-) production of relational ties and their mutually effecting and reinforcing impacts."[57] This approach, I argue, helps us understand the relationality of ethnoracial statistics, the chief instrument of racial arithmetic. It helps register that statistical claims about a particular population necessarily imply and are related to claims about other populations. These relations are a major source of their meaningfulness and discursive significance. However, I should note that binary juxtapositions, such as those that anchored Chicago's redistricting negotiations, are not the only form these relations can take.

Beyond its purchase for the study of racial arithmetic, a relational approach opens terrain for the study of ethnoracial politics more broadly. As Natalia

Molina argues, this approach invites us to rethink our questions, units of analysis, and assumptions about racial identity and group formation.[58] In a social horizon marked by growing diversity, we especially need analytic frameworks that make visible the contextually specific conflicts, collaborations, and connections out of which ethnoracial politics arise and transform.

ACKNOWLEDGMENTS

I thank Michelle Mejía for her research assistance.

NOTES

1. The term *racial arithmetic* trades on the notion of *political arithmetic,* which was coined by the seventeenth-century British political philosopher William Petty. For Petty, political arithmetic was a method for "handling economic and political matters mathematically." Patrick Carroll, *Science, Culture, and Modern State Formation* (Berkeley: University of California Press, 2006), 87.

2. Melissa Nobles, *Shades of Citizenship: Race and the Census in Modern Politics* (Stanford, CA: Stanford University Press, 2000); Kenneth Prewitt, *What Is Your Race? The Census and Our Flawed Efforts to Classify Americans* (Princeton, NJ: Princeton University Press, 2013).

3. John David Skrentny, *The Minority Rights Revolution* (Cambridge, MA: Belknap Press of Harvard University Press, 2002); Ann Morning and Daniel Sabbagh, "From Sword to Plowshare: Using Race for Discrimination and Antidiscrimination in the United States," *International Social Science Journal* 57, no. 183 (2005): 57–73; Debra Thompson, *The Schematic State: Race, Transnationalism, and the Politics of the Census* (Cambridge: Cambridge University Press, 2016).

4. For an example on Latinx civil rights, see G. Cristina Mora, *Making Hispanics: How Activists, Bureaucrats, and Media Constructed a New American* (Chicago: University of Chicago Press, 2014).

5. *Investigation of the Ferguson Police Department* (Washington, DC: U.S. Department of Justice, Civil Rights Division, 2015), 4.

6. Natalia Molina, *How Race Is Made in America: Immigration, Citizenship, and the Historical Power of Racial Scripts* (Berkeley: University of California Press, 2014), 3. For other relational accounts of race, see Tomás Almaguer, *Racial Fault Lines: The Historical Origins of White Supremacy in California* (Berkeley: University of California Press, 1994); Claire Jean Kim, *Bitter Fruit: The Politics of Black-Korean Conflict in New York City* (New Haven, CT: Yale University Press, 2000); David Theo Goldberg, "Racial Comparisons, Relational Racisms: Some Thoughts on Method," *Ethnic and Racial Studies* 32, no. 7 (2009).

7. A note on terminology. This chapter employs both *Latino* and *Latinx* (a gender-nonbinary version of *Latino/a*). When referring to ward politics or redistricting, the former will be used, since this is the term of choice within this political context. The latter, however, will be used when the subject is the population as a whole (e.g., Latinx population growth).

8. On substantialism, see Mustafa Emirbayer, "Manifesto for a Relational Sociology," *American Journal of Sociology* 103, no. 2 (1997): 281–317.

9. Matthew Desmond, "Relational Ethnography," *Theory and Society* 43, no. 5 (2014): 551.

10. Goldberg, "Racial Comparisons," 1272.

11. Desmond, "Relational Ethnography," 554.

12. Michael Omi and Howard Winant, *Racial Formation in the United States: From the 1960s to the 1980s* (New York: Routledge, 1986).

13. Prewitt, *What Is Your Race?*

14. Prewitt, *What Is Your Race?*, 26.

15. Prewitt, *What Is Your Race?*, 6.

16. The City Council does not have any Latina members, hence the use of the term *Latino*.

17. John Byrne and Hal Dardick, "City Population Loss, Race Issue Make Council Remap Tricky," *Chicago Tribune,* July 6, 2011.

18. Art Golab, "Shrinking Chicago," *Chicago Sun-Times,* Febuary 16, 2011.

19. William Mullen and Vikki Ortiz-Healy, "Chicago's Population Drops 200,000," *Chicago Tribune,* February 15, 2011.

20. Like other major cities, Chicago's African American population decline has numerous contributing factors, including unemployment, gentrification, violence, and labor market opportunities in other regions.

21. Monica Davey, "Chicago Is Now Smaller and Less Black, Census Shows," *New York Times,* February 15, 2011.

22. Golab, "Shrinking Chicago."

23. For example, Andrea Zopp, "Black Chicago: Where Have You Gone?," *Chicago Defender,* February 23–March 1, 2011.

24. "Census: Hispanics Surpass Blacks in Most U.S. Metros," *USA Today,* April 14 2011.

25. Matt Sledge, "Chicago's Black Population Dwindles, Census Numbers Show," *Huffington Post,* August 4, 2011.

26. Prewitt, *What Is Your Race?*, 94.

27. Hal Dardick, "Latino Numbers 'Speak Louder Than Ever,'" *Chicago Tribune,* November 11, 2011.

28. Hal Dardick and Kristen Mack, "Latino Aldermen Want More Chicago City Council Seats," *Chicago Tribune,* September 8, 2011.

29. In another article, Mack and Dardick are even more direct: "Latino aldermen, who stand to gain three wards under a proposal being discussed, have been pleased with the still evolving plan. Latino gains, however, would come largely at the expense of African-American aldermen, who could lose two seats." Kristen Mack

and Hal Dardick, "Message to Emanuel: Black Aldermen Not Happy with Remap," *Chicago Tribune,* December 2, 2011.

30. Fran Spielman, "Black Caucus Map Hits Daley's 11th Ward," *Chicago Sun-Times,* December 8, 2011.

31. Abdon M. Pallasch, "Committeeman Candidates May Find They're Barely in Ward Where Most Signatures Collected," *Chicago Sun-Times,* September 12, 2011.

32. Fran Spielman, "Dispute over Boundaries Could Get Ugly: Black Caucus Hires Lyle in Ward Fight," *Chicago Sun-Times,* August 2, 2011.

33. Spielman, "Dispute over Boundaries."

34. Fran Spielman, "Brookins to Lead Black Caucus," *Chicago Sun-Times,* May 19, 2011; "Alderman Howard Brookins to Head Black Caucus after Affordable Housing Battle," *Huffington Post,* May 19, 2011, https://www.huffingtonpost.com/2011/05/19/alderman-howard-brookins-_n_864283.html.

35. Claims about the diffuse nature of Latino (and Asian American) populations were not limited to the Black Caucus and were made throughout redistricting.

36. Mark Brown, "Black, Hispanic Aldermen Battle for Their Share of City's Pie—Sort of Confused by Ward Remap Fight," *Chicago Sun-Times,* December 20, 2011.

37. Hal Dardick and Kristen Mack, "Latino Aldermen Want More Chicago City Council Seats," *Chicago Tribune,* September 8, 2011.

38. Fran Spielman, "Hispanics Demand More Council Seats in Power Battle," *Chicago Sun-Times,* July 7, 2011.

39. Jacqueline Urla, "Cultural Politics in an Age of Statistics: Numbers, Nations, and the Making of Basque Identity," *American Ethnologist* 20, no. 4 (1993): 820.

40. Dardick, "Latino Numbers 'Speak Louder Than Ever.'"

41. Fran Spielman, "Ex-HDO Chief Reyes to Help Boost Hispanics on Council," *Chicago Sun-Times,* September 9, 2011.

42. Urla, "Cultural Politics," 831.

43. Hal Dardick, "Black Aldermen Are United on Remap," *Chicago Tribune,* September 20, 2011.

44. Dardick, "Black Aldermen Are United on Remap."

45. Fran Spielman, "Hispanics Expecting More Wards: Black Caucus Map Called 'Laughable,'" *Chicago Sun-Times,* September 20, 2011.

46. Hal Dardick, "Latino Map Would Put 2 Aldermen's Seats at Risk," *Chicago Tribune,* November 18, 2011.

47. Fran Spielman, "Opposition to Primary Plan Could Force Referendum," *Chicago Sun-Times,* December 1, 2011.

48. Spielman, "Opposition to Primary Plan."

49. John Byrne, "Remap Fight Pivots on Back of the Yards," *Chicago Tribune,* December 4, 2011.

50. Sam Hudzik, "Tensions Grow over City Council Remap as Caucuses Introduce Proposals," WBEZ, December 16, 2011, https://www.wbez.org/shows/wbez-news/tensions-grow-over-city-council-remap-as-caucuses-introduce-proposals/786f7be9-634e-4495-80fe-8811e337612c.

51. Editorial Board, "Let's See the Doomsday Map," *Chicago Tribune,* December 17, 2011.

52. Fran Spielman, "Mayor Would Push Ballot Question Asking Voters If City Should Have Only 25 Aldermen," *Chicago Sun-Times,* December 20, 2011.

53. Edward McClelland, "Mexican-American Legal Defense Fund Draws Ward Map," NBC Chicago, January 9, 2012, https://www.nbcchicago.com/blogs/ward-room/Mexican-American-Legal-Defense-Fund-Draws-Ward-Map--136815108.html.

54. Hal Dardick, "City Council Passes New Ward Map, 41–8," *Chicago Tribune,* January 19, 2012.

55. The map did not consolidate the Back of the Yards area into one ward, an initial demand of some community groups and the Latino Caucus, nor did it create an "Asian" ward anchored by Chinatown.

56. Fran Spielman, "The Eye of the Storm," *Chicago Sun-Times,* December 6, 2011.

57. Goldberg, "Racial Comparisons," 1276.

58. Natalia Molina, "Examining a Chicana/o History through a Relational Lens," *Pacific Historical Review* 82, no. 4 (2013): 520–41.

FOURTEEN

The Relational Positioning of Arab and Muslim Americans in Post-9/11 Racial Politics

Julie Lee Merseth

At the advent of the twenty-first century and in the perennial aftermath of 9/11, Arabs and Muslims in the United States have been intensely targeted as presumptively suspect and threatening members of social and political life. In the name of antiterrorism and national security, Arab and Muslim communities, including American citizens, have been increasingly subjected to racial profiling and police surveillance, as well as to routine and at times unbridled vilification in the mainstream media.[1] Through a combination of policy making and public discourse, Arabs and Muslims have experienced an intensified "othering" that reflects a deepening marginal status similar to that of groups in the United States that are racialized as minorities, people of color, or nonwhites.[2] Indeed, that Arabs and Muslims have been targeted relentlessly by the government and in the public sphere as not only un-American but presumably anti-American makes scant the post-9/11 possibility of locating these communities within "whiteness," the dominant category in the American racial order.[3] Rather, the state-sanctioned and discursive othering of Arabs and Muslims has increasingly positioned these groups qua groups as racially subordinate or lesser than. At the same time, it is not obvious that Arab and Muslim communities are targeted and viewed in ways consistent with the perceptions and stereotypes attached to other existing racial(ized) groups, including Asian Americans and African Americans.

This chapter investigates whether and how the post-9/11 othering of Arab and Muslim communities is changing the collective or group-based terrain of American racial and ethnic politics. Employing a relational lens and focusing on racial(ized) political discourse in the mainstream news, I examine the extent to and ways in which Arabs and Muslims have been distinctly racialized and potentially positioned as a group in relation to multiple other groups. Based on a content analysis of more than sixty thousand articles in the *New York Times* over a span of fifteen years, this chapter examines the frames through which Arabs and Muslims have been racialized. First, I explore the conflation of these communities and, second, observe framing differences in comparison to Asian Americans and African Americans. I further show consistency in these framing patterns across time. Ultimately, I argue that the post-9/11 racialization of Arabs and Muslims in the United States has helped advance the formation of a new racial(ized) group, an emergent political construction relationally positioned in twenty-first-century racial politics.[4]

ARAB AND MUSLIM RACIALIZATION
IN THE UNITED STATES

Studies of Arab and Muslim racialization in the American political context remain relatively few, but they have established a number of critical underpinnings: in particular, the conflation of Arabs and Muslims (as well as Middle Easterners) and the role of religion in not only racializing but also dividing Arab and Muslim communities.

The Conflation and Classification of Arab
and Muslim Communities

Many scholars of Arab and Muslim racialization have argued that the racial othering of Arabs and Muslims in the United States rests on the conflation of the two communities, a conflation fueled by the persistent residues of Orientalism in contemporary American politics, society, and culture.[5] Drawing on Edward Said's influential work on the "binary opposition between East and West" and the "immutable 'essence'" of the Orient, Nadine Naber writes,

> Government policies that were directed at individuals who were associated with a constructed "Arab enemy" came to be directed at a constructed "Arab Muslim" enemy. Thus particularly since the 1970s, government and media discourses on "the Arab" tended to be constituted by a conflation of the categories "Arab" and "Muslim" and a refashioning of European discourses that portrayed Islam as homogenous, uncivilized, and culturally backward, and violently misogynistic.[6]

Indeed, the terms *Arab* and *Muslim* have become nearly indistinguishable in U.S. policy making and public discourse, advanced in part through post-9/11 media representations that have relentlessly advanced the conflation.[7] This is striking because, by conventional definitions, Arabs and Muslims are not the same type of identity-based group. To identify as Arab is to link one's ancestry with a region spanning parts of western Asia and northern Africa, including what is often described as the "Middle East."[8] Because the so-called Arab world encompasses a large and diverse set of nation-states (e.g., Lebanon, Egypt, Syria, Palestine, Jordan, Morocco, Iraq), *Arab* is often understood either as a panethnic group or as a single ethnic group based on, for example, Arabic as a common language. On the other hand, self-identification as a Muslim is a religious identification. To be a practicing Muslim is to practice Islam, a religion with an immense and fast-growing global presence. The worldwide Muslim population is expected to increase to 2.8 billion by 2050, reaching near parity with the Christian population.[9]

Furthermore, the terms *Arab* and *Muslim* refer to populations that, when defined separately, have little overlap. Contrary to widespread stereotypes, many Muslims are not Arab. Worldwide, only one in five Muslims resides in the Middle East–North Africa region, whereas the largest Muslim populations continue to be located in Asia, mainly in Southeast and South Asian countries such as Indonesia and India.[10] In the United States, too, the majority of the Muslim population is nonwhite, with the two largest groups reported as black and Asian and notable differences along lines of nativity: while native-born Muslims are 56 percent black and 2 percent Asian, foreign-born Muslims are 28 percent Asian and 10 percent black.[11] By the same token, most Arabs in the United States are not Muslims. Among Arabs in the United States, as many as two-thirds are Christian, while only one-third are Muslim, although the majority of recent Arab immigrants are Muslim.[12]

Nevertheless, the terms *Arab* and *Muslim* are constantly conflated or interchanged in many domains of American politics. It is unclear the extent to which this stems from feigned ignorance or calculated self-interest among political leaders and everyday citizens. For instance, during the 2016 election, two presidential candidates—frontrunners of a major political party, including Donald Trump, the eventual Republican nominee who continued on to win the presidency—called for "a total and complete shutdown of Muslims entering the United States," casting suspicion on all communities of immigrants from the Middle East after a deadly act of terrorism in the United States by two Pakistani Muslims, including a native-born American citizen, and the need "to patrol and secure Muslim neighborhoods before they become radicalized" as a national security measure.[13] Although these proposals were met with fierce criticism and debate in the public sphere, the voters' response was not to penalize but to reward those candidates, demonstrating that conflating Arabs and Muslims remains acceptable in mainstream American politics fifteen years after 9/11 and is increasingly effective as a campaign strategy.

The interchangeability of Arab and Muslim communities also remains an alarming feature of post-9/11 policy making. Consistently throughout the "War on Terror," which has been advanced through overseas military and domestic media campaigns, the conflation of Arabs and Muslims has been perpetuated through the political actions of the state. For example, detailing the consequences of the government's brazen racial profiling practices in the immediate wake of 9/11, Leti Volpp writes,

> Subsequent to September 11, over twelve hundred noncitizens have been swept up into detention. The purported basis for this sweep is to investigate and prevent terrorist attacks, yet none of the persons arrested and detained have been identified as engaged in terrorist activity. While the government has refused to release the most basic information about these individuals— their names, where they are held, and the immigration or criminal charges filed against them—we know that the vast majority of those detained appear to be Middle Eastern, Muslim, or South Asian. We know, too, that the majority were identified to the government through suspicions and tips based solely upon perceptions of their racial, religious, or ethnic identity.[14]

Repeatedly, federal and local enforcement policies have treated Arabs and Muslims as a single entity by effectively identifying all members of both communities as political targets not just abroad but also domestically, alleging the need to apprehend Islamist radicals who have secretly infiltrated unsuspecting American communities.[15]

Nevertheless, while the U.S. government may at times seem to formally use "Arab/Muslim" as a distinct category, it does not. Neither community, Arab or Muslim, is designated as an institutionalized racial or ethnic category. Because *Muslim* refers to a religious identity, the case of Arabs has received greater attention in debates over racial classification.[16] Within the current system of classifying race and ethnicity—a distinction itself contested in theory and mutable in practice, as the case of Latinos and "Hispanic origin" aptly demonstrates[17]—neither Arabs nor any combined grouping of Arabs and Muslims has existed as an institutionally recognized group.[18]

Rather, for Arab Americans the assumed default racial category is white, and indeed many Arabs in the United States have identified with whiteness, both in the past and in the present day.[19] For example, to gain access to naturalization and citizenship privileges, Arab immigrant communities pursued and won court cases seeking to be categorized as white rather than "Chinese-Mongolian" during periods of Asian exclusion in the twentieth century.[20] The post-9/11 American political context has, however, cemented a "growing rift between 'Arab' and 'white' identities," creating a set of choices that can seem to present no choice at all. As Andrew Shryock writes, "Arab Americans might identify *with* 'people of color,' but they very rarely identify *as* Asian or black. Instead, Arabs accept or reject the label 'white.'"[21]

In response, Arab American community leaders agitated for the inclusion of an "Arab" category on the U.S. Census in 2000 and again in 2010, to no avail.[22] In fact, the word *Arab* did not even appear on the 2010 census form. The Census Bureau's position on racial classification and Arab background was made explicit only in the instructions: "'White' refers to a person having origins in any of the original peoples of Europe, the Middle East, or North Africa. It includes people who indicated their race(s) as 'White' or reported entries such as Irish, German, Italian, Lebanese, Arab, Moroccan, or Caucasian."[23] With efforts refocused on the possibilities for Census 2020, Arab American organizations then worked to mobilize community support for a proposed new category for those of Middle Eastern or North African descent, or MENA, also to no avail.[24] Those who identify as "Arab" or "Arab American" have continued to be counted as racially white, an institutional practice that many view as incongruent with experiences of escalated state-sanctioned discrimination and everyday threats of anti-Arab and anti-Muslim violence.

Religion and Religious Difference in Arab and Muslim Communities

Studies of Arab and Muslim racialization also have made central the role of religion, attending to how it shapes racialization processes, including calls to view the Muslim American experience as fundamentally racialized[25] and, at the same time, to view religious difference as a formidable political cleavage. Indeed, the othering of non-Christian religions—namely Islam—features prominently in the conflation of Arabs and Muslims discussed above. Enabled by Orientalist narratives of these communities as perpetually foreign, exotic, and culturally backward, the elision through which these communities come to be viewed as one and the same profits from obscuring the possibility of religious variation. It firmly attaches Islam (religion) to the Middle East (region), and then seizes on the public imagination.

In fact, religious identities cross-cut Arab communities, which include Christians, Muslims, and Jews,[26] and scholars have observed important differences in political behavior based on religious divisions. For instance, in the post-9/11 context of heightened racial profiling and police surveillance, Arab Muslims and Arab Christians have responded in divergent ways to the conflation of Arab and Muslim communities. Jen'nan Ghazal Read argues that some Arab Christians have responded through a strategy of emphasizing their religious identity in an effort to escape the harsh Islamophobia that has likewise defined their post-9/11 experiences.[27] Arab Muslims, on the other hand, lack this "ethnic option," which affords their Christian counterparts greater access to "the American mainstream":

> [9/11] created a cultural wedge that factionalized the Arab American community along religious lines. . . . Christian Arab Americans are able to emphasize cultural aspects of their Arab identity (for example, celebrating Arabic holidays) and play down political aspects (for example, being active in Middle Eastern politics) to distance themselves from the events of September 11 and demonstrate that they are neither terrorists nor terrorist sympathizers.[28]

Further, there appears to be a generational dimension to this response. The political beliefs of Muslim youth, for example, clearly reflect their membership in a cross-generational religious community, yet many have responded to post-9/11 Islamophobia by rejecting what they perceive as their parents' aims of Islam-American hybridity.[29] More specifically, some Muslim youth activists have politically organized by firmly opposing Arab cultural authenticity narratives through claims of "Muslim First, Arab Second."[30]

In addition, studies of Arab and Muslim racialization in nation-state contexts outside the United States or through cross-national case studies have begun to expand this literature in promising comparative directions.[31] Muslim populations in France, for example, present a particularly illuminating case in contrast with those of the United States that can "shed light on the multi-threaded historical trajectories that Islam's racialization has followed in North America and Europe."[32] A comparative lens rightly places Arab and Muslim racialization processes in a broader global context, with such studies issuing additional challenges to the notion of American exceptionalism on questions of racism and racial hierarchy.

Thus, research on Arab and Muslim racialization continues to emphatically underscore the conflation of Arab and Muslim communities and the consequences of religious differences within and across them. Yet despite these and other important contributions, much remains to be understood about the racialization of Arabs and Muslims in the United States and, in particular, its impact on the dynamic construction of groups and categories in post-9/11 racial and ethnic politics.

ARAB AND MUSLIM RACIALIZATION: A RELATIONAL ANALYSIS

To examine whether and how Arab and Muslim racialization is changing the group-based contours of American racial politics, I employ a relational lens. The American racial order historically has been and continues to be both variable (with shifting positions among groups racialized as nonwhites or people of color) and tenacious (with those racialized as white consistently positioned with more status and advantage than other groups). A relational lens is useful in studying these patterns and changes because it instructs that the racialization of each group occurs in dynamic relation to the racialization of all other groups. Natalia Molina underscores the group-based intersections inherent in anti-essentialist notions of race:

> A relational treatment of race recognizes that the construction of race is a mutually constitutive process and demonstrates how race is socially constructed, hence fighting against essentialist notions. Furthermore, it attends to how, when, where, and to what extent groups intersect. It recognizes that there are limits to examining racialized groups in isolation.[33]

Indeed, too often studies focus on a single racial group as if its formation takes place in isolation from that of others. That groups are racialized in different ways and relative to one another is a fundamental premise of studying race relationally. A relational lens prescribes attention to multiple groups, compelling us to consider how other groups are politically constructed in order to understand the positioning of any particular group in a given historical context.

This analysis thus attends to how Arab and Muslim communities are racialized and positioned in relation not to one group, such as whites, but to multiple groups, including nonwhite groups such as blacks, Latinos, and

Asians.[34] Specifically, it draws on the theory of *racial triangulation*.[35] This influential relational framework articulates an alternative to problematic notions of racial hierarchy understood as a binary, single-scale vertical ranking along which Asians in the United States are typically located somewhere between blacks and whites. Presenting a multiaxis "field of racial positions," Asian Americans are positioned as "racially triangulated" vis-à-vis blacks and whites. This triangulation results from simultaneous processes of "relative valorization" and "civic ostracism,"[36] whereby blacks and Asians are maintained in lower-ranking positions compared with whites. Claire Jean Kim writes,

> Since the field of racial positions consists of a plane defined by at least two axes—superior/inferior and insider/foreigner—it emphasizes both that groups become racialized in comparison with one another and that they are differently racialized. As a normative blueprint for who should get what, this field of racial positions profoundly shapes the opportunities, constraints, and possibilities with which subordinate groups must contend, ultimately serving to reinforce White dominance and privilege.[37]

Further, while the field of racial positions is discursively generated within a particular context of time and place, the processes of racial triangulation nevertheless explain how (white) "racial power" is continually reproduced and thus has remained an enduring feature of social and political life in the United States.[38]

To be sure, racial groups are far from monolithic, and racial triangulation theory is limited by an inability to capture the nuanced dimensions of power within groups. As a multiaxis intervention, it has demonstrated substantial reach across fields and literatures; however, incorporating other axes of difference is a challenge that scholars have rightly sought to address.[39] It is simply not possible for a two-dimensional field of racial positions to account for variation within groups along several markers of difference such as class, gender, sexuality, religion, language, ethnic/national origin, nativity, citizenship status, and legal status. As a result, critical differences in access to power, status, and privilege are obscured between poor versus wealthy Asian Americans, for instance, or undocumented versus second-generation Asian Americans (who are native-born citizens). The relational positioning of African Americans is likewise complicated by myriad intragroup differences as well as notions of, for example, second-class citizenship, which raise questions about the relative "insider" status of black communities. Nevertheless, these shortcomings do not overshadow the fundamental contributions of racial triangulation as a framework for studying relational racialization, nor do they preclude its use in expanding our understanding of groups beyond its original focus on Asian Americans—indeed, this study offers evidence of this.

Empirically, I focus on one key component of racialization: *racial(ized) political discourse.* Here, I refer to national or macro-discussions about race—including racism and racial inequality, racial(ized) policy, racial/ethnic identity and group membership, and race-centered political mobilization. "Postracial" discourse is one contemporary example, which I discuss below. This study centers on the characteristics and content of such discussions and, more specifically, on how groups such as Arabs and Muslims have been described and characterized in the mainstream news. As an influential source of racial messages and stereotypes among everyday people, the media play a significant role in producing racial(ized) political discourse on Arab and Muslim communities.[40] To constrain the scope of analysis, I focus primarily on the period since 9/11, noting the important caveat that Arab and Muslim racialization processes can and should be traced much further back.

Based on a vast sample of more than sixty thousand articles, I conducted a quantitative content analysis of the *New York Times,* one of the most nationally prominent mainstream newspapers in the United States.[41] First, I examined all news and editorial stories that discussed Arabs and Muslims published from January 1, 1997, to December 31, 2011, a fifteen-year period that both predates and extends well beyond the events of September 11. Whereas studies analyzing media portrayals of Arabs and Muslims have focused most closely on the few intense weeks after 9/11, I seek to gain some traction on how 9/11 may have impacted Arab and Muslim racialization in the longer term. I obtained these data through ProQuest newspaper archives by identifying all articles and editorials that included the words "Arab" or "Muslim."[42] Second, I added two other large samples of articles to the analysis, one focused on Asian Americans and the other on African Americans. These stories span the full twelve months of 2001 and 2011 for a combined period of two years, which also allows me to observe some degree of consistency across time. These data were obtained via the same newspaper archives based on searches for sets of words referencing each racial group and the largest ethnic/national origin groups within them.[43]

With each sample, I conducted a computer-assisted, descriptive content analysis in which the findings were generated by an algorithm that counted the frequencies of occurrences of certain words that represent a set of raciali-

TABLE 14.1. Racialization frames and group-based stereotypes

Inferior frames

Incapable: dependent, lazy

Criminal: lawbreaking

Foreigner frames

Unassimilable: culturally "other"

National threat: attack/betray U.S.

---

zation frames. To derive these, I conceptually unpacked the two hierarchical axes of "superior/inferior" and "insider/foreigner" from racial triangulation theory into a set of frames to code and analyze. The influence of such frame occurrences on the contours of group-based politics is potentially powerful because "[b]y rendering events or occurrences meaningful, frames function to organize experience and guide action, whether individual or collective."[44] The underlying intuition is that the frequency count of a frame in a nationally prominent mainstream newspaper is a simple indicator of its presence in the public sphere, and it provides information about the potential impact of the content or message attached to that frame, with higher frequency counts being more likely to yield greater impact. Importantly, the aim is not to confirm this impact on mass attitudes—for example, frame occurrence data do not show that a frame or set of frames causes perceptions of Arabs and Muslims to move in one direction or another. In this study, frame occurrences concern discursive impact. Each time a racialization frame appears (or occurs), it receives exposure, with repeated occurrences increasing that exposure and leading to an amplified presence. It is thus through exposure and amplification that the frame shapes racial(ized) political discourse.

As shown in table 14.1, the set of racialization frames I examine aims to capture the variation in group-based stereotypes that shape American racial discourse at the intersection of being nonwhite and nonnative. I do not mean to suggest that these are the only such frames; rather, I hold that these frames reflect the lower ends of each axis in racial triangulation theory ("inferior" and "foreigner"), where "racial power" is sustained through the discursive (re)production of the notion that nonwhite, or racially subordinate, groups tend to be less capable (dependent and lazy, not self-sufficient and hardworking), more criminal (lawbreaking, not law-abiding), less assimilable (culturally "other," not "American"), and a greater threat to the United States (likely to attack or betray the country, not protect or defend it). The frames were operationalized by developing a coding scheme based on group-based stereotypes that have been shown to have significant, persistent influence on racial(ized) political discourse.[45] I call these frames *incapable, criminal, unassimilable,* and *national threat.*

Using this set of frames, I examine the extent to and ways in which (a) Arabs and Muslims have been racialized through similar frames and (b) Arabs and Muslims have been racialized through frames differently than Asians and blacks—the two existing nonwhite groups in which most Arabs and Muslims are otherwise located. I expect to find evidence that the framing of Arabs is similar to the framing of Muslims, reinforcing the conflation of the two communities, and that the framing of Arabs and Muslims is different from the framing of blacks and Asians. In so doing, I do not seek to conflate definitions of relational and comparative; rather, I hold that comparison is a tool to employ in a relational analysis. In other words, a relational analysis—that is, an analysis with expectations, evidence, and conclusions grounded in a relational framework—can and often does involve making observations across units.

RACIALIZATION FRAMES: COMMONALITY, CONSISTENCY, DIFFERENCE

The findings confirm two central patterns that both hold across time: the conflation of Arabs and Muslims through common racialization frames; and distinct differences in frames across groups (Arabs and Muslims, blacks, Asians).

Common Racialization Frames: Arabs and Muslims

First, to investigate the discursive conflation of Arabs and Muslims in the United States, I examine variation in frames across these communities. Because each article in the sample included "Arab" or "Muslim," some articles include one of these words and some articles include both, making possible an analysis across three subcategories: (1) those that discuss only Arabs ("Muslim" is not mentioned); (2) those that discuss only Muslims ("Arab" is not mentioned); and (3) those that refer at least once to both Arabs and Muslims. Broken down between these subcategories, the proportions of the total sample that discussed only Arabs and only Muslims were almost equal

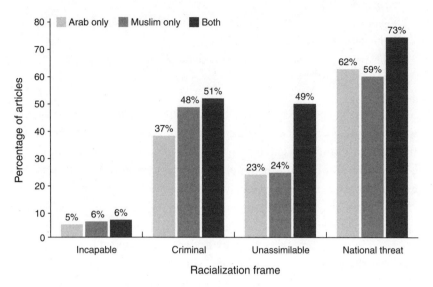

FIGURE 14.1. Percentages of *New York Times* articles (1997–2011) with occurrences of racialization frames for Arabs and Muslims by subcategory.

(40 percent and 39 percent, respectively), while the remaining one-fifth (21 percent) included references to both Arabs and Muslims.

Figure 14.1 shows the percentages of newspaper articles that included words consistent with each racialization frame, broken down by subcategories. Overall, the ordered pattern of frame occurrences did not vary across articles that discussed Arabs only, Muslims only, or both. Portrayals of Arabs and Muslims, whether separately or together, were always most consistent with attacking or betraying the United States and least consistent with dependence or laziness. For example, whether focused on Arabs and Muslims in the United States or abroad, the headlines that appeared in the *New York Times* in the years after 9/11 repeatedly established and reinforced contemporary stereotypes of Arabs and Muslims as suspicious/dangerous, discontent /angry, and aggressive/violent:

"Who Seethes and Why: Despair beneath the Arab World's Rage" (October 14, 2001)
"Justice Department Wants to Query More [Muslim] Foreigners" (March 21, 2002)
"The Arab World: Anger at U.S. Said to Be at New High" (July 11, 2002)
"Poll Finds U.S. Muslims Thriving, but Not Content" (August 2, 2009)

"Egypt Sentences Muslim to Death in Killings of Christians" (January 17, 2011)

"Embattled Arab Leaders Decide It's Better to Fight than Quit" (April 28, 2011)[46]

Moreover, when both Arabs and Muslims were discussed, words consistent with the foreigner frames became even more prevalent. For example, for frames of unassimilable and national threat, there was almost no difference between Arab-only and Muslim-only results; when both groups were discussed, however, the presence of words such as "Arabic," "mosque," and "hijab" more than doubled, and words such as "terrorism" and "bomb" appeared in 11 to 14 percent more articles. In fact, Islam-specific references appeared in more than twice as many stories that discussed both Arabs and Muslims than in stories that discussed Muslims only (49 percent versus 24 percent, respectively). This suggests a striking discursive shift when Arabs and Muslims are discussed in combination, as the conflation of these communities appears to take on a distinctive force of its own.

Consistent Racialization Frames: 1997–2011

Second, the data show remarkable consistency in the patterns of racialization frames over time. Figure 14.2 presents this set of findings. From 1997 to 2011, a very large percentage of articles that discussed Arabs and Muslims included words consistent with the frame of national threat (52 to 77 percent), which accords with the findings above and with previous studies. Not only did this frame appear in a larger percentage of stories compared with the other three frames, its dominance remained constant across all fifteen years. For example, in the year immediately after 9/11, 77 percent of stories that discussed Arabs or Muslims included words such as "terrorist," "spy," and "attack," while 47 percent referred to lawbreaking, and 23 percent facilitated associations with cultural "otherness." On the other hand, an insubstantial 5 percent included words consistent with dependence or laziness.[47] This follows intuition in tandem with the national threat frame, as those who plot terrorist attacks are generally viewed as resourceful and motivated.[48] By some accounts, this is what makes these communities an even greater threat—for example, the Bush administration repeatedly invoked this to make a case for defending America at any cost, whether through racial profiling in the United States and unlawful domestic surveillance or deploying military troops abroad.[49]

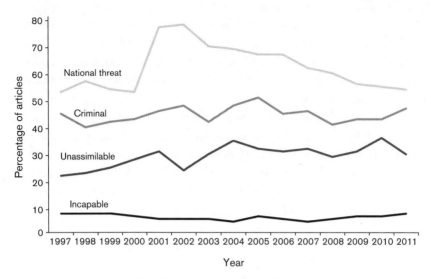

FIGURE 14.2. Percentages of *New York Times* articles (1997–2011) with occurrences of racialization frames for Arabs and Muslims across time.

Notably, among the two most common and consistent frames across time in articles discussing Arabs or Muslims, one is a foreigner frame and one is an inferior frame. This further suggests that the contemporary racialization of Arab and Muslim Americans may follow a process of racial triangulation similar to that of other groups comprising large foreign-born populations— that is, racialization occurs simultaneously along multiple dimensions based on perceptions of both foreignness and inferiority, including criminality or moral inferiority. In the case of Asian Americans, for example, it was historically taken as fact that Asians were inferior to whites overall, but it was also believed that "Orientals" cannot and will not assimilate partly because their own civilizations are too highly developed.[50] In the early twenty-first century, Asians in and outside the United States are still perceived as threatening when they are viewed as skillful, competitive, and unscrupulous. These stereotypes are reinforced by narratives of imminent danger conveyed through steady depictions of North Koreans as devious and petulant, obscuring distinctions between a population and its leaders, or the Chinese as shrewdly strategic in stories such as "China Maneuvers to Avoid Debate on Its Rights Record in U.N." and "China Quietly Extends Its Footprints Deep into Central Asia."[51]

Importantly, while the difference between racialization frames for Arabs and Muslims appeared the largest in the year immediately after 9/11, the ordered pattern—*national threat, criminal, unassimilable, incapable*—was well established at least five years earlier and has continued without disruption. This observation supports the view that 9/11 did not single-handedly cause a dramatic shift in the racialized experiences of Arabs and Muslims; rather, it deepened the political marginalization that these communities had long confronted owing to the intensified anti-Arab, anti-Muslim political context.[52] At the same time, the immediate spike in national threat representations is consistent with chilling statistics about sharp increases in violence against Arab and Muslim communities immediately following the terrorist attacks—for example, "in 2001, the U.S. Department of Justice recorded a 1,600 percent increase in anti-Muslim hate crimes from the prior year"[53]— and in this way supports a view of 9/11 as an unmistakable inflection point in contemporary Arab and Muslim American politics.

Different, Consistent Racialization Frames: Arab/Muslim, Asian, Black

Lastly, figure 14.3 presents results from the analysis across three groups: Arab and Muslim combined or "Arab/Muslim," Asian, and black. Foremost, among all articles examined, the frame of national threat appeared overwhelmingly more frequently in stories having to do with Arabs and Muslims compared with Asians or blacks. Notably, in 2001, both blacks and Asians were likewise discussed in a large number of articles (nearly one-third) that included words consistent with the frame of national threat (for blacks, 28 percent of stories and for Asians, 30 percent of stories). These findings likely reflect the overlap between Arab, Muslim, Asian, and black populations, such that some national threat frames are applied also to the latter two. In 2011 the overall pattern of group differences remained for this frame, though the occurrences were lower across all three groups. Ten years after 9/11, Arab and Muslim communities were still discussed alongside words such as "terrorism" and "assassin" more than half the time. Once again, the presence of national threat frames in articles discussing African Americans compared with Asian Americans varied little (22 percent for blacks and 20 percent for Asians), and in both cases this was dramatically lower than for Arabs and Muslims (53 percent).

Furthermore, while the overwhelming dominance of the national threat frame for Arab and Muslim communities lessened over time, decreasing 23 percent from 2001 to 2011, the data reveal extremely little change in any of

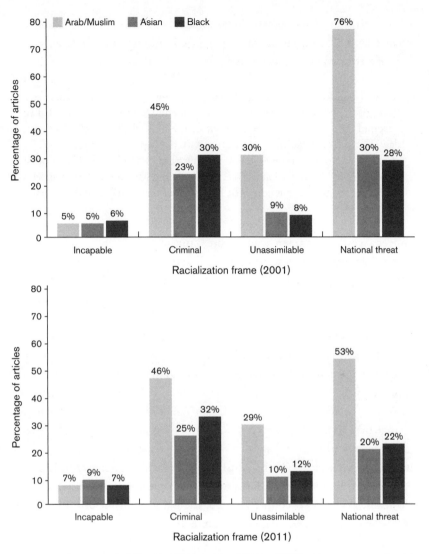

FIGURE 14.3. Percentages of *New York Times* articles (2001 and 2011) with occurrences of racialization frames across groups and time.

the other racialization frames, showing differences of only 1 to 2 percent. For Asians and blacks, the only sizable change was observed in the national threat frame (30 to 20 percent and 28 to 22 percent, respectively). Notably, the criminal frame remained prominent across all three groups and most of all for Arabs and Muslims. In particular, lawbreaking stereotypes of Arabs and Muslims loom large in the vast majority of terrorism-related articles before and after 9/11—observe, for example, the effective linking of noncompliance with U.S. antiterrorism initiatives with immigration violations in the lede of a 2001 *New York Times* article:

> Federal and local investigators began searching today for more than 200 young foreign men believed to be living in the Detroit area who failed to respond to letters sent last month inviting them to schedule interviews with law enforcement officials in connection with the Sept. 11 terrorist attacks. . . . The switch [from sending letters to dialing phones and knocking on doors] has infuriated immigration lawyers and Arab and Muslim leaders here, who say many of those who ignored the letters have visa violations and fear being arrested.[54]

Indeed, words that referenced lawbreaking such as "crime," "prison," and "arrest" appeared in close to half of all articles that discussed Arabs and Muslims (45 to 46 percent), compared with nearly one-third of all articles that discussed blacks and, perhaps less expectedly, approximately one-quarter of articles about Asians.

While it is not possible to discern from these data whether one group was the substantive focus of a particular article and, if so, which specific group, it is possible to examine how frequently more than one group appeared in the same story. In articles that discussed Arabs and Muslims, 14 percent also included the terms "black" or "African American" in 2001 and 2011 (no change over time), while the terms "Asian" or "Asian American" appeared in just 6 percent in 2001 and an even smaller 4 percent ten years later. In short, it was rare that either Arabs/Muslims *and* blacks or Arabs/Muslims *and* Asians were discussed in the same story. Thus, in the vast majority of articles, the frame occurrences counted for a particular group were unlikely to refer instead to one of the other groups examined.[55]

"ARAB/MUSLIM": RELATIONAL POSITIONING, RELATIONAL POSSIBILITIES

Taken together, these findings indicate that post-9/11 racialization frames of foreignness and inferiority have appeared in the mainstream media in ways similar for Arabs and Muslims yet distinct from other existing racial(ized) groups. Simultaneous processes of conflation and differentiation appear to take place: the racialization of Arabs and Muslims is converging while at the same time diverging from the racialization of Asian Americans and African Americans, with remarkable consistency across time. First, these data provide further evidence of the conflation of Arab and Muslim communities in the United States that previous scholars have observed, based on Orientalist underpinnings that powerfully elide religious and geographic differences. Second, the data confirm that frames of foreignness, with a pronounced focus on threats to the nation, have consistently dominated representations of Arabs and Muslims in one of the most nationally prominent mainstream newspapers since at least the late 1990s and firmly into the early 2000s. Specifically, Arabs and Muslims have been discussed overwhelmingly in the context of stories that also speak of terrorism, bombs, and attacks. This national threat frame is striking in both its greater prevalence relative to other racialization frames and its persistence across time. Third, the findings suggest that the post-9/11 racialization of Arabs and Muslims, at least in racial(ized) political discourse, has taken place distinctly from that of either Asian Americans or African Americans, again with persistence across time. Evidence across frames of foreignness and inferiority reveals that Arabs and Muslims are consistently discussed in larger percentages of stories related to terrorism and crime as well as being culturally different from what is considered mainstream American culture (e.g., English-speaking, Christian).

These findings point to the possible emergence of a new racial(ized) group in the contemporary United States, one that might be called "Arab/Muslim," and they demonstrate the usefulness of a relational lens for studying the changing terrain of post-9/11 racial politics. Making clear that we have much to learn not only about Arabs and Muslims but also about other groups in relation to Arabs and Muslims, these findings have important implications for collective or group-based mobilization in response to a post-9/11 political context in which racism and xenophobia have not attenuated but deepened.

For example, a counterview to the possible emergence of Arab/Muslim as a new racial category holds that Arab and Muslim communities can already claim membership in existing groups—as previously noted, black Muslims and South Asian Muslims account for nearly half of the Muslim population in the United States.[56] In this view, Arab American and Muslim American issues are properly understood as African American and/or Asian American issues, and therefore political support for Arabs and Muslims in the United States can and should be located among already established racial groups—in other words, within the fields of black politics and Asian American politics. However, this objection may too optimistically presume consistent, reliable support from Asian American and black communities on issues targeting Arabs and Muslims. The definition and practice of both African American politics and Asian American politics have long been contested and repeatedly fractured by disagreements about which issues the group "owns," how to apportion scarce organizational resources across competing interests within the group, and where to draw the boundaries of group membership. Indeed, while South Asians overwhelmingly represent the Asian Muslim population, South Asian membership within the category of Asian American has been contested for decades.[57]

Thus, the assumption that Arab and Muslim political marginalization will be addressed from within other racial groups may be flawed. As the political targeting and scapegoating of Arab and Muslim communities continue more than a decade after 9/11, with further escalation during and since the 2016 election over a proposed Muslim registry and temporary ban on Muslim immigrants, the stakes remain too high to assume that other racial groups will arrive at a consensus of support on these issues and, more demanding still, prioritize taking action on them. To be sure, some organizations have provided this leadership, such as the Asian American Legal Defense and Education Fund, which responded to the extensive surveillance of Muslim communities in New York City, and Asian Americans Advancing Justice, which condemned the Trump administration's repeated attempts to restrict or halt the arrival of immigrants and refugees from Muslim-majority nations.[58] To date, however, there is little evidence that either black or Asian American communities have reliably owned or sustained a collective response to issues of racialized, Islamophobic antiterrorism policy, even after 9/11. It may be that the most pressing political needs and interests of Arabs and Muslims cannot be addressed within the current purview of either African American or Asian American politics. Rather, there may exist greater potential for the issues facing Arab and Muslim communities to be confronted within the scope of an emergent Arab/Muslim American politics that decidedly overlaps with the politics of other groups.[59]

At the same time, these findings draw attention to the potential of post-9/11 political coalitions by identifying the discursive foundations of collective mobilization across groups. That racial(ized) groups can be distinct yet not strictly discrete is and has always been inescapable in the complicated terrain of U.S. racial and ethnic politics. In this regard, the case of Arabs and Muslims offers an affirming example of how this might be leveraged toward positive ends, in particular, because the overlap of Arab and Muslim communities with black and Asian American communities offers a propitious foundation for multiracial coalitions. For example, political observers across the ideological spectrum have drawn comparisons between the terrorist attacks on September 11, 2001, and the World War II attack on Pearl Harbor on December 7, 1941.[60] Conservatives and liberals alike have emphasized similarities not only between the attacks themselves—which, given the deaths of thousands of people, were objectively devastating—but also between the U.S. government's response in their aftermath. Parallels between the state-sanctioned internment of Japanese Americans in the wake of Pearl Harbor and the racial profiling and egregious detention of Arab and Muslim Americans after 9/11 have also been advanced by group-based organizations. Within the Asian American community, the most outspoken advocates and supporters of Arab/Muslim political resistance, such as the Japanese American Citizens League, have explicitly referenced those parallels. African American communities, too, have long been the targets of government-sponsored surveillance and violence, including the suppression of many black-led political movements, including the civil rights and Black Power movements and the Nation of Islam. These findings thus suggest that there is in place a foundation for strong alliances between a twenty-first-century Arab/Muslim American politics, African American politics, and Asian American politics. All three groups (qua groups) have experienced a marginal positioning partly based on racialization frames that are, taken together, perhaps most aptly understood as "criminalized national threat." To this end, that some individuals may claim membership in more than one group could even strengthen ties across communities.

This study also has broader implications for debates over the contemporary relevance of race and racial(ized) groups. Underlining the fluidity of racial categories and, when needed, redrawing those categories altogether have long been and will remain dynamic features of American racial politics. The schema of racial and ethnic classifications prescribed by the U.S. Census is itself a political construction, routinely shifting in response to demographic changes and mobilizations for group-specific recognition. The claims advanced here about the potential formation of a new racial category offer more fodder for ideological debates concerning the role of racial classifications in American politics and society. In the late twentieth century, this conflict was widely characterized as race-neutral or "colorblind" versus race-conscious; in the early twenty-first century, it has shifted to heated disputes over the term *postracial*. In particular, the historic election of the first black president seemed to convince many Americans that racism had been decisively dismantled, and the public sphere bustled with postracial arguments against the need to recognize race as an indicator of constrained or unequal life chances.[61] In this contemporary iteration of colorblind discourse, the United States is a nation where race, viewed as a divisive historical artifact, no longer figures into the social, economic, and political opportunities and outcomes of its citizens. Opponents maintain that it is necessary to address racial issues directly and that evidence of structurally embedded racial disparities and everyday acts of racial prejudice controverts postracial rhetoric. Set against this backdrop, post-9/11 Arab and Muslim racialization carries even greater significance because it takes place in an era when the value of talking about race at all has been increasingly questioned. As debates continue over whether racial classifications have become irrelevant, the findings presented here suggest that a new racial(ized) group may be emerging. Such an emergence further challenges the notion of a postracial America: not only do existing categories remain relevant in the early twenty-first century, but it is also still possible for new categories to form.

Lastly, this analysis provides initial or partial evidence of the contemporary construction of an Arab/Muslim racial(ized) group. As discussed above, racial(ized) political discourse is a key component of racialization processes, but it is one part of a much larger picture. Racial group formation takes place on both micro- and macro-levels, shaped by a combination of social practices and social structures, including individual beliefs and actions, institutions, and ideologies.[62] Similarly, while the *New York Times* is one of the most nationally prominent mainstream newspapers in terms of reputation and circulation, there exist many other sources of racial(ized) political discourse. Building from this study, future research might broaden the scope of analysis to include other national newspapers and local or community-based newspapers; they might also compare these findings with other forms of media, such as television or radio.

RELATIONAL MOBILIZATION IN POST-9/11 RACIAL POLITICS

This study has presented a large-scale, across-time content analysis of articles in the *New York Times* showing that the post-9/11 racialization of Arab and Muslim communities in the mainstream media points toward the possible emergence of a new racial(ized) group. Although Islam is practiced by some members of black and Asian communities in the United States, Arabs and Muslims, or "Arabs/Muslims," *as a group,* have been othered differently in racial(ized) political discourse from either African Americans as a group or Asian Americans as a group. To the extent that the framing of Arabs and Muslims in the mainstream media has helped advance the formation of a new racial(ized) group or racial category, it is certainly an imperfect aggregation of individuals from heterogeneous backgrounds who hold a simultaneous multiplicity of politically salient identities; this is, however, no different than any other group, whether existing or emerging. It is increasingly clear that Arab and Muslim racialization is changing the group-based terrain of American racial and ethnic politics.

This study also affirms that a relational lens is a vital tool in advancing our understanding of this new terrain, with great consequences for political mobilization and policy agendas that are necessarily multiracial. Consider contemporary immigration issues, for example. These findings show that the post-9/11 racialization of Arabs and Muslims has been shaped most relentlessly through the racialization frame of national threat, providing discursive foundations for collective political work not only within but also across groups. To further underscore the point, national threat is a dimension of foreignness with manifest connections to immigration issues, yet Arab and Muslim communities too often have been perceived and positioned on the margins of contemporary immigrant politics. A relational lens reveals why this is flawed in theory and limiting in practice. Other communities also greatly impacted by immigration debates, such as Latinos and Asian Americans, have been racialized similarly, though of course not identically, as "perpetual foreigners" and the putative "enemy within."[63] If the political marginalization and political empowerment of Latinos and Asian Americans partially depend on those of Arabs and Muslims and vice versa, it is not possible to realize or sustain a transformative movement for immigrant rights or immigration reform without the deliberate and meaningful inclusion of Arab and Muslim communities. This conceptual and practical interdependence is rightly illuminated by a relational lens. If each racial(ized) group is positioned in relation to all other groups, attention to the racialization of Arab and Muslim Americans is nothing less than essential to advancing our understanding of post-9/11 racial politics, and it is, ultimately, a critical step toward dismantling racial hierarchies in the twenty-first century.

ACKNOWLEDGMENTS

The author wishes to thank Claire Kim, Taeku Lee, Nitasha Sharma, Michael Dawson, Tianna Paschel, the Reproduction of Race and Racial Ideologies Workshop at the University of Chicago, the editors of this volume, and anonymous reviewers for their helpful comments and suggestions.

NOTES

1. Lori Peek, *Behind the Backlash: Muslim Americans after 9/11* (Philadelphia: Temple University Press, 2011); Peter Morey and Amina Yaquin, *Framing Muslims: Stereotyping and Representation after 9/11* (Cambridge, MA: Harvard University Press, 2011).

2. Susan M. Akram and Kevin R. Johnson, "Race, Civil Rights, and Immigration Law after September 11, 2001: The Targeting of Arabs and Muslims," *New York University Annual Survey of American Law* 58, no. 3 (2002): 295–356; Nadine Naber, "Arab Americans and U.S. Racial Formations," in *Race and Arab Americans before and after 9/11: From Invisible Citizens to Visible Subjects,* ed. Amaney Jamal and Nadine Naber (Syracuse, NY: Syracuse University Press, 2008), 1–45.

3. I do not mean to suggest that some Arabs and Muslims do not prefer this end and/or do not self-identify as white—to be sure, some do, and scholars have examined how these communities must navigate the ideology of "whiteness" as those who "hold a precarious position on the racial hierarchy." Sawsan Abdulrahim, "'Whiteness' and the Arab Immigrant Experience," in Jamal and Naber, *Arab Americans before and after 9/11,* 145. I refer here to the racialization of a group qua group and its group-based position in the racial order.

4. Naber, "Arab Americans and U.S. Racial Formations"; Amaney Jamal, "Arab American Racialization," in Jamal and Naber, *Arab Americans before and after 9/11,* 318–26; Louise A. Cainkar, *Homeland Insecurity: The Arab American and Muslim American Experience after 9/11* (New York: Russell Sage Foundation, 2009). I am not suggesting that Arab and Muslim racialization began after 9/11; on the contrary, scholars have clearly demonstrated that the othering of Arab and Muslim communities was established long before that. I begin from 9/11 because this is a point when racialized policy making and public discourse concerning Arabs and Muslims intensified significantly, marking a new contemporary era in the racialization of Arab and Muslim communities.

5. Khaled A. Beydoun, "Between Muslim and White: The Legal Construction of Arab-American Identity," *New York University Annual Survey of American Law* 69, no. 1 (2013): 29–76.

6. Naber, "Arab Americans and U.S. Racial Formations," 32.

7. Evelyn Alsultany, *Arabs and Muslims in the Media: Race and Representation after 9/11* (New York: New York University Press, 2012).

8. Michael W. Suleiman, "The Arab Immigrant Experience," in *Arabs in America: Building a New Future,* ed. Michael W. Suleiman (Philadelphia: Temple University Press, 1999), 1–22.

9. Pew Research Center, *The Future of World Religions: Population Growth Projections, 2010–2050* (Washington, DC: Pew Research Center, 2015).

10. Pew Research Center, *Future of World Religions.*

11. Pew Research Center, *Muslim Americans: Middle Class and Mostly Mainstream* (Washington, DC: Pew Research Center, 2007). As the Pew Research Center report discusses, an unfortunate and confounding dynamic of studying Arab and Muslim communities in the United States is the difficulty in acquiring accurate demographic information. For example, the U.S. Census does not collect information specifically about being Arab (as later discussed) or about being Muslim.

12. Jen'nan Ghazal Read, "Family, Religion, and Work among Arab-American Women," *Journal of Marriage and Family* 66, no. 4(2004): 1042–50.

13. Jenna Johnson and David Weigel, "Donald Trump Calls for 'Total' Ban on Muslims Entering United States," *Washington Post,* December 8, 2015; Philip Bump, "Ted Cruz Wants to Nationalize an NYPD Muslim Surveillance Program That the NYPD Says Didn't Work," *Washington Post,* March 23, 2016.

14. Leti Volpp, "The Citizen and the Terrorist," *UCLA Law Review* 49, no. 5 (2003): 1577–78.

15. Akram and Johnson, "Race, Civil Rights, and Immigration Law."

16. While the absence of a Muslim racial category on the census is less perplexing, it is not necessarily as straightforward as it seems—it is often argued, for example, that Jewish people are a race or that Jewish communities have been racialized.

17. G. Cristina Mora, *Making Hispanics: How Activists, Bureaucrats, and Media Constructed a New American* (Chicago: University of Chicago Press, 2014).

18. Helen Hatab Samhan, "Not Quite White: Race Classification and the Arab-American Experience," in *Arabs in America: Building a New Future,* ed. Michael W. Suleiman (Philadelphia: Temple University Press, 1999), 209–26.

19. Jamal, "Arab American Racialization."

20. Sarah Gualtieri, *Between Arab and White: Race and Ethnicity in the Early Syrian American Diaspora* (Berkeley: University of California Press, 2009).

21. Andrew Shryock, "The Moral Analogies of Race: Arab American Identity, Color Politics, and the Limits of Racialized Citizenship," in Jamal and Naber, *Arab Americans before and after 9/11,* 99–100; italics in original.

22. Samhan, "Not Quite White"; Cainkar, *Homeland Insecurity.*

23. U.S. Bureau of the Census, *Overview of Race and Hispanic Origin: 2010* (Washington, DC: U.S. Bureau of the Census, 2011), http://www.census.gov/prod /cen2010/briefs/c2010br-02.pdf.

24. To be sure, much debate surrounded the proposed category within Arab American communities—see, for example, Arab American Institute, *2020 Census: Reaching an Accurate Count* (Washington, DC: Arab American Institute, 2018); Tara Bahrampour, "A U.S. Census Proposal to Add Category for People of Middle

Eastern Descent Makes Some Uneasy," *Washington Post,* October 21, 2016. Announcing its decision, the Census Bureau cited the mixed viewpoints from within these communities and the need for more research—see, for example, Hansi Lo Wang, "No Middle Eastern or North African Category on 2020 Census, Bureau Says," NPR, January 29, 2018, www.npr.org/2018/01/29/581541111/no-middle-eastern-or-north-african-category-on-2020-census-bureau-says.

25. Saher Selod and David G. Embrick, "Racialization and Muslims: Situating the Muslim Experience in Race Scholarship," *Sociology Compass* 7, no. 8 (2013): 644–55.

26. Yvonne Yazbeck Haddad, *Becoming American? The Forging of Arab and Muslim Identity in Pluralist America* (Waco, TX: Baylor University Press, 2011).

27. Jen'nan Ghazal Read, "Multiple Identities among Arab Americans: A Tale of Two Congregations," in *Being and Belonging: Muslims in the United States Since 9/11,* ed. Katherine Pratt Ewing (New York: Russell Sage Foundation, 2008), 107–27; Jen'nan Ghazal Read, "Discrimination and Identity Formation in a Post-9/11 Era: A Comparison of Muslim and Christian Arab Americans," in Jamal and Naber, *Arab Americans before and after 9/11,* 305–17.

28. Read, "Multiple Identities," 124–25.

29. Katherine Pratt Ewing and Marguerite Hoyler, "Being Muslim and American: South Asian Muslim Youth and the War on Terror," in Ewing, *Being and Belonging,* 80–104.

30. Nadine Naber, *Arab America: Gender, Cultural Politics, and Activism* (New York: New York University Press, 2012).

31. Steve Garner and Saher Selod, "The Racialization of Muslims: Empirical Studies of Islamophobia," *Critical Sociology* 41, no. 1 (2015): 9–19.

32. Juliette Galonnier, "The Racialization of Muslims in France and the United States: Some Insights from White Converts to Islam," *Social Compass* 62, no. 4 (2015): 579.

33. Natalia Molina, "Examining Chicana/o History through a Relational Lens," *Pacific Historical Review* 82, no. 4 (2013): 522.

34. Throughout the chapter, I use the following terms interchangeably: *Asian* and *Asian American; black* and *African American.* In the former case, *Asian* is simply an abbreviated version of *Asian American,* and it also offers a nod to the large foreign-born population within Asian American communities.

35. Claire Jean Kim, "The Racial Triangulation of Asian Americans," *Politics and Society* 27, no. 1 (1999): 105–38.

36. Kim defines *relative valorization* as the process by which "dominant group A (Whites) valorizes subordinate group B (Asian Americans) relative to subordinate group C (Blacks) on cultural and/or racial grounds in order to dominate both groups, but especially the latter"; *civic ostracism* is the process by which "dominant group A (Whites) constructs subordinate group B (Asian Americans) as immutably foreign and unassimilable with Whites on cultural and/or racial grounds in order

to ostracize them from the body politic and civic membership." Kim, "Racial Triangulation," 107.

37. Kim, "Racial Triangulation," 107.

38. For example, Kim delineates the impressive persistence of "the American racial order and, specifically, the racial triangulation of Asian Americans within that order" from the mid-1800s to the present, shifting only "cosmetically" in response to the ascendancy of post-1965 colorblind discourse. Claire Jean Kim, *Bitter Fruit: The Politics of Black-Korean Conflict in New York City* (New Haven, CT: Yale University Press, 2000).

39. Taeku Lee, "Bringing Class, Ethnicity, and Nation Back to Race: The Color Lines in 2015," *Perspectives on Politics* 3, no. 3 (2005): 557–61.

40. Peter Morey and Amina Yaqin, *Framing Muslims: Stereotyping and Representation after 9/11* (Cambridge, MA: Harvard University Press, 2011).

41. As a methodology, content analysis has no single or dominant definition. There are disagreements particularly over whether to approach quantitative and qualitative content analyses differently. Classical definitions focus on the former—for example, Berelson famously defined content analysis as "a research technique for the objective, systematic, and quantitative description of the manifest content of communication." Bernard L. Berelson, *Content Analysis in Communications Research* (Glencoe, IL: Free Press, 1952). Similarly, Holsti defined the method as "any technique for making inferences by objectively and systematically identifying specified characteristics of messages." Ole R. Holsti, *Content Analysis for the Social Sciences and Humanities* (Reading, MA: Addison-Wesley, 1969), 14.

42. The total number of all articles and editorials published in the *New York Times* from January 1, 1997, and December 31, 2011, that include the words "Arab" or "Muslim" is nearly 30,000 ($N = 29,889$).

43. The search for these data was based on the following words: (a) asian, asian-american, china, chinese, philippines, filipino, filipina, india, indian, vietnam, vietnamese, korea, korean, japan, japanese ($N = 17,629$); (b) black, african-american, jamaica, jamaican, haiti, haitian, trinidad, trinidadian, nigeria, nigerian, ghana, ghanaian, ethiopia, ethiopian ($N = 12,696$).

44. David A. Snow, E. Burke Rochford Jr., Steven K. Worden, and Robert D. Benford, "Frame Alignment Processes, Micromobilization, and Movement Participation," *American Sociological Review* 51, no. 4 (1986): 464–81.

45. I developed a coding scheme for the following stereotypes: *incapable*—welfare, TANF, Medicaid, food stamps, Section 8, unemployed, unemployment, jobless; *criminal*—crime, fraud, theft, drug(s), gang(s), murder, jail, prison, detention, arrest; *unassimilable*—Arabic, mosque, hijab, burka, temple, shrine, palace, Oriental, tribal, primitive; and *national threat*—terrorism, terrorist, spy, assassin, bomb, attack.

46. Susan Sachs, "Who Seethes and Why: Despair beneath the Arab World's Rage," *New York Times,* October 14, 2001; Philip Shenon, "Justice Department Wants to Query More Foreigners," *New York Times,* March 21, 2002; Jane Perlez,

"The Arab World: Anger at U.S. Said to Be at New High," *New York Times,* July 11, 2002; Laurie Goodstein, "Poll Finds U.S. Muslims Thriving, but Not Content," *New York Times,* August 2, 2009; Mona El-Naggar, "Egypt Sentences Muslim to Death in Killings of Christians," *New York Times,* January 17, 2011; Michael Slackman and Mona El-Naggar, "Embattled Arab Leaders Decide It's Better to Fight Than Quit," *New York Times,* April 28, 2011.

47. To further clarify, these percentages can be interpreted as telling us something about the messages that the public has received about Arab and Muslim communities. As the political psychology literature has demonstrated, the messages we receive about racial(ized) groups can significantly inform how we think about and subsequently stereotype those groups.

48. Notably, the meaning of "terrorism" itself and the racialization of Arabs and Muslims in the United States are processes of construction that proceeded hand in hand, not only in the years leading up to 9/11 but also originating decades earlier when, after the Cold War, Islamic terror became the priority of policy makers and experts alike. Lisa Stampnitzky, *Disciplining Terror: How Experts Invented "Terrorism"* (Cambridge: Cambridge University Press, 2014). That over time these processes have clearly and steadily converged is reflected in these findings—specifically, the degree to which Arab/Muslim racialization is shaped by a national threat frame.

49. Adam Hodges, *The "War on Terror" Narrative: Discourse and Intertextuality in the Construction and Contestation of Sociopolitical Reality* (New York: Oxford University Press, 2011).

50. Edward W. Said, *Orientalism* (New York: Vintage Books, 1978); Kim, "Racial Triangulation."

51. Barbara Crossette, "China Maneuvers to Avoid Debate on Its Rights Record in U.N.," *New York Times,* April 19, 2001; Edward Wong, "China Quietly Extends Its Footprints Deep into Central Asia," *New York Times,* January 3, 2011.

52. Naber, "Arab Americans and U.S. Racial Formations"; Jamal, "Arab American Racialization"; Cainkar, *Homeland Insecurity.*

53. Nazli Kibria, Cara Bowman, and Megan O'Leary, *Race and Immigration* (Cambridge: Polity Press, 2014), 156.

54. Jodi Wilgoren, "200 Muslims Are Sought in Michigan," *New York Times,* December 12, 2001.

55. Frame occurrence findings by subcategory, across groups, and across both groups and time are also presented in tables 14.A1, 14.A2, and 14.A3 in this chapter's appendix.

56. Pew Research Center, *Muslim Americans.*

57. See, for example, Lavinia Dhingra Shankar and Rajini Srikanth, eds., *A Part Yet Apart: South Asians in Asian America* (Philadelphia: Temple University Press, 1998).

58. For example, in 2011: Asian American Legal Defense and Education Fund, "AALDEF, Brennan Center, and Muslim Advocates Request NYPD Records to

Investigate Post-9/11 Racial Profiling," September 22, 2011, http://aaldef.org/press-releases/press-release/aaldef-brennan-center-and-muslim-advocates-request-nypd-records-to-investigate-post-911-racial-profi.html; in 2017: Asian Americans Advancing Justice, "Asian Americans Advancing Justice, the CAIR, and NIAC Action Condemn the Government's Attempt to Make the 'Backdoor Muslim Ban' Permanent," September 1, 2017, http://www.advancingjustice-chicago.org/asian-americans-advancing-justice-the-cair-and-niac-action-condemn-the-governments-attempt-to-make-the-backdoor-muslim-ban-permanent/.

59. Some authors view the post-9/11 racialization of Arab and Muslim communities as part of a broader process, such as the racialization of South Asians, Muslims, and Arabs as well as Latinos into the category "Brown" or the formation of "a new racial category called AMEMSA (Arab, Middle Eastern, Muslim, and South Asian) or MASA (Muslim, Arab, and South Asian)." Nitasha Sharma, "Racialization and Resistance: The Double Bind of Post-9/11 Brown," in *South Asian Racialization and Belonging after 9/11: Masks of Threat,* ed. Aparajita De (Lanham, MD: Lexington Press, 2016), 137–48; Deepa Iyer, *We Too Sing America: South Asian, Arab, Muslim, and Sikh Immigrants Shape Our Multiracial Future* (New York: New Press, 2015). Empirically, the extent to which a Brown category and a "post-9/11 Brown" politics may be emerging is a closely related but separate question, and as such the findings of this analysis neither support nor counter this view. Theoretically, because a Brown category cross-cuts even more currently existing nonwhite racial(ized) groups, it is burdened by substantial challenges in group formation, including consensus on what defines the group and how Brown as a new racial formation affects the broader group-based terrain of American racial politics.

60. See, for example, Michelle Malkin, *In Defense of Internment: The Case for Racial Profiling in World War II and the War on Terror* (Washington, DC: Regnery, 2004); Natsu T. Saito, "Internments, Then and Now: Constitutional Accountability in Post-9/11 America," *Duke Forum for Law and Social Change* 2, no. 4 (2010): 71–102.

61. See, for example, Stephen Ansolabehere and Charles Stewart III, "Amazing Race: How Post-racial Was Obama's Victory?," *Boston Review,* January/February 2009; Ward Connerly, "Obama Is No 'Post-racial' Candidate," *Wall Street Journal,* June 13, 2008; Michael Crowley, "Post-racial: Even White Supremacists Don't Hate Obama," *New Republic,* February 12, 2008; Juan Williams, "Obama's Color Line," *New York Times,* November 30, 2007. Bill Clinton, on the campaign trail, said that "we have the largest percentage of Americans we've ever had who are literally aching to live in a post-racial future." Charles Babbington, "Obama Walks a Tricky Racial Line," Associated Press, January 26, 2008.

62. Michael Omi and Howard Winant, *Racial Formation in the United States,* 3rd ed. (New York: Routledge, 2015).

63. Lisa Lowe, *Immigrant Acts: On Asian American Cultural Politics* (Durham, NC: Duke University Press, 1996); Frank Wu, *Yellow: Race in America beyond Black and White* (New York: Basic Books, 2003).

TABLE 14.A1. Arab and Muslim racialization frames, by subcategory

Frames	Arab only	Muslim only	Both
"Inferior"			
Incapable	5%	6%	6%
Criminal	37%	48%	51%
"Foreigner"			
Unassimilable	23%	24%	49%
National threat	62%	59%	73%
Number of articles	11,969	11,576	6,344

TABLE 14.A2. Arab and Muslim racialization frames, across time

Frames	1997	1998	1999	2000	2001	2002	2003	2004	2005	2006	2007	2008	2009	2010	2011
"Inferior"															
Incapable	7%	7%	7%	6%	5%	5%	5%	4%	6%	5%	4%	5%	6%	6%	7%
Criminal	44%	39%	41%	42%	45%	47%	41%	47%	50%	44%	45%	40%	42%	42%	46%
"Foreigner"															
Unassimilable	21%	22%	24%	27%	30%	23%	29%	34%	31%	30%	31%	28%	30%	35%	29%
National threat	52%	56%	53%	52%	76%	77%	69%	68%	66%	66%	61%	59%	55%	54%	53%

TABLE 14.A3. Racialization frames, across groups and time

	2001			2011		
Frames	Arab/ Muslim	Asian	Black	Arab/ Muslim	Asian	Black
"Inferior"						
Incapable	5%	5%	6%	7%	9%	7%
Criminal	45%	23%	30%	46%	25%	32%
"Foreigner"						
Unassimilable	30%	9%	8%	29%	10%	12%
National threat	76%	30%	28%	53%	20%	22%
Number of articles	2,660	10,088	7,245	2,448	7,541	5,451

FURTHER READING

The scholarship on the relational formation of race is wide ranging and difficult to delineate with precision. This bibliography captures a selection of this work and is not exhaustive. There are other rich works not listed here, including graduate dissertations and theses, non-English-language sources and scholarship, and scholarship examining topics and locations outside the United States and Mexico.

Alexander, M. Jacqui. "Remembering *This Bridge Called My Back,* Remembering Ourselves." In *Pedagogies of Crossing: Meditations on Feminism, Sexual Politics, Memory, and the Sacred,* 275–86. Durham, NC: Duke University Press, 2006.

Alfaro-Velcamp, Theresa. *So Far from Allah, So Close to Mexico: Middle Eastern Immigrants in Modern Mexico.* Austin: University of Texas Press, 2007.

Almaguer, Tomás. *Racial Fault Lines: The Historical Origins of White Supremacy in California.* Berkeley: University of California Press, 1994.

Alvarez, Luis. "From Zoot Suits to Hip Hop: Towards a Relational Chicana/o Studies." *Latino Studies* 5, no. 1 (2007): 53–75.

———. *The Power of the Zoot: Youth Culture and Resistance during World War II.* Berkeley: University of California Press, 2008.

Alvarez, Luis, and Daniel Widener. "A History of Black and Brown: Chicana/o–African American Cultural and Political Relations." *Aztlán: A Journal of Chicano Studies* 33, no. 1 (2008): 143–54.

Anzaldúa, Gloria. *Borderlands: The New Mestiza/La Frontera.* San Francisco: Spinsters/Aunt Lute, 1987.

Aragon, Margarita. "'The Mexican' and 'the Cancer in the South': Discourses of Race, Nation and Anti-Blackness in Early Twentieth-Century Debates on Mexican Immigration." *Immigrants and Minorities* 35, no. 1 (2017): 59–77.

Araiza, Lauren. *To March for Others: The Black Freedom Struggle and the United Farm Workers.* Philadelphia: University of Pennsylvania Press, 2014.

Arredondo, Gabriela F. *Mexican Chicago: Race, Identity, and Nation, 1916–39.* Champaign-Urbana: University of Illinois Press, 2008.

Bailey, Kristian Davis. "Black-Palestinian Solidarity in the Ferguson-Gaza Era." *American Quarterly* 67, no. 4 (2015): 1017–26.

Bald, Vivek. *Bengali Harlem and the Lost Histories of South Asian America.* Cambridge, MA: Harvard University Press, 2013.

Barker, Joanne. *Native Acts: Law, Recognition, and Cultural Authenticity.* Durham, NC: Duke University Press, 2011.

Bayoumi, Moustafa. *How Does It Feel to Be a Problem? Being Young and Arab in America.* New York: Penguin, 2009.

Behnken, Brian D., ed. *Civil Rights and Beyond: African American and Latino/a Activism in the Twentieth-Century United States.* Atlanta: University of Georgia Press, 2016.

———. *Fighting Their Own Battles: Mexican Americans, African Americans, and the Struggle for Civil Rights in Texas.* Chapel Hill: University of North Carolina Press, 2011.

———, ed. *The Struggle in Black and Brown: African American and Mexican American Relations during the Civil Rights Era.* Lincoln: University of Nebraska Press, 2011.

Bennett, Herman L. *Colonial Blackness: A History of Afro-Mexico.* Bloomington: Indiana University Press, 2009.

Bernstein, Shana. *Bridges of Reform: Interracial Civil Rights Activism in Twentieth-Century Los Angeles.* New York: Oxford University Press, 2010.

Bow, Leslie. *Partly Colored: Asian Americans and Racial Anomaly in the Segregated South.* New York: New York University Press, 2010.

Briggs, Laura. *Reproducing Empire: Race, Sex, Science, and U.S. Imperialism in Puerto Rico.* Berkeley: University of California Press, 2003.

Brilliant, Mark. *The Color of America Has Changed: How Racial Diversity Shaped Civil Rights Reform in California, 1941–1978.* New York: Oxford University Press, 2010.

Brooks, James F., ed. *Confounding the Color Line: The Indian-Black Experience in North America.* Lincoln: University of Nebraska Press, 2002.

Browne, Irene, and Mary Odem. "'Juan Crow' in the Nuevo South? Racialization of Guatemalan and Dominican Immigrants in the Atlanta Metro Area." *Du Bois Review: Social Science Research on Race* 9, no. 2 (2012): 321–37.

Cacho, Lisa Marie. *Social Death: Racialized Rightlessness and the Criminalization of the Unprotected.* New York: New York University Press, 2012.

Camarillo, Albert. "Black and Brown in Compton: Demographic Change, Suburban Decline, and Intergroup Relations in a South Central Los Angeles Community, 1950–2000." In *Not Just Black and White: Historical and Contemporary Perspectives on Immigration, Race, and Ethnicity in the United States,* edited by Nancy Foner and George M. Fredrickson, 358–75. New York: Russell Sage Foundation, 2004.

Carbado, Devon W. "Racial Naturalization." *American Quarterly* 57, no. 3 (2005): 633–58.

Castañeda, Antonia. "Women of Color and the Rewriting of Western History: The Discourse, Politics, and Decolonization of History." *Pacific Historical Review* 61, no. 4 (1992): 501–33.

Chang, Jason Oliver. *Chino: Anti-Chinese Racism in Mexico, 1880–1940*. Champaign-Urbana: University of Illinois Press, 2017.

Chang, Kornel. *Pacific Connections: The Making of the U.S.-Canadian Borderlands*. Berkeley: University of California Press, 2012.

Chávez-García, Miroslava. *States of Delinquency: Race and Science in the Making of California's Juvenile Justice System*. Berkeley: University of California Press, 2012.

Cheng, Wendy. *The Changs Next Door to the Díazes: Remapping Race in Suburban California*. Minneapolis: University of Minnesota Press, 2013.

Crenshaw, Kimberlé. "Mapping the Margins: Intersectionality, Identity Politics, and Violence against Women of Color." *Stanford Law Review* 43, no. 6 (1991): 1241–99.

Criollo, Manuel. "Palestinian and Chicano Peoples Share a History of Resistance to Colonization, Racism, and Imperialism." *American Quarterly* 62, no. 4 (2010): 847–54.

Daulatzai, Sohail. *Black Star, Crescent Moon: The Muslim International and Black Freedom beyond America*. Minneapolis: University of Minnesota Press, 2012.

———. *Return of the Mecca: The Art of Islam and Hip-Hop*. Los Angeles: Razor Step, 2014.

Davis, Angela. *Women, Race, and Class*. New York: Vintage, 1983.

Day, Iyko. "Being or Nothingness: Indigeneity, Antiblackness, and Settler Colonial Critique." *Critical Ethnic Studies* 1, no. 2 (2015): 102–21.

De Genova, Nicholas, ed. *Racial Transformations: Latinos and Asians Remaking the United States*. Durham, NC: Duke University Press, 2006.

De Genova, Nicholas, and Ana Yolanda Ramos-Zayas, eds. *Latino Crossings: Mexicans, Puerto Ricans, and the Politics of Race and Citizenship*. New York: Routledge, 2004.

Delgado, Grace. *Making the Chinese Mexican: Global Migration, Localism, and Exclusion in the U.S.-Mexico Borderlands*. Stanford, CA: Stanford University Press, 2013.

Desmond, Matthew. "Relational Ethnography." *Theory and Society* 43, no. 5 (2014): 547–79.

Du Bois, W. E. B. *The Philadelphia Negro: A Social Study*. New York: Schocken Books, 1967.

Fabian, Ann. *The Skull Collectors: Race, Science, and America's Unburied Dead*. Chicago: University of Chicago Press, 2012.

Feldman, Keith P. "On Relationality, on Blackness: A Listening Post." *Comparative Literature* 68, no. 2 (2016): 107–15.

———. *A Shadow over Palestine: The Imperial Life of Race in America*. Minneapolis: University of Minnesota Press, 2015.

Fernández, Lilia. *Brown in the Windy City: Mexicans and Puerto Ricans in Postwar Chicago*. Chicago: University of Chicago Press, 2012.

Ferreira, Jason. "From College Readiness to Ready for Revolution!" *Kalfou: A Journal of Comparative and Relational Ethnic Studies* 1, no. 1 (2014): 117–44.

Fishbach, Michael. *Black Power and Palestine: Transnational Countries of Color*. Palo Alto, CA: Stanford University Press, 2018.

Foley, Neil. *The White Scourge: Mexicans, Blacks, and Poor Whites in Texas Cotton Culture.* Berkeley: University of California Press, 1997.

Forbes, Jack. *Africans and Native Americans: The Language of Race and the Evolution of Red-Black Peoples.* Champaign-Urbana: University of Illinois Press, 1993.

Franco, Dean. *The Border and the Line: Race, Literature, and Los Angeles.* Palo Alto, CA: Stanford University Press, 2019.

Frazier, Robeson Taj. *The East Is Black: Cold War China in the Black Radical Imagination.* Durham, NC: Duke University Press, 2014.

Fujino, Diane Carol. *Heartbeat of Struggle: The Revolutionary Life of Yuri Kochiyama.* Minneapolis: University of Minnesota Press, 2005.

———. *Samurai among Panthers: Richard Aoki on Race, Resistance, and a Paradoxical Life.* Minneapolis: University of Minnesota Press, 2012.

Fusté, José I. "Containing Bordered 'Others' in La Frontera and Gaza: Comparative Lessons on Racializing Discourses and State Violence." *American Quarterly* 62, no. 4 (2010): 811–19.

García, David G. *Strategies of Segregation: Race, Residence, and the Struggle for Educational Equality.* Oakland: University of California Press, 2018.

Garcia, Matthew. "The Importance of Being Asian: Growers, the United Farm Workers, and the Rise of Colorblindness." In *Racial Formation in the Twenty-First Century,* edited by Daniel HoSang, Oneka LaBennet, and Laura Pulido, 75–89. Berkeley: University of California Press, 2012.

Glenn, Evelyn Nakano. *Unequal Freedom: How Race and Gender Shaped American Citizenship and Labor.* Cambridge, MA: Harvard University Press, 2002.

Goldberg, David Theo. "Racial Comparisons, Relational Racisms: Some Thoughts on Method." *Ethnic and Racial Studies* 32, no. 7 (2009): 1271–82.

Gómez, Laura E. *Manifest Destinies: The Making of the Mexican American Race.* New York: New York University Press, 2018.

González, Fredy. *Paisanos Chinos: Transpacific Politics among Chinese Immigrants in Mexico.* Berkeley: University of California Press, 2017.

Guerrero, Perla M. *Nuevo South: Latinas/os, Asians, and the Remaking of Place.* Austin: University of Texas Press, 2017.

Guevarra, Rudy P., Jr. *Becoming Mexipino: Multiethnic Identities and Communities in San Diego.* New Brunswick, NJ: Rutgers University Press, 2012.

Guridy, Frank. *Forging Diaspora: Afro-Cubans and African Americans in a World of Empire and Jim Crow.* Chapel Hill: University of North Carolina Press, 2010.

Guterl, Matthew Pratt. *Seeing Race in Modern America.* Chapel Hill: University of North Carolina Press, 2013.

Gutiérrez, Ramón A. "Introduction—Race and Immigration in the American City: New Perspectives on Twenty-First Century Intergroup Relations." *Du Bois Review: Social Science Research on Race* 9, no. 2 (2012): 3–7.

———. *When Jesus Came, the Corn Mothers Went Away: Marriage, Sexuality, and Power in New Mexico, 1500–1846.* Stanford, CA: Stanford University Press, 1991.

Hernández, Kelly Lytle. *City of Inmates: Conquest, Rebellion, and the Rise of Human Caging in Los Angeles, 1771–1965*. Chapel Hill: University of North Carolina Press, 2017.

Ho, Fred, and Bill V. Mullen, eds. *Afro Asia: Revolutionary Political and Cultural Connections between African Americans and Asian Americans*. Durham, NC: Duke University Press, 2008.

Hodes, Martha, and Ann Laura Stoler, eds. *Haunted by Empire: Race and Colonial Intimacies in North American History*. Durham, NC: Duke University Press, 2006.

Hong, Grace Kyungwon, and Roderick A. Ferguson, eds. *Strange Affinities: The Gender and Sexual Politics of Comparative Racialization*. Durham, NC: Duke University Press, 2011.

Horne, Gerald. *The Apocalypse of Settler Colonialism: The Roots of Slavery, White Supremacy, and Capitalism in 17th Century North America and the Caribbean*. New York: New York University Press, 2018.

———. *Black and Brown: African Americans and the Mexican Revolution, 1910–1920*. New York: New York University Press, 2005.

———. *Facing the Rising Sun: African Americans, Japan, and the Rise of Afro-Asian Solidarity*. New York: New York University Press, 2018.

HoSang, Daniel Martinez. "The Changing Valence of White Racial Innocence: Black-Brown Unity in the 1970s Los Angeles School Desegregation Struggles." In *Black and Brown in Los Angeles: Beyond Conflict and Coalition*, edited by Josh Kun and Laura Pulido, 115–42. Berkeley: University of California Press, 2013.

———. *Racial Propositions: Ballot Initiatives and the Making of Postwar California*. Berkeley: University of California Press, 2010.

HoSang, Daniel Martinez, Oneka LaBennett, and Laura Pulido, eds. *Racial Formation in the Twenty-First Century*. Berkeley: University of California Press, 2012.

Hu-DeHart, Evelyn. "Chinatowns and Borderlands: Inter-Asian Encounters in the Diaspora." In *Sites of Asian Interaction: Ideas, Networks and Mobility*, edited by Tim Harper and Sunil Amrith, 191–215. Delhi: Cambridge University Press, 2014.

———. "Race Construction and Race Relations: Chinese and Blacks in Nineteenth-Century Cuba." In *Alternative Orientalisms in Latin America and Beyond*, edited by Ignacio López-Calvo, 82–94. Newcastle, U.K.: Cambridge Scholars, 2007.

Hu-DeHart, Evelyn, and Kathleen Lopez, eds. "Afro-Asia." Special issue, *Afro-Hispanic Review* 27, no. 1 (2008).

Ioanide, Paula. *The Emotional Politics of Racism: How Feelings Trump Facts in an Era of Colorblindness*. Stanford, CA: Stanford University Press, 2015.

Jacoby, Karl. *Shadow at Dawn: An Apache Massacre and the Violence of History*. New York: Penguin, 2009.

Johnson, Gaye Theresa. "Constellations of Struggle: Luisa Moreno, Charlotta Bass, and the Legacy for Ethnic Studies." *Aztlán: A Journal of Chicano Studies* 33, no. 1 (2008): 155–72.

———. *Spaces of Conflict, Sounds of Solidarity: Music, Race, and Spatial Entitlement in Los Angeles*. Berkeley: University of California Press, 2013.

Joshi, Khyati Y., and Jigna Desai. *Asian Americans in Dixie: Race and Migration in the South.* Urbana: University of Illinois Press, 2013.

Jun, Helen Heran. *Race for Citizenship: Black Orientalism and Asian Uplift from Pre-Emancipation to Neoliberal America.* New York: New York University Press, 2011.

Jung, Moon-Ho. *Coolies and Cane: Race, Labor, and Sugar in the Age of Emancipation.* Baltimore: Johns Hopkins University Press, 2006.

Jung, Moon-Ho, ed. *The Rising Tide of Color: Race, State Violence, and Radical Movements across the Pacific.* Seattle: University of Washington Press, 2014.

Jung, Moon-Kie. *Beneath the Surface of White Supremacy: Denaturalizing U.S. Racisms Past and Present.* Stanford, CA: Stanford University Press, 2015.

—. *Reworking Race: The Making of Hawaii's Interracial Labor Movement.* New York: Columbia University Press, 2006.

Kajikawa, Loren. "The Sound of Struggle: Black Revolutionary Nationalism and Asian American Jazz." In *Jazz/Not Jazz: The Music and Its Boundaries,* edited by David A. Ake, Daniel Goldmark, and Charles H. Garrett, 190–216. Berkeley: University of California Press, 2012.

Kauanui, J. Kēhaulani. "Tracing Historical Specificity: Race and the Colonial Politics of (In)Capacity." *American Quarterly* 69, no. 2 (2017): 257–65.

Kelley, Robin D. G. "The People in Me." *ColorLines,* Winter 1999, 79–81.

—. "Roaring from the East: Third World Dreaming." In *Freedom Dreams: The Black Radical Imagination,* 60–109. Boston: Beacon Press, 2002.

Kim, Claire Jean. *Bitter Fruit: The Politics of Black-Korean Conflict in New York City.* New Haven, CT: Yale University Press, 2000.

—. "The Racial Triangulation of Asian Americans." *Politics and Society* 27, no. 1 (1999): 105–38.

Klopotek, Brian. *Recognition Odysseys: Indigeneity, Race, and Federal Tribal Recognition Policy in Three Louisiana Indian Communities.* Durham, NC: Duke University Press, 2011.

Kun, Josh. *Audiotopia: Music, Race, and America.* Berkeley: University of California Press, 2005.

—. "What Is an MC if He Can't Rap to Banda? Making Music in Nuevo LA." *American Quarterly* 56, no. 3 (2004): 741–58.

Kun, Josh, and Laura Pulido. *Black and Brown in Los Angeles: Beyond Conflict and Coalition.* Berkeley: University of California Press, 2013.

Kurashige, Scott. *The Shifting Grounds of Race: Black and Japanese Americans in the Making of Multiethnic Los Angeles.* Princeton, NJ: Princeton University Press, 2008.

Lee, James Kyung-Jin. *Urban Triage: Race and the Fictions of Multiculturalism.* Minneapolis: University of Minnesota Press, 2004.

Lee, Julia H. *Interracial Encounters: Reciprocal Representations in African and Asian American Literatures, 1896–1937.* New York: New York University Press, 2011.

Lee, Sonia Song-Ha. *Building a Latino Civil Rights Movement: Puerto Ricans, African Americans, and the Pursuit of Racial Justice in New York City.* Chapel Hill: University of North Carolina Press, 2014.

Leonard, Karen. *Making Ethnic Choices: California's Punjabi Mexican Americans.* Philadelphia: Temple University Press, 2010.

Lipsitz, George. "Blood Lines and Blood Shed: Intersectionality and Differential Consciousness in Ethnic Studies and American Studies." In *A Concise Companion to American Studies,* edited by John C. Rowe, 151–71. Oxford: Wiley-Blackwell, 2010.

———. "Introduction: A New Beginning," *Kalfou: A Journal of Comparative and Relational Ethnic Studies* 1, no. 1 (2014): 7–14.

———. "Like Crabs in a Barrel: Why Interethnic Racism Matters Now." In *American Studies in a Moment of Danger,* 117–38. Minneapolis: University of Minnesota Press, 2001.

———. *The Possessive Investment in Whiteness: How White People Profit from Identity Politics.* Philadelphia: Temple University Press, 2006.

Lloyd, David, and Laura Pulido. "In the Long Shadow of the Settler: On Israeli and U.S. Colonialisms." *American Quarterly* 62, no. 4 (2010): 795–809.

Loewen, James W. *The Mississippi Chinese: Between Black and White.* Long Grove, IL: Waveland Press, 1971.

Lopez, Ian Haney. *White by Law: The Legal Construction of Race.* New York: New York University Press, 1997.

Lowe, Lisa. *Immigrant Acts: On Asian American Cultural Politics.* Durham, NC: Duke University Press, 1996.

———. *The Intimacies of Four Continents.* Durham, NC: Duke University Press, 2015.

Lowery, Malinda Mayor. *Lumbee Indians in the Jim Crow South: Race, Identity, and the Making of a Nation.* Chapel Hill: University of North Carolina Press, 2010.

Lubin, Alex. *Geographies of Liberation: The Making of an Afro-Arab Political Imaginary.* Chapel Hill: University of North Carolina Press.

Luk, Sharon. *The Life of Paper: Letters and a Poetics of Living beyond Captivity.* Berkeley: University of California Press, 2017.

Lye, Colleen. "The Afro-Asian Analogy." *PMLA* 123, no. 5 (2008): 1732–36.

Maira, Sunaina. "Belly Dancing: Arab-Face, Orientalist Feminism, and U.S. Empire." *American Quarterly* 60, no. 2 (2008): 317–45.

———. *Desis in the House: Indian American Youth Culture in New York City.* Philadelphia: Temple University Press, 2002.

Márquez, John D. *Black-Brown Solidarity: Racial Politics in the New Gulf South.* Austin: University of Texas Press, 2014.

Marrow, Helen B. *New Destination Dreaming: Immigration, Race, and Legal Status in the Rural American South.* Stanford, CA: Stanford University Press, 2011.

———. "New Immigrant Destinations and the American Colour Line." *Ethnic and Racial Studies* 32, no. 6 (2009): 1037–57.

Medak-Saltzman, Danika. "Empire's Haunted Logics: Comparative Colonialisms and the Challenges of Incorporating Indigeneity." *Critical Ethnic Studies* 1, no. 2 (2015): 11–32.

Medak-Saltzman, Danika, and Antonio T. Tiongson Jr. "Racial Comparativism Reconsidered." *Critical Ethnic Studies* 1, no. 2 (2015): 1–7.

Meeks, Eric V. *Border Citizens: The Making of Indians, Mexicans, and Anglos in Arizona.* Austin: University of Texas Press, 2007.

Menchaca, Martha. *Recovering History, Constructing Race: The Indian, Black, and White Roots of Mexican Americans.* Austin: University of Texas Press, 2001.

Miles, Tiya. *The House on Diamond Hill: A Cherokee Plantation Story.* Chapel Hill: University of North Carolina Press, 2010.

———. "Taking Leave, Making Lives: Creative Quests for Freedom in Early Black and Native America." In *IndiVisible: African-Native American Lives in the Americas,* edited by Gabrielle Tayac, 139–51. Washington, DC: Smithsonian Institution's National Museum of the American Indian, 2009.

———. *Ties That Bind: The Story of an Afro-Cherokee Family in Slavery and Freedom.* Berkeley: University of California Press, 2005.

Miles, Tiya, and Sharon Patricia Holland, eds. *Crossing Waters, Crossing Worlds: The African Diaspora in Indian Country.* Durham, NC: Duke University Press, 2006.

Mohanty, Chandra Talpade. *Feminism without Borders: Decolonizing Theory, Practicing Solidarity.* Durham, NC: Duke University Press, 2003.

Mohanty, Chandra Talpade, Ann Russo, and Lourdes Torres, eds. *Third World Women and the Politics of Feminism.* Champaign-Urbana: Indiana University Press, 1991.

Molina, Natalia. *Fit to Be Citizens? Public Health and Race in Los Angeles, 1879–1939.* Berkeley: University of California Press, 2006.

———. *How Race Is Made in America: Immigration, Citizenship, and the Historical Power of Racial Scripts.* Berkeley: University of California Press, 2014.

Moraga, Cherríe, and Gloria Anzaldúa, eds. *This Bridge Called My Back: Writings by Radical Women of Color.* 4th ed. Albany: State University of New York Press, 2015.

Mugabo, Délice. "On Rocks and Hard Places: A Reflection on Antiblackness in Organizing against Islamophobia." *Critical Ethnic Studies* 2, no. 2 (2016): 159–83.

Mullen, Bill V. *Afro-Orientalism.* Minneapolis: University of Minnesota Press, 2004.

Muñoz, José Esteban. *Disidentifications: Queers of Color and the Performance of Politics.* Minneapolis: University of Minnesota Press, 1999.

Nelson, Jennifer. *Women of Color and the Reproductive Rights Movement.* New York: New York University Press, 2003.

Ngai, Mae M. *Impossible Subjects: Illegal Aliens and the Making of Modern America.* Princeton, NJ: Princeton University Press, 2004.

Nieva, Chrisshonna Grant, and Laura Pulido. "Beyond Conflict and Competition: How Color-Blind Ideology Affects African Americans' and Latinos' Understanding of Their Relationships." *Kalfou: A Journal of Comparative and Relational Ethnic Studies* 1, no. 1 (2014): 87–116.

Nobles, Melissa. *Shades of Citizenship: Race and the Census in Modern Politics.* Stanford, CA: Stanford University Press, 2000.

Ocampo, Anthony. *The Latinos of Asia: How Filipino Americans Break the Rules of Race.* Stanford, CA: Stanford University Press, 2016.

Okihiro, Gary. *Margins and Mainstreams: Asians in American History and Culture.* Seattle: University of Washington Press, 1994.

———. *Third World Studies: Theorizing Liberation.* Durham, NC: Duke University Press, 2016.

Omi, Michael, and Howard Winant. *Racial Formation in the United States: From the 1960s to the 1980s.* New York: Routledge, 1986.

Onishi, Yuichiro. *Transpacific Antiracism: Afro-Asian Solidarity in 20th-Century Black America, Japan, and Okinawa.* New York: New York University Press, 2013.

Ortiz, Paul. *An African American and Latinx History of the United States.* Boston: Beacon Press, 2018.

Pascoe, Peggy. *Relations of Rescue: The Search for Female Moral Authority in the American West, 1874–1939.* New York: Oxford University Press, 1990.

Paulin, Diana Rebekkah. *Imperfect Unions: Staging Miscegenation in U.S. Drama and Fiction.* Minneapolis: University of Minnesota Press, 2012.

Pérez, Hiram. *A Taste for Brown Bodies: Gay Modernity and Cosmopolitan Desire.* New York: New York University Press, 2015.

Prashad, Vijay. *The Darker Nations: A People's History of the Third World.* New York: New Press, 2008.

———. *Everybody Was Kung Fu Fighting: Afro-Asian Connections and the Myth of Cultural Purity.* Boston: Beacon Press, 2002.

———. "Genteel Racism." *Amerasia Journal* 26, no. 3 (2000): 21–33.

Puar, Jasbir K. *Terrorist Assemblages: Homonationalism in Queer Times.* Durham, NC: Duke University Press, 2007.

Pulido, Laura. *Black, Brown, Yellow, and Left: Radical Activism in Los Angeles.* Berkeley: University of California Press, 2006.

Pulido, Laura, and David Lloyd. "From La Frontera to Gaza: Chicano-Palestinian Connections." *American Quarterly* 62, no. 4 (2010): 791–94.

Raphael-Hernandez, Heike, and Shannon Steen, eds. *AfroAsian Encounters: Culture, History, Politics.* New York: New York University Press, 2006.

Reagon, Bernice Johnson. "Coalition Politics: Turning the Century." In *Home Girls: A Black Feminist Anthology,* edited by Barbara Smith, 343–56. New York: Kitchen Table: Women of Color Press, 1983.

Roberts, Tamara. *Resounding Afro Asia: Interracial Music and the Politics of Collaboration.* Oxford: Oxford University Press, 2016.

Rodríguez, Juana María. *Queer Latinidad: Identity Practices, Discursive Spaces.* New York: New York University Press, 2003.

Román, Miriam Jiménez, and Juan Flores, eds. *The Afro-Latin@ Reader: History and Culture in the United States.* Durham, NC: Duke University Press, 2009.

Sakai, J. *Settlers: The Mythology of the White Proletariat from Mayflower to Modern.* Oakland, CA: PM Press, 2014.

Salaita, Steven. *Inter/Nationalism: Decolonizing Native America and Palestine.* Minneapolis: University of Minnesota Press, 2016.

Saldaña-Portillo, María Josefina. *Indian Given: Racial Geographies across Mexico and the United States.* Durham, NC: Duke University Press, 2016.

Sánchez, George J. *Becoming Mexican American: Ethnicity, Culture, and Identity in Chicano Los Angeles, 1900–1945.* New York: Oxford University Press, 1993.

———. *Bridging Borders, Remaking Community: Racial Interaction in Boyle Heights, California in the 20th Century.* Berkeley: University of California Press, forthcoming.

———. "Disposable People, Expendable Neighborhoods." In *A Companion to Los Angeles,* edited by William Francis Deverell and Greg Hise, 129–46. Malden, MA: Wiley-Blackwell, 2010.

———. "Reading Reginald Denny: The Politics of Whiteness in the Late Twentieth Century." *American Quarterly* 47, no. 3 (1995): 388–94.

———. "'What's Good for Boyle Heights Is Good for the Jews': Creating Multiracialism on the Eastside during the 1950s." *American Quarterly* 56, no. 3 (2004): 633–61.

Schleitwiler, Vince. *Strange Fruit of the Black Pacific: Imperialism's Racial Justice and Its Fugitives.* New York: New York University Press, 2017.

Seijas, Tatiana. *Asian Slaves in Colonial Mexico: From Chinos to Indians.* Cambridge: Cambridge University Press, 2014.

Sexton, Jared. "People-of-Color-Blindness: Notes on the Afterlife of Slavery." *Social Text* 28, no. 2 (2010): 31–56.

Shah, Nayan. *Contagious Divides: Epidemics and Race in San Francisco's Chinatown.* Berkeley: University of California Press, 2001.

———. *Stranger Intimacy: Contesting Race, Sexuality, and the Law in the North American West.* Berkeley: University of California Press, 2011.

Sharma, Nitasha Tamar. *Hip Hop Desis: South Asian Americans, Blackness, and a Global Race Consciousness.* Durham, NC: Duke University Press, 2010.

Shih, Shu-Mei. "Comparative Racialization: An Introduction." *PMLA* 123, no. 5 (2008): 1347–62.

Sifuentez, Mario Jimenez. *Of Forests and Fields: Mexican Labor in the Pacific Northwest.* New Brunswick, NJ: Rutgers University Press, 2016.

Simpson, Leanne Betasamosake. "Indigenous Resurgence and Co-resistance." *Critical Ethnic Studies* 2, no. 2 (2016): 19–34.

Skwiot, Christine. *The Purposes of Paradise: U.S. Tourism and Empire in Cuba and Hawai'i.* Philadelphia: University of Pennsylvania Press, 2010.

Smith, Andrea. "Indigeneity, Settler Colonialism, White Supremacy." In *Racial Formation in the Twenty-First Century,* edited by Daniel M. HoSang, Oneka LaBennett, and Laura Pulido, 66–90. Berkeley: University of California Press, 2012.

Solis, Gabriel. "The Black Pacific: Music and Racialization in Papua New Guinea and Australia." *Critical Sociology* 41, no. 2 (2015): 297–312.

Stern, Alexandra Minna. *Eugenic Nation: Faults and Frontiers of Better Breeding in Modern America.* Berkeley: University of California Press, 2005.

Stoler, Ann Laura, ed. *Haunted by Empire: Geographies of Intimacy in North American History.* Durham, NC: Duke University Press, 2006.

Takaki, Ronald T. *A Different Mirror: A History of Multicultural America.* Boston: Little, Brown, 1993.

Tang, Eric. *Unsettled: Cambodian Refugees in the New York City Hyperghetto.* Philadelphia: Temple University Press, 2015.

Tawil, Randa. "Racial Borderlines: Ameen Rihani, Mexico, and World War I." *Amerasia Journal* 44, no. 1 (2018): 85–104.

Tayac, Gabrielle. *IndiVisible: African-Native American Lives in the Americas.* Washington, DC: Smithsonian Institution's National Museum of the American Indian, 2009.

Tiongson, Antonio T., Jr. "Afro-Asian Inquiry and the Problematics of Comparative Critique." *Critical Ethnic Studies* 1, no. 2 (2015): 33–58.

Tomlinson, Barbara, and George Lipsitz. "American Studies as Accompaniment." *American Quarterly* 65, no. 1 (2013): 1–30.

Umemoto, Karen. "Korean and African-American Relations: Integrating the Symbolic with the Structural." *Trotter Review* 7, no. 2 (1993): 8–11.

Valerio-Jiménez, Omar S. *River of Hope: Forging Identity and Nation in the Rio Grande Borderlands.* Durham, NC: Duke University Press, 2013.

Varzally, Allison. *Making a Non-white America: Californians Coloring outside Ethnic Lines, 1925–1955.* Berkeley: University of California Press, 2008.

Volpp, Leti. "Immigrants Outside the Law: President Obama, Discretionary Executive Power, and Regime Change." *Critical Analysis of Law* 3, no. 2 (2016): 385–404.

Wailoo, Keith. *How Cancer Crossed the Color Line.* Oxford: Oxford University Press, 2010.

Weise, Julie M. *Corazón de Dixie: Mexicanos in the U.S. South since 1910.* Chapel Hill: University of North Carolina Press, 2015.

White, Richard. "Race Relations in the American West." *American Quarterly* 38, no. 3 (1986): 396–416.

Willoughby-Herard, Tiffany. "More Expendable Than Slaves? Racial Justice and the After-Life of Slavery." *Politics, Groups, and Identities* 2, no. 3 (2014): 506–21.

Wolfe, Patrick. "Settler Colonialism and the Elimination of the Native." *Journal of Genocide Research* 8, no. 4 (2006): 387–409.

———. *Traces of History: Elementary Structures of Race.* New York: Verso, 2016.

Wu, Judy Tzu-Chun. *Radicals on the Road: Internationalism, Orientalism and Feminism during the Vietnam Era.* Ithaca, NY: Cornell University Press, 2013.

Young, Cynthia. *Soul Power: Culture, Radicalism, and the Making of a U.S. Third World Left.* Durham, NC: Duke University Press, 2006.

CONTRIBUTORS

LAURA E. ENRIQUEZ is Assistant Professor of Chicano/Latino Studies at the University of California, Irvine. She earned her PhD in sociology from the University of California, Los Angeles. Her research explores the role that immigration laws play in the lives of undocumented young adults and their family members.

RODERICK FERGUSON is Professor of African American and Gender and Women's Studies at the University of Illinois at Chicago. He is the author of *The Reorder of Things: The University and Its Pedagogies of Minority Difference* and *Aberrations in Black: Toward a Queer of Color Critique*. He is coeditor of the Difference Incorporated series at the University of Minnesota Press.

ALYOSHA GOLDSTEIN is Associate Professor of American Studies at the University of New Mexico. He is the author of *Poverty in Common: The Politics of Community Action during the American Century,* the editor of *Formations of United States Colonialism,* and the coeditor of "On Colonial Unknowing," a special issue of *Theory & Event,* and of "Settler Colonialism," a special issue of *South Atlantic Quarterly.*

PERLA M. GUERRERO is Assistant Professor of American Studies and U.S. Latina/o Studies at the University of Maryland, College Park. Her research and teaching interests include relational and comparative race and ethnicity, space and place, immigration, labor, and U.S. history. She has received multiple fellowships, including two from the Smithsonian Institution and a postdoctoral fellowship from the Ford Foundation, and she has published several book chapters and articles.

RAMÓN A. GUTIÉRREZ is Preston and Sterling Morton Distinguished Service Professor of American History at the University of Chicago. His research and publications focus on race and ethnic relations in the Americas from 1492 to the present, religion and spirituality in the hemisphere, ethnic Mexican culture and politics on both sides of the border, immigration and adaptation in the United States, and inequality and diversity in American society. He is the author of several books, among them *When Jesus Came, the Corn Mothers Went Away: Marriage, Sexuality, and Power in New Mexico, 1500–1846.*

KELLY LYTLE HERNÁNDEZ is Professor of History at the University of California, Los Angeles. She is the author of *Migra! A History of the U.S. Border Patrol* and *City of Inmates: Conquest and the Rise of Human Caging in Los Angeles, 1771–1965*.

DANIEL MARTINEZ HOSANG is Associate Professor of American Studies and Ethnicity, Race & Migration at Yale University. He is the author of *Racial Propositions: Ballot Initiatives and the Making of Postwar California* (University of California Press, 2010) and coeditor, with Oneka LaBennett and Laura Pulido, of *Racial Formation in the 21st Century* (University of California Press, 2012). His research and teaching explore the contradictory labor of race within U.S. political culture across a wide range of sites, including electoral politics, social movements, and academic discourse.

RAOUL S. LIÉVANOS is a faculty affiliate at the University of Washington Center for Studies in Demography and Ecology and Assistant Professor of Sociology at the University of Oregon. His research focuses on the organizational, institutional, demographic, and spatial dynamics of environmental and housing market inequalities and on the social movements and policy processes that attempt to address such inequalities in the United States.

GEORGE LIPSITZ is Professor of Black Studies and Sociology at the University of California, Santa Barbara. His publications include *How Racism Takes Place, Midnight at the Barrelhouse, The Possessive Investment in Whiteness,* and *A Life in the Struggle: Ivory Perry and the Culture of Opposition.* Lipsitz is senior editor of the journal *Kalfou,* editor of the Insubordinate Spaces series at Temple University Press, and coeditor of the American Crossroads series at the University of California Press.

JULIE LEE MERSETH is Assistant Professor in the Department of Political Science at Northwestern University. Her areas of specialization are situated in the field of American politics with a dual and overlapping focus on race and immigration. Her research is especially animated by questions of how racial and ethnic politics in the United States are changing as a result of fast-growing populations of immigrants, largely from Latin America, Asia, Africa, and the Middle East.

TIYA MILES is a Professor of History and Radcliffe Alumnae Professor at Harvard University. She is the author of three prizewinning works of history: *Ties That Bind: The Story of an Afro-Cherokee Family in Slavery and Freedom* (2005), *The House on Diamond Hill: A Cherokee Plantation Story* (2010), and *The Dawn of Detroit: A Chronicle of Slavery and Freedom in the City of the Straits* (2017). She has also published a narrative study of ghost tourism titled *Tales from the Haunted South: Dark Tourism and Memories of Slavery from the Civil War Era,* and a novel, *The Cherokee Rose,* set on a haunted plantation in the Cherokee territory of present-day Georgia. She is coeditor, with Sharon P. Holland, of the collection *Crossing Waters, Crossing Worlds: The African Diaspora in Indian Country.* Her work has been funded by the MacArthur Foundation, the Mellon Foundation, and the National Endowment for the Humanities.

NATALIA MOLINA is Professor of American Studies and Ethnicity at University of Southern California. Her work lies at the intersections of race, gender, culture, and citizenship. She is the author of two award-winning books, *Fit to be Citizens? Public Health and Race in Los Angeles, 1879–1939* and *How Race Is Made in America: Immigration, Citizenship, and the Historical Power of Racial Scripts.* Her current book project examines eight decades of place making, community formation, and gentrification in the historically multiethnic LA community of Echo Park.

CATHERINE S. RAMÍREZ is Associate Professor of Latin American and Latino Studies and Director of the Chicano Latino Research Center at the University of California, Santa Cruz. She is the author of *The Woman in the Zoot Suit: Gender, Nationalism, and the Cultural Politics of Memory.* Her current book project is entitled *Assimilation: An Alternative History.*

MICHAEL RODRÍGUEZ-MUÑIZ is Assistant Professor of Sociology and Latina/ Latino Studies at Northwestern University. He has published on the politics of censuses, Latino identity formation, and ethnographic methods, and he is currently completing a book manuscript on the role of demographic statistics in contemporary national Latino civil rights.

STEVEN SALAITA is the author of several books, among them *Anti-Arab Racism in the USA: Where It Comes from and What It Means, The Holy Land in Transit: Colonialism and the Quest for Canaan,* and *Arab American Literary Fictions, Cultures, and Politics.* He is the former Edward W. Said Chair of American Studies at the American University at Beirut and a former faculty member of the English Department at Virginia Tech.

GEORGE J. SÁNCHEZ is Director of the Center for Democracy and Diversity and Professor of American Studies & Ethnicity and History at the University of Southern California. He is the author of *Becoming Mexican American: Ethnicity, Culture, and Identity in Chicano Los Angeles, 1900–1945.* He is coeditor of the American Crossroads series from the University of California Press.

TIFFANY WILLOUGHBY-HERARD is Associate Professor of African American Studies at the University of California, Irvine. She researches Black political thought and the material conditions of knowledge production, Black radical movements, and raced gender consciousness and queer and trans sexualities internationally. She has several roles in publishing as the Managing Editor of the *National Political Science Review* and is one of the History/Social Science Book Review Editors for *Safundi: The Journal of South African and American Studies.* She is the author of *Waste of a White Skin: The Carnegie Corporation and the Racial Logic of White Vulnerability.*

JEFFREY T. YAMASHITA received his PhD in Ethnic Studies from the University of California, Berkeley. His historical research examines the racialization of Asian American patriarchal identity formations, such as the war hero, gentleman, and athlete, in relation to other racial, ethnic, and indigenous groups.

INDEX

NOTE: Page numbers in *italics* indicate maps, tables, or illustrations.

AMEMSA (Arab, Middle Eastern, Muslim, and South Asian), as racial category, 323

American Indian Policy Review Commission (1977), 66

American Indian studies. *See* inter/nationalist scholarship: American Indian studies and importance of Palestine; Native American studies

American Israel Public Affairs Committee (AIPAC), 109

American studies, transnational turn in, 4

Anderson, Benedict, 199n4

anticolonialism as relational project: anti–U.S. imperialism and, 85–86; Bandung conference (1955) and, 84–85; gender and sexual contradictions in nationalist formations, 86–89, 92; and internal colonial model (U.S.), 86; race as disciplined in discourse of, 89; and race as global vs. national category, 86; *World 3* stamp project illuminating, 83–84, 92. *See also* inter/nationalist scholarship: American Indian studies and importance of Palestine; queer of color formations; women of color feminism

Antin, Mary, *The Promised Land,* 25, 41n7

antiracist relational analyses and politics: overview, 13–14, 81, 83–84; coalition building and, 13; and global vs. national construction of race, 81, 86; and relational race lens, 34–35, 81, 89–92; as resource for movements, 14; and unity, meaning of, 13. *See also* anticolonialism as relational project; queer of color formations; racialized immigration and slavery/anti-Black racial subjection, relationality of; women of color feminism

anti-Semitism, contestation of Zionism read as, 106

Aoki, Richard, 29

appropriation: multiculturalism and, 111; of Native identity, 198

Arab American studies, 99

Arab and Muslim Americans in post-9/11 racial politics: overview, 9, 256, 296–97, 316–17; *Arab,* as identity-based group, 298; conflation of Arab and Muslim

communities, 297–99, 313; conflation of, and religion/religious differences, 298, 300–302; difficulty of acquiring accurate demographic information about, 319n11; generational differences and, 301; media coverage and, 296, 298, 304; *Muslim,* as religious identification, 298; "othering" of, 296–97, 317; postracial discourse, 304, 315–16; prior to 9/11 attacks, 318n4, 322n48; and Trump proposed ban on travel/immigration, 298–99, 314; U.S. Census and, 319n11, 319n16; and "War on Terror"/racial profiling policy, 299; and whiteness, 296, 300, 318n3

—ARAB/MUSLIM AMERICAN AS NEW RACIAL(IZED) GROUP: overview, 316–17; conflation of Arab and Muslim and de facto treatment as, 297–99; counterview to, that issues are best dealt with in the Asian American or African American communities, 313–14; formal categorization of Arab/Muslim as not recognized, 219n16, 299–300; and postracial/colorblind discourse, 316–17

—METHODOLOGY: comparison as relational tool, 306; content analysis, 304, 321n41; *New York Times* content analysis method, 304–6, 321n42–43,45; racial(ized) political discourse, 304; racial triangulation, 303–4, 305–6, *305,* 309, 320–21nn36,38; relational lens for, 302–3, 317. *See also* —racialization frames as methodology

—RACIALIZATION FRAMES METHOD: overview/discussion, 312–16; applicability to other political discourse, 316; common frames as confirming conflation of Arabs and Muslims, 306–8, *307,* 313, *324;* consistent frames over time of Arabs and Muslims, 308–10, *309,* 313, 322nn47–48, *324;* design of frames, 304–6, *305,* 321nn41–43,45; different/consistent frames in relational analysis, 310–12, *311,* 313, 317, *324;* exposure and amplification of discourse revealed by, 305, 322n47; group-based stereotypes operationalized in, *305,* 306; reliability

of frame occurrence counts, 312; tabulated results, *307, 309, 311, 324*
—IN RELATION WITH BLACK AND ASIAN AMERICANS: overview, 302–3; different/consistent frames in relational analysis, 310–12, *311*, 313, 317, *324*; and intragroup differences, 303; solidarity and coalitions with Arab and Muslim Americans, 313–15; terms used in, 320n34

Arabs and Arab Americans: Brown/AMEMSA/MASA as proposed racial categories for, 323n59; as Christians, 298, 301; as Jews, 301; MENA (Middle Eastern or North African descent) as proposed census category for, 300; population percentage of Muslims, 298; and the U.S. Census, 300, 319–20nn11,24; and whiteness, 296, 300, 318n3. *See also* Arab and Muslim Americans in post-9/11 racial politics

Arapaho people, 170
Arce Pagán, Emilio de, 174
archives: activism and broadening of, 29; as masking relational interdependencies, 10–11; Native American slaves as absent from, 127; Native American women represented in, 134–35; new sources, development of, 34, 48–49, 51–52, 58nn22,29; parochialism of the academy and narrowness of, 32; solo work in, vs. community collaboration, 34–35; well-known and heavily used, moving beyond, 49–50, 58n22
area studies, vs. American Indian studies, 116
Argentina, undocumented immigrants from, 261
Arkansas: and Cuban refugees, 205, 206, 218; desegregation of schools, 208; Japanese internment camps in WWII, 185–86, 196, 207, 208; and Latina/o immigration, 205, 206, 218–19; and state-sponsored anti-Black violence, 207. *See also* Vietnamese refugees in Arkansas, racialization of
Armstrong, Samuel Chapman, 170–71, 179
Asahina, Robert, 185

Asian American Legal Defense and Education Fund, 314
Asian Americans Advancing Justice, 314
Asian Pacific Islanders (API): as term, 261, 277n26. *See also* undocumented students (Latinas/os and Asian Pacific Islanders)
Asians and Asian Americans: assimilation stereotypes about, 309; on Chicago City Council, 284, 290, 295n55; and the Chicano community, 25; defined as racial group, 260; as excluded/restricted from immigration, 48, 52, 61, 213, 227, 300; intragroup conflicts, 314; as Muslims, 298, 313–15; number of undocumented immigrants in U.S., 257; and relational racialization, 226–27; and spatial racialization in Stockton (CA), 225, 235, 238–40, *239*, 244; structural racism and, 48. *See also* Arab and Muslim Americans in post-9/11 racial politics—in relation with Black and Asian Americans; Chinese and Chinese Americans; Japanese American soldiers (AJA), racialization as Hawaiian; Japanese and Japanese Americans; Japanese internment in World War II; Koreans and Korean Americans; racial triangulation; undocumented students (Latinas/os and Asian Pacific Islanders); Vietnamese refugees in Arkansas, racialization of
assimilation: and Asians, stereotypes about, 309; as blocked for persons of African descent, 151–52, 159nn25,27; "civilization" and, 167–70, 177, 178–79; as disappearance, 171, 179; as policy replacing genocide of Native Americans, 64–65, 67–68; prevention of, followed by blaming of groups for lack of, 25; questioning of Indian policy of, 177–78; relationality, generally, 11; segmented, 260–61; "spatial," 244; whiteness as move of, 178. *See also* Arab and Muslim Americans in post-9/11 racial politics—racialization frames method; Carlisle Indian Industrial School—assimilation and

Atshan, Sa'ed Adel, 98
authority. *See* methodologies of relational framework

Bachmann, Michele, 63
Baldwin, James, 38
Balfour, Lawrie, 72
Bandung conference (1955), 4, 84–85
Bankhead-Jones Farm Tenant Act (1937), 70
Barker, Joanne, 65
Barrelli, Adela, 174
Bascara, Victor, 149, 150
Belize, undocumented immigrants from, 261, 268
Bell, Genevieve, 179–81nn2,12, 184n78
Benjamin, Orly, 102
Berelson, Bernard L., 321n41
Berlant, Lauren, 159n23
Berlin, Ira, 124, 127, 143n39
Bhandar, Brenna, 73–74
biracial/bicultural consciousness, Black Indians and, 130, 132–33
Black culture: drama and fiction, 14; as point of entry for Mexican immigrants, 25
Black Elk, Wallace, 2
Black farmers: numbers of, over time, 69–70; USDA discriminatory lending practices to, *Pigford* lawsuits on, 60, 68–73
Blackness: as categorical antagonist to white nationalism, 148–49; internationalism of, 27–28, 148–49; and undocumented students, 268
Black Panther Party, 28, 86–87, 88
Black political consciousness, modern canard dismissing, 15, 153
Black Power movements, 315
Black press: on anti-Black racism during WWII, 190, 191, 192, 193–94; and Black internationalism, 27–28; and Blackness, 27–28; on Indigenous Hawaiians as a vanishing people, 197; and support for Sleepy Lagoon defendants, 54–55. *See also* media
Black press and relationality, and imperialism, critique of, 4

Black radical tradition/internationalism and anti-imperial politics: the Black press and, 27–28; as categorical antagonist to white nationalism, 148–49; as forerunner of relational study of race, 4; as form of world-transcending citizenship, 27; and post-Emancipation racial labor hierarchy, 151, 159nn25,27
Black subjugation: as difference, and relational framework, 150; immigration histories as flattening, 31; lynching, and WWII, 192, 195; racial-cleansing programs of the South, 207; racial triangulation and, 227; relational politics and sensitivity to, 15, 148. *See also* racialized immigration and slavery/anti-Black racial subjection, relationality of; racism
Black Twitter, 38
Black-white racial binary: California conditions as defying, 46; Chicana/o history and disruption of, 45–46; the South and complication of, 205
blight as discourse, 228
Border Patrol, U.S., Black perception of, 26
Boyle Heights (Los Angeles neighborhood): Black-Mexican relationship in, 28; ethnoracial diversity of, 50–51; FHA description of, as "diverse and subversive," 39, 51; Japanese American National Museum, *Boyle Heights: The Power of Place* (2002 exhibition), 50, 58n28; and Japanese internment, effect of, 51; structural discrimination and, 51
Bradley, Tom, 24
Brazil: Indigenous peoples in slavery in, 125; racial subjugation in, 158n14
Breitbart, Andrew, 76n12
Brendel, Caroline L., 209
British empire, slavery and, 125, 126, 160n35
Brookins, Howard, 285, 286, 289
Brown, as racial category, 323n59
Brown, Elaine, 88
Brown, Mark, 286
Brumbaugh, Martin Grove, 173
Buffalo Soldiers, 170

Bureau of Indian Affairs (BIA), 65, 66, 143n40, 169, 177

Bush administration (George H. W., Bush I), and Black farmers' *Cobell* suit, 68

Bush administration (George W., Bush II), post-9/11, 308

Byrd, Jodi, 103

Byrne, John, 281

Caddo people, 170

California: ethnoracial diversity in, 46–47, 50–51, 224–25; gold rush, 231–32; laws and policies to support undocumented college students, 259, 276nn14,17; Proposition 187, 27, 41n9; as territory of Mexico, 46, 61, 231

Camarillo, Albert, 47

Camp Pendleton (CA), 209

Camp Shelby (Hattiesburg, Mississippi): and acquittal of white lynching defendants, 192, 195; anti-Black racism and conditions of soldiers in, 190–91, 192–93; local media coverage of, 193. *See also* Japanese American soldiers (AJA), racialization as Hawaiian

Canada, number of undocumented immigrants in U.S., 257

capitalism: slavery as imbricated in, 153–54; women of color feminist and queer of color formations as transcending limits of, 94

Carbado, Devon, 164, 176

Caribbean: Indigenous peoples in slavery in, 125; number of undocumented immigrants from, 257

Carlisle Indian Industrial School: family separation/natal alienation as goal of, 168–69; funding for, and racialization, 173–74; and Hampton school, co-education of Negroes and Indians at, 168, 170–72, 173, 177, 181n27; history of the school, 166, 168–71; and interracial relationships and marriage, 171–72, 182n38; number of graduates of, 178, 184n78; number of pupils, 166, 169, 179–80n2, 180–81n12; pan-Indianism as fostered by, 178

—ASSIMILATION AND: as a relational process, 163–64, 168, 178–79; before-and-after portraits of students, 169; as "civilizing," 167–70, 177, 178–79; "killing the Indian and saving the man," 169–70; "outing program" as tool of, 169; as racialization, 163–64, 167–68, 172–78; segmented, 168; slavery and, 172; "under duress," 172; whiteness as move of, 178

—PUERTO RICAN STUDENTS AT: overview, 166–68; class status of students, 173, 176–77; gender and, 166–67; manual laborers and domestic servants, focus of training on, 166–67, 176–77, 178; number of graduates of, 178; number of pupils, 166, 173, 179–80n2; Puerto Ricanness of students as reinforced by, 178; racial and cultural ranking of students, 173–78; student recollections of, 166, 173, 174–77, 178

Castañeda, Antonia, 45

Castro, Fidel, 205

Central America: disease as decimating Indigenous population, 125; Indigenous peoples in slavery in, 125; repression and genocide in, 30–31, 102–4

Césaire, Aimé, 32

Champagne, Duane, 115

Change, David, 65

Charlottesville, VA, white supremacist rally, 155

Chatterjea, Partha, 85

Cheng, Wendy, 204

Cherokee people, 128, 132–34, 136–37, 139, 142n24

Cheyenne people, 170

Chiapas insurgency, 103

Chicago. *See* racial arithmetic—Chicago redistricting of 2011

Chicana/o history: foundational works of, 56n5; and new sources, development of, 49–50, 58n22; and reconsideration of existing research, 52–55; relational turn in, 45–46, 55, 56–57nn6–7; Sleepy Lagoon murder, 52–53, *53–54*, 54–55; women of color, turn toward centering of, 45; Zoot Suit riots, 23, 53–54

Chicana/os: and intersectionality, awareness of, 43; nationalism of, and demographic change of 2040, 35–36; as term, 55–56n1. *See also* Mexicans and Mexican Americans

Chicana/o studies, as term, 55–56n1

Chickasaw people, 142n24

China, Black internationalism and, 28

Chinese and Chinese Americans: overview, 2–3; excluded/restricted as immigrants, 48, 52, 61, 226–27, 227; and the gold rush, 231; racialization of, 48, 57n19; and spatial racialization in Stockton (CA), 225, 235, 238, *239, 241,* 244, 245; undocumented immigrants from, 261; viewed as "greatest threat" to Los Angeles, 47; violence against, 4

Chinese Exclusion Act (1882), 48, 61, 227

Choctaw people, 128

Christianity, values of, and Vietnamese refugee settlement, 203–4, 206, 208, 209–10

Christian Right, 206, 210

citizenship: Black radical tradition and world-transcending form of, 27; ethnic group interest politics and false ideal of, 149–50, 153; "infantile," 159n23; of Mexicans, in wake of Mexican-American War, 227; racialization as dependent on constructions of, 3; second-class, African Americans and, 303; as whitening, 148, 151–52, 160n36. *See also* racialized immigration and slavery/anti-Black racial subjection, relationality of—citizenship and citizens and

"civilization": assimilation and, 167–70, 177, 178–79; slavery and, 172. *See also* assimilation; segregation

civil rights: liberal settlers of West Bank and, 104–7; *Pigford II* as largest settlement for, 60

Civil Rights Act (1964), 70

civil rights movement: and interrelatedness, 1, *2;* and racial arithmetic, 278; Second Reconstruction of, 207–8; and USDA discriminatory lending practices, 70

Civil War: Black troops in, 170; establishment of schools for newly freed slaves, 173

Claims Resolution Act (CRA, 2010): overview, 11, 20–21, 60–61; *Cobell v. Salazar,* 60, 64–68; Congressional debate on, 62–63, 64, 74, 76n12; as extinguishing further recourse, 67–68; as foreclosing the salience of historically fraught relations, 21, 62, 68, 69, 72–75; and formal equality, language of, 72; *Pigford II* (2010), 60, 68–73; as reconciliation, 21, 73–74; reparations and, 63, 72, 74–75; signing by Barack Obama, 63–64, 67

class: accountability displaced from wealthy to working class, 62; differential racialization and, 226; as intragroup difference, 303; and Puerto Rican students at the Carlisle Indian School, 166–67, 176–77, 178; and Vietnamese refugees, 210, 213–15, 221

Clyburn, James, 64

Cobell, Elouise, 64

Cobell v. Salazar (1996), 60, 64–68

collaboration among researchers, 51

collaboration with communities: overview, 19; books written by nonacademics, 38; creation of local democracy, 38; and history, people seeing themselves in, 39–40

Colombia, immigrants from, 261

colonialism: internal colonial model (U.S.), 86; modern, definition of, 61. *See also* anticolonialism as relational project

colonialism and white supremacy, relationality of: overview, 3, 11, 21; Bandung conference (1955) and recognition of, 85; and "indebted servitude" of Black peonage and sharecropping, 61–62; slavery as entwined in, 61–62, 75, 124–26. *See also* Claims Resolution Act; imperialism; Indigenous dispossession; settler colonialism; slavery

colonization (Back-to-Africa) movement, opposition to, 171, 179

colorblind discourse, 315–16, 321n38

Columbia University, 18–19n23
Comanche people, 170
comparative study of race: definition of, 8; as reifying categories of race, 44; relational study distinguished from, 8, 44, 279–80, 291; relational study using tool of, 306
Consolidated Farmers' Home Administration Act (1961), 70
Continued Dumping and Subsidy Offset Act (2000), 74
contract rights, and burdens of citizenship, 154
Cotler, Irwin, 110–11
Cox, Oliver Cromwell, 29
Cragin, Ellen, 136
Craven, Kimberly, 67
Creek people, 128, 132, 133, 142n24
Crenshaw, Kimberlé, 13, 30, 32
criminality, as stereotype. *See* Arab and Muslim Americans in post-9/11 racial politics
criminal justice system, discrimination in: Scottsboro case, 54–55; Sleepy Lagoon murder, 52–53, *53–54*, 54–55
Crisis (journal), 23
Crisotomo, Paula, 28
critical ethnic studies, 4
Crost, Lyn, 185
Cruz-Jansen, Marta, 160n36
Cuba, 4, 151; refugees from, 205, 206, 218
cultural productions, and antiracist formations, 14

Dagenette, Charles, 166
Daley, Richard M., 282
Danticat, Edwidge, 145
Daraphant, Boonyarit, *Targeted or Overlooked*, 272, *273*
Dardick, Hal, 281, 284, 293–94n29
Darrows, Mary Allen, 126
Daulatzai, Sohail, 14
Davey, Monica, 282
Davis, Angela, 88
Davis, Lucinda, *122*
Dawes Act (General Allotment Act, 1887), 64–65, 67, 168–69, 177

decolonization: American, and American Indian studies/Palestine studies relationship, 98, 99, 101, 108–9, 110; of the university, 116–17. *See also* inter/nationalist scholarship: American Indian studies and importance of Palestine
deed restrictions (racially restrictive covenants): declared unenforceable by Supreme Court, 246; definition of, 233; FHA as mandating use of, 233; general use of, by 1920s, 233; HOLC and, 233, 234, 236, 238–40, *239*, 245, 246; Los Angeles and, 50; mortgage lending discrimination and, 240
Deloria, Vine Jr., 123
democracy, lack of, 38
demographics, change in 2040 of, 35–36
desegregation: of the academy, 32; of schools, 208
Desmond, Matthew, 8, 279
Deutsch, Sally, 51
Devils Tower, WY (Mato Tupilak), 107, 118n22
Díaz, José, 53
differences and relational framework: Black subjugation/slavery and, 150; intragroup differences, 303; methodological concern for, 12–13; sensitivity to, politics and necessity of, 15–16; unity and, 13. *See also* Black subjugation
the disciplines: deterritorialization of, and inter/nationalist scholarship, 116; and parochialism of the academy, 32
dispossession: historical Jewish, 108, 118–19n23; slavery and, 11, 70, 74–75. *See also* Indigenous dispossession
diversity: discourses of, as recentering whiteness, 72–73; and Indigenous Hawaiians as vanishing people, 197. *See also* ethnoracial diversity
Dominican Republic, 151
Downes v. Bidwell (1901), 184n82
Dred Scott v. Sanford (1857), 61
DuBois, Ellen Carol, 4

Du Bois, W. E. B.: anticolonialism and, 27; *The Philadelphia Negro: A Social Study,* 5; and social movements, 29

Duus, Masayo, 199n9

Eaton, John, 173

"ecological theory" (Hoyt), 233

economic crisis of 2008, and CRA, passage of, 62–63, 64

education: and assimilation of Indians, questioning of federal policy of, 177–78; Hampton Normal and Agricultural Institute, 168, 170–72, 173, 177, 181n27; tracking of students, 43, 56n2. *See also* Carlisle Indian Industrial School

Educational Council for Foreign Medical Graduates (ECFMG), 216

Eglin Air Force Base (FL), 209

Eichelberger, Leslie, 195

El Salvador: repression and genocide in, 102; and Trump's racist anti-immigrant statements, 154, 155

El-Tayeb, Fatima, 90–91

emancipation, indebtedness of the freed for, 74

Emanuel, Rahm, 290

encomienda system, 125

English language: as second language, assumed for Chicana/o students, 43, 56n2; and stereotypes of undocumented students, 266; in U.S.-style schools in Puerto Rico, 173; and Vietnamese refugees, 210, 211, 218–19, 223nn45,54

Enriquez, Laura E., 9–10, 255, 256, 337

Esch, Betsy, 28

essentialism, as strategic survival mechanism, 164, 187

ethnic group interest politics, and false ideal of citizenship, 149–50, 153

ethnic studies: social movements and development of, 5–6; subfield paradigm and, 6, 44; substantialist perspective and, 6–7; transnational turn in, 4

ethnoracial diversity: of Boyle Heights, 50–51; in California, 46–47, 50–51, 224–25; as defying Black-white racial

binary, 46; and finding commonalities within neighborhoods, 43; as generative of relational study of race, 43–44, 46–48; in Los Angeles, 46–47, 50–51

ethnoracial politics: comparative analytic approach to, 279–80, 291; group-centric analytic approach to, 279, 291; relational analytic approach to, 280. *See also* relational study of race

eugenics, 278

Europe, number of undocumented immigrants in U.S., 257

family formations, and welcome of refugees, 218

family separation/natal alienation: Carlisle Indian Industrial School and goal of, 168–69; racialized immigration and, 147–48, 152, 154, 158n14

Fanon, Frantz, 83, 84–85, 176

Farmers' Home Administration Act (1946), 70

farms: number of Black- vs. white-owned, 69–70; small farmers as disappearing, 72. *See also* Black farmers; USDA

Farrington, J. R., 189–90, 197

Faubus, Orval, 208

Federal Housing Administration (FHA): on Boyle Heights as "diverse and subversive," 39, 51; and racially restrictive covenants, 233; and redlining, 232–33; segregation promulgated by, 39

feminism: Afro-German, 90–91. *See also* women of color feminism

Ferguson, MO: police department, 278; uprising in, 38

Ferguson, Roderick, 4, 13, 14, 15, 81, 150, 337

Figueroa, Vicente, 166, 174, 175, 176

Fiji, undocumented immigrants from, 261

Filipinos and Filipino Americans: and spatial racialization in Stockton (CA), 225, 235, 238, *239, 241,* 244, 245–47, 248; in Zoot Suit riot, 54

Finch, Earl, 193

"Five Civilized Tribes," 128, 142n24

Flora, Cornelia Butler, 114

Foley, Neil, 45–46

Forbes, Jack, 4, 123, 129
Fort Indiantown Gap (PA), 209
Fort Marion (St. Augustine, FL), 170
Foulkes, Toni, 289
Foxx, Virginia, 63
France: and construction of race, 176;
    Muslim populations of, 301; and slav-
    ery, 125
Franklin, John Hope, 123
Fredrickson, George, 8
Freedmen's Bureau, 69
freedom discourse, and Vietnamese refu-
    gees, 210–11, 222n31
free people of color, 130, 143n39
Freeze, Jack, 203
Friedman, Moses, 166
Friedman, Paul L., 69
Fujino, Diane, 29
futurity, 150–51

Garvey, Marcus, 27
Gasteyer, Stephen P., 114
Gates, Darryl, 24
gender: nationalist formations and contra-
    dictions of, 86–88, 92; racialization as
    dependent on constructions of, 3;
    women of color feminism and queer of
    color critical formations as fostering
    catalysts via, 91–92. See also feminism;
    intersectionality; women of color
    feminism
General Allotment Act (Dawes Severalty
    Act, 1887), 64–65, 67, 168–69, 177
generational experiences and differences:
    Arab and Muslim Americans in post-
    9/11 racial politics, 301; and genocide,
    30–31; and social movements, 28–29
genocide: assimilation of Native Ameri-
    cans as policy replacement for, 64–65,
    67–68; Black labor in context of, 31;
    generational impacts of, 30–31; of
    Indigenous Hawaiians, 197–98; paro-
    chialism of the academy and, 32; role of
    Israel in Central American repression
    and, 102–4
Gentleman's Agreement (1907), 48
gentrification, history as destroyed
    through, 39

Georgia, racial cleansing campaigns in,
    207
Germany, Black movement of, 90–91
Giago, Tim, 114–15
Giddings, Paula, 138
Gillam, Cora, 121–22, 128, 138–39
Gilmore, Ruth Wilson, 29
Glenn, Evelyn Nakano, 32
Goldberg, David Theo, 291
Goldstein, Alyosha, 4, 11, 20–21, 337
Gonzalo, José, 174
Gotham, Kevin Fox, 226
Goto, Masaichi, 196
Gottdiener, Mark, 247
Grant, Gary, 68
Great Depression. See New Deal
group-centric analysis, 279, 291
Guam, 184n82, 210
Guatemala: and genocide, intergenera-
    tional effects of, 30; genocide of Indig-
    enous people (1982–83), 102–4
Guerrero, Perla M., 8–9, 164–65, 337
Guevara, Che, 85
guilt: colonial algorithms of, 113; as per-
    formance of whiteness, 73
Gutiérrez, Ramón A., 86, 337

Hagel, Chuck, 109–10, 119n27
Haiti, 151, 154, 155
Hampton Normal and Agricultural
    Institute, 168, 170–72, 173, 177, 181n27
Handlin, Oscar, 26
Harland, Leland, 212
Harlow, Barbara, 87
Harmon, Andrew, 193
Harris, Cheryl, 61
Hartman, Saidiya, 61–62, 74, 82, 146,
    152–54
Hastie, Judge, 190
Hastings, Doc, 63
Hattiesburg, MS. See Camp Shelby (Hat-
    tiesburg, Mississippi)
Hawai'i: anti-Black racism/segregation
    during WWII, 191–92; Indigenous
    Hawaiians, and spatial racialization in
    Stockton (CA), 235; Indigenous
    Hawaiians, as vanishing people, 197–
    98; "Local" culture and identity of

Hawai'i *(continued)*
  Japanese Americans in, 187–88. *See also* Japanese American soldiers (AJA), racialization as Hawaiian
Hayt, Ezra A., 65
Hershey, Lewis B., 193
Herskovits, Melville, 129
Hertz, Allen Z., 111
heteromasculinist notions of political struggle: Black movement in Germany as eschewing, 91; as hindrance, 88, 89; homophobia and sexism and, 88; and race, regulation of, 88–89
Hillier, Amy, 230, 232–33
Himes, Chester, 23; *If He Hollers Let Him Go,* 23
Hirschhorn, Sara, 105–6
history: early works centering relational notions of race, 52; Native Americans in slavery, exclusions and inaccuracies in, 123–24; people as understanding themselves through, 39–40
Hitler, Adolf, 32
Holocaust, 32
Holsti, Ole R., 321n41
Home Owners' Loan Act (1933), 232
Home Owners' Loan Corporation. *See* space as relationally racialized in Stockton, Home Owners' Loan Corporation (HOLC)
homophobia, in anticolonialist movement, 87–89
Honduras, repression and genocide in, 104
Hong, Grace, 4, 13, 90, 150
Hoover, J. Edgar, 88
HoSang, Daniel Martinez, 338
Hoxie, Frederick, 177–78
Hoyt, Homer, 233
Huckabee, Mike, 205
Hu-DeHart, Evelyn, 4
human rights, and principle of self-determination, 85
Hume, David, 92–94
Hutchison, Ray, 247
Hyperresearch program, 261–62

illegality: as master status, 272. *See also* undocumented immigrants; undocu-

mented students (Latinas/os and Asian Pacific Islanders)—racialized illegality
Illinois, racial cleansing campaigns in, 207
Imada, Adria, 194
immigrants and immigration: segmented assimilation and importance of coethnic communities, 260–61. *See also* racialized immigration and slavery/ anti-Black racial subjection, relationality of; undocumented immigrants; undocumented students (Latinas/os and Asian Pacific Islanders)
immigration history, as flattening Black subjugation, 31
immigration policy: Chinese Exclusion Act (1882), 48, 61, 227; Gentleman's Agreement (1907), 48; racial arithmetic used for racial quotas, 278; Donald Trump's racist anti-immigration policy, 154–55, 158n14, 160–61n45, 298–99, 314; and "whiteness" of Arab immigrants, 300
imperialism: anticolonialism and, 85–86; Black press on, 4; Israel as proxy for, 103, 104. *See also* anticolonialism; Black radical tradition/internationalism and anti-imperial politics; colonialism
Indians. *See* inter/nationalist scholarship: American Indian studies and importance of Palestine; Native Americans; Native American studies
Indian Wars: assimilation efforts for Indian prisoners of, 170; Buffalo Soldiers in, 170
indigeneity, and inter/nationalist scholarship of American Indian studies and Palestine, 98–99, 110–12
Indigenous Americans in slavery. *See* Native Americans in slavery
Indigenous dispossession: allotment policy and, 64–65; and economic crisis of 2008, 64; and inter/nationalist scholarship: American Indian studies and important of Palestine, 98–99, 100, 101–4, 106–8, 111; neoliberal practices as framework of, 100, 102–4; origins of white supremacy in, 226–27; slaveown-

ing Native Americans as hoping to avoid, 128; and Stockton, CA metropolitan area, 231; treaty abrogation and, 64. *See also* Claims Resolution Act (CRA, 2010); racialization, "one-drop rule" (hypodescent) for Blacks and blood quantum ratio method for Native Americans

Los Angeles Department of Public Health: archives of, 49; and medical racialization, 46, 47–48, 57nn14,18–19; origins of, 47, 57n14

Los Angeles riots (1992), 24

Louisiana, and Black Indian people, 143n39

Lovett, Laura, 138–39, 140

Lowe, Lisa, 10, 94

Ludlow, Helen, 171

Lyle, Freddenna, 285–86, 289

Lytle Hernández, Kelly, 22, 338; *City of Inmates,* 22, 34–35; *Migra!,* 22, 26; in roundtable discussion, 7–8, 19, 22–40

Mabalon, Dawn Bohulano, 231

McClellan, John L., 208–9

McGill, Kim, 34

McGrath, Alice, *54,* 55

Mack, Kristen, 284, 293–94n29

McLoughlin, William, 133–34

McNickle, Darcy, 98, 117n2

McWilliams, Carey, 51–52, 55

Major Crimes Act (1885), 65

Maldonado, Roberto, 287

Manifest Destiny lore, 47

Marcos, Subcomandante, 103–4

Margolis, Ben, *54*

Martínez, Providencia, 174

Marx, Anthony, 8

Marx, Karl, 125

MASA (Muslim, Arab, and South Asian), as racial category, 323n59

mass incarceration, settler colonialism as lens for, 34–35

master status, illegality as, 272

Matthews, Phil, 212

Mayan people, genocide of, 103–4

media: and Arab and Muslim Americans, racialization of, 296, 298, 304; and Chicago redistricting of 2011, 281, 282–83, 284–86, 288, 289, 290, 291, 293–94n29; and Japanese American soldiers (AJA), racialization as Hawaiian, 189–94, 197–98; justifications of Indigenous dispossession in, 112; *New York Times* content analysis methodology, 304–6, 321n42–43,45; role in

anti-Black racism in Hawai'i, 192; and Vietnamese refugees in Arkansas, 208–10; and War on Terror, 299. *See also* Black press

Medicine, Bea, 134

Mell, Richard, 287, 289, 290

Merseth, Julie Lee, 9, 256, 338

messianism, as term, 106

methodologies of relational framework: overview, 9–13, 48–50; and authority/expertise of instructor, pushing beyond, 11–12, 24–25, 34, 40; and authority/expertise of researcher, pushing beyond, 9–10, 19, 33–34; collaboration among researchers, 51; comparative approach distinguished from, 8, 44, 279–80; content analysis, 304–6, 321n41–43,45; and going beyond the academy, 34–35; group-centric approach distinguished from, 279, 291; Hyperresearch program, 261–62; and internal distinctions and hierarchies of gender and sexuality, 13; new sources, development of, 34, 48–49, 51–52, 58nn22,29; and positionality of groups, differentials of, 12–13, 303; ProQuest newspaper archive, 304; reconsideration of existing research, 52–55; reconsideration of unit of analysis, 50–52; sociospatial approach, 228–29, 247–48; and study of different groups, even separated by space and time, 10, 52; for undocumented students, 261–62. *See also* Arab and Muslim Americans in post-9/11 racial politics—racialization frames method; archives; racial arithmetic; racial triangulation; research

Mexican American Legal Defense and Educational Fund, 290

Mexican-American War (1846–1848), 46, 227, 231

Mexicans and Mexican Americans: as Arkansas immigrants, 205, 206, 218–19; and Black culture, 25; ethnoracial diversity and, 47; and Japanese internment, 51; as "legally white but racially other," 227; medical racialization of,

46, 47–48, 57nn18–19; population fluctuations of, 46, 48; social divisions and differential racialization of, 226–27; and spatial racialization in Stockton (CA), 235, 238, *239, 241,* 244, 245–47, 248. *See also* Chicana/os; undocumented immigrants; undocumented students (Latinas/os and Asian Pacific Islanders)

"Mexican Scottsboro Boys," 53–55, *53–54*

Mexico: Israeli involvement in Chiapas insurgency, 103; Native American dispossession and, 231; U.S. capital penetration into, 25; U.S. seizure of northern Mexico, 46, 61, 231

Middle East studies, and Palestine studies, 110, 116

Miles, Tiya, 7, 82, 338

military: Native American prisoners of, 170; Zoot Suit Riots, 23, 53–54

miscegenation. *See* interracial relationships and marriage

Mississippi: racial cleansing campaigns in, 207. *See also* Camp Shelby (Hattiesburg, Mississippi)

Missouri, racial cleansing campaigns in, 207

Mittelstaedt, R. E., 195

Miwok people, 231

mixed-race persons: as especially vulnerable to enslavement, 127, 130. *See also* interracial relationships and marriage; Native Americans—kinship of Black Indians

model minority myth, and racialized immigrants vs. descendants of enslaved Africans, 151

Mohanty, Chandra, 93

Molina, Natalia, 8, 10, 20, 84, 188–89, 227, 273–74, 291–92, 302, 339; *Fit to be Citizens?,* 48

Mongolia, undocumented immigrants from, 261

Montt, Efraín Ríos, 103, 104

Moraga, Cherríe, 4, 13, 89–90

Moral Majority, 206, 210

Morgan, Edmund, 126

Morgensen, Scott, 103

Morris, Colonel, 216

mortgage lending discrimination: HOLC maps and, 234; racially restrictive covenants and, 240; redlining, 232–33

mortgages, by HOLC, 232, 233

multiculturalism: appropriation and, 111; and individualist logic of racism, 106

Muñoz, Ricardo, 287

music: and antiracist formations, 14; as point of entry into America, 25

Muslims: global population of, 298; as identity, 298; othering of, 300–301; percentage of, as Arabs vs. non-Arabs, 298, 313; and racialized immigration in relation to slavery, 159n27; Trump proposed registry, travel ban, immigration ban, 298–99, 314; as undocumented immigrants, 261, 262–63; U.S. Census, absence of racial category of, 319n16. *See also* Arab and Muslim Americans in post-9/11 racial politics

Myrdal, Gunnar, 86

Naber, Nadine, 297

natal alienation. *See* family separation/natal alienation

national liberation movements. *See* anticolonialism as relational project; inter/nationalist scholarship: American Indian studies and importance of Palestine

Nation of Islam, 315

nation-state: empty promises of, 149; inter/nationalist scholarship and challenges to probity of, 115; as mechanism for administering coercion and contracts, neoliberalism and, 62; thinking beyond, women of color feminism and queer of color formations and, 92

Native Americans: adoption into tribes, 133–34; blood-quantum and tribal membership of, 65, 143n40; federal assimilation policy as replacing genocide policy, 64–65, 67–68; federal mismanagement as trustee of allotments of, lawsuit for (*Cobell v. Salazar,* 1996), 60, 64–68; and liberal colonial logic at

Native Americans *(continued)*
Devils Tower (Mato Tipila), 107, 118n22;
mortgages and commercial banking as
disadvantaged for, 68; sovereignty of,
allotment as dismantling, 65, 67–68;
sovereignty of, named as source of
poverty, 68; and spatial racialization in
Stockton (CA), 225, 235, 252n66; treaties
abrogated by federal government, 64, 65,
68; violence against, 4; women, as
neglected topic, 134–35. *See also* Carlisle
Indian Industrial School; Claims Resolution Act; Indigenous dispossession;
Native American studies; racialization,
"one-drop rule" (hypodescent) for
Blacks and blood quantum ratio
method for Native Americans; United
States—Indian policy
—IN SLAVERY: overview, 82, 121–24;
Black Indian women and, 134–38; and
Blackness as synonymous with bondage, 126; categorization of Indian slaves
as Africans, 127, 130–32, 143nn38–39;
conquest and racialization of Black and
Red people, 124–26; decrease of practice over time, 126–27; disease and, 125,
127; escaped slaves, 127, 130–31, 143n38;
exclusions and inaccuracies in histories, 123–24, 127, 131; exclusions and
inaccuracies in popular culture, 121,
122–23; interviews and narratives
about, 121–22, 127, 128, 132–37, 138–40;
mixed-race persons as especially vulnerable to enslavement, 127, 130; and
privileging of Indian vs. Black identity,
138–40; as slaveowners, 127–28, 132–33,
136–37, 142n30; written records,
absence from, 127
—KINSHIP OF BLACK INDIANS: overview, 128; and adoption into tribes,
133–34; biracial/bicultural identities
and, 130, 132–33; Black relatives and,
130; definition of Black Indian, 130;
importance of kinship, 128–29; matri-
lineality/patrilineality and belonging
to tribe, 129–30, 142n30; percentage of
African American population reporting Native ancestry, 129; slaveholding

Natives and, 132–33, 137, 142n30;
women and, 135, 137–38
Native American studies: and the field,
commitment to, 108–9; intertribal/
pannational focus in, 97–98, 117n2. *See
also* inter/nationalist scholarship:
American Indian studies and importance of Palestine
nativism, 213
Navarro-Rivera, Pablo, 179–80n2
Nave, Cornelius Neely, 132–33
Nehru, Jawaharlal, 27–28
neoliberalism: and economic crisis of
2008, 64; Indigenous dispossession
as situated in framework of, 100,
102–4; the state as reduced to
administering coercion and contracts
under, 62
Netherlands, and slavery, 125–26
Newcomb, Steven, 115
New Deal: agricultural legislation, 70;
Home Owners' Loan Act (1933), 232;
housing policy of, generally, 225, 232.
See also Federal Housing Administra-
tion (FHA); space as relationally
racialized in Stockton, Home Owners'
Loan Corporation (HOLC)
New England Committee to Defend
Palestine, 111
New York Police Department, branch in
Israel, 118n11
New York Times content analysis method-
ology, 304–6, 321n42–43,45
Nieves, Delores, 174, 176
Nkrumah, Kwame, 85
nonwhite as racial category: Hume's
exclusion of, from principles of the
mind, 93; as Others, 125; racial scripts
and, 227; slavery as synonymous
with, 126
North Korea, Black internationalism and,
28
North Koreans, stereotypes of, 309

Obama, Barack: AIPAC speech (2012),
109; and Cobell settlement, 63–64, 67;
and immigration, 158n14; and postracial rhetoric, 315–16

Ogbu, John U., 231, 245
Okihiro, Gary Y., 51, 196
Oklahoma, racial cleansing campaigns in, 207
Omi, Michael, 7, 46, 57n20, 124–25, 226, 280
Ong, Aihwa, 172–73
Orientalism, 228, 297, 300–301, 313
Osborne, Rick, 216
Osuna, Juan José, "An Indian in Spite of Myself," 176–77, 178
Otolith Group: World 3, 83–84

Painter, Nell Irvin, 138
Pakistan: terrorism by, 298–99; undocumented immigrants from, 261, 262–63
Palestine studies: liberatory ethos of, 108–9; Middle East studies and, 110, 116. *See also* inter/nationalist scholarship: American Indian studies and importance of Palestine
Pan Africanism, 83
pan-Indianism, 98, 178
Park, Lisa Sun-Hee, 229, 248
Paulin, Diana, 14
Pellow, David N., 229, 248
Pence, C. W., 189
Perdue, Theda, 134, 135
Perez, Shimon, 109
Perlmutter, Ed, 63
Peru, immigrants from, 261
Petty, William, 292n1
Philippines, 4, 184n82; undocumented immigrants from, 261, 263, 265
Pigford II (2010) (*In re Black Farmers Discrimination Litigation*), 60, 68–73
Pigford v. Glickman (1999, "*Pigford I*"), 60, 68–73
Plummer, Brenda Gayle, 159n25
plutocratic conduct, and Indigenous dispossession, 102, 103
Plyler v. Doe (1982), 259
police and policing: anti-Black brutality, and use of archives, 34; Border Patrol, Black perception of, 26; Ferguson, MO, 278; Israel offering for hire, 103;

118n11; New York PD branch in Israel, 118n11
political arithmetic, 292n1
political practice of relationality: overview, 4, 15. *See also* antiracist relational analyses and politics
popular culture: and correlation of enslavement with Black people, 122–23; as point of entry into America, 25; and women's engagement in insurgent struggles, 87. *See also* music
population: of African Americans in California, 46; of Mexican immigrants, 46, 48
Portugal, and slavery, 125
postracial discourse, 304, 315–16
Prado, José, 174, 177
Prashad, Vijay, 14
Pratt, Richard Henry, 168–71, 172–73, 177, 178–79
Prewitt, Kenneth, 280, 283
Proposition 187, 27, 41n9
ProQuest newspaper archives, 304
proxies for race, blood quantum of Native Americans, 65
Pryor, David, 203–4, 209, 215–17
Puar, Jasbir, 103
Public Law 280 (1953), 65
Puerto Rico: education system installed by U.S., 173; imperialism and, 4; students brought to Hampton and Tuskegee Institutes, 173; as territory of U.S., 166, 173, 179, 184n82. *See also* Carlisle Indian Industrial School—Puerto Rican students at
Pulido, Laura, 14, 226, 229, 248

queer of color formations: as fostering gender/sexuality catalysts, 91–92; and gender/sexuality contradictions in anticolonialist movement, 87–89, 92; and intersectionality, 13; and liberal capitalism, transcendence of relational limits of, 94; and the mind, principles and capacities for association of, 92–93; and race as relational, 81, 91–92; and thinking beyond the state, 92
Quiquivix, Linda, 103

racialization, "one-drop rule" (hypodescent) for Blacks and blood quantum ratio method for Native Americans: definition of terms, 131, 143n40; as ensuring ever-growing slave population while ensuring fewer Native people to claim land and tribal sovereignty, 131–32, 182n38; and miscegenation policies, differentials in, 172, 182n38; as originating outside Black and Native communities, 132; percentage blood quantum defined by BIA, 143n40

racialized illegality. *See* undocumented students (Latinas/os and Asian Pacific Islanders)—racialized illegality

racialized immigration and slavery/anti-Black racial subjection, relationality of: overview, 15, 82, 145–49; abolitional consciousness/Black consciousness and, 150, 153, 154, 156; and "afterlife of slavery," 146, 151–52; assimilation as blocked for persons of African descent, 151–52, 159nn25,27; differences in, respect for, 150; and futurity/model minority myth, 150–51; and multiple sites as categorical antagonists to white nationalism, 148–49; and the nation-state/national project, 149, 155, 156; positionality of researcher as activist in, 157n5; and *sankofa* (return to the source), 146–47; and "second slavery," 146, 153, 160n35; and slavery as anchoring form of social explanation for the modern state and its practices, 152–54, 155–56; Trump's racist anti-immigrant discourses and, 154–55, 160–61n45; violence and, 146, 148, 149, 151–52, 154, 155–56, 159n27

—CITIZENSHIP AND CITIZENS AND: overview, 147–48; contract rights and burdens of, 154; as escape, 156; as false ideal, 149–50; family separations/disruption of kinship/natal alienation and, 147–48, 152, 154, 158n14; as temporary and contingent status, 150, 151–52; violence and, 148, 151–52; as whitening, 148, 151–52, 160n36

racially restrictive covenants. *See* deed restrictions

racial naturalization, 164, 176
racial projects, 7
racial scripts, 227
racial stereotypes: Asian Americans as "perpetual foreigner," 260; of criminal/illegal vs. law abiding status, 258, 260, 262–64, 272; exclusion vs. inclusion and, 260; Latinas/os as "illegal aliens," 257–58, 260, 262–64, 268, 272; of Muslims, as terrorists, 262–63, 299; structural racism as based on, 48. *See also* Arab and Muslim Americans in post-9/11 racial politics—racialization frames method

racial triangulation: and Arab and Muslim Americans in post-9/11 racial politics, 303–4, 305–6, *305*, 309, 320–21nn36,38; of Asian Americans, 227–28, 303, 309, 321n38; Black subjugation and, 227; citizenship and, 156; and colorblind discourse, 321n38; and intragroup differences, inability to account for, 303–4; of Mexicans, 227; persistence of the American racial order and, 303, 321n38; in racialization frames analysis, 305–6; and relative valorization/civic ostracism, 303, 320–21n36; of space, 227–28, 247

racism: African American soldiers during WWII and, 190–94; anti-Black, and federal housing programs, 233–35, 238–40, *239*, 247–48; anti-Black, and Vietnamese refugees, 204, 206–8, 217–18; anti-Japanese, and internment during WWII, 188; and individualism, logic of, 106; police brutality, 34; postracial/colorblind discourse and claims of disappearance of, 315–16; Puerto Rican students at Carlisle Indian school and expressions of, 174–76; racial arithmetic and, 278; yellow peril (anti-Asian), and Vietnamese refugees, 205, 206, 208, 211–13, 218, 220n10. *See also* antiracist relational analyses and politics; Japanese American soldiers (AJA), racialization as Hawaiian—and anti-Japanese racism; systemic discrimination

Rahall, Nick, 63
Ramírez, Catherine S., 11, 163–64, 339
Read, Jen'nan Ghazal, 301
Reagan administration, closure of USDA Office of Civil Rights Enforcement and Adjudication, 68, 71
reconciliation, as enclosing and containing the past, 21, 73–74
Reddy, Chandan, 62
redistricting: as site of racial arithmetic, 281. *See also* racial arithmetic—Chicago redistricting of 2011
redlining, 232–33
Reel, Estelle, 177
refugees: and relationality of race, 149–50. *See also* racialized immigration and slavery/anti-Black racial subjection, relationality of
reggae music, 14
relational study of race: overview, 1–5, 23–24, 291–92; as act of intervention, 36–37; and the Black radical tradition, 27–28, 148–49; breadth and depth questions of, 36; community studies tradition contrasted to, 5–6; comparative framework distinguished from, 8, 44, 279–80, 291; comparison as tool in, 306; and complexity of the evidence, fidelity to, 29–30; definition of, 44; as epistemic shift, 84, 86; ethnoracial diversity as generative of, 43–44, 46–48; exclusions and inaccuracies in history as addressed by, 123–24; forerunners of, 3–5; and intergenerational learning, 28–29; and locality as ancillary to relationality, 8; Los Angeles as particular site for, 24–26, 28, 46–47; and the middle word, xi, 36–37; MLK and, 1, *2*, 3; and multiple sites as categorical antagonists to white nationalism, 148–49; and single group, understanding of, 20, 44, 84; subfield paradigm contrasted to, 6, 44; substantialist perspective contrasted to, 6–7; and time for looking at things apart, 23–24, 44; and the twenty-four-year plan (demographics change of 2040), 35–36; uninterrogated privileging of

whiteness as disrupted by, 7–8, 23; and "your freedom is my freedom," 19, 27. *See also* academy, the; knowledge production; methodologies of relational framework; racialization as mutually constitutive process; social movements
religion: categories of, not used in U.S. Census, 319n16; of Vietnamese refugees, 210. *See also* Christianity; Muslims
Remnick, David, 113
research: and authority/expertise of researcher, pushing beyond, 9–10, 19, 33–34; definition of subject as shaping process and question, 49; possibilities for interested researchers, 52, 248–49, 273–74. *See also* methodologies of relational framework
Rexach, Emanuel Ruiz, *175*
Reyes, Victor, 287
Rice, Monsignor, *2*
Rivera, Luis Muñoz, 177
Roberts, Dorothy, 158n14
Roberts, James, 232
Rodney, Walter, 29
Rodríguez-Muñiz, Michael, 7, 255–56, 339
Rohwer incarceration camp (Arkansas), 185–86
Roosevelt, Franklin D., and WWII, 188, 245
Rothschild, Emma, 92–93
Ruiz, Vicki, 4

Said, Edward, 97, 297
Salaita, Steven, 12, 81–82, 339
Sánchez, George J., 22, 50–51, 339; *Becoming Mexican American*, 22, 24, 25, 31, 50; and *Boyle Heights: The Power of Place* (2002 exhibition), 50, 58n28; "Contemporary Peoples/Contested Places" (with Sarah Deutsch and Gary Y. Okihiro), 51; in roundtable discussion, 7–8, 9, 19, 22–40
Sanders, Frank, 107, 118n22
San Francisco, Fillmore District redevelopment project, 227–28
sankofa, 146–47
Santano, Juan, 173
segmented assimilation, 260–61

social sciences: community studies tradition in, 5–6; subfield paradigm and, 6. *See also* ethnic studies

social welfare benefits, 212, 222n35

sociospatial approach, 228–29, 247–48

Soil Conservation and Domestic Allotment Act (1936), 70

Solis, Danny, 287, 288, 289

Solis, Gabriel, 14

South America: disease as decimating Indigenous population, 125; Indigenous peoples in slavery in, 125

South Asians: contested membership in Asian American category, 314; as Muslims, 298, 313

Southern Homestead Act (1866), 69

the South, U.S.: and Black-white racial binary, complication of, 205; white dispossession of Black farmers, 70. *See also* Black subjugation; Japanese American soldiers (AJA), racialization as Hawaiian; Vietnamese refugees in Arkansas, racialization of

space, as unit of analysis, 50–51

space as relationally racialized in Stockton (CA): overview, 165, 224–26; academic theories (e.g. "ecological theory") and, 228, 233, 247; anti-Asian sentiment and racial exclusivity, 225, 235, 238–40, *239*, 244; definition of, 228; economic status and, *239*, *242*; environmental inequality and, 229, 248–49; and "green" spaces model of racial exclusivity, 236, 238; history of Stockton, 231–32; immigration patterns and, 225, 231, *241*, 244, 252n70; and Lipsitz's "how racism takes place," 247; manufacturing growth and decline in, 231–32; population, ethnoracial percentages, 225, 235, 238, *241*, 252n66; pro-growth coalitions and, 228, 245–46; racial triangulation model and, 227–28, 247; real estate industry and, 226, 228, 229, 233, 235, 246, 247; research implications of, 248–49; research strategy/sources used, 229–31; Sanborn fire insurance survey maps and, 229, 232, 235–36; and segregation-

ist ideology, 226, 233, 247; sociospatial approach to, 228–29, 247–48; as state-sponsored project, 226, 228, 229, 246, 247; and University of the Pacific (UOP) and proximity, 236, 238, 240, 243, 244, 246, 248, 252n66; urban renewal and, 245–46; and the white elite, 228, 231, 235–36, 244, 248; and whites, foreign born (Italians), 235, 235–36, 238, 244; World War II and, 245

space as relationally racialized in Stockton, Home Owners' Loan Corporation (HOLC) residential appraisals: overview, 225–26; and Black residents viewed as paramount racial threat, 233–35, 238–40, *239*, 247–48; as confidential residential survey surveys (RSSs), 232; and deed restrictions (racially restrictive covenants), 233, 234, 236, 238–40, *239*, 245, 246; developmental context, 238–40, *239*; and mortgage financing availability, 238–40, *239*; number of mortgages by HOLC, 232, 233; population and housing conditions, 238–40, *239*, *241–42*, 242, 246; redlining and, 232–33; restricted access to surveys, 233; as source, 229, 230–31; and urban-industrial boundaries as containment of nonwhites, 229, 235, 238, *239*, *242*, 246–47, 248–49; and "white spatial imaginary," 233

—GRADE AREAS: overview and definition of, 232, 234; areas of Stockton, 235–38, *237*, 252n57; attributes consistently referenced in, 238–40, *239*; contemporary economic/housing/land use characteristics based on 1938 grade, 242, *242*; contemporary map of Stockton overlaid on 1938 grade, 242, *243*; contemporary neighborhood economic status as clearly related to, 242–47, 252nn66,70; contemporary racial-ethnic and immigrant population based on 1938 grade, 240–42, *241*

Spain: and conquest, 231; and construction of race, 176; and slavery, 125

Spanish-American War (1898), 166, 173

Spanish language: Black study of, 26–27; and resource awareness in undocumented Latina/o community, 269; whitening references in, 160n36

Spielman, Fran, 285–86

Spock, Benjamin, 2

statistics: statistical races (ethnoracial statistics), 280; as transparent, belief in, 287. *See also* racial arithmetic

Statue of Liberty, 210–11

Stewart, Ollie, 190

Stimson, Henry L., 88

Stockton, CA. *See* space as relationally racialized in Stockton (CA)

Stockton, Robert F., 231

Stowe, Harriet Beecher, *Uncle Tom's Cabin,* 121

structural discrimination: Asian Americans and, 48; Federal Housing Administration (FHA) and, 51; stereotypes as basis of, 48; subfield paradigm as documenting, 44. *See also* racism; systemic discrimination

Strum, Circe, 132

Student Nonviolent Coordinating Committee, 86–87

"Studying Race Relationally" conference (2016), xii

Suarez, Ray, 287

substantialist ontology, 6–7, 279

suburbanization, 207, 229

sundown towns, 207

Supplemental Nutrition Assistance Program (SNAP, food stamps), 72

Suzuki, Chiyo, 196

systemic discrimination: individualistic logic of racism as denial of, 106; judicial declaration on, as "over" in federal government, 69; of USDA, against Black Farmers, 68–73. *See also* criminal justice system, discrimination in; racism; structural discrimination

Tadiar, Neferti X. M., 100, 101

Taino people, 178

Takaki, Ronald, 123–24

Takei, George, 38

TallBear, Kimberley, 3

Tapscott, Horace, 28

teaching race relationally: association and accountability, questions of, 40; and authority/expertise, pushing beyond, 11–12, 24–25, 34, 40; positionality of teacher and, 40

terrorism: as construction, 322n48; Muslims and stereotypes of, 262–63, 299. *See also* Arab and Muslim Americans in post-9/11 racial politics

Terry, John, 189–91, 192, 193

Thatch, Lam Van, 203

Third World Gay Revolution, 87–88

Third World solidarities, Bandung conference (1955) and, 4

Thompson, Mamie, 136

Tillman, Dorothy, 286

Tomich, Dale, 82, 146, 153–54, 160n35

Tomlinson, Barbara, 30; "the middle word," xi, 37

Tompkins, Jane, 121

Tong, C. T., 195

Tran, Hoa Thi Kim, 214

transnational study of race: comparative vs. relational frameworks and, 8; race as transnational category, 81, 86; as turn within disciplines, 4; women of color feminism and, 90–91. *See also* anticolonialism; inter/nationalist scholarship; American Indian studies and importance of Palestine

Travis, Hannah, 135

Trinh, Hong Thi Cam, 215

Trump, Donald: and immigration, 154–55, 158n14, 160–61n45, 298–99, 314; proposed Muslim registry and travel ban, 298–99, 314; on "shithole" countries, 154, 160–61n45

Tudó, Angela Rivera, 174–75, 178

Turner, Jerry, 214–15

Tuskegee Institute, 173

"Uncle Tom," dual images of, 121–22, 138, 139–40

undocumented immigrants: and coethnic communities, importance of, 260, 268–69; denial of social services to

undocumented immigrants *(continued)*
(Prop 187), 27, 41n9; and immigrant
illegality as concept, 258; master status
as concept in study of, 272; population
of, 257; segmented assimilation and,
260–61; stereotypes linking Latinas/os
to, 257–58, 260, 262–64, 268, 272. *See
also* undocumented students (Latinas/
os and Asian Pacific Islanders)
undocumented students (Latinas/os and
Asian Pacific Islanders): overview,
9–10, 255, 257–58, 271–72; and access to
information about post–high school
options, 259–60; age of entry into U.S.,
266; and API as term, 261, 277n26;
college attendance statistics, 259;
guaranteed access to K–12 education,
259; and identification documents, lack
of, 267; and Latinas/os as term, 260,
261, 274–75n1, 277n26; methodology
and data of study, 261–62, *273*; population of, 259; state laws and policies for
tuition and financial aid, 259,
276nn14,17
—RACIALIZED ILLEGALITY: overview,
271–74; acculturation and, 265–66;
additional research possibilities, 272–
74; Black students and, 268; definition
of, 258; and inclusion/exclusion in
educational resources and support
structures, 258, 260–61, 264, 268–71,
272; and inclusion/exclusion in interpersonal interactions, 258, 260–61,
264–68, 272; master status distinguished from, 272; relationality of, 258,
272–74, 275n7; self-presentation/
phenotype and, 264–65, 266–68; and
stereotypes of criminal/illegal vs. law
abiding status, 258, 260, 262–64, 272;
white students and, 268
unemployment benefits, 212
United States: civil rights enforcement by,
207–8; and foreign policy, racial categorizations of, 155, 160–61n45; internal colonial model of, 86; and post-9/11
racial profiling policy, 299; segregation
as promulgated by, generally, 39; spatial
racialization in Stockton (CA) as

project of, 226, 228, 229, 246, 247;
Vietnamese refugee settlement and
resentment of government, 208–9
—INDIAN POLICY: assimilation as
replacement for genocide as, 64–65,
67–68; assimilation, questioning of,
177–78; General Allotment Act,
Dawes Severalty Act (1887), 64–65, 67,
168–69, 177; Individual Indian Money
(IIM) Trust Fund, 65–68; Major
Crimes Act (1885), 65; Public Law 280
(1953), 65
United States Academic and Cultural
Boycott of Israel, 100
universality, the law and, 62
the university: influence of, 37; inter/
nationalist scholarship and decolonization of, 116–17; scholarship limited to
environs of, 101; supporting the work
of colleagues, 37–38; supporting works
from outside of, 38. *See also* teaching
University of Arizona, American Indian
Studies program, 108
University of Arkansas Medical Center, 216
University of Hawai'i at Manoa (UH), 195
University of Puerto Rico, 173, 176
University of Texas, indigenous studies
program, 108
urban redevelopment: and racial triangulation of space, 227–28; and Stockton
(CA) spatial racialization, 245–46
Urla, Jacqueline, 287
U.S. Census: advocacy for "Arab" category
on, 300, 319–20n24; information on
Arabs and Muslims not collected by,
319n11; racial/ethnic classifications of,
as construction, 315; religious/racial
categories not used in, 319n16. *See also*
racial arithmetic—Chicago redistricting of 2011
U.S. Commission on Civil Rights, 70–71
U.S. Constitution, Three-Fifths Compromise, 278
USDA (U.S. Department of Agriculture):
discriminatory lending practices
against Black farmers, 68–73; Office of
Civil Rights Enforcement and Adjudication, 68, 71

white supremacy *(continued)*
    rhetoric and, 155. *See also* colonialism
    and white supremacy, relationality of;
    genocide; Indigenous dispossession;
    slavery
Wilderson, Frank, 150
Williams, Francis, 93
Willoughby-Herard, Tiffany, 15, 82, 339;
    "Learning from the 'The Whatever
    that Survived'" (poem), 147, 158n13
Wilson, James Q., 37
Wilson, Sarah, 134, 136–37
Winant, Howard, 7, 8, 46, 57n20, 124–25,
    226, 280
Wolfe, Patrick, 3, 167, 172, 182n38
women: engaged in anticolonial struggles,
    86–89. *See also* gender
women of color: Chicana/o history and
    turn toward centering of, 45; definition
    of, 93
women of color feminism: as fostering
    gender/sexuality catalysts, 91–92; and
    liberal capitalism, transcendence of
    relational limits of, 94; and the mind,
    principles and capacities for association
    of, 92–93; and race as relational, 81,
    89–92; and thinking beyond the
    state, 92

women of color scholarship: as forerunner
    of relational study of race, 3–4. *See also*
    intersectionality
Works Progress Administration (WPA),
    Slave Narratives, as source, 141n3
World War II: African American soldiers
    in and anti-Black racism during, 190–
    94; Pearl Harbor attack, 188, 315. *See
    also* Japanese American soldiers (AJA),
    racialization as Hawaiian; Japanese
    internment in World War II
Wright, J. Leitch, 126
Wright, Richard, *The Color Curtain,* 4
Wyoming, Devils Tower, 107, 118n22

Yamada, Masao, 197
Yamashita, Jeffrey T., 12, 164, 339
yellow peril: definition of, 220n10. *See also*
    Vietnamese refugees in Arkansas,
    racialization of
Yenne, Bill, 185
Yokut people, 231
Young Lords, 86–87
Young, Robert J. C., 85

Zamora, Rodolfo Lobos, 104
Zapatistas, 103
Zoot Suit Riots (1943), 23, 53–54